To Bill
With best regards

Weiying Zhang

Jan 28, 2015.

THE
Logic
OF THE
Market

THE
Logic
OF THE
Market

AN INSIDER'S VIEW OF CHINESE ECONOMIC REFORM

WEIYING ZHANG
TRANSLATED BY MATTHEW DALE

CATO INSTITUTE
WASHINGTON, D.C.

The Logic of the Market was originally published in 2010 by Century Publishing Group (Shanghai: Shanghai People's Press).

ISBN: 978-7-208-09343-0

Translated by Matthew Dale.

Library of Congress Cataloging-in-Publication Data

Zhang, Weiying, 1959-
    The logic of the market : an insider's view of Chinese economic reform / Weiying Zhang; translated by Matthew Dale.
        pages cm
    Includes bibliographical references and index.
    ISBN 978-1-939709-59-2 (hardback : alk. paper) — ISBN 978-1-939709-60-8 (pbk. : alk. paper) 1. China—Economic policy—1976-2000. 2. China—Economic policy—2000- 3. China—Commercial policy. 4. Financial crises—China. 5. Economic development—China. I. Title.

HC427.92.Z4374 2014
338.951—dc23

                                                                    2014043702

eBook ISBN: 978-1-939709-61-5

Cover design: Jon Meyers.
Printed in the United States of America.

CATO INSTITUTE
1000 Massachusetts Ave., N.W.
Washington, D.C. 20001
www.cato.org

Contents

List of Tables and Illustrations

Tables

Figures

Preface to the English Edition

China's economic reforms that started in 1978 have had a tremendous impact on China, and even the world. On the one hand, after 30 years of high-speed economic growth, the living standards of the average person have greatly improved. There are more choices and more liberties. The international ranking of the Chinese economy has increased from 13th place before the reforms to 2nd place today. China has a greater voice in the international community. G2 has become part of the international vocabulary. There is even talk of the eastern transition of global leadership. On the other hand, with that high-speed economic growth, the various contradictions of Chinese society have become more prominent. Issues such as income inequality, regional differences, serious corruption in officialdom, health and education inequality, and environmental pollution have caused people's feelings of dissatisfaction to increase instead of decrease along with the improvements in living standards.

Corresponding with these two phenomena are two groups with two ways of thinking about how to evaluate reforms of the past and guide reforms of the future that have arisen. I disagree with both. The first group, the China Model Theorists, believe that the source of the Chinese economic miracle was the unique "China Model." Its basic characteristics are strong government intervention and a dominant state-owned economic sector. It is completely different from the road taken by Anglo-American and other Western countries. It is different from the free competition and private enterprise system advocated by the "Washington Consensus." The second group, the Reform Failure Theorists, believe that China's current social contradictions are caused by marketization. They believe that 30 years of marketization reform policies were a mistake.

The China Model Theory was originally proposed by overseas scholars who researched developing countries (including China). After the 2008 Global Financial Crisis, certain Chinese scholars, and especially government officials, put faith in the idea. The Reform Failure Theory is mainly advocated by certain leftist Chinese scholars but has a significant following among ordinary people, and has even been acknowledged by certain high-ranking government officials.

In my view, these two ways of thinking, although they may appear different at first glance, are in essence the same. Both have blind faith in government power and distrust the logic of the market, have blind faith in the foresight of government officials but distrust the judgments of entrepreneurs, have blind faith in authority but distrust liberty, and have blind faith in "national conditions" and "characteristics" but do not accept universal values. The difference between the two is that the Reform Failure Theorists negate the market reforms of the past as a starting point to advocate returning to the era of central planning, government allocation of resources and incomes, eradication of private entrepreneurs, and state-owned enterprise dominance of the economy. To this they add a little abstract "direct democratic participation" from the masses. The China Model Theorists negate the marketization and democratic reforms of the future. They advocate solidifying the current system and power structure, relying on industrial policy to guide development, and using state-owned enterprises to guide the economy. As to whether their advocacy is based on principles or private interests, I do not know, but it is probably both.

On the surface, both of these ways of thinking have a certain basis in reality, but their understanding of reality is incorrect. Yes, if we compare China to Anglo-American developed countries, the biggest difference is that the Chinese government does intervene in economic and social affairs more, the proportion of state-owned enterprises is higher, and China has not established true democracy and rule of law. However, if because of this we attribute the past 30 years of China's economic growth to government intervention and state-owned enterprises, as the China Model Theory advocates do, we are wrong. China's reforms started with an all-powerful government under the planned economy. The reason China could have sustained economic growth during the process of reform was because the government managed less and the proportion of state-owned enterprises decreased, not the other way around. It was precisely the relaxation of government control that brought about market prices, sole proprietorships, town and village enterprises, private enterprises, foreign enterprises, and other non-state-owned entities. Not only did the Chinese economy not collapse, in fact it maintained a relatively high rate of growth. It should also be pointed out that the past 30 years of China's economic growth relied on technology and management practices that had accumulated in Western developed countries over the last few hundred years. These technologies and management practices could not possibly have been created by China's high levels of government intervention and economy dominated by the state-owned sector.

High levels of government intervention and state-owned enterprise dominance are not the reasons for the Chinese economic miracle. In fact, those things are the reason for the contradictions and unfairness in Chinese society that the Reform Failure Theorists exaggerate. Government control over large amounts of resources and excessive intervention into the economy are the direct cause of cronyism between officials and businessmen, are a breeding ground for official corruption, seriously corrupt commercial culture, and damage the market's rules of the game. The monopoly profits extracted by monopolistic state-owned enterprises allow state-sector employment compensation to far exceed fair market levels. It is an important contributor to income distribution inequality. If China opened up the medical market earlier, allowing nongovernment capital to freely enter instead of maintaining the monopoly status of state-owned hospitals, it would not be so difficult and expensive to see a doctor. If nongovernment schools could open freely, China's education quality would not be as poor as it is. If China could establish the absolute authority of the constitution and the law, putting government power below the law, there would not be as many cases of barbaric relocation as there are. If farmers truly held the right of land ownership, there would not be as many instances of unfair expropriation of farm land. If starting a business was the equal right of every person, instead of being a privilege bestowed on a group of people by government examinations and approvals, cronyism would not be as common as it is. If citizens had the right to vote and freedom of the press, government corruption would not be as unrestrained as it is today.

Unfortunately, during the 10-year reign of President Hu and Premier Wen, the China Model Theory and Reform Failure Theory were not limited to essays and catchphrases—they were put into practice. This has seriously impacted the direction of government policy, causing reform to stagnate and even regress. Over the last 10 years, the pace of reform has been obstructed by anti-reform sentiments and policy. Some traditional methods of the planned economy have been resurrected under the name of macroeconomic adjustments and industrial policy. Prices that have been liberalized are now subject to price controls. "Private advance and state retreat" as the mainline of ownership structure adjustment has given way to "state advance and private retreat." For many years, government revenues have far outpaced the growth of the national economy and residential incomes. Government investment has begun to squeeze out private capital. Entrepreneurial fervor to do business has been replaced by a zeal to emigrate. Countless other examples have created institutional deficits for future economic growth and caused Chinese society to be less harmonious.

Therefore, if China is to maintain sustained economic growth, understand the various social contradictions that it faces, or establish a truly harmonious society, it must be persistent in its reforms toward marketization, reduction of government control over resources and intervention into the economy, and the establishment of a true rule-of-law-society and democratic politics.

All debates over issues of China's reforms reflect people's common misunderstanding of the market. This misunderstanding is related to traditional economics. Traditional economics sees the market as only a means of efficiently allocating resources, not as an institutional arrangement for human beings to pursue happiness via the division of labor and cooperation. To prove the efficiency of markets, traditional economists made many assumptions. These assumptions are all unrealistic and unfounded and have destroyed the reputation of the market. They have also provided reasons for the government to intervene in the economy. The failure of market theory is mistaken as the failure of the market per se. In reality, the efficient operation of the economy does not require the assumptions of traditional economics. As an institutional arrangement for the pursuit of happiness via the division of labor and cooperation, the orderly operation of the market only relies on liberty, private property, and the rule of law. Economists have a duty to work toward establishing a better market theory.

Weiying Zhang
August 20, 2014

Preface to the Second Chinese Edition

This book was first published in July 2010, and I am gratified by the response. Pirated copies were even found, a possibility that never occurred to me.

This revised version includes three new articles. "Introduction: The Logic of the Market and China's Reforms" gives an overview of the core content of the book, especially the first two parts. I hope it will help the reader better understand my market ideals. "Good Policy and Bad Policy" provides a standard for judging the superiority and inferiority of economic policies. "The Market and Morality" attempts to settle some misunderstandings about the relationship between the markets and morality.

Ludwig von Mises claimed that everything that people do stems from the allocation of reason, science, creed, and spirit. In human history, beyond the mind, nothing is true or substantive. A general belief considers the struggles discussed by sociologists as struggles between interest groups. If that theory is correct, then human cooperation is hopeless. However, the effect of Deng Xiaoping's 1992 Southern Tour on Chinese society proves that von Mises was right.

Human errors occur either because of ignorance—when bad things are done for good reasons—or because of unscrupulousness—when others are harmed for personal gain. Unscrupulousness can also be interpreted as a manifestation of ignorance.

I believe that the market is humanity's most effective tool for handling the majority's ignorance and limiting the minority's unscrupulousness, and it is especially useful for reducing the disasters that are caused by the combination of the two. I hope that the logic of the market becomes every person's ideal. That is my reason for writing this book.

Weiying Zhang
January 2012
Beijing

Preface to the First Chinese Edition

The market economy is humanity's greatest creation. It provides the best rules of the game for human progress.

The logic of the market's foundation is that if people want to be prosperous, they must first make others prosperous. To use an old Chinese saying, "Benefit yourself by benefiting others." For example, the producer wants to earn profit, so the consumer must be satisfied with a good or service. Value must be created for the consumer. The entrepreneurs want to hire employees, but they must provide those employees with sufficient wages and working conditions for employees to be willing to work. Then an entrepreneur must take responsibility for their actions. Workers want job opportunities that can provide for their families' livelihood and improve their standard of living. Thus, they must produce goods or services that customers are willing to purchase.

Market competition is really just competition to create value for others. Enterprises that cannot create value for others must be eliminated through competition. The market uses such reasoning to take individual pursuit of prosperity and happiness and to transfer it into the driving force of production for society's prosperity and progress. Only through that approach did the Western world advance over the past 200 years. It is also the reason for China's economic marvel over the past 30 years.

The market is not just an invisible hand; it is also an invisible eye. The invisible hand directs people to do the right thing. The invisible eye watches over people to make sure they do it well, which, in turn, will build a good reputation. Specifically, that invisible hand and invisible eye make strangers—who are separated by great distances and who have never seen each other—work together. That division of labor allows them to serve each other, improve people's lives, and promote human progress.

Private property, unhampered prices, enterprises, entrepreneurs, and profit are the basic institutional arrangements put into motion by the invisible hand and invisible eye of the market. Only those institutional arrangements guarantee that—in a market economy—enriching oneself at the expense of others cannot be done. Each person must be responsible for his or her own actions, and the pursuit of happiness becomes the premise for providing benefit to others.

Of course, the market is never actually perfect; it will have all kinds of problems. Problems arise for several main reasons: (a) the market operates in an imperfect legal environment, (b) people's knowledge is limited, and (c) various kinds of anti-market forces such as vested interests and governments often interfere with the market. For those reasons, the market is often criticized and questioned. People are accustomed to blaming market dysfunctions for the troubles they encounter in their daily lives. For example, after the current financial crisis that started in the United States in 2008 and swept across the globe, the market became the scapegoat, and government assistance became the savior.

The market is not an invention of economists; it is the creation of ordinary people. The market is the result of the spontaneous behavior of innumerable people. Often, those ordinary people who create the market and live in the market do not see the forest for the trees. They are easily bewitched by anti-market views. Understanding any market mechanism requires a rational and scientific mindset. The market economy needs people to protect it. That protection is the basic responsibility of economists. Moreover, the professional economist is certainly a steadfast supporter of the market economy. Without a market economy, we do not need economists.

Of course, understanding the market is no easy task. Since Adam Smith, the debate about the market economy has never stopped, even among economists. The Neoclassical economists attempted to provide a perfect theoretical structure for the market mechanism. Their pursuit of mathematical perfection led them to make some unrealistic assumptions, which provided excuses for market criticism. Those unrealistic assumptions even provided theoretical support for the centrally planned economy and government intervention. Discussions of "market failure" became very fashionable among economists. Even someone such as Nobel Prize–winning economist Joseph Stiglitz has an understanding of the market that is not up to current standards. He incorrectly takes the defects of Neoclassical economics as defects in the market itself. Such a pity!

In reality, the so-called defects of the market are in large part the result of market critics' subjective imagination and the government interventions they cause. That conclusion is especially the case when the market economy's normal operations are damaged by inappropriate intervention by the government or by some other sort of power. When the market economy's performance is hampered, people often misjudge the abnormality as something inherently wrong with the market itself.

The same holds true with people. They may be perfectly healthy, but if someone keeps telling them that they have an illness and must take medication, they will ultimately take the medication and become ill. That same reasoning is the subject of Chinese comedian Zhao Benshan's *Maiguai (Selling Crutches)*. The victim's leg was fine, but the crutch seller repeatedly told him that it was broken. In the end, the victim was convinced his leg was broken. His only recourse was to buy crutches. In today's society, the "crutch" is government's willful intervention in the marketplace. The crutch sellers sold us the majority of the defects in the so-called market economy.

My understanding of the market economy began with reading about the subject. When I was a graduate student at the Northwestern University of China in 1982, I read Adam Smith's *The Wealth of Nations* for the first time. It started to build my belief in the market economy. In 1984, I wrote two papers. One proposed how to use the dual-track price system to incrementally bring about price liberalization, and the other discussed entrepreneurs' role in the market economy.

Since then, I have summed up the market economy as an equation: the market = prices + entrepreneurs. All my further research developed along that line. After graduate school, I began working at the State Commission on Economic System Restructuring where I was directly involved in research about the Chinese economic reform policies. Subsequently, I went to Oxford University. While at Oxford, I tried to provide a theoretical framework for the capitalist enterprise system from the view of the relationship between ownership and entrepreneurs. On returning to China, I became a professor at Peking University, and I applied the theories that I had learned and developed to my continuing research of China's reform issues.

My understanding of the market economy deepened as China's economic reforms were put into practice. My faith in the market economy has also continuously strengthened. The challenges to the market economy by critics and others inside and outside China—as well as the issues that Chinese reform has encountered—have been sources of inspiration for my research. One could say that over the past 26 years, the vast majority of my papers have tackled real issues and have put forward my own ideas to help people understand the market economy and the market reforms that China is currently undertaking.

This book includes 16 of my papers. Two of them, "China's Gradual Reform: A Historical Perspective" and "Taking Price Reform as the Center of Systemic Economic Reform" (a chapter appendix) were written in 1994 and 1984, respectively. The other 14 papers were written in the past five years. I have divided this book into four parts. Part One, "Understanding the Market Economy," includes five chapters. It primarily discusses the basic reasoning of the market economy, especially how the market uses the systemic constructs of enterprises, entrepreneurs, and profit to make individuals responsible for their own actions and to create a system of accountability for cooperation between strangers. I attempt to settle a few common misunderstandings about the market economy. Special attention is paid to clarifying ideas about profit and corporate social responsibility. I also discuss the contradictions between state ownership and the market economy.

Part Two, "Reflecting on China's Economic Reform," includes six chapters and one appendix. It mainly analyzes how China's reforms were implemented. These chapters prove that no one has the ability to design the market economy. China's economic reform is a process of continuous adjustments and sustained evolution. Many situations "scored a lucky hit," as if an invisible hand was in control. The major accomplishment of China's reforms has been becoming good at using spontaneous forces and turning spontaneous forces into conscious policy. I also prove that the transition from position-based rights to property-based rights, as well as the rise of entrepreneurs, is the key to understanding China's rapid economic growth. Problems such as corruption and income disparity must be viewed as part of a process.

Part Three, "Understanding the Financial Crisis," includes three chapters. It discusses how the financial crisis happened, and what the correct policy choices are. I believe that mistakes in government policy caused the financial crisis, and the best way to solve it is to let the market adjust itself. Governments' use of Keynesian policies to stimulate the economy will be effective for a while, but that approach will bring about serious long-term negative consequences. I must admit that my understanding of the financial crisis is basically attributable to the Austrian school of economics' theory of the business cycle. I believe the Austrian school of economics has the most convincing theory on the market economy. It differs from the Neoclassical school of economics. The Austrian school believes that the market is made up of innumerable economic actors existing in an uncertain environment and constantly in the process of collecting and processing dispersed information to make a decision with a goal in mind. Entrepreneurs are the main driving force of the market. Artificial government interventions in the market process distort price signals and lead to inefficiency, even crises. Precisely because of uncertainty and incomplete information, the free market is necessary, and it is the only efficient system. The Neoclassical school's assumption of complete information is an issue with the economists themselves, not an issue with the market.

Part Four, "The Pulse of Future Development," includes one chapter. It discusses the potential of Chinese economic development and the prospects for reform. I believe that the key for China, as the country with the world's largest population, to return to being the largest economy lies in allowing the entrepreneurial spirit to develop the potential of the domestic market. For that to happen, China must continue to reduce the state-owned economy, to reduce government control over the economy, and—over the next 30 years—to emphasize political reform to build a system of constitutional democracy. I predict that China's historical transition, starting in 1840, will be complete by 2040. At that time, China will be a true market economy and a country under the rule of law.

Some of the chapters in this book came from lectures I gave to students at Peking University. Mr. Cen Ke and others made important contributions to the early revisions and presentations, for which I am very grateful. Three articles were translated from English, for which I would like to thank Mr. Hongbo Wang and Mr. Zhijing Niu for their outstanding translations.

This book came about because of a proposal by Mr. Hongjun Shi. The finishing work was also under his supervision. The success of this book's publication could not have come about without the high-quality and highly effective editing of Ms. Wenqing Li. Here, I would like to thank them both.

If this book allows the reader to better understand the market economy and to have solid confidence in China's market reforms, that understanding is all I can ask.

Weiying Zhang
April 5, 2010, Qingming Festival
Guanghua School of Management, Peking University

Introduction: The Logic of the Market and China's Reforms

Renewed Interest in the Outstanding Ideas of Classical Economics

Recently, I have been reading about the history of ideas. In the history of science, there is an idea called Whig history, which purports that science is always progressing. Today's discoveries are more correct than yesterday's discoveries. If that is the case, those of us who engage in scientific research do not need to read the old literature; we just need to read whatever has been published most recently. The idea of Whig history is completely incorrect. Science does not absolutely always progress in a straight line. It often detours. For example, the ancient Greek astronomer Aristarchus proposed heliocentric theory 300 years before the Common Era. His theory was not accepted because Ptolemy's geocentric theory had reigned supreme for more than 1,500 years. Aristarchus's theory was accepted only after Copernicus published *On the Revolutions of the Heavenly Spheres* in 1543.

Classical economics began when Adam Smith wrote *The Wealth of Nations* in 1776. It has made a lot of progress, but it has also taken a torturous path. That is to say, the economic theories that appeared after Adam Smith's time were not necessarily more correct or deeper than classical economics.

I have also been studying Keynesianism recently. In some respects, Keynesian theories represent progress, but perhaps overall they represent regression. Our planned economy theories of the past were a giant step backward compared with the market theories of classical economics. Therefore, I recommend that those who study economics should sometimes look back and reexamine the classics. The outstanding ideas of classical works can help us understand our current problems. We now focus only on some mathematical and statistical models. But to my knowledge, very few people in the field of economics today have truly surpassed Adam Smith. Adam Smith's

1

basic idea was to research the essence and reasons for the growth in a nation's wealth. Economics later turned into research about resource allocation and equilibrium. It turned into a kind of static research, not research into progress and change. Thus, we put a lot of focus on unimportant things.

In the few thousand years of written history, civilization made little progress before the Industrial Revolution. The rate of annual technical progress did not surpass 0.05 percent. It took 1,500 years for per capita income to double. Over the past 200 years, humanity's rate of annual technical progress averaged 1.5 percent. Per capita income for the entire world can double every 50 years.[1] Why did the progress made over the past 200 years far exceed the progress made over the past few thousand years? That is the question I would like to explain using the logic of the market.

Adam Smith's theory was that wealth creation came from productivity increases. Productivity increases came from technological progress and innovation. Technological progress and innovation came from division of labor. Division of labor is limited by market scale. Thus, the larger the market scale is, the higher the degree of division of labor and specialization will be. The higher the degree of division of labor is, the faster the speed of technological progress will be. The faster the speed of technological progress is, the wealthier the country will be. An increase in national wealth further expands the scale of the market. That process then repeats itself, leading to sustained economic growth. That is the basic logic of social progress.

In ancient times, technology spread very slowly. The speed of technological progress was even slower. The Stone Age lasted more than 2 million years. Archeological discoveries reveal that more than 10,000 years ago, there was little difference in the stone tools used worldwide. After the Bronze and Iron Ages, technological progress and the spread of technology accelerated, but they were still slow. For example, Cai Lun improved the papermaking process in about 100 AD during the Han dynasty. However, the papermaking process did not spread to the Islamic world until 751 AD during the Tang dynasty. That technology transfer was accidental: the Tang dynasty was at war with the caliphate at that time, and Tang soldiers who were taken prisoner imparted their knowledge of papermaking to their captors. The spread of papermaking technology from China to the Islamic world took more than 650 years. It took another 200 to 300 years for the process to reach Europe.

Today, the speed of technological progress is extremely fast, and technology spreads even faster. Today, the speed of technological progress cannot keep up with the speed at which technology spreads. As soon as a new technological innovation emerges, the entire world can begin using it, and that speed has had a very important effect on humanity. Regardless of whether we are discussing the speed of technological progress or the speed at which technology spreads, they are actually a process of market globalization.

The Logic of the Market and the Logic of Robbery

Why does the market have such power? To answer that question, we must return to human nature. From ancient times to the present, human nature has been to pursue happiness. Even though different people have different understandings of happiness—with some seeing it as money, some as fame, some as power, and some as contentment—all people pursue happiness, regardless of what they call it.

The ways in which people pursue happiness can be separated into two methods. The first leads to happiness by causing others to be unhappy, such as theft, robbery, or war—taking from others to make oneself happy. That pursuit is the logic of robbery. The second method leads to happiness by causing others to be happy. That pursuit is the logic of the market.

Since ancient times, both logics have existed. The Roman Empire's conquests resulted from the logic of robbery. The Silk Road was a result of the logic of the market. The First Emperor of Qin used the logic of robbery to unify China. The European Union was formed on the logic of the market.

The progress of humanity could be called a process of gradually replacing the logic of robbery with the logic of the market. The logic of robbery can only allocate wealth or even destroy wealth. Only the logic of the market can truly create wealth. Over the past 200 years, the reason humanity underwent such a huge change was that the logic of the market replaced the logic of robbery. Although the logic of robbery still exists between countries, increasingly more people recognize that all people can win only if they transact according to the logic of the market. Only then can humanity continuously improve everyone's living standards.

A classic example from recent history is Japan and Germany. Japan and Germany started World War II in an attempt to use the logic of robbery to improve the interests of their own countries. They failed and were almost destroyed. After World War II, the reason the two countries could rise again to become world economic powers was that they transitioned to the logic of the market. In other words, they produced goods and provided services that people in the rest of the world valued, so they became economic powers.

The Foundation of the Market: Liberty and Private Property Rights

All people who study economics know that any enterprise that wants to earn money in the market must first produce goods or services that consumers are willing to purchase. A person can pursue happiness only by making others happy. If someone wants to be a boss, but his or her employees are unhappy, there is no way for the boss to be happy. At the same time, if the employer is not happy, the employees cannot be happy. Therefore, the market economy is an impetus for everyone to pursue happiness. The market turns that impetus into a system that creates wealth and creates value for others. In the market, one person does not decide what is good or bad; that decision is made by others. Competition between enterprises in the market economy can be understood as competition to create happiness for consumers. Whoever can create more happiness for consumers, whoever can expand the market, is the one who ultimately makes a profit.

Why must the market abide by that logic? To answer the question, we must return to a more basic issue: liberty and property rights. In the market, no one can force someone else to buy anything. The buyer must agree to pay a certain price. That price will not be more than the value the buyer will receive from that product or service. Therefore, liberty is the first priority. Without liberty, the market cannot operate. We could even say that liberty and markets are two sides of the same coin. Respect for the system of private property is a guarantor of liberty. The property rights system includes material things, human rights, and intellectual property. If everyone's rights and liberties are fully respected, then one can attain happiness only by making others happier.

We can explain that conclusion from another perspective. Today, only one organization in the world legally does *not* have to make others happy but can be happy on its own. That organization is government. Government receives revenue through taxes. Taxes are forced, not voluntary, because the government has the power to collect taxes forcefully. Even if in theory we require government to serve the people and to provide public goods to citizens, we have no way of guaranteeing that the taxes collected by the government are not higher than the value of the public goods provided while serving the people. In fact, taxes collected by government often exceed the value of services provided. For example, the government collects Y 100 in taxes, but the value of the services provided is only Y 80. However, enterprises in a competitive market cannot provide goods or services whose value is less than the prices paid because enterprises can receive earnings only through transactions.

We can consider this issue in yet another way. Imagine that an enterprise that produces mineral water is allowed to collect taxes. The government grants that privilege with the stipulation that the enterprise must continue to provide mineral water to society. We can foresee that the enterprise will collect taxes from us every year, but the amount of mineral water provided and its quality will decrease. In the end, we may have nothing to drink.

Enterprises and governments are two completely different types of organizations. One must create value, but the other will not necessarily create value. If the government wants to have unlimited power to tax, then we citizens have no way to truly limit the government. Understanding democratic politics from that perspective shows why budget restrictions are so important. Therefore, in the process of building democratic systems in the West, the way to restrict the government's power to tax became a very important issue.

Laissez Faire and Noninterference

People often believe that laissez faire is a Western ideal and that China has lacked market ideals since ancient times. That view is biased. In ancient China, the philosopher Laozi was perhaps the world's first true classical liberal. His ideas regarding rule by noninterference could be considered the quintessence of the market economy. Adam Smith's laissez faire ideas possibly stemmed from Laozi.

While in France, Adam Smith met François Quesnay, a representative of the physiocratic school, and Smith stayed in contact with him. Without question, Quesnay influenced Smith's way of thinking. Quesnay himself was influenced by ancient Chinese philosophers, such as Laozi and Confucius, among others. In the last chapter of *Tao Te Ching,* Laozi said, "The more we give to others, the more we have ourselves." That statement completely encompasses the logic of the market that I described. Of course, Laozi did not understand the market economy, nor did he have an idea of what the market was.

Another example from ancient China is the distinguished second-century BC historian Sima Qian of the Western Han. He was perhaps the first market liberal in human history.[2] His *Biographies of Usurers* in the *Records of the Grand Historian* is an excellent defense of the market economy. It states that human nature is the pursuit of wealth and happiness and cannot be changed. Therefore, a great ruler should let things be and make the best of circumstances. The worst kind of government benefits itself at the expense of the people. He said, "The best is to allow others to follow their pursuits; ... they can be led to their pursuits or can be taught or regulated, but the worst is to fight against their pursuits." If only the government will not interfere, labor could be divided among agriculture, industry, commerce, mining, and fishing, "with everyone encouraged to pursue their own business and enjoy what they do." Wealth will flow like water from high points to low points.

Many phenomena in contemporary Chinese society do not result from free competition between individuals and enterprises that truly adhere to market rules. Instead, they are caused by the government's using force to benefit itself at the expense of the people. Much of the theft committed by state-owned enterprises today is not new; it existed in China 2,000 years ago. State-owned enterprises also are not new. After states came into existence, so too did state-owned enterprises. Of course, the enterprise ideal of ancient times is not the same as today's.

Much of China's academic research and education has a "Eurocentric" perspective. That is something we need to reconsider. From a global perspective, using Eurocentric methods to explain many current issues is problematic. Marx himself was a classic Eurocentrist. In Marx and Engels's *The Communist Manifesto*, the peoples of China and India are designated as barbaric and semibarbaric. When we accepted Marxism, we also believed China was inferior, closed, barbaric, irrational, unscientific, and despotic. Those ideas had a tremendous effect on our way of thinking. With the rise of China, we have a reason—and a responsibility—to reconsider the developmental track of the history of human thought.

The Ancient Implication System and Joint Responsibility Today

Adam Smith said that market extent (scale) is very important. If a market is very small, division of labor cannot be very specialized. For example, in the countryside, there are few professional hairstylists. Those rural hairstylists have to perform all services related to hairstyling. In the city, hairstyling's labor is divided: some people specialize in washing hair, and some specialize in cutting hair. Another example is the foot-washing business in the city. Different people handle the water and wash the feet, someone else clips toenails, and another person cleans ears.

Only after division of labor becomes specialized can jobs be done relatively well. The larger the scale of the market, the more people there will be to participate in transactions. Division of labor in the market will become more specialized so technological progress and wealth accumulation will happen more quickly.

However, the larger the scope of the market, the number of people who know each other will decrease. The majority of transactions will be between people who do not know each other. The modern market is a kind of transaction between strangers. Because it involves transactions between strangers, trust becomes extremely important. That is especially the case for vital goods because without trust, no one would risk buying or selling. For example, who produced the mineral water I drink? Who is the owner of the enterprise, and who are its employees? They are all people I do not know. So how can I drink that mineral water confidently?

Borrowing from the many systems used to rule ancient China will help us understand the modern market economy. Since the Qin dynasty, even though China has been split, overall it had been unified until today. When the First Emperor of Qin unified China, the country had 20 million people. At the peak of the Han dynasty, China had 63 million people. For more than 1,000 years following the Han dynasty, China's population basically fluctuated between 20 million and 60 million. During that time, developed means of communication did not exist (unlike today, where the Internet and telephones allow us to get news from anywhere quickly). When General Wu Sangui (1618–1678) revolted in Yunnan in the early Qing dynasty, two months passed before the Kangxi Emperor knew about it.

Considering that the spread of information was so backward in ancient China, effectively managing such a large area and population was an amazing feat. I believe a very important system during that time was the implication system, designed by the statesman Lord Shang (395–338 BC) during the reign of Duke Xiao of Qin. Under the implication system, "when one person commits a crime, the whole family is implicated." For example, if one person rebelled in a village with 100 people, all 100 would be killed. People had to bear joint liability for family and community members. Under that system, the emperor did not need to watch over every person because they had to supervise each other. For the past 2,000 years, the management of China has basically relied on such a system. The implication system, of course, is not the only reason ancient China succeeded, but it is a very important reason. That linked responsibility became a system in which everyone mutually supervised each other.

In my view, trust in the modern market economy in essence is built on "the implication system," but we refer to it as "linked responsibility." Therefore, linked responsibility is the key to understanding the operation of the market economy. The basic difference is that the ancient linked responsibility was based on bloodlines and location. The individual had no choice. Our linked responsibility today is built on a foundation of contractual relationships. It is formed on a voluntary basis. When someone enters an organization, that person forms a linked responsibility relationship with the other people in the organization. The individual must bear responsibility for the behavior of the other people in the organization, and the others must bear responsibility for each individual's actions. That responsibility is related not only to the law but also to reputation.

Of course, in reality, some linked responsibility systems are rooted in location and voluntary associations. Commercial organizations founded on origin are an example. There are 31 provinces, municipalities, and autonomous regions in mainland China. On the international stage, we are Chinese, but in China, we are also Henanese, Shandongese, Zhejiangese, and so on. The Henanese can also be separated into Luoyangese, Zhumadianese, Zhoukouese, and so on. People from the same village or city have linked responsibility. If someone from Shaanxi misbehaves, it may affect the reputation of all Shaanxiese. Because of linked responsibility, each Shaanxiese must bear a certain responsibility for the actions of other Shaanxiese. Therefore, some restrictions will form between Shaanxiese. There is a Shaanxi Commercial Association in Beijing. To join, people must meet certain standards. If an applicant is a fraud or has a bad reputation, that person will be refused membership—thus preventing "one mouse from ruining a pot of porridge." Such is the meaning of linked responsibility. It is precisely that type of linked responsibility that causes commercial associations to play an important role in maintaining market order.

Profit Comes from Responsibility

Enterprises in the market economy can be understood as organizations that establish trust by linked responsibility. The ownership of enterprises and their profit system can be understood as a type of linked responsibility system. That system allows consumers to supervise producers more effectively, so trust in the market can be established.

An enterprise is a production team formed by many people. To better assign responsibility and to make all people responsible for their own actions, an enterprise must have an owner. Being a so-called owner means that if other people's problems are not discovered, they become the owner's problems. Being a so-called employee means that if no one else discovers the employee's problems, that person does not have to take responsibility.

Take a restaurant, for example. If a customer gets food poisoning—perhaps the vegetables were not washed well enough, or some ingredient was contaminated—the restaurant owner must take responsibility. Even if away at the time, the owner must still bear responsibility. Because of such responsibility, the owner will design various types of management systems. In this case, the restaurant owner makes the wait staff get regular medical checkups, even though regulations do not require those checks. An infectious disease carried by a server could cause the restaurant to go out of business. The owner must bear linked responsibility for each person's behavior. That is the basic meaning of being an owner. That meaning should help in understanding the design of an enterprise's internal property rights structure and management system. Ultimately, a management system, or a system of linked responsibility, is designed with the objective of making everyone responsible for his or her own actions.

Here is another case. A downstream branded enterprise must bear linked responsibility for all upstream enterprises. Imagine that a BMW's bearings break, causing an accident. BMW must take responsibility, even if it did not produce the bearings. Because downstream enterprises must bear linked responsibility for upstream enterprises, BMW designed many quality standards to guarantee that the parts purchased from its suppliers are up to standard. Another example is Alibaba.com. It must bear linked responsibility for tens of millions of traders, which is where its true value lies.

It is in that sense that I say profit is responsibility. In other words, for people to earn money, they must certainly take on more responsibility. The ability to take on responsibility will determine the size of a person's business and how much money he or she can earn. Take, for example, the melamine milk powder incident in 2008. The dairies did not add the melamine. Dairy farmers or milk depots added it. The reason we want the dairies to take responsibility is that part of the money they earn encompasses the responsibility taken for those dairy farmers and milk depots. If the dairies do not bear responsibility for dairy farmers and milk depots, they should not earn as much money.

The Telunsu brand of milk made by Mengniu did not contain melamine because that milk came from cows owned by Mengniu. If only the milk from company cows were guaranteed free of melamine, milk production would be determined by the number of company cows. Corporate scale would be limited. To have melamine-free milk, the enterprise must have the ability to supervise all dairy farmers and milk depots, even feed suppliers. That analysis means that the size of a country's enterprise scales is determined by the legal and cultural environment in society. If the degree of trust in all of society is very low and if dairy companies must start producing their own feed, then corporate scope cannot possibly be large.

Real estate companies are the same. One year, a media company exposed a real estate development that had ammonia levels over the legal limit. The owner protested; he believed that it was the construction company's problem and that it had nothing to do with him. If high ammonia levels are the construction company's responsibility, how can that owner have the nerve to sit in his office and earn so much money?

Banks are another example of linked responsibility. If a customer is robbed after entering a bank but the bank does not take responsibility, certainly, no one will deposit money in that bank. If the bank guarantees that it will take responsibility if customers lose money after entering the premises, then more people will deposit money at that bank, and perhaps the bank will also earn more money. That is why banks hire security guards.

This point is very important to our understanding of the current market structure. It also has an important implication for antitrust policies. One enterprise wants to acquire another, but its market share surpasses a certain scale, so the government intervenes. That interference is absurd. An enterprise is not only a production unit but also an organization that establishes trust.

Economics textbooks speak of so-called perfect competition. It cannot possibly be a truly effective market structure. If an industry had an infinite number of suppliers, perhaps no one would be trusted. Therefore, whether an industry produces milk, vehicles, or televisions, the result of competition is that only a few large branded manufacturers exist. That is the basic characteristic of the market structure. The few countable branded manufacturers will monitor their upstream suppliers, who, in turn, will monitor their own upstream suppliers. Our society will naturally form a good monitoring network. One Walmart must bear responsibility for the actions of millions, or even tens of millions, of people. If there were 100 Walmarts in the market, all with different names, that market would certainly be ineffective.

One reason intellectual property is so significant is because it is an important foundation for trust in commercial society. If any company could call itself Walmart, then Walmart would not have the ability, nor the incentive, to bear responsibility for all those people. The business would certainly fail. Trust between consumers and vendors would not exist. Therefore, a truly effective market is composed of different enterprises on each level of the value chain. A small number of large branded enterprises face the consumer directly. Behind one large enterprise are dozens of smaller enterprises supporting it. Behind those dozens of smaller enterprises are hundreds, thousands, or even tens of thousands of small enterprises overlaying the levels of linked responsibility, forming an effective market.

From the Position-Based Economy to the Property-Based Economy

The past 200 years of economic development in the West surpassed the previous 5,000 years. The transition over the recent 30 years of the Chinese economy also perhaps surpassed our transition over the past 5,000 years. In 1800, the average Britton had the same common standard of living as that of an ancient Roman. His projected lifespan was not longer than that of an ancient Roman, and his calorie intake was not higher. Similarly, the standard of living of the average Chinese 30 years ago was certainly not as good as that of the average Chinese in the Sui and Tang eras, nor even in the Qin and Han eras. The quality and variety of food were not much different. If Emperor Taizong of Tang (598–649) had come back to life 30 years ago, he would have been accustomed to this country, because it was pretty much the same as when he died.

China's reforms over the past 30 years have progressed from the logic of robbery to the logic of the market. The planned economy was in essence the logic of robbery. The government owned all production materials, and the government decided what to produce and how to produce it. People had no basic liberties, especially the freedom to start a business. The so-called price set by the government was nothing more than a tool for government plunder and allocation of wealth. It was not much different from taxes.

We Chinese have constantly been hard working, with everyone pursuing his or her own happiness. During the planned economy of the past, individual pursuit of happiness often led to mutual harm. In the end, no one was happy. We gradually moved toward the logic of the market after Reform and Opening. The household-contract responsibility system, the liberalization of prices, the rise of private enterprise, and the reformation of state-owned enterprises into private enterprises were all part of the gradual process toward the logic of the market. Over the past 30 years, increasingly more resources, energy, and time have transitioned to creating value for others. They increased society's wealth, and everyone's standard of living improved.

What is the difference between the planned economy (state-owned economy) and the private economy (market economy)? It is generally believed that assets and rights in the private economy belong to individuals, whereas in the state-owned economy, assets and rights belong to the state or the collective. That is a misunderstanding.

Consider that in any society, no matter what ideal it calls itself or what system it uses, rights are exercised by individuals. Only people with the ability to think can exercise those rights. The only difference between the state-owned economy and the private economy is that the foundation for individual rights is different. Under the planned economy, or state-owned economy, individual rights are granted according to a person's position (status) in government and society. Rights are separated according to administrative level. Generally, the higher the level, the more rights a person has. So everyone competes for positions. For example, when people rode the train, whether they had a ticket for a hard seat or a soft sleeper was decided by position. Cars and telephones are another example. A division cadre could have a telephone extension, and a department cadre could have a direct line, but average people could not have telephones at all. Even the type of newspaper someone could read was determined by rank. High-level leaders read reference materials, but common people could read only newspapers such as *People's Daily*. In other words, each type of right was related to a person's position.

Under the planned economy, we did not pursue happiness by making others happy. Instead, we pursued happiness by making others unhappy. Our energies were spent fighting for power and gain. We were competing, even competing for life and death, but we were not creating value. The well-known Chinese cartoonist Hua Junwu once drew a cartoon titled "Who Says We Aren't Hardworking?" It showed two people using a saw, but the teeth were pointed upward, so the wood would not be cut. At the time, we had to struggle not only against the living but also against the dead (such as the Criticize Lin, Criticize Confucius Campaign). All our energies were focused on the struggle. Our struggles against the dead were tools to struggle against the living.

Under the market economy, rights are defined by property. Reform and Opening changed the singular class system. With individual property, as long as people have money, they can also enjoy the majority of services that only people with power could enjoy before.

13

With money, farmers too can travel in soft sleeper compartments on trains, fly on airplanes, buy cars, have telephones, or read various types of media online. Today, the head of the State Council uses the Internet; in that regard, he and the common people are equals. But that would not have been the case in the past. Under the planned economy, farmers could not even decide what crops to plant; commune cadres made that decision.

The foundation of rights in today's Chinese society has already experienced a tremendous change. Sima Qian once said more than 2,000 years ago, "Those with one thousand jin [gold] live as well as a magistrate, and those with tens of thousands of jin live as well as kings." He was referring to that phenomenon during his own time, but it also describes that phenomenon in today's society. For example, a mayor may have many privileges, but the living standards of China's wealthy are no worse than that of the mayor; they might even be better. If a mayor has excessive material pleasures, they were more than likely attained through corruption, whereas those of private business owners are derived from money. They can have higher-quality cars and larger houses than the mayor, and they can also hire more nannies. That status was impossible in the past. To hire a nanny, one had to reach a certain level. Of course, perhaps I am exaggerating a bit. Bureaucrats still have many privileges, but at least now to attain happiness, we do not need to attain a certain level in government.

Precisely because of that kind of transition in the system of property rights, happiness can be attained by creating value. Thus, the process in which each person pursues happiness became a process of continuously creating wealth. And that is exactly how China's wealth accumulated year after year. Now, China has already become the world's second-largest economic system. Some economists like the production function ideal. They believe that China's growth relies mainly on increases in inputs, not increases in productivity. However, a basic fact is that with the same natural resources, China's per capita income has increased 10 times! Capital is also created by people.

The foundation of rights continues to change. If people's viewpoints do not change with it, much maladjustment will occur. In the 1980s, many people were dissatisfied with reform, and their dissatisfaction was directly related to the change in rights. For example, when taking the train, the people in the soft sleeper car—even if they did not know each other—had their rank in common and were comfortable with each other. After Reform and Opening, a drastic change occurred. A sole proprietor could ride in the soft sleeper car, which perhaps made those with special privileges feel uncomfortable. We Chinese are accustomed to status differences based on government rank rather than income differences based on market competition. We are accustomed to considering issues using the logic of robbery rather than the logic of the market.

Entrepreneurs Are the Core of Wealth Creation

The activities in which the best and brightest of a society are engaged—such as being officials, being cadres, or doing business—are vital to a country's accumulation of wealth and economic development. In a backward country, the best and brightest are all government officials. In a developed country, the best and brightest are primarily engaged in business. The Bureaucrat-Rank Standard (*guan benwei*) prevails in our society. In the power-via-position economy, the best and brightest all go into the government. The best and brightest are skilled in the art of the power struggle. Our government has accumulated a large number of bright people, so the best minds are all concentrated in government, but they are not engaged in productive activities.

However, under the planned system in China, one group of people had no such opportunity: the farmers. They were excluded from entering the city, from being state workers, and from being cadres. Therefore, the brightest people in the countryside of the past were of two types: (a) production team leaders, or directors of mass revolutionary committees, who enjoyed special privileges and (b) people engaged in speculative buying and selling, who would perhaps ultimately be arrested and serve jail time. After Reform and Opening, those two types basically set up the private economy and rural enterprises in the countryside.

We have a hard time determining whether many matters are good or bad. An example is the household-registration system (*hukou*). Today, it is regarded as a very bad system. But in view of the process of reform, it was the household-registration system that preserved the timbers of reform and entrepreneurship. If we had at the time attracted all the rural best and brightest into the government, the initial steps of reform in China would have been very difficult. Because the rural best and brightest did not enter the government, the first generation of entrepreneurs came from the countryside. Later, with the further liberalization of the economic system and the legalization of private enterprises, some urban residents and government officials entered the private market, becoming the second generation of entrepreneurs. Then, we attracted overseas talent, the returnee entrepreneurs—such as Yanhong Li, the cofounder of Baidu, and Chaoyang Zhang, the founder of Souhu—who are our third generation of entrepreneurs. Since Reform and Opening, China's entrepreneurial pool expanded through this process.

If we look back, our country has many issues related to the co-existence of the two types of economies: the power-via-position economy and the power-via-property economy. The combination of the two will lead to corruption. People with power turn power into property, and those with property use it to buy power, which they then use to seek more property. Thus, corruption appears, leading to popular discontent.

People of China have different views about the three generations of entrepreneurs since Reform and Opening.

Many people look down on the first generation of entrepreneurs. They are regarded as uncouth. They have money, but no culture, and are uncivilized. They are rich, which, of course, disgusts us, even though they produce the things we like, bringing us happiness.

Because the second generation of entrepreneurs came out of the government, they have close connections with the government, which they often used to obtain resources. Therefore, we believe they did not rely on ability or diligence to make their fortunes.

People view the third generation of returnee entrepreneurs more positively. They brought back overseas capital to invest. They created "high technology" that we did not understand and that had a sense of mystery. They were well educated, with doctorates and master's degrees from overseas. Chinese people respect those who have been well educated. Therefore, the majority of people have nothing against the returnees' becoming millionaires or billionaires.

People are still not very accepting of the first and second generations of entrepreneurs and may even hate them. I believe we can understand the whole process of China's reforms from this angle:

how the Chinese view the three types of entrepreneurs. Regardless of whether we are discussing price reform, state-owned enterprise reform, or other aspects of reform, this angle will allow us to be more rational.

Reform Is a Reduction of Government Power

China's reforms over the past 30 years have been a huge success. However, over the past few years, reform has stagnated or even relapsed. Whether or not high economic growth in the future is sustainable will be determined to a large degree by whether or not we can get back on the path to market reforms. It will also be determined by whether or not the rule of law and democracy can truly move forward.

The overall objective of future reform should be to reduce the scope of the power-via-position economy and expand the power-via-property economy. The market economy needs government. The basic function of government is to protect individual liberty and property. If the government exists, so will a power-via-position economy, but the problem is that now the proportion of that economy is much too large. The government controls too many resources, and government officials have too much power. The result is not only that individual liberty and property are ineffectively protected but also that they are seriously threatened. To resolve that issue, we must gradually push forward the establishment of the rule of law and the democratization of politics. If the political system reforms of the future cannot be effectively implemented, we could even lose some of the progress we have already made.

Unfortunately, the 2008 Global Financial Crisis caused the power of our government to expand again. The 1998 Asian Financial Crisis led to a reduction in government power and an increase in private property. Leaders at the time were worried that if state-owned enterprise losses continued, they would cause the collapse of the country's financial system. A transition was implemented for the state-owned enterprise system.

After the 2008 financial crisis, the government had an opposite response. It was believed that only government investment and state-owned enterprises could solve the problem. Now, we have some private enterprises that were rapidly merged into state-owned enterprises. Of course, some private enterprises sought out acquisitions by state-owned enterprises. Under the current circumstances, private enterprises often feel unsafe, so they want to ally with state-owned enterprises. That approach is called "wearing a red hat," and it is the logic of robbery. It is very dangerous to continue in that direction.

When considering China's issues, or when resolving China's issues, we should view the long term, not confuse ourselves with short-term issues. To push the gross domestic product over 8 percent in 2009, the government implemented a large amount of state investment. From the long-term perspective, the damage may possibly be enormous. Excessive stimulus leads to inflation, so then the government begins to interfere with prices that had already been liberalized. Various types of administrative control measures are strengthened, leading to a relapse of the economic system.

I hope that the logic of the market can become everyone's ideal. Our future, the country's future, even humanity's future depends on what we believe in and what we do not believe in. From the 1950s to 30 years ago, we believed in the planned economy. The result was a tremendous disaster. If we continue to pin our hopes on the government plan and to use large, state-owned enterprises to develop China's economy, we have absolutely no prospects for the future.

Only if we move toward the logic of the market will China's future be bright!

PART ONE

THE NATURE OF THE MARKET

1. Understanding and Safeguarding the Market Economy

Economics is a science that receives a lot of criticism, as do the economists who study it. One might say that economics is the most easily attacked of the social sciences. Criticism of economics is not a new phenomenon, nor is it a phenomenon limited to China. Since the birth of economics more than 200 years ago, some people have viewed economics as *scientia non grata*. A recently published book by William Oliver Coleman, titled *Economics and Its Enemies*, analyzed the views of anti-economic thought since Adam Smith founded economics to the present day.[1] It is very comprehensive and well worth the read. The articles by Chinese economists who scold economics are, in contrast, too superficial.

Safeguarding the Market Economy Is the Duty of Economists

Because economics is such an unwelcome science, questions arise: Why does society need economists? Why do we need to put up the money to support so many economists? These questions could be answered in many ways. My own answer is that society needs economists because the market economy needs people to safeguard it. If we did not need a market economy, we would not need economists.

Why does the market economy need safeguarding? First, special interests and the privileged classes do not like the market economy. Throughout human history, the market economy has proved to be the fairest system. It gives every person opportunity and rejects special privileges. It can turn rags into riches, but it can also turn riches into rags. Therefore, people who have special privileges, people who would like special privileges, and people who want to gain through special privileges are not willing to accept the challenges of the market economy. The market economy opposes their special interests. Throughout history, we can see that the largest anti-market economy forces have been the privileged classes and special interests.

Second, we need economists because of people's ignorance. When I use the word "ignorance," I do not mean it in the negative sense. I want to emphasize its importance to scientific and rational thought. Rational thought is an important pillar of modern society. Since the Renaissance, each successive generation of scientists has taught us to use scientific methods to rationally consider issues. However, in daily life, most people do not consider issues in this way. They use their intuition instead. With respect to intuition, the market economy has a defect: When people can enjoy its benefits, they probably will not see its shortcomings. When people do not have the opportunity to enjoy the benefits of a market economy, they have no way of seeing what its advantages are. That is especially the case when the market economy's normal operations are damaged by inappropriate intervention by the government or some other sort of power. When the market economy's performance is hampered, people often misjudge the abnormality as something inherently wrong with the market itself.

Third, opportunists can easily take advantage of people's ignorance. Because most people use intuition rather than rational thought to view issues that will occur in society, those playing to the gallery have an opportunity to gain their favor. Those who criticize the market economy may not believe deep down that the market economy is bad; they just know that criticizing the market economy is a good way to gain public acclaim and support. Perhaps the critic is a so-called scholar or a politician. Since ancient times, politicians have asserted that a market economy is bad. They know that proposing anti-market mottos and policies can bring them more acclaim and more votes. Politicians like to promise people a free lunch, because people desire a free lunch—but economics tells us that there is no such thing as a free lunch. Therefore, whether in the past or in the present, whether inside China or in other countries, there have always been many people who oppose the logic of the market and see economists as their enemies.

China's Anti-market Signs Today

China's establishment of the market economy has not been easy. During the era of central planning, we completely disavowed the market. After the Reform and Opening policies were implemented, we partially recognized the market. After Deng Xiaoping's Southern Tour in 1992, we completely acknowledged the market. Complete acknowledgment happened because of the hard work of multiple generations. It even came at the cost of blood. Now, misunderstandings about and lack of trust in the market economy are starting to spread again throughout society. If lack of trust in the market evolves into national policy, it will have a huge negative effect on China's future economic development and social progress. Therefore, I am concerned about the spread of distrust toward the market.

Examples of such distrust are numerous; the recent price restriction on Lanzhou noodles is just one. In a market economy, why does the government need to restrict the price of a bowl of noodles? People who lack rational thinking skills believe that such restrictions will benefit the consumer. In reality, the only protection for the consumer's interest is market competition, not the government. If a government department limits competition while saying it wants to protect the consumer from exploitation by the seller, that action conflicts with logical reasoning. When the government restricts prices on noodles, a restaurant might reduce the quantity or quality of noodles; in the end, the consumer receives no benefit. Even worse, controlling the price of noodles can become a way for the government to rent-seek (for example, deciding which restaurants can sell a bowl of noodles for Y 4 and which can sell a bowl for Y 6). Restaurant owners must then find a bureaucrat to help them circumvent the restrictions, which leads to corruption.

Housing is another example. Because the price of housing is high, people complain. Thus, the government implements policies to create affordable housing and even to limit the price of housing. Many people believe that approach will resolve the average person's housing needs. If the market value of those houses is high, the people who get to live in them receive a substantial subsidy. Who gets to live in those houses? Except for the few average people who wait in line for housing, the majority of the houses are given to people with special privileges or people with connections, such as government employees and their friends and family. The best way to help low-income earners is to give them monetary subsidies directly.

Another example is the new Labor Contract Law. It includes a few sections that indicate a high level of distrust of the market. It places too many limitations on employing and laying off workers. China's common laborers receive no benefit from such a law. Excessive limitations on an enterprise's ability to hire and fire people will impede its development, and workers will have more difficulty in finding employment. Research of various countries demonstrates that euphemistically called labor protection laws ultimately victimize the workers themselves. The best way to protect workers is to promote competition between enterprises. The more ample the competition, the fairer the treatment the laborers will receive.

China's antitrust law will go into effect on August 1 of next year (2008). Frankly speaking, I am not at all optimistic about its prospects. Both the law's theoretical foundation and its impact concern me. The business behavior that the antitrust law targets and limits is actually a part of market creation and reputation. As for breaking up government-protected industries, this law has little use. I am concerned that laws with the goal of stopping monopolies will become a tool to oppose market competition.

Many people understand this reasoning, but few are willing to talk about it. I believe that if the misunderstandings about the market economy continue to spread in society, they will evolve into anti-market policies. China's economic development will face substantial risks, such as increased environmental damage. At this time, economists need to stand up, clarify, and safeguard the market economy.

The Marvel of the Market Economy throughout History

To examine the market economy's contribution to humanity, we must look back on history. Economist J. Bradford Delong from the University of California, Berkeley, researched 2.5 million years of human history from the Paleolithic era to 2000 AD. Until about 15,000 years ago, it took 99.4 percent of humanity's existence for the world's per capita gross domestic product (GDP) to reach 90 international dollars. (The international dollar is a unit of wealth measurement based on international purchasing power in 1990.) Then, in another 0.59 percent of humanity's history, until about 1750, the world's per capita GDP doubled to 180 international dollars. From 1750 until 2000, in less than 0.01 percent of the time, the world's per capita GDP grew 37 times, reaching 6,600 international dollars. In other words, 97 percent of humanity's wealth was created over the past 250 years, or 0.01 percent of its history.[2]

If Delong's research were depicted on a graph, it would show that over the past 2.5 million years, throughout 99.99 percent of humanity's time, the world's per capita GDP basically did not change. Over the past 250 years, though, there was suddenly straight-line vertical growth. The world's principal developed countries—whether they are derivatives of Western Europe, such as the United States, Canada, and Australia; the 12 countries of Western Europe; or even late-start Japan—experienced their main economic growth within the past 200 years. China's economic growth primarily occurred over the past 30 years.

Just citing numbers cannot fully explain the issue. Think for a moment about our ancestors. The goods an ordinary Chinese person was able to consume 100 years ago differed little from those in the Qin-Han-Sui-Tang era and was even less than from the Song dynasty. In Europe, it was the same. The goods an ordinary Briton could consume in 1800 were the same goods an Ancient Roman could enjoy, and the Ancient Roman consumed even more of those goods. The goods we can consume today are goods that people 100 years ago could not have dreamed of.

Estimates of consumer goods have been made from the records of retailers. Two hundred and fifty years ago, the number of types of products measured by stock-keeping units (SKUs) that people could enjoy was about 10^2, or only 100 types of products. Today, the number of SKUs of products we can consume is on the order of 10^{10}, or tens of billions.[3]

In 1820, the world's average life expectancy was 26 years, the same as Ancient Rome. By 2002, it had become 67 years. Now, the life expectancy in China is estimated at 70 years.

Some young people do not understand history and are probably unaware that China's grain-rationing tickets were in use until 1994. Before the ration ticket system ended, a person had to have grain tickets to buy grain, oil tickets to buy oil, and fabric tickets to buy fabric. Thirty years ago, a low-level cadre's salary was about Y 60 a month. At that time, 0.5 kilograms of eggs cost 60 cents. In other words, a cadre's monthly salary could buy about 50 kilograms of eggs. Today, a nanny's salary in Beijing is about Y 1,200 and can buy 150 kilograms of eggs. When I was in the countryside, farmers earned 20 cents for a day's work, which was equal to the value of 0.25 kilograms of wheat flour. Today, in my hometown, a person with no skills and an elementary school education can earn Y 55 per day. That Y 55 can buy a 25-kilogram bag of wheat flour. Such is the change brought about by China's Reform and Opening.

Why did the marvel of the market economy appear only in the past 250 years? Why did China's economic growth appear only in the past 30 years? Have people become smarter or wiser? Of course not; there has been little progress in people's IQs or wisdom over the history of written records. Of all the intelligent Chinese today, I doubt that there is anyone who could surpass Confucius, Mencius, or Laozi. In the West, it is the same. Humanity's wisdom over the past 2,000 or 3,000 years has changed little.

Did resources increase? Humanity's resources have not increased; instead, resources related to land are slowly decreasing. What changed? My only answer is that humanity implemented a new type of economic system, and that system is the market economy. Western countries began to implement the market economy more than 200 years ago, so they began to take off more than 200 years ago. China began to move toward the market economy 30 years ago, so over the past 30 years, China has made a giant leap forward.

The First Characteristic of the Market Economy: Compete to Create Value for Others

Why can the market economy create enormous wealth? The father of economics, Adam Smith, expressed a concept in the *Wealth of Nations* known as "the invisible hand." He said that in the market economy, each person pursues his own self-interest. Self-interest is very broad; it includes pursuing wealth and even pursuing renown. When people pursue their own self-interest, an invisible hand leads them to create value for others at the same time. Self-interest creates more value for society than someone who subjectively wants to contribute to society. And that is the wonder of the market economy.

What is the market? The market is a system in which the value of a product (good or bad) is decided by others, not by the individual who makes it. In the market, no one can receive an income unless he creates value for others. A person must work hard to create value for others. Prices provide us with a signal that informs us about which products and services have value, and which have no value. Value is tested on the market and decided by the buyer. No one willingly pays for a service unless its value exceeds its price. When two enterprises compete and we say one has the advantage, we mean that one enterprise can create more surplus value for the consumer. Competition between enterprises is competition to create surplus value for consumers.

Looking further, how do enterprises create more surplus value? They rely on creativity. Market competition is not simply price competition. Instead, it is a competition to see who has the ability to produce new products, or who uses new ways to produce products at a lower cost. It is a competition to see who can find new markets, discover new raw materials, and use new forms of organization to create higher value for the consumer. Whoever can do so will receive a larger market share. Business competition gave impetus to humanity's rapid development and allowed us over the past few hundred years to create wealth as never before.

A common misunderstanding is that improvements to humanity's standard of living have come from technological progress. But why has technology progressed under some systems but not under others? What promoted the progress of technology? The real proof of historical development has shown that only the market economy can promote the progress of technology. It quickly brings new technology into operation and influences human life. In ancient times, a few technological advances appeared but very few created value for the consumer or created wealth for society. Because they were not created under the pressure of market competition, those advances were hard to commercialize. The products or services that intelligent people rely on inspiration to create do not always satisfy consumers' real needs.

The Second Characteristic of the Market Economy: Division of Labor and Cooperation Between Strangers

The second special characteristic of the market economy is cooperation between strangers. The outcome of two people doing work cooperatively is greater than the outcome of their working independently. In other words, cooperation can create value, which is a basic principle of economics. Cooperation between strangers is different from cooperation in the people's communes, where everyone gets together to do the same thing. It is cooperation founded on division of labor and specialization. Division of labor and specialization can maximize each person's superior skills. It can maximize the use of people and materials to propel technological advancement; therefore, it can create more value.

Division of labor and specialization are interconnected with transactions. Division of labor is possible only because humans are willing to exchange. Because information is asymmetric, people who were familiar with each other in traditional society were often the only ones who cooperated. People related by blood, such as brothers and sisters, or people from the same village or temple initiated cooperation. Cooperation between strangers was rare. Today's cooperation is already interregional, across national boundaries, and increasingly global. Of all the commodities we consume today, 99 percent of the producers are people unknown to the consumer. When a business sells its products, most of its consumers are strangers. Precisely because of this kind of large-scale, large-scope cooperation is the world's wealth able to grow at a surprising speed.

For strangers to cooperate, an extremely important issue must be resolved—the issue of trust. If we do not trust others, we are reluctant to buy their products. If producers cannot sell their products, specialization has no benefit. In the end, they have no option but to produce for themselves and to return to the self-sufficiency model of the natural economy.

Therefore, I want to emphasize another ideal: the market economy has not only an invisible hand but also an invisible eye. In other words, if two strangers cooperate, they do so because an invisible eye is watching over them. Each person must perform well and must be responsible for his own actions. Critics of the market economy have often focused on the invisible hand, but they have not seen the use of the invisible eye, so they believe that swindlers will undoubtedly be in the market. That view reflects China's traditional bias against merchants. In reality, people in countries with more developed market economies care more for their own reputations. That is especially the case for businesses. If they want to succeed on the market, businesses must first build their reputation. If their reputation is not good, no one will trust them, and they will be eliminated.

The Key to Building Market Trust: Firms, Profit, and Entrepreneurs

How is market trust built? I will stress three ideals: firms, profit, and entrepreneurs. Those three ideals are the key to understanding the market economy.

For example, China has 1.3 billion people. If each person produces his own goods to sell on the market, who can trust whom? Let us re-phrase the question: if all labels were taken off all goods on the market, what goods would consumers risk buying? Perhaps they would risk buying simple commodities, such as potatoes, rice, and fruit. Would they risk buying products whose quality and functions are not easily discernable, such as vehicles, computers, mineral water, or projectors? They would not; thus, consumers would not risk buying 99 percent of the goods on the market.

There is a way to resolve that situation. We separate the 1.3 billion people into groups, for example, by where they live: Henanese, Hubeiese, Shandongese, Shaanxiese, Beijingers, and so on. After we have established those groups, we may not know every person, but we do know some are Shandongese and others are Guangdongese. So we can make some sort of judgment. Enterprises are just like social groups; each one has a name. Therefore, we can prosecute whoever cheats us. If they cheat us this time, we will not buy from them the next time, and they will go out of business. When society is separated into enterprises, each enterprise must be responsible for its own actions. Only then can we build credibility. If there were no enterprises, everyone would have to produce their goods by them-selves, and that production could not be done.

How can enterprises earn our trust? The answer is related to ownership and profit. Assume that 10,000 people form an enter-prise. In theory, each person could become a co-owner. The enter-prise earns Y 100 million annually and spreads its earnings evenly among the 10,000 people, or Y 10,000 per person per year. That is fair. But if a problem arises, which person is responsible? If we require each of them to be responsible, it is possible that no one will take responsibility.

Enterprises use another way to distribute responsibility. Some people bear responsibility for their own mistakes only (in legal ter-minology, negligence liability), and some bear strict responsibility (in legal terminology, strict or residual reliability). Those who bear responsibility for their own mistakes receive a contracted wage. For example, as long as they do not come to work late and leave early, are not absent, and do not violate work rules, they will receive their salary at the end of each month. They are the staff or the employees.

What is an employee? Simply put, an employee is one who has no responsibility if no one else notices his mistakes. Another group, the owners, must bear strict responsibility. An owner is one with all the responsibility, even if he or she does not notice others' mistakes. Owners do not have the right to demand earnings from consumers because of the fact that they themselves have made no mistakes. However, the employees have the right to demand earnings from the owner even if he himself has made no mistakes. That is the difference between owners and employees.

The owner receives profits but has a responsibility to the consumer. Profit is the surplus of earnings minus costs. Profit may be either positive or negative, so it is an incentive mechanism. When an enterprise produces a product, the consumer does not know the workers who produce the good, so why should the consumer trust them? The consumer trusts them because he knows someone in the enterprise bears the residual liability. A simple example would be the owner of a restaurant. If the chef does not clean the food properly and a patron becomes ill, the owner is liable. Because profit is a way to receive income, it makes the owner of an enterprise bear residual and strict responsibility. The owner must assume liability for any mistakes his employees make; therefore, the owner must seriously supervise and standardize his employees' behavior. That way, customers can buy the enterprise's products with confidence.

Furthermore, the owner bears responsibility not only for the enterprise's employees but also for its suppliers. For instance, if a consumer buys a brand-name computer but part of the computer malfunctions—such as the microchip or the fan—or the batteries even explode, someone needs to take responsibility for the problem. Initially, the computer manufacturer, not the spare parts supplier, is liable for compensating the unlucky consumer. In other words, a brand-name enterprise uses its brand as an oath to consumers. It guarantees that if the product has a problem, it will take responsibility. Only then can everyone have trust in the market, can strangers cooperate, and can society's wealth continuously increase.

Therefore, I say that the market economy is a system of responsibility, and profit is a system of appraisal. The market uses enterprises as differentiated accounting units, and it uses profit to trace responsibility to make each person eventually responsible for his actions.

When we discuss the market economy, we must not forget the entrepreneurs. We cannot understand the market economy from the viewpoint of price only. It is a pity that the entrepreneur has no standing in all of the older mainstream economic textbooks. Joseph Schumpeter once criticized economists' discussions of economic growth as being like *Hamlet* without a prince. In the cases of both resources allocation and growth, the main character is missing. The person who receives the profit is the entrepreneur. He shoulders the task of organizing, producing, and supervising others for the whole society. Of course, the entrepreneur is not just the person per se; it is a function of behavior. In the market economy, the entrepreneur acts as an important character. Not recognizing entrepreneurship, not valuing profit, and not accepting the market economy are one in the same.

The Plight Faced by Chinese Entrepreneurs

Generally speaking, the entrepreneur's work is twofold: facing uncertainty and promoting innovation in society. Facing uncertainty is what American economist Frank H. Knight[4] proposed in 1921. He proved that there is no profit, in the economic meaning of the term, without uncertainty. Profit is compensation for uninsurable uncertainty.

The second part of the entrepreneur's work is to promote innovation in society. Innovation is the responsibility of entrepreneurs, not the responsibility of technicians. Technicians invent, but innovation turns the inventions into an item valued by the consumer. Innovation is "creative destruction." For example, we currently use MP3 players to store and play our music. MP3 players destroyed Sony's Walkman, but Sony's Walkman destroyed the cassette player. Each new type of product destroys a previous type of product. Schumpeter[5] proposed this important viewpoint in *The Theory of Economic Development*.

Are Chinese entrepreneurs and entrepreneurs of the developed Western market economies the same? In the broader sense, they are the same. No matter whether an entrepreneur is Chinese or Western, they both face uncertainty and advance innovation. However, after we analyze the details, we will discover their differences. Uncertainty can be differentiated into two categories: (a) market uncertainty and (b) policy uncertainty. Innovation can also be differentiated into two categories: (a) technological and commercial innovation, such as releasing a new product, using a new production method, or using a new business model; and (b) institutional innovation, such as designing new institutional arrangements, possibly while gaming the system.

Using those categories, Western entrepreneurs mainly face market uncertainty and mainly advance technological and commercial innovation. Therefore, they use most of their energy projecting future consumer tastes, future technological development trends, and the kinds of new products that will win in the market. In contrast, Chinese entrepreneurs spend too much energy on facing policy uncertainty: Can we do this today? What can we do tomorrow? Can we issue bonuses? Can we place stock options for employees and management? Most of their energy is spent reacting to the government. They need to think of ways to get around current policies and to push forward so-called institutional innovation. (On a matrix, Western entrepreneurs would be in the northwest corner, and Chinese entrepreneurs would be in the southeast corner. This concept will be discussed further in chapter 10.)

In view of their spending too much time on policy uncertainties, Chinese entrepreneurs are at a disadvantage on the stage of global competition. Consumers do not care what entrepreneurs do all day or how difficult their job is. They will not give more money to Chinese entrepreneurs because they are busier than American entrepreneurs. In making their decisions, consumers care only about whether one product is better than another and whether it creates more value than other products. Therefore, Chinese entrepreneurs face a much larger challenge.

This is not just empty rhetoric; anyone can research whether or not Chinese entrepreneurs are busier than foreign entrepreneurs. No matter how large their business, foreign entrepreneurs all have time to rest and be with their families. By contrast, Chinese entrepreneurs have very little time to rest; they do not even take Sundays off. Why? They have to react to too many policy uncertainties. Chinese entrepreneurs have a hard time telling you what they are doing next month.

Government Intervention Causes the Dysfunction of the Market

The market has several segments: the product market, the labor market, the capital market, the land market, and the technology market. In China, the market with the least government intervention has developed the best.

Speaking overall, the product market has developed the best. For example, the government stopped interfering with the home-appliance market early on, so it developed very well. By comparison, the government interfered heavily with China's automobile manufacturers before China joined the World Trade Organization. For example, Mr. Shufu Li, the founder of the Geely Group, wanted to produce cars in the 1990s but needed government approval to be listed in the industrial catalog. However, the government did not approve. If entrepreneurs want to produce vehicles but the government rejects their catalog listing, they cannot legally sell vehicles. That is the reason China's automobile market today is filled with foreign brand-name vehicles. Detailed research will show that the product markets that government restricts most are the product markets with the most problems.

Our labor market's development can also be considered relatively good. There is a relationship between the ability of China's economy to develop so well and the competition and flexibility of the labor market. But the labor market is not perfect because we still have the household-registration restrictions and restrictions on immigration. Many farmers have become workers, but we do not call them workers; we call them rural migrant workers. According to their identity cards, they are farmers, but according to their profession, they are workers. This phenomenon is caused by institutional distortions as a result of the *hukou* system (or household-registration system), which limits migration within China.

The capital and land markets have the most problems. In the capital market, policy primarily decides who can get loans and who can list on the stock market. Sometimes, even individual officials make those decisions. That was especially the case early on. When an enterprise wanted to list on the stock market to raise capital, it needed approval from multiple departments. Whoever could get the qualifications received monopoly status. Only people with good connections with relevant departments are able to get qualifications, so the capital market is very unhealthy. Bank loans are the same. To whom should ordinary people's money be loaned? The government makes that decision. It is not easy for privately owned profitable companies to get funding, but state-owned enterprises with huge losses still get funding. The capital market is very inefficient.

When we view the land market, we see no real private transactions, only government-enforced transactions. If one is to build a house on agricultural land, the land must be taken from farmers. The government acquires that land at very low prices and then resells it. People with connections can get land, but people without connections cannot unless they are willing to pay very high prices. The land market is corrupt and ineffective. If we implemented a system of free property rights, with housing prices as high as they are, a lot of land would be developed, so the upward price of housing would be controlled.

The remaining market, the technology market, is very important. Innovation is the fountainhead of economic growth, and it is directed by enterprises and the market. In a real market economy, if one has a good invention, one can create its value by starting a business, selling the invention, or authorizing others to use it. In China, individuals, not companies, submit most technology patents. Innovation has not become an institutional, daily behavior of companies. This important element influences China's ability to have original innovations, which has to do with our lack of protections for intellectual property.

How the Government Can Improve the Market: Protect Property and Promote Competition

What should the government do to improve the market? It should clearly define property and protect property rights. The government really needs to do only those two things in order to protect people's liberty. Only then can each person use his advantages, exchange on the market, and cooperate. All of society will become prosperous very quickly.

Without a government, economic development is impossible because government is also a market need. The problem is that governments raise money differently from enterprises. Enterprises that do not create value do not receive revenues. Even though the government does not produce value, it can raise revenue through taxes. Therefore, the behavior of government easily exceeds the limits of its responsibilities. In another aspect, as was mentioned earlier, many people lack rational thought. When they see a problem in society, they do not understand the real reason for it and often ask for government intervention. In most situations, problems become worse the more government interferes. When a problem becomes worse, there are more demands for government intervention, and a vicious cycle begins.

The effectiveness of competition is not decided by how many firms are in an industry, or the so-called degree of concentration, but by whether or not the government allows free entry into that industry. In China, industries such as petroleum and telecommunications are often criticized. What is the real issue? The real issue is that the government did not open up those industries. It allows only some state-owned enterprises to enter but not others. If the goal is to make China's telecommunications and petroleum companies serve society better, the only effective method is to eliminate the barriers to entry for those industries. In that way, even if no enterprises rush into the industry immediately, the threat of potential competition will make the incumbent work hard to cater to the consumer.

Any restriction on competition is beneficial to only a very small number of people. Resource allocation can either depend on the market or depend on special privileges. If the market does not decide resource allocation, it will undoubtedly be decided by special privileges. Any method that limits competition or artificially sets prices will ultimately benefit only a small number of people with special privileges.

How to Turn Poor People's Assets into Capital

Peruvian economist Hernando de Soto's classic *The Mystery of Capital* provides proof of the significance of property rights protection and the enrichment of poor people.[6] Why are ordinary people of backward countries so poor? They are poor because those countries lack a system for turning assets into capital. Why are developed economies so well-developed? They are well-developed because their definitions of property are very clear, and anyone can turn assets into capital.

Those reasons sound very abstract, so here is an example: Assume I own a house and want to do business, but I need money. If I have clear title to my house, I can get a collateralized loan from the bank. My house is worth Y 1 million, and the bank lends me Y 600,000 so I can start my business. Ten years later, I have become a very rich person. In a backward country, however, I cannot do the same. De Soto visited about a dozen countries and conducted large-scale statistical research. He discovered that the poor people of the Third World have a lot of accumulated assets, such as residential real estate worth $9.5 trillion. Those assets are all half-legal and half-illegal. They can be used, but they cannot be sold.

Are China's farmers the same? Farmers are the lowest level of China's society, but they own very valuable assets, such as land, dwellings, and homesteads. However, they cannot sell them. Even if they move to the city, they must leave those assets behind. On the one hand, they have very valuable assets sitting there; on the other hand, they have nowhere to live in the city. That situation is ridiculous. If farmers earned landownership rights, they could sell their homesteads and buy a house in the city, as urban residents can. At the moment, they cannot, because the government does not allow them to. They can only use the land; they have the right to farm it but not to sell it.

Societal backwardness occurs not because we have no assets but because we have no way to turn our assets into capital. Many people are stuck "begging for food with golden bowls." The concept of the capital market is that it allows people to transfer the future to today. What does that mean? Today, I have nothing, only an idea or a plan. But because I can turn my idea into big money in the future, people will lend me money today. If property rights are not well-defined or protected—even if you have an entrepreneurial plan—but the government does not allow you to borrow money or if the banks won't give you a loan, you lose the possibility to enrich yourself.

Therefore, it does not matter whether it is the Third World or emerging markets like China; the first imperative to allow poor people to enrich themselves is to define property clearly so that poor people can turn their assets into capital. Otherwise, relying on the government and the World Bank for relief—or relying on charity— cannot offset the losses brought on the poor by an irrational system.

How to Trust the Market: Allow Nongovernmental Poverty Alleviation

Of course, in any society, even in the market economy, relatively poor people will always need assistance. The issue is how to assist them.

Many people believe that poverty alleviation relies on the government. In China, I have discovered through research that the areas where government expenditures are a larger part of GDP have higher disparities of income. Right now, the government is building a new countryside. Providing subsidies to poor people in the countryside is initially a good policy. But we should take a detailed look at where the money goes. Most of the money does not go to the poorest people or to the people who need it most. It goes to the relatives of the leader of some county or government department. The government has spent a lot of money, but it has had not helped alleviate poverty.

That is not to say that the government is useless. We should just believe that the market itself would provide many methods to alleviate poverty. In the United States, tuition for a decent university costs $40,000 a year, but students from families below a certain economic level can have their tuition waived. The reason is the schools can receive higher tuition from wealthy students to subsidize poorer students. Subsidies are also partly financed by voluntary donations. Maybe people believe that the government should solve the issue. Government should support education, but remember that the government itself cannot create wealth; it can only collect taxes. Would it be better to have the universities adjust themselves, or would government subsidies be better? I believe it would be better to go through the universities, but there should also be a two-pronged approach. Of course, the specifics of implementing the approach need further research. When we look at private schools, we will have a better understanding. Private schools are willing to offer free education to students from poor families. They do so because they hope to develop a good reputation and to attract more students. That is the result of competition.

People often say that governments should do what the market cannot. But a lot of what the market cannot do is not because it really cannot do it; it is because the government does not allow it to. Today's philanthropy exposes a lot of unfair situations. When China has more wealthy people in the future, philanthropy will increase. But today, our institutional environment is bad for developing philanthropy. I have personally experienced that situation. Three years ago, Professors Yushi Mao, Jinglian Wu, Yifu Lin, a dozen or so other people, and I started the Fuping Foundation. It has two goals: (a) to help migrant workers with training and (b) to support microfinance in the countryside. Even today, the fund has not been registered because the government will not give it a permit.

The same logic applies to the issues that exist in the health care system. I have said before that although the government has a responsibility to provide minimum medical care, it does not have the authority to prevent private medical care. If the government would allow private medical care, more government resources spent on health care could reach the lower classes. High-income earners will spend more to go to private hospitals with better services and no lines. In addition, the government could still collect taxes from the private hospitals and could, therefore, subsidize the people in need. Thus, allowing private medical care kills two birds with one stone. But if we look at the present situation in Beijing or the entire country, the better hospitals are used by and more money is spent on the people with special status or special connections.

A Fatal Misunderstanding: The Market Causes Inequality

Most people are worried about the phenomenon of income differences in society. Some attribute that phenomenon to market reforms; others even believe that the market economy will widen the income gap between the rich and the poor. They are mistaken.

Historically, ordinary people are the biggest beneficiaries of the market economy. For a simple example, look at Thomas Edison's invention of the light bulb, which benefited everyone. A light bulb is less valuable to a rich person than a poor person. Rich people have money, so even if there were no light bulbs, they could buy a lot of candles. But poor people could not afford to buy even one. Another example is the television. Today, the ordinary person can watch celebrities sing or act. But before, only wealthy people and the nobility could enjoy performances on stage. Vehicles are the same. In the past, wealthy people rode in carriages; today, everyone has means of transportation. All new products and new technologies are similar. Ordinary people are the biggest beneficiaries of the market economy, not the privileged classes.

Take another look at the history of China's reforms. I entered the university in 1977. That year, only 280,000 new undergraduates were enrolled in the entire country. At that time, fewer than 5 percent of high school students had the opportunity to go to a university. Of those students, a portion of them had bad family backgrounds, or their parents had historical issues. They could not join the military or go to work, so they had no choice but to study at home. After the college entrance examination was suddenly reinstated, those students got into a university. In the 1980s, most of the small private businesses in the city were owned by the lower classes. People with even a little privilege went into the military, the government, or state-owned enterprises. What could those without privileges or connections do? All they could do was scavenge or set up a fruit stand. In the end, the latter became prosperous.

Those examples illustrate that reform has improved our society's upward mobility. The research of two professors at Stanford University shows that of the lowest-earning one-fifth of China's population in 1990, a lower proportion was still in that group by 1995 compared with a similar population in the United States.[7] In other words, China's vertical mobility was higher than the United States' for that period. That conclusion is understandable because China is in the process of rapid change, whereas American society is relatively stable. In China, though, a person who was originally a member of the lower classes can enter the middle class after working hard or starting a business. Such people are more prevalent in China than in the United States. I have calculated the statistics on the Gini coefficient and China's provinces, municipalities, and autonomous regions. On average, the areas with the most developed market economy, with the least state-owned enterprises, and with the least proportion of government spending as a part of GDP are the areas with the least income disparity.

What is the explanation for that fact? If government involvement in economic activity is minimal and if people are free to engage in commercial activity, then competition will be fierce, and profits from commercial activity will be low. If only people with privileges and government connections are allowed to do business—or only people with extreme courage will risk doing business—the profit from doing business will be very high. For example, Zhejiang Province has many businesspeople. Many of them are wealthy, but profits are thin. An area such as northeast China has few businesspeople, and they earn a lot of money. They can do so because their market environment is bad. Therefore, we can see that areas with a more open market and less government intervention also have less income disparity.

In addition, equality is not just something that appears as monetary income. It also includes other aspects, such as liberty, rights, and choice. What freedoms did the ordinary people of the past have? When I was in the countryside, farmers would take their watermelons and apples to market to sell them. If they were discovered, they were considered profiteers. They would be denounced and sometimes even imprisoned. The basic right to be a person did not exist. At that time, peasants could not eat meat all year, nor could they afford dough. However, when a cadre from the commune came to the village, everyone rushed to treat him. Any available noodles and meat were given to the cadre, because only when a family had good relationships with the cadre did their children have the opportunity to join the military or get a job—even though the probability was very small. Therefore, I do not believe Reform and Opening has made Chinese society less equal; instead, it has made it more equal.

How to Refuse the "Crutch Sellers": Believe in the Market Economy

Over the past 30 years of China's Reform and Opening, per capita GDP has doubled every nine years. That is an amazing accomplishment. American scholar William J. Bernstein recently published a book called *The Birth of Plenty*.[8] It views the modern West's rise from economic, military, and historical institutions. He proposes that a modern society's economy has four requirements for success: (a) a system of property rights, (b) scientific rationality, (c) capital markets, and (d) a reduction in transportation costs. I believe those requirements deserve our consideration.

Over the past 30 years of China's Reform and Opening, there has been progress in many aspects. Take property rights, for example. Early on, farmers could contract the land for only one year, so no one was willing to invest. Therefore, the government changed the contract to five years, but there was still a problem: no one was willing to develop irrigation. So the contract was extended to 10 years. However, no one was willing to plant trees. Finally, the contract was extended to 30 years. Today, a problem still exists because if land cannot be transferred, most farmers have no way of becoming urban residents. Our capital markets are also continuously developing. State-owned enterprises and state-owned banks are listing shares domestically and overseas. In the short term, not much can be changed. However, for the long term, we are moving in the right direction. Of course, society still has a lot of problems, which need more reform to solve.

Here, I want to emphasize how economists look at issues and policies. With respect to rational thinking and probing issues, our society is still deficient. Some discussions analyze economists' standpoints—who represents whose interests, or who speaks from what position—but they have no significance. Emotional discussions of issues do not help promote social progress. Taking a position and speaking from it is not the way economists consider issues. Economists consider (a) whether a policy can satisfy the conditions it is meant to solve and (b) whether it can really achieve its goal.

That consideration brings us back to my initial question: why does society need economists? The market economy needs people to safeguard it because it is too fragile and too easily criticized. To reiterate: when people enjoy the benefits of a market economy, they will see its faults. But when they do not have the opportunity to enjoy its benefits, they have no way of knowing what its benefits are. When it breaks, people scold it for being broken.

The same holds true with people. They may be perfectly healthy, but if someone continuously tells them that they have an illness, they will take the medication and get sick. That same reasoning is the subject of Chinese comedian Zhao Benshan's *Maiguai* (*Selling Crutches*). The victim's leg was fine, but the crutch seller repeatedly told him that his leg definitely had a serious problem. In the end, the victim was induced to believe his leg was broken, so his only option was to buy crutches. In today's society, a lot of people are "selling crutches." What is that crutch? It is the huge amount of anti-market opinions. The crutch sellers sold us the majority of so-called market failures.

My only goal here is for everyone to better understand what the market economy is and to maintain our belief in the market economy. What should we be worried about in China's future? It is not the issues of resources or the environment. Although they are important, they are not the most important because market competition will promote technological progress and can undoubtedly find an answer. We do not need to be as pessimistic as Malthus was more than 200 years ago or the Club of Rome was more than 30 years ago. China's future development depends on our beliefs, both what we believe and what we do not believe. If we staunchly believe in the market economy, continuously promote reform, and perfect the market, China's future will be extremely bright. If we lose our belief in the market and introduce progressively more government interventions, China's future will face complications and crises.

41

2. Profits and Corporate Social Responsibility

Over the past year, "corporate social responsibility" has become a very popular topic. Academic, business, and government circles all like to discuss it. Searching for "social responsibility" on Baidu yields 7.5 million results. Searching for "corporate social responsibility" produces 4.8 million results.

The emphasis of CCTV's Economic Person of the Year reflects an important trend related to the state of China's economic development. In 2002, it emphasized innovation, challenges, and influence. In 2003, the emphasis was on influence, looking forward, and innovation. In 2004, it was on innovation, responsibility, and health. In 2005, it was on innovation, responsibility, influence, and promotion. And in 2006, "responsibility" was emphasized first. Other media have emphasized responsibility as well. In 2006, *The Talents* (*Yingcai*) and *Beijing Youth Daily* (*Beijing Qingnianbao*), as well as 10 other publications, selected 100 top Chinese managers. Social responsibility was the first indicator.

That emphasis is not limited to China. Internationally, we find the same. Basically, any conferences having to do with business are also discussing social responsibility. Not long ago, I went to the United States to participate in Cisco's conference on leadership. It too dedicated a portion to social responsibility.

Although everyone is discussing "corporate social responsibility," different people understand the subject differently. Its meaning also changes with time. In the past, when people talked about corporate social responsibility, they meant donations to alleviate poverty and to help "Hope schools." Later, environmental protection and resource conservation were added. Recently, another viewpoint has emphasized the multiplicity of corporate social responsibility. It includes responsibility to stockholders, employees, customers, suppliers, communities, and so on. This idea is very influential internationally.

English speakers use the word "stakeholder," but Chinese speakers use the phrase "lìyì xiāngguānzhě" ("interest holder"). Traditionally, people emphasized that shareholders own corporations, so the corporation's goal was to maximize the shareholders' interests. The idea of a stakeholder is that the corporation should serve all interest holders.

Why People Are Keen to Discuss Social Responsibility

At some economic forums, well-known entrepreneurs sit on the stage and speak eloquently—first about the importance of corporate social responsibility and second about what social responsibilities their business has undertaken. By highlighting his business's social responsibility, the speaker is shaping the image of his company. If a company courageously takes on social responsibility, it will likely receive more respect and recognition from consumers and customers. Respect and recognition improve its competitiveness, which also benefits its shareholders.

Another aspect of social responsibility is that the Chinese government is promoting the building of a harmonious society. Corporations' social responsibility could assist in realizing that goal. At the same time, corporate social responsibility is an international trend. A considerable number of organizations are committed to promoting this movement. Their commitment has created a very strong force of public opinion. Everyone lives in society's public opinion. When a person says or does something, it often does not reflect what he or she values, but what other people value. Public opinion is especially important to entrepreneurs because businesses must cater to public opinion. Under the pressure of public opinion, an entrepreneur may say things that he or she does not personally believe.

Frankly speaking, clarifying the ideal of social responsibility is very difficult. However, after corporate social responsibility became trendy, everyone rushed to fashionably support it. That trend concerns me. I think that when a lot of people discuss corporate responsibility, there is much preaching and sensationalism with limited rational analysis. And the lack of limited analysis will mislead people. Misleading people in such a way will perhaps make our business environment worse, not better. Therefore, I think that clarifying this topic is necessary.

The Confusions and Paradoxes of the Corporate Social Responsibility Idea

The ideal of corporate social responsibility—if it is the same as the shareholder ideal—cannot make a business take on social responsibility. In one respect, logically speaking, if a manager wants to avoid responsibility, the best way to do so is to proclaim responsibility to everyone's interests. Accordingly, that manager would actually not be responsible for anyone. If the business loses money, the manager could say that it was lost in the interest of the consumer. Conversely, when prices are raised, the manager also has ample justification. The manager not only must be responsible to the customer but also must consider the stockholders' interests. Of course, when the managers lay off people, they have a reason: they need to take care of the shareholders' interests. With that kind of ideal, "responsible to all" really means responsible to no one.

Conversely, when formulating a policy decision, that decision often needs to have a relatively unique goal. If a business wants to consider many goals, it often cannot make a decision. For example, if a company is losing too much money, from the shareholders' perspective, it should close. But from the perspective of other stakeholders, it cannot close because closure will result in people losing their jobs. Assume that a business has 2,000 employees, but it owes the government millions in taxes. If the entrepreneur pays taxes according to the law, the business will be bankrupt, and 2,000 employees will lose their jobs. But if the entrepreneur does not pay the taxes, the business can continue to operate, and its employees will still have their jobs. From the socially responsible viewpoint, should the business pay taxes or not?

We can ask an even simpler question. Assume a business really takes care of the consumer and provides its products for free. Is that a good or a bad move? Take oil companies as an example. If they provide free oil, it would result in the overconsumption of oil, too many vehicles on the road, traffic jams, serious environmental pollution, and the rapid exhaustion of oil resources. In other words, if a business starts from the ideal of "social responsibility" and provides consumers with free products, the result is actually not socially good. It could possibly damage society, not bear responsibility for it.

Those examples illustrate the complexity of defining corporate social responsibility, which has a lot of misperceptions and paradoxes that need our clarification.

With regard to the goal of an enterprise, viewpoints differ. For example, economists tell us that the goal of enterprises is to maximize profits. Scholars of management tell us that creating value for the customer is the most important goal for the survival and growth of enterprises. Public opinion calls for enterprises to focus most on social responsibility. Some people believe a contradiction exists among the three viewpoints, such as those who say that an enterprise cannot pursue only profit; it must also pay attention to social responsibility. The implied meaning is either that profit is socially irresponsible or that it is not a part of social responsibility.

Next, I would like to emphasize that in a complete market system, the pursuit of profit, creation of value for customers, and bearing of societal burdens not only have no contradictions but instead are basically the same thing. Profit is society's most important indicator for checking whether enterprises, as well as entrepreneurs, are really fulfilling their responsibilities. Without this indicator, we have no way of judging whether an enterprise's actions actually harm or help society. However, in a society with serious institutional defects, profit is probably not the best indicator to assess entrepreneurs. At this time, we should think of a way to improve the institutions and to allow profit to really reflect enterprises' and entrepreneurs' contributions to society. We should not lay aside changes to society's institutions and then try to resolve contradictions by preaching.

How to Understand Profits, Revenues, and Costs

Anyone with business sense knows that so-called profit is a business's revenues minus costs. Although that formula sounds simple, it is a bit more complicated. People familiar with management know that costs, revenues, and accounting can all be manipulated. Some businesses lose money, but through creative accounting, their practices show earnings. Some businesses have earnings, but their accounting practices can turn those earnings into losses. In this section, we will assume that such manipulations do not exist, and then we will analyze the internal relationship among revenues, costs, and profit.

First, let us define "revenue." Revenue is a part of a business that creates value for consumers. I stress "a part of" because in a market of voluntary exchange, the amount of revenue a business makes absolutely cannot surpass the value it creates for consumers. The exception is when fraud exists. Even with a monopoly, if the business creates 100 units of value for the consumer, it might be able to receive 99 units, but it cannot receive 101 units. Generally speaking, the fiercer the competition, the less value a business can keep from the consumer, so the consumer receives more of the surplus.

We need to remind ourselves that in a system where individual property rights are sufficiently protected, no one can force others to buy and sell. The only exception is government. Government's revenue comes from taxes. In theory, government exists to serve the public. But government is different from business. Business must satisfy consumers' desires in order to receive revenue. A government is not constrained by the people and can collect taxes as revenue, regardless of whether or not the people agree. Even democratic politics have no way to guarantee that the government's activities create more value than they take from taxes.

That is to say, whether in a competitive market or not, the amount of revenue a business receives absolutely cannot exceed the value it creates for the consumer. This point is very important. Operators of businesses should understand that the more value that they create for consumers, the larger the share of it they can enjoy. Of course, how much the specific share is depends on pricing strategy and negotiation skills. Nevertheless, if a business does not create value for the consumer, receiving revenue is unthinkable.

Next, let us define "cost." Speaking from intuition, a business spends a lot of money ordering goods, buying materials, and hiring people during the course of its operations. Those expenditures are its costs. For example, if a business hires an employee for Y 5,000, its cost is Y 5,000. Why would hiring someone cost Y 5,000? That person has a price tag on the market. In a competitive market, regardless of whether we are discussing staff, materials, or resources, they all have their own price. That price is the opportunity cost of the enterprises using them. Assume a person works for a business and creates not less than Y 5,000 in value. If he cannot create Y 5,000 in value at another business, that business should not hire him. In other words, the second business cannot use him. If it does, it will simultaneously waste society's resources and lose its own money.

After understanding the definitions of revenue and cost, let us define "profit." In reality, profit is a yardstick. It measures whether or not the value created for the consumer is larger than the cost of using society's resources. If consumers are willing to pay a price that is lower than the cost of using society's resources, a loss will occur, and social responsibility will not have been fulfilled. By contrast, if the same resources are used, but the value created is more than anyone else can create, that means the business has created more value for society. From this point of view, we can see that profit itself is an important indicator of corporations' fulfilling their social responsibility.

Suppose two enterprises are in the same market and have the same resources. One enterprise creates Y 10 million in profit, but the other creates only Y 2 million in profit. The second enterprise donates that Y 2 million to charity. Which of the two enterprises fulfilled its social responsibility? It clearly is not the second one.

How did those two companies in the same market using the same resources create different value? That question will be answered in the next section. Now, we will discuss two questions: What is the source of profit? Why does profit exist?

The Source of Profit

In 1921, American economist Frank Knight wrote a book called *Risk, Uncertainty, and Profit.*[1] In his book, he proposed a very important view: profit comes from uncertainty. That viewpoint indicates that if a market had certainty, all revenue that could be gained from consumers would be society's opportunity cost. At that moment, product prices would equal the sum of costs; there would be no profit to speak of. Because that view sounds abstract, I will provide some examples.

Assume that there is a certain piece of land. Everyone knows that no matter whether a shopping center or residential property is built on it, it will create Y 100 million in revenue, excluding materials and labor costs. If someone wants to use that land, how much should he pay? The answer is Y 100 million. If that person offers Y 90 million, someone else will be willing to pay Y 91 million, and then a third person will be willing to pay Y 92 million. After the competitive bidding ends, the price of the property will certainly be Y 100 million. Because the land also creates Y 100 million in revenue, there is no profit.

Each person's judgment is different. Judgment is conjecture about the future and embodies uncertainty. The judgment may be correct or incorrect. If the majority of people believe a piece of land will create Y 100 million in revenue, but someone else is more farsighted and believes it will create Y 200 million in revenue, that person will pay more. If that person has judged correctly, and the development is later sold for Y 200 million, the difference is the seller's profit. And that is the meaning of "profit comes from uncertainty." Only because people judge the future differently, will profit exist. Some people have better vision, decisionmaking ability, and management ability than others. Those abilities make success easier, and those people are the entrepreneurs.

Anyone with business experience knows that the products and services that everyone believes will make money are the products and services that ultimately do not make money. Most people do not understand what will make money, but some people do understand. To make money, a person must assume risk and the consequences of uncertainty. That statement does not contradict what I said earlier. Without uncertainty, all revenue will become costs, so there will be no profit. Because of uncertainty, there is a difference between costs and revenues. Earnings are possible, but so are losses. On average, the people with good judgment skills will still make a profit.

Because uncertainty exists, investments must take on risk. Profit is also a type of compensation for risk. Most people fear risk; otherwise, insurance companies would not be necessary. But even if no one feared risk, uncertainty would still exist, so investors' compensation would still be different. Imagine that 10 people are pursuing a business opportunity, and each invests Y 1 million. The possibility of success is only 10 percent; in other words, only 1 of the original 10 will succeed. How much income must they project before they are willing to pursue the opportunity? Without considering one's risk preferences, it needs to be at least Y 10 million. Because Y 10 million is the projected revenue, it will compensate for the 90 percent chance of losing Y 1 million. If in the end, the 10 people—regardless of whether they succeed or fail—divide the Y 10 million in earnings equally, so that each person receives Y 1 million, they would have no reason to invest in the first place. If we are unwilling to bear the difference in income between outcomes, then we nullify the value of entrepreneurs.

The second source of profit is innovation. Innovation is the view proposed by Austrian-American economist Joseph Schumpeter.[2]

Innovation in the commercial sense does not mean inventions; it means using the same type of resources to create more value than someone else. Or it means a person produces the same amount of value as someone else but uses fewer resources. If someone can do that, that person earns money. In a competitive market, how does one earn more money than others? The answer is simple. Given a set cost, a person must sell more than someone else to earn money. Conversely, if the person is given a set sales revenue, his costs must be lower than someone else's. If one enterprise uses 10 people to do something, but another uses 8, they earn money. That is innovation.

When a new technology or business model is developed, few people risk using it because of uncertainty. But the people who risk using it could possibly make money from it. If the technology or business model is widely used, the profit will average toward opportunity costs, and people will not earn from it. A few years ago, an article in the *Harvard Business Review* said that information technology is not a competitive advantage.[3] The author did not mean that information technology is unimportant. He meant that once everyone realizes the value of information technology, no one can be more competitive by using it. Electricity is the same. Because everyone uses it, it is no longer an advantage, so it has become a cost. In other words, in a competitive market, any business needs to be devoted to innovation. If it lacks innovation, it cannot earn money, and it will be eliminated.

The third source of profit—which I believe is very important—is enterprises' maintenance of the market order. We often talk about the power of brands, and many enterprises are branding themselves. Brands are valuable because they create consumer trust. Consumers are willing to pay more for trustworthy products. Because there is no need to haggle, transaction costs are reduced. Part of those savings will return to the producer as the brand premium. Brand premiums come from their maintenance of the market order.

Imagine the kind of market we would have if we tear the labels off all the products on the market. Except for potatoes, rice, radishes, and other simple commodities whose quality can be judged by eye, we would not risk buying most other products. The market would shrink significantly. For businesses, if the consumer trusts one business more than another, it can earn more money than its competitors. Speaking of social significance, without that kind of trust, the market order has no way of maintaining itself. Companies like Yili and Mengniu bring us not only milk but also market order, so we can drink milk without concern. They use branding to reap huge profits.

To sum up, the source of profit comes from the three aspects mentioned earlier. Does a business have the ability to face uncertainty? Does a business have the ability to innovate? Are some businesses more trustworthy than others? If a business does all three well, it will make a profit.

The next question is this: after a business earns revenues, why are some people's earnings considered costs, but other's earnings are considered profit? In other words, why do only some people earn profit, and why is profit not evenly distributed among them all?

Why Profit Is a Responsibility

Imagine for a moment that 100 people form a business. Without first discussing how much they contribute, how should the revenue of the business be divided? One method is to divide it equally. If the business has an annual revenue of Y 20 million, each person would receive Y 200,000. Each person's incentive for creating value might be very limited, but there is an incentive for laziness. The business has a problem because no one really bears responsibility.

In another arrangement, 99 people could have a fixed contracted income, and the 100th person could receive the remaining income. The so-called residual income is the part left over after costs of raw materials, interest, salaries, and so forth are subtracted from sales revenue. That is the profit. The person who receives the residual revenue is the owner, and the people who receive salaries are employees.

What is the benefit of that arrangement? It allows the person who receives the residual revenue to better bear responsibility, as well as to supervise others to ensure that they also bear their own responsibilities. The entrepreneur receives the residual revenue, but he takes on the residual responsibility. The employees receive contracted incomes and take on responsibility for mistakes.

In other words, as employees, people have no responsibility if they do not make mistakes, or if the owner does not discover that they have made a mistake. In contrast, if the owner does not discover other people's mistakes, any problems that happen are entirely the owner's fault. After employees work for a certain amount of time—as long as they have made no mistakes—the owner must pay their salary. Otherwise, the owner has violated the contract, and the workers can sue him. The owner cannot use business losses as a justification for not paying salaries. If the business is not managed well, and if the owner does not discover others' mistakes, all the mistakes are the owner's fault. The owner cannot tell the consumer that he or she has worked much harder this year so this year's profit needs to be high and, therefore, consumers need to give the owner more money.

At this point, most people can understand that in the enterprise system, the people receiving the profit are the ones who bear final responsibility. The owner receives the profit and so must bear associated responsibility for the behavior of staff. The owner must take responsibility for any problems that arise. Therefore, the owner must supervise the employees with the utmost caution so they do not get into trouble. When employees get into trouble, owners cannot deny responsibility. If owners do, either they do not want to be the owner or they are unaware that they are the owner. For example, when someone opens a restaurant, and some of the patrons get food poisoning, who bears responsibility? The owner bears responsibility, not the cook or the purchasing agent. Because the owner must bear that responsibility, that person must be cautious when hiring staff. If a staff member is sick and infects the customer, the owner must also compensate the customer.

Previously, we mentioned that brands are a source of profit. Actually, the value of brands per se is formed by a series of responsibilities. For example, an automaker does not produce most of the parts for its cars. One vehicle has over 10,000 parts, so the automaker has a large number of suppliers. To a branded enterprise, any problem in the supply chain is something it must bear liability for. For example, a tier five supplier's raw materials have quality issues. When the car goes on the road, a steel shaft is defective. Who bears liability for the consumer's damage? The automaker does, not the business that produces the steel shaft. The consumer settles the issue with the automaker, not the supplier. Because the business must bear final responsibility, it must find a way to supervise the supplier. If it does not have the ability to supervise the supplier, if the raw materials it purchases are not up to standard, and if the assembled car has a defect, the automaker will soon find itself at a dead end.

A brand enterprise taking responsibility for suppliers in its supply chain is similar to an owner taking responsibility for employees. The supply chain is layered. If a car has a problem because of steel quality issues, the automaker does not go to the steel producer. It goes to the supplier that makes parts with that steel, and then the parts maker discusses the issue with the steel manufacturer. The problem is investigated layer by layer. That is both a responsibility system and a value system. The more responsibility a business takes, the bigger its share of the value chain. If that were not the case, producers would not work hard to establish their own brands. If a car has a problem and the consumer must resolve the issue with the parts maker, few people would be willing to purchase a car.

How many people are in society? How many people do we have to transact with? It is hard to say. Inspect the products used in daily life. Who produced them? Although we do not know them, we can still shop with confidence. That is the wonder of the market system. It separates everyone into different groups. Those groups then face the consumer, so the group with a problem can be recognized at a glance. If someone buys a computer from Toshiba, and the computer has a problem, the purchaser goes back to Toshiba, not to Sony. Naming each enterprise is a sacred affair. The goal is to make the owner bear responsibility to establish a brand and receive a profit. Inside the enterprise, profit, as a type of residual income, makes some people assume residual liability. Assuming that residual liability forces them to make each link exert more effort and bear responsibility for its related responsibility. Therefore, I say that profit is responsibility.

Looking back, what are the salaries, debts, and interests that an enterprise pays for? They are all some form of opportunity cost. In other words, an employee who works at one company cannot work at another company. A bank that loans money to one person cannot loan that same money to someone else. Speaking from this perspective, the entrepreneur's most important responsibility is contract fulfillment. If the entrepreneur promises to pay the workers Y 10,000 and promises to pay the suppliers within one month, the entrepreneur needs to honor those promises. If wages and debt are owed, or if the receipt and delivery of goods are not done according to schedules, then social responsibility has not been fulfilled. Therefore, no one should deviate from contract behavior and then abstractly talk about social responsibility. That approach will solve nothing.

The Social Meaning of Profit

Further, let us examine a more macroview. How does profit lead to the efficient allocation of resources? What decides a society's economic status? The so-called efficient use of people and resources decides it! How do we know what a business should and should not produce? Profit is a signal! If an industry's profit is on average higher than the profits of other industries, that profit means the industry lacks resources and competition. Businesses pursuing profit will naturally enter that industry, and that entry will cause society's resources to flow rationally. What kind of talents should society foster? If mechanics' salaries rise quickly, but if average university graduates' salaries do not, that difference means society lacks mechanics, so more people should learn those skills. Profit takes on this leading role.

If profit as a measurement were not used, should factory boilers use oil, coal, or alcohol? Only profit can tell us which methods are correct and which are wasteful. If a factory should use coal but uses oil instead, its costs will be too high; either profit will decrease, or a loss will occur. After a time, the factory would close, and the wasteful behavior would naturally disappear. China has a saying, "The car will find a way around the mountain when it gets there." That sentence means the scarcer a resource is, the higher its price. More effort must be made to develop replacement resources. Today, the world's supply of oil is strained. If the price of oil rises, replacement energy will increase. Innovation in new energy sources also relies on the profit system.

We emphasize innovation, but whether or not innovation can create social value is also measured by profit. To scientists and engineers, the importance of innovation is to satisfy their curiosity. For example, when Beijing's Olympic Stadium was being built, the architect did not care about cost; he only hoped that his work could last through the ages and become a great achievement. Whether that is beneficial to society is uncertain. We will know only after we measure profit. Innovation without commercial value is doomed to be a flash in the pan or an exhibition piece.

In short, a country's resource usage, technological progress, and sustainable development all rely on the guidance of the market economy and the profit mechanism. Which countries squander resources, have the slowest technological development, and suffer the most serious environmental pollution? They are not the countries that emphasize "social responsibility" less. They are the countries with unclear property rights and distorted price signals. Without a proper system, our empty talk about this and that responsibility is useless.

In contrast, who does the ideal of corporate social responsibility suit most? First, it suits government most. As stated earlier, businesses cannot receive revenue if they do not create value for the consumer. The government receives revenue regardless of whether or not it creates value. Therefore, governments especially need to be reminded of social responsibility. The government does not have a profit target. We can only continuously encourage it to serve the people and work harder.

Second, social responsibility suits nonprofit organizations. Society has no way to directly measure the contribution of universities and research institutions. A professor or researcher is not like the CEO of a company in that profit can immediately show whether or not the CEO performs well. Therefore, social responsibility must be emphasized.

Third, social responsibility suits government-imposed monopolistic organizations. The profit of a monopolistic organization does not represent its contribution to society. If it earns a lot of money, it does so not because of innovation or risk but because it has a monopoly on resources. Monopolistic industries such as oil and telecommunications especially need to understand social responsibility.

In the end, whether or not a person or business contributes to society should be viewed not by their stated responsibility but by the accountability of their responsibility. English has two related words: "responsibility" and "accountability." It is very important to understand those two words. If responsibility does not include accountability, a person who professes responsibility to everyone is actually responsible to no one. We have no way of judging whether that person has fulfilled his duty, nor do we know if a business is doing good or bad things. Under the command economy, each store has a sign hanging at its door that says, "Serving the people." The Ministry of Propaganda stresses serving the people. What is the real result? The quality of service is terrible. The key issue is not that our emphasis on serving people is lacking; rather, it is that the rules of the game and the system do not give us any positive incentives for people to behave well.

Choices under a Defective System

We already know that in a robust market system, there is no contradiction between businesses pursuing profit and bearing responsibility; they are basically the same. In other words, earning money means contributing to society and is a measurement for the standard of completeness of a system. In a nearly perfect system, earning money basically equals contributing to society. In a bad system, earning money often harms society's interests. Of course, in reality, those two extremes are rarely seen. A system is always somewhere between a state of perfection and the worst possible state. At this time, anything we do—such as produce or not produce—will have four possible outcomes: (a) it will have social value and also make money, (b) it will make money but have no social value, (c) it will have social value but not make money, and (d) it will neither make money nor have social value.

When facing this kind of situation, if one speaks for the whole society, the first priority is to attempt to perfect the system so that society moves toward the first possibility. That outcome will—to the greatest extent—avoid differences between individual and social interests. But we can imagine that no matter how hard we work, creating a perfect system is impossible. Therefore, companies that pursue profit as their goal will possibly face this dilemma: If something is valuable to society but cannot make money, should it be done? Or if something can make money but has no social value, should it be done?

Classical Chinese is very interesting, and we can borrow a few metaphors from it to describe the four possible outcomes. The kind of person in the first category, which has social value and makes money, is a *jūnzĭ*, or a gentleman. The ancients used to say, "The gentleman loves wealth, but properly." To love wealth "properly" means to make money by creating value for society. The person in the second category, who makes money doing things without social value, is a *xiǎorén*, or a bad man (or small man). A so-called gentleman does not act like a bad man. The third type of person is a *shèngrén*, or a sage. The sage is valuable to society but loses money and has a hard life. Sages are great; we respect them but cannot pin our hopes on them. The fourth kind of person is a *shǎzi*, or an idiot. Only idiots would do things that harm others with no benefit to themselves. Everyone worries about the idiots, but few exist.

By comparing the four types of people, we should appeal to everyone to do something that contributes to society even if that something makes no profit. For example, if an area suffers pestilence or is very poor, a pharmaceutical company should send it some free medication. Conversely, if something will provide a modicum of profit but will harm society, it should not be done. For example, if the medication has expired or has side effects, but the consumer is unaware, the company could sell it to make money, but it should not do so. At this time, the social responsibility ideal has meaning, which includes the pollution issue. Currently, the legal system is not robust, and some industry codes of practice have not been established. If a business knows for certain that producing a product will cause serious pollution and will cause damage to society but does it anyway to pursue profit, it has not fulfilled its social responsibility.

A society can promote the sage spirit but cannot pin its hope on being sage. A better system would encourage gentlemen and punish bad men through systemic design. Such a system would turn more bad men into gentlemen and would allow gentlemen to do more business. In other words, we should not ramble on about social responsibility; we should focus on improving our system to make everyone take on social responsibility. Responsibility can be guaranteed only if it is assessable. Therefore, the most important step is to set up a system of property rights and prices to invigorate the incentive mechanism. Only this kind of society is healthy because all people can receive what they deserve. When we discover a dislocation between business profit and social value, we should analyze where the problem lies: Does the system of property rights have a problem so business leaders pursue only short-term interests without considering the long-term impact? Is our price system irrational? Are prices set too low so that resource distribution is distorted?

Take, for example, the current issue over mining deaths. If extraction rights for coal mines were extended from 3 years to 30 years, the effect would be greater than educating the mine owners to care about the miners. The focus should not be on education; it should be on solving institutional issues. If a business opens a mine today but is unsure of whether the mine can be worked tomorrow, why would it want to buy safety equipment? If safety equipment costs Y 10 million, but Y 2 million is not earned back, what is the mine to do? If mining companies are given 30-year leases or even permanent property rights, sooner or later the government inspections would be unnecessary because the companies would be more cautious. That is the basic principle of Adam Smith's invisible hand. In a competitive market with adequate protections for property, people each pursue their own interests; in turn, the benefits brought to society are larger than if each person tried to benefit society directly.

To sum up, social responsibility makes sense because systems cannot be perfect. Social responsibility's significance is limited because good systems are lacking and because responsibility is hard to assess and implement. For entrepreneurs, their real responsibility is to create value for customers and to earn profit based on honesty and trustworthiness. At the same time, they give people employment opportunities and pay more taxes to the government. An enterprise should not produce something without considering profit. In the end, it would have a big pile of products, but it would also be a mess. And that is lack of responsibility toward all of society.

3. Is State Ownership Consistent with a Market Economy? The Chinese Experience

What is market socialism? Although different scholars might hold different views, a generally accepted definition is that market socialism is an economic system in which the public (all of the people) own the enterprises, but their economic decisions are coordinated by market prices. Simply speaking, market socialism is public ownership plus the market mechanism.[1] In practice, public ownership usually takes the form of state ownership; that is, the state (government) is the legal owner of all firms. Here, ownership is defined by who can lay claim to residual earnings and control over management.

With this definition, the Chinese economic reform process can be taken as an unprecedented experiment of market socialism in human history. So far, the Chinese government has never intended to give up socialism, and the Chinese Communist Party's official ideology has always insisted that state ownership is the cornerstone of socialism. However, the Chinese government has indeed tried to introduce a market price mechanism into its state ownership–dominated economy since 1979. It is in this sense that scholars both inside and outside China interpret Chinese reform as a "market-oriented reform." Before 1984, the official reform objective was to improve and perfect the public ownership–based planned economy by introducing some market elements at margin. In 1984, the Third Plenary Session of the 12th Central Committee of the Chinese Community Party officially adopted the "planned commodity economy" as the objective model of reform. In the Chinese vocabulary at the time, "commodity economy" was more or less a "soft" version of "market economy regulated by the state." The attributive "planned" was added partly to avoid ideological controversy and partly because the government did not have full confidence in market mechanisms. In

1992, 13 years after the reform began, the 14th Chinese Communist Party Congress eventually adopted the "socialist market economy" as the objective model for reform, and thus the "market economy" was legitimized.

Here, I need to point out that although I interpret the Chinese economic reform as an experiment of "market socialism," I do not mean that the Chinese government has ever intended that the economy should be purely state owned. To the contrary, even in the pre-reform era, nonstate sectors (mainly collectively owned enterprises and farms) coexisted with state sectors in China. Since reform, the private businesses, rural enterprises, and foreign-invested enterprises have developed rapidly. As a result, today's Chinese economy is more like a "mixed economy" in ownership structure. In industrial sectors, state-owned enterprises account for about one-third, or even less, of output. Furthermore, even some so-called state-owned enterprises have some nonstate shareholders. However, in Chinese official statements, nonstate sectors could only "supplement" state ownership, and state ownership must permanently maintain its dominant position in the whole economy. It is in this sense that I say the Chinese reform is an experiment with market socialism rather than one of a "mixed economy." I will argue later that the diminishing of the state sector is itself strong evidence of inconsistency between state ownership and market competition.

The key issue of market socialism is whether state ownership is consistent with market competition. Within China, economists hold different or even opposite views on the issue. Some economists (called the "competition school") think that ownership is irrelevant as long as there is "full competition" in product markets and that state ownership can be consistent with a market economy. And it is competition, rather than ownership, that is the indispensable component of the market economy. Thus, what the government needs to do with state-owned enterprises is to separate firms from government control (*zhengqi fenkai*), to give firms full autonomy, and to create a level playing field for competition.[2] Another group of economists (called the "ownership school") has argued that a market economy cannot be based on state ownership and that only under private ownership does a market economy work efficiently! Therefore, privatization is inevitable in order for a market economic system to be established successfully.[3]

The astonishing performance of Chinese economic reform (in the growth rate of the GDP as well as other economic indexes) is also cited by some economists beyond China as evidence that market competition can be independent of the ownership structure and that an economy can be very successful even in the absence of well-defined property rights. This view is particularly echoed by Joseph Stiglitz,[4] among others.

Drawing on Chinese reform experiences, as well as on my previous research, this chapter argues that state ownership is inconsistent with a market economy, and that the competitive behaviors of firms cannot be independent of the ownership structure. I share Louis Putterman's argument that the Chinese experience has demonstrated that market socialism has little chance of long-run viability unless strong barriers to the growth of private enterprises are afforded by constitutional or policy constraints.[5] In particular, I show the following:

1. In a state-owned economy, "full competition" must be excessive competition, and competitive behaviors of state-owned enterprises can be very destructive with regard to social efficiency.

2. Competition under state ownership can result in extremely excessive entry.

3. The reputation mechanism in the market order is not workable under state ownership.

4. State-owned enterprises could not survive long under market competition, and competition would eventually lead to privatization of state-owned enterprises.

Excessive (or Vicious) Competition

According to the fundamental theorems of welfare economics, every competitive economy is Pareto efficient, and every Pareto-efficient allocation could be attained through the use of market mechanisms. Efficiency of a market economy depends greatly on the firm's behavior with regard to the maximization of profit. In the competitive market, the optimal pricing rule of a profit-maximizing firm implies that the price equals the marginal cost, which is a condition for the social optimum. In reality, because of externality and market power, attempting to maximize profit does not always lead to Pareto efficiency, and the market could fail. However, with proper government interventions, market competition can still approximate an efficient allocation of the economy.

It is widely accepted that a planned economy is inefficient, partly because the central planner has insufficient information to make the correct decisions and partly because enterprises are not maximizing profits. Market socialism does not reject the fundamental theorems of welfare economics. It is, rather, based on fundamental theorems.[6] It presumes that market competition could be perfectly installed in a state-owned economy and that, as long as state-owned enterprises are motivated by the maximization of profit, socialism could attain the same efficiency as a capitalist market economy.

Although it was not explicitly stated, that presumption has been the underlying doctrine that has guided the Chinese economic reform process. State-sector reform in China began with (a) granting decision rights (i.e., those over production, investment, and pricing) to managers and (b) providing bonus and profit-sharing incentive schemes. For a considerable period, the degree of managerial autonomy was a basic official measure of the reform process and its success. Various reform policies were subsequently implemented to increase managerial autonomy and market competition.[7] It was assumed that once state-owned enterprise managers were able to make their own decisions and compete with one another in the market, the reform would be complete.

Roughly speaking, by 1995 in most sectors, state-owned enterprises were almost free to make their own production decisions and to compete with one another. They did not even need to deliver dividends to the government (the "owner"). In other words, they enjoyed as much freedom as their capitalist counterparts in product markets but bore no equity costs. However, the consequence was surprising and was very different from that which had been expected. Particularly in the second half of the 1990s, it was frequently reported that many state-owned enterprises undercut one another's prices and that product prices were deliberately set below marginal costs. The state sector experienced massive losses. The Chinese media called that kind of pricing behavior "vicious competition." I refer to it as "excessive competition." Excessive (or vicious) competition had become so serious that in mid-1998, the State Economic and Trade Commission of China had to issue a regulatory document forbidding state-owned enterprises to cut prices, a major reversal of the liberalization of pricing policy.

In the Western market economy—except in the case where dominant firms try to monopolize the market by driving out their competitors—we hardly observe such massive excessive competition in competitive sectors where no firm has any prospect of monopolizing the market. Why does excessive competition exist in the transitional Chinese economy? What is the particular condition under which a state-owned enterprise will engage in such pricing behavior?

In Zhang and Ma,[8] we set up a theoretical model to address those issues. Our basic argument is that distortion by virtue of ownership might induce managers to conduct excessively competitive practices. In the traditional theory, the objective of the firm is summarized by a profit function or by some variable proportional to profit. Profit maximization could be a good approximation for the objective of a classic capitalist firm or even a listed private firm. However, it is definitely not a good approximation of the objective of a state-owned enterprise. Let me provide a detailed explanation.

Any economic decision will generate both benefit and cost. Full private ownership can be understood as the decisionmaker's full internalization of the benefit and cost of economic decisions. Thus, in the context of the firm, we can measure ownership distortion by a ratio of the manager's share in the firm's sales revenue to his or her share of the firm's cost. Here, in a static model, both the revenue and the cost should be interpreted as the discounted present values of lifetime cash flows of a production decision. The manager's share of revenue is denoted by β, and the share of cost by α.[9] Then, ownership distortion can be measured by $\gamma = \beta/\alpha$: $\gamma = 1$, meaning no ownership distortion; when $\gamma \neq 0$, distortion occurs. The further γ is from 1, the greater the distortion.

Let us assume that managers maximize their own utility (equal to their personal revenue minus personal cost), whatever the ownership of the firm. In a private owner-controlled firm, $\beta = \alpha = 1$, $\gamma = 1$; that is, the manager is fully responsible for both revenue and cost, and there is no ownership distortion. Profit-maximizing behavior would not lead to excessive competition, whatever the structure of the market. Even under separation of control from ownership where $\beta < 1$, $\alpha < 1$, as long as $\beta = \alpha > 0$, $\gamma = 1$ still holds, and there is no ownership distortion. In this case, the manager's objective function is still equivalent to profit maximization, and excessive competition would not occur.

However, in the case where the managers' revenue share is not equal to their cost share—that is, $\alpha \neq \beta$, and thus $\gamma \neq 1$—each manager's utility-maximizing behavior is different from that of profit maximization. In a static Cournot model, it is easy to show that when ownership is sufficiently distorted (that is, γ is sufficiently large), a manager will optimally set the price below marginal cost, and excessive competition will occur. That model is demonstrated in Figure 3.1, where the manager's optimal price is lower than marginal cost. Furthermore, the greater the number of firms with $\gamma > 1$, and the more elastic the demand, the more likely competition will be excessive.[10]

This theoretical model fairly captures the competitive behavior of state-owned enterprises in the transitional Chinese economy. In pre-reform China, both the revenues and costs of state-owned enterprises were centrally budgeted, and production decisions were

Figure 3.1
OWNERSHIP DISTORTION AND EXCESSIVE COMPETITION

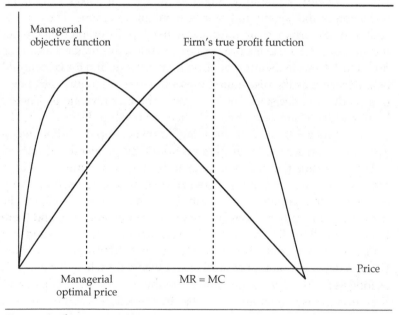

SOURCE: Author's compilation.

made and prices fixed by government departments.[11] Since the reform, managers have acquired considerable production decision rights. At the same time, various incentive systems have been introduced into the state sector.[12] Although many incentive contracts are usually profit based, both pecuniary bonuses and nonpecuniary perks for managers are considerably more dependent on the revenue than on the cost. The reason is that measuring sales revenue is much easier than measuring costs. Typically, revenue is realized in accounting records immediately after sale, whereas production costs can be easily spread over a much longer period. Furthermore, given that the managerial appointment of state-owned enterprises is based on short-term contracts (explicit or implicit), a manager has every incentive to make money quickly, which can be achieved by manipulating accounting entries through putting off losses, as demonstrated in Figure 3.2. For instance, it is widely reported that state-owned enterprise managers often underreport fixed asset depreciation as well

Figure 3.2
Cost Manipulation Behavior

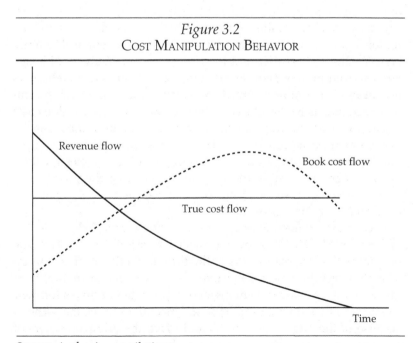

Source: Author's compilation.

as other kinds of measurable costs, thereby delaying the updating of technology. They even "make" profit by defaulting on state bank loans. In addition, many costs are often unaccountable unless the manager is an owner of the firm. As a result, the state-owned enterprise manager's share in sales revenue is typically larger than that in the production costs the manager has to bear, even if the incentive contract is accounting profit based. Thus, we can naturally refer to today's state-owned enterprise as the firm where $\gamma > 1$. That explains why excessive competition occurs in most competitive industries.

We can also reinterpret excessive competition of state-owned enterprises in the context of Holmström and Milgrom's multitask model.[13] Within this setting, the manager has two tasks: revenue growth and cost control. Given that the cost is more difficult to observe, revenue-based incentives outweigh cost-based incentives. The overall incentive would be distorted in favor of revenue maximization rather than profit maximization. Excessive competition will follow.

To complete my argument, I must address the issue of why the separation of ownership from management in Western private economies does not lead to pervasive excessive competition, as experienced by state ownership in China. I believe that the fundamental reason is the nature of ownership. There is an essential difference between the state owner and the private owner. Truly, as Sklivas[14] argues, even in a Western-listed company, given that shareholders do not manage the firm directly, the separation of ownership from management, as well as the complexities of operation decisions that separation leads to, could make the firm deviate from the choice of profit maximization. However, private shareholders in those companies have sufficient incentive to design incentive schemes for their managers and to monitor those schemes so as to make γ as close to 1 as possible, because their personal interests are strongly related to the firm's long-run performance.

In contrast, ownership of a state-owned enterprise belongs to "all of the people." That all are owners means there is no owner at all. The people, as the original owners of the firm, not only lack relevant information but also have no effective means by which to monitor their managers. They cannot be motivated to provide incentives for their agents, and they do not even have self-incentives (to be the owners) because of the "free-rider" problem. In fact, the original owners of a state-owned enterprise do not have "behavioral abilities." That is particularly true when the size of the owner population and the size of the state sector are extensive, as is the case in China.[15]

By means of a long chain of delegation, the state is the legal owner of state-owned enterprises; however, politicians and bureaucrats run the state. Neither politicians nor bureaucrats have any legal claim on a firm's profits. Bureaucrats, as agents, suffer from the same distortion of incentives as state-owned enterprise managers. They are also short-lived in their positions. Why should they behave as private owners to make γ close to 1? It is not surprising that bureaucrats often collude with managers in the misappropriation of state assets, rather than monitoring the managers. Even if bureaucrats have the intention of designing an incentive-compatible contract for managers, lack of sufficient information implies that such an incentive is inevitably of the "one-size-fits-all" type. Given that enterprises differ in many respects from one another, a one-size-fits-all contract can contain only very limited control variables. As a result, managerial autonomy means insider control, and managers will enjoy excessive freedom to manipulate accounting entries. Excessive competition is more likely to occur.

Another important difference between the state-owned economy and Western private economies is that in the Western economy, both the capital market and the managerial labor market play very important roles in disciplining and motivating managers. However, neither of those two mechanisms exists in the state economy, given that all means of production are owned by the single state-owner. That conclusion implies that the state-owner has much less information and fewer means by which to discipline managers. When managerial reputation is not valued in markets, how can managers have any incentive to build up a good reputation, as seen in Western economies?

To summarize, in this section, I have argued that the excessive competition in product markets (i.e., setting prices below marginal costs) observed in China is a natural phenomenon of state ownership when state-owned enterprises are granted the autonomy to make decisions. A general implication is that in a state-owned economy, "full" competition must be excessive competition, and "perfect" competition is inconsistent with a Pareto optimum. When the competition school argues that ownership is irrelevant as long as there is sufficient competition in product markets,[16] it is implicitly assumed that competitive behavior is independent of the ownership structure. However, the Chinese experience has shown that competitive behavior cannot be independent of the ownership structure. Without a fundamental change of ownership, "sufficient competition" can be very destructive.[17]

Given that price is set below marginal cost, how could state-owned enterprises survive in the long run? The answer is that state-owned enterprises are, explicitly or implicitly, subsidized by the government—that is, because of soft budget constraints.[18] Without government subsidies, excessive competition would eventually result in the collapse of state-owned enterprises. One implication is that as the government's budget becomes exhausted, privatization of state-owned enterprises will follow. I shall discuss privatization later in this chapter.

Excessive Entry

The efficiency of markets depends not only on the behavior of existing firms but also on the entry of new firms and the exit of inefficient firms. The process of entry and exit determines the dynamics of market structure and efficiency. In particular, as envisioned by Schumpeter,[19] economic development involves a process of "creative destruction," in which competition in the innovation of technology performs the role of a filter—selecting the winners and driving out the losers.

However, no general theory has emerged to show that the market equilibrium number of firms in a private economy will necessarily be socially efficient. To the contrary, some theoretical models have shown that market equilibrium tends to generate excessive entry—that is, too many firms with regard to the social optimum.[20] In particular, it is often argued that there should be restricted entry into industries with economies of scale because free entry could lead to the undesirable duplication of fixed costs.[21]

For many proponents of socialism, excessive entry and duplication are evils of private ownership. They claim that excessive entry and duplication could be eliminated under state ownership, because no conflict of interests exists between different firms and because all firms have a common goal. Even when excessive entry and duplication do occur for any reason, the government can successfully solve the issues through administrative interventions (such as closedowns, mergers, and acquisitions).

Ironically, Chinese experiences have demonstrated the opposite. State ownership has not only failed to eliminate excessive entry and duplication but also led to further excessive entry and duplication when compared with Western economies. Even under the pre-reform regime, when the government made all decisions regarding entry and exit, excessive entry and duplication caused the most serious and lasting headache for the government. Several cyclical administrative restructurings were launched to deal with the problem.

Since the beginning of reform, many entry restrictions have been gradually abolished, and both local governments and state enterprises have acquired considerable investment decision rights. Progressively more industries are also open to private investors and foreign investment. As a result, excessive entry and duplication have worsened. What we observe today is that, except for a few state-monopolized sectors (such as petroleum, railroads, airlines, and banks), most Chinese industries contain too many small "atomic" firms, with no dominant players. With regard to the number of firms, the Chinese economy might be the most "competitive" economy. Compared with Western and even many developing economies, most Chinese industries are much less concentrated. For example, in 15 manufacturing sectors, only the petroleum-refining sector has a 4-firm concentration ratio that exceeds 40 percent, 3 sectors are between 20 percent and 30 percent, and the remaining 11 sectors are all below 20 percent with 5 of those sectors below 8 percent.[22]

Along with excessive entry and duplication, we also find that it is more difficult for efficient mergers and acquisitions to take place. Failing state-owned firms are extremely resistant to being taken over or closed down. Even insolvent firms have no need to exit. As Ruiming Zhang, CEO of Haier Group, vividly described, as long as it has one breath remaining, a state-owned firm would not be willing to be swallowed up.

Why is entry more excessive and duplication more serious under state ownership? Why is it more difficult to achieve mergers and acquisitions in state sectors? A conventional Chinese argument is that excessive entry and duplication originate from "regional, departmental, and firm self-interests." For example, under the Chinese tax-sharing system, local governments blindly make investments and build new factories only to increase their local tax revenues and employment, in ignorance of social efficiency. Managers are resistant to being taken over because they are concerned about losing their positions and power. However, this type of argument merely illustrates the existence of the problem, rather than providing an answer. After all, one cannot say that interests under state ownership are more dispersed than those under private ownership. In a private economy, every enterprise is an independent entity with its own objective, and it makes investment decisions to maximize its own profit. However, we have not observed excessive entry to be as pervasive as it is in China. Rather, merger and acquisition—either friendly or hostile—frequently happen.

In a 1998 article, I explained that the pervasive phenomenon of excessive entry and duplication in a state economy is rooted in the nature of the state ownership of the firm.[23] As widely recognized by scholars of the theory of the firm, the firm generates two types of return: cash flow (called "profit" for simplicity) and control benefits.[24] The difference between cash flow and control benefits is that cash flow can be distributed in a formal ownership structure, and it is transferable; control benefits are attached, are nontransferable, and can be enjoyed by only managers or controlling shareholders. Here, control benefits can be understood as all private returns related to the managerial position that managers privately value, including perks, nepotism, power, social prestige, and so on. The condition of entry equilibrium depends on how cash flow is matched (or mismatched) with control benefits.

In an owner-managed economy, managers appropriate both profit and control benefits. When there is free entry, the market equilibrium number of firms is given by the condition that the marginal firm's total value (the sum of cash flow and control benefits) equals zero.[25] In an economy where ownership and control are separated, cash flow and control benefits are vested in different people, and the condition of equilibrium is more complicated, depending on incentive schemes and the allocation of authority.

In a state-owned economy, cash flow belongs to "all the people" (or the state), and managers can enjoy only control benefits.[26] Even when managers share some of the cash flow (either explicitly or implicitly), their share of cash flow is still attached to their position and is nontransferable. Therefore, we can still refer to this situation as relating to control benefits.

In the pre-reform regime, bureaucrats made the investment decisions. In the Chinese transitional economy, as state-owned enterprise managers have obtained more autonomy, state-owned enterprise investment decisions are made jointly by managers and bureaucrats. However, in both situations, within certain limits, decisionmakers are driven by private benefits. Therefore, we can reasonably assume that entry equilibrium is determined by the condition that further entry brings about zero control benefits, rather than zero total value or zero profit.

Figure 3.3 shows how cash flow, control benefits, and total value change with the number of firms in an industry. When the number of firms is very low, a small number of oligopolists have substantial market power, and both the cash flow and the control benefits are considerable. As the number of firms increases, markets become more competitive, and both cash flow and control benefits fall.

Figure 3.3
EQUILIBRIUM NUMBER OF FIRMS

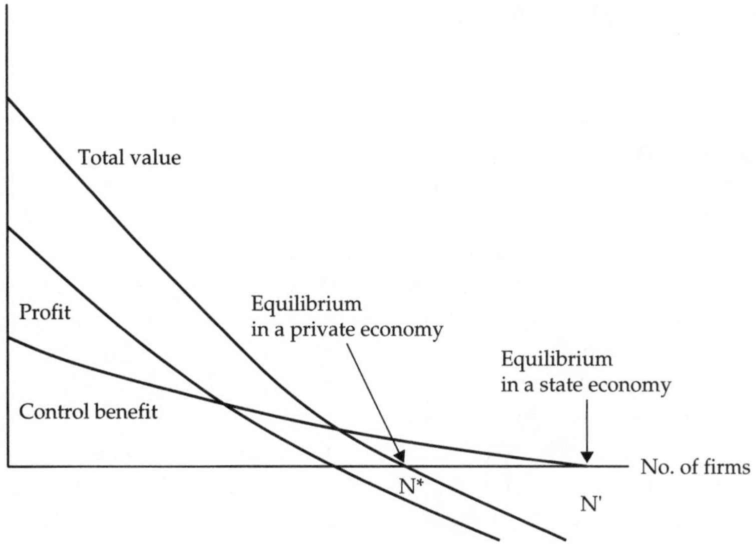

Total value

Equilibrium
in a private economy

Equilibrium
in a state economy

Profit

Control benefit

No. of firms

N*

N'

SOURCE: Author's compilation.

Control benefits fall for two reasons: (a) a lower level of cash flow, meaning there are fewer available perks; and (b) a greater number of managers, meaning that being employed as a manager carries less prestige. We can further assume that cash flow falls faster than control benefits. After all, even when the firm takes a loss, the manager can still appropriate some control benefits. Thus, the cash flow and the total value diminish to zero earlier than the level of control benefits. The equilibrium number of firms in a private economy (denoted by N^*) is lower than that in a state economy (denoted by N').[27]

Thus, I have shown that the state-owned economy suffers far more from excessive entry and duplication. Casual observations strongly support this argument. For example, assume that the social optimal number of car manufacturers is 5 but the government officials in charge choose to increase that number to 50 because they can now appoint 50 general managers and can, therefore, bestow greater favors on their relatives and friends. Although the whole industry, which is attempting to support 50 car manufacturers, takes a loss, no one cares.

The same logic can also explain why mergers and acquisitions in the state sector are more difficult to achieve. In a private economy, the manager of the target firm may lose control benefits after the merger. However, if the merger is efficient in terms of maximizing total value, as an owner, the manager can be compensated by increases in cash flow. The merger can be a Pareto improvement for all parties concerned. In contrast, in a state-owned economy, the loss of control benefits by the manager of the target firm cannot be compensated for in any legal manner through increases in cash flow. Thus, target managers have every incentive to resist mergers in order to protect their control benefits, unless the government offers each manager another equivalent position.

I now turn to discuss the private economy, with separation of control from ownership. Truly, such separation can lead to various managerial discretionary behaviors. However, for the following reasons, that discretion might not be very serious in cases of entry and acquisition when compared with state ownership. First, even when the shareholders are not the managers, it is the shareholders or the board of directors, rather than managers, who, in the main, make entry and merger decisions. This allocation of authority actually implies that the state of equilibrium is more likely to "break even." That is, when compared with an owner-managed economy, there might be too few entries and too many mergers.

Second, in most listed private firms, CEOs hold some shares and, in some cases, are even the largest shareholders. Thus, even though the merger wipes out their control benefits, they can still be partly compensated by cash flow increases. Third, in the interest of their own cash flow, the shareholders of the target firm have incentives to buy out the manager through cash compensation (such as a golden parachute) to mitigate the manager's resistance. In contrast, the "owners" (the people) of state firms have neither a legal right nor an incentive to buy out the manager who will lose control. Fourth, in a market economy with private ownership, many mergers and takeovers can be conducted by making direct offers to shareholders in stock exchanges. This type of mechanism is not available in the state-owned economy.

My argument is also supported by certain empirical studies. For example, using panel data from a Chinese high-tech park, Li, Zhang, and Zhou[28] show that, although efficiency has become an important factor for the survival of all high-tech firms, ceteris paribus, state-owned firms are less likely to exit than are nonstate firms. In particular, the financial distress has a lesser negative effect on the survival of state-owned firms than of nonstate firms, and the least effect is on firms controlled by the central government.

Lack of a Reputation Mechanism

Markets are coordinating devices of transactions and economic activities. In almost all cases, transactions are nothing more than exchanges of promises, and economic activities are nothing more than performing promises. Markets cannot work effectively and efficiently without sufficient mutual trust between the transacting parties. For example, if a buyer does not trust a seller regarding the promised quality of a particular product, he would be reluctant to pay for it. If investors do not believe what an investment bank has said about a company in need of capital, it is unlikely that they would buy that company's stocks. Furthermore, if a bank has no confidence in the borrower to repay, it would be foolish to make a loan. In all those cases, without trust, potential Pareto efficiencies could not be realized. In general, without trust, division of labor and specialization would not occur, and cooperation through markets becomes impossible.

Trust is important but it is also difficult to build. The main reasons for that difficulty are (a) asymmetry of information between the transacting parties and (b) the informed party's behavior with regard to moral hazard. As Akerlof[29] demonstrates, information asymmetry can lead to market failure. Nevertheless, one should not rush to conclude that the asymmetry of information would necessarily result in a market collapse. The assumption of perfect information is the flaw of Neoclassical market economics, but it is definitely not the flaw of the market mechanism itself. We must realize that markets not only are an invisible hand, but also are an "invisible eye" that observes and polices agents' behavior.[30] That is the reputation mechanism.

Although the government-supported legal system might be necessary for agents to keep their promises in certain cases, everyday experience and numerous scholarly studies suggest that official contract enforcement is often costly and impractical. It is the market-based reputation that maintains the integrity of activities in most cases. Anyone who intends to survive in competitive markets for any length of time must build a good reputation for trustworthiness; otherwise, markets would drive them out. In a market economy, reputations and brand names are the most valuable assets and competitive advantage for a firm.

As Adam Smith said a long time ago, honesty is the best business policy. Markets have created numerous intermediaries (such as firms, investment banks, credit rating institutions, etc.) that make possible cooperation that would otherwise be impossible, even cooperation between strangers. In human history, there has been no other institution where reputation is so valuable and plays such an important role as that in market economies. In contrast to the conventional argument—that markets may not work when there is asymmetric information—I would like to argue that asymmetry of information might simply be another or, probably, the main justification for a need for market mechanisms. Without information asymmetry, a planned economy might be just as efficient as a market economy! With information asymmetry, markets could work much better! It is extremely unfortunate that neither Neoclassical economics nor market socialism has put sufficient emphasis on the reputation mechanism of a market economy.

With regard to firms' autonomy and price liberalization, one may claim that the Chinese economy has been greatly affected by the market mechanism. However, Chinese markets are very disorderly. Scams and fakes are pervasive, contracts are often not honored, and state-owned enterprises frequently default on bank loans (resulting in bad debt that accounts for about 25 percent of total bank loans). Disorders exist not only in the product and credit markets but also in the securities markets. Since the establishment of the two stock exchanges (Shanghai and Shenzhen) in 1990, state-owned enterprises have been dominant players in raising capital. Listed state-owned enterprises have taken the stock exchanges as their cash machines. They manipulate accounting entries, cheat private investors, and care little for their reputation. A great many listed firms have committed fraud. Since 1993, about 200 listed firms out of 1,200 have been subject to enforcement action by the China Security Regulation Committee, the Shenzhen Stock Exchange, and the Shanghai Stock Exchange. The ratio of firms committing fraud of all listed firms in China far exceeds the ratio of firms causing scandals in other countries, such as the United States.[31] As a result, the 13-year-old stock exchanges are almost ruined by state-controlled listed companies.

Why are Chinese markets so disorderly? Why do state-owned enterprises care so little about their reputation? One may argue that the reason is that market-friendly legal systems have not been well developed in China. Although that argument is partly true, I deeply believe that the problems originate in the nature of state ownership.[32] The reputation could come only from repeated games. For one to have incentives to build a good reputation, one must have a long-run expectation and must be willing to sacrifice short-term interests in exchange for future returns. Clearly defined private property rights provide owners with proper incentives to play a repeated game. By contrast, under state ownership, everyone plays a one-shot game, and reputation has no value. Making quick money is their best strategy.

In particular, as Kreps[33] points out, in a market economy, the firm is the bearer of reputation. However, for the firm to bear reputation, the following three conditions must hold:

1. The firm must have real owners. As previously stated, reputation is the most important (intangible) asset in a market economy. The most tangible assets of a firm are actually its operation costs, not the true value of the firm. Ownership of the firm

is actually defined by who has a claim to the residual reputation of the firm. The role of owners is to maintain and enhance the firm's reputation. That role is particularly true when the firm employs many people and when anyone's misconduct could damage its reputation. Without true owners, no one would take care of the firm's reputation, and the reputation would be lost.

2. The name of the firm must be tradable in markets. The value of reputation is embedded in the firm's name. It can be fully appropriated only when the owner has freedom to transfer it for economic return. How much incentive the owner has for maintaining and enhancing the firm's reputation depends greatly on tradability. For example, if McDonald's were not franchisable, the firm would not be worth as much.

3. There must be free entry and exit in markets. In the absence of free entry and exit, the firms with good reputations could not drive out a firm with a bad reputation. As a result, an incumbent firm could enjoy great monopoly rents. When consumers cannot punish a firm's dishonest behavior, reputation is less valuable.

Thus, we can easily explain why state-owned firms do not care for their reputation. When a firm is owned by the state, no one has a residual claim over its reputation. The name of the state-owned enterprise is usually not tradable. Even when traded, it could not be correctly priced because the "seller" could not appropriate the sale revenue. The restriction of the entry of private firms and soft budget constraints also make the survival of state-owned enterprises less dependent on their reputations. When government bureaucrats' interests are not related to the firm's reputation, why should they care about it? Given that the bureaucrats have no proper incentive to make managerial appointments on the basis of merit, state-owned enterprise managers feel very insecure about their positions, and they have no future to care about. Therefore, they have every incentive to play the one-shot game to make quick money. All those factors lead to a failure of reputation. Using an analogy, reputation is like a tree. The manager of a state-owned enterprise might have an incentive to grow grass but definitely not to plant trees.

To conclude, the "invisible hand" of the free price system and the "invisible eye" of the reputation mechanism, together, make markets work. In a state economy, even if the price system is set free, the reputation mechanism could not work well. Therefore, disorder is inevitable in state ownership–based markets.

Competition-Driven Privatization

Although many scholars have claimed that Chinese economic reform is a transition to a market economy, unlike most eastern European and former Soviet Union countries, the Chinese government has never intended to give up state-owned enterprises. For the Chinese Communist Party, state ownership is the cornerstone of the socialist market economy; without state ownership, China would no longer be a socialist country. The goal of reform has simply been to improve the public ownership–based economy by introducing market competition, rather than to establish a private ownership–based market economy. Privatization has never been adopted as official reform policy. The scholars who argue for privatization are often denounced as "bourgeois liberals."

However, the consequences of the reform are far beyond what they were supposed to be. Today's reality is that, although state-owned enterprises are still dominant in some key industries (i.e., the petroleum, electricity, telecommunications, and financial sectors), and although the government still insists that state ownership should play a dominant role in the whole economy, nonstate sectors (i.e., foreign-owned, joint-venture, mixed-ownership, and domestic private enterprises) have already become—or are becoming—leading players in many industries.

In 1978, nearly four-fifths of total industrial output in China came from state-owned enterprises. By 1997, the state-owned enterprise share had shrunk to little more than a quarter.[34] More surprisingly, since the early 1990s, spontaneous and local government-initiated privatization of both state-owned firms and collective-owned firms has been accelerating through various ways—including public offerings, open sale, management and employee buyouts, leases, and joint ventures—under the official name of *gaizhi*.[35] By the end of 1998, more than 80 percent of state and collective firms at or below the county level had undergone *gaizhi*, which involved direct privatization in most cases.[36] A 2002 national survey of industrial state-owned enterprises estimated that 86 percent had been through *gaizhi* by the end of 2001, and that about 70 percent had been partially or fully privatized.[37]

Southern Jiangsu is a particularly interesting case. Up until the early 1990s, the Southern Jiangsu model (*Sūnán móshì*) was widely thought to be an "economic model of a new type of public ownership" compared with the private ownership–dominated Zhejiang model. However, by the end of 2000, nearly 100 percent of village-owned firms, 95 percent of township firms, 90 percent of county-owned firms, and 85 percent of city-owned firms had already been privatized.[38] The Zhejiang private-ownership model eventually claimed victory over the Jiangsu public-ownership model.

Interestingly, Chinese economic reform began (a) with decentralization rather than with the development of a private-ownership system and (b) with the revitalization of state firms rather than with their privatization. What are the driving forces behind the unintended and accelerating rise of a private-ownership system in China? What has motivated local governments to privatize the enterprises under their control?

In Li, Li, and Zhang,[39] we developed a theoretical model to address those issues. In that article, firm ownership is defined by who holds the residual claim.[40] Privatization is the process of shifting residual claims from government to managers. For ease of exposition, we focus on how cross-regional competition in the product market triggers privatization of state-owned enterprises through the interaction between bureaucrats and managers in regional government-controlled public economies.[41] We find that when cross-regional competition is sufficiently intense, each region has to cut production costs. Given that the efforts of managers are not verifiable, local governments might have to grant total or partial residual shares to the managers. In general, intense product competition stimulates the rise of a private property system. We then submit our theory to a vigorous empirical test using China's industrial census data of more than 400,000 firms. The test strongly supports our postulation that cross-regional competition is the driving force behind China's transition toward the private economic system.

While Li, Li, and Zhang[42] focus on how competition induces privatization of existing state-owned enterprises, we believe that the same logic can be applied to analyzing how cross-regional competition induces the establishment of new private enterprises. As I have pointed out, official open privatization in China has never been adopted as a central government policy. However, competition is far more powerful than ideology. Regardless of whether or not the central government will draw up a blueprint for full privatization, both our theory and reality show that the privatization process will continue to accelerate with its own logic and vigor.

The Chinese experience demonstrates not only that the "invisible hand" is powerful in allocating resources, but also that it is powerful in creating institutions. Once decentralization begins, market competition could precipitate a self-enforcing development of a private-ownership system. The newly founded and privatized firms, in turn, intensify market competition, which is a major lesson from China's experience.

More generally, the relevance of our theory extends beyond China and former socialist economies. According to a recent World Bank report, the output of state-owned enterprises still accounts for a large share of the gross domestic product in many countries, including not only transition economies but also developing economies and even industrial economies.[43] But across countries and time, state-owned enterprises are generally poor performers. In the past decade or more, privatization of state-owned enterprises has taken place not only in socialist and developing economies but also in developed economies. It is our conjecture that the intensifying cross-country competition resulting from globalization has been—and will continue to be—one of the most fundamental driving forces behind the worldwide movement toward privatization and the transition to the market economy.

Conclusion

Drawing on China's reform experiences, as well as on my previous research, this chapter has shown that state ownership is inconsistent with a market economy and that competitive behavior in markets cannot be independent of the structure of ownership of firms. In particular, I have shown the following:

1. In a state-owned economy, competition can be excessive (or destructive) in the sense that the state-owned firms are more likely to set prices below marginal costs as competition intensifies.

2. Competition under state ownership could result in extreme excessive entry—that is, too many firms in industries, compared with private economies.

3. In a state ownership–dominated economy, market disorder is inevitable, and building trust is more difficult, because the reputation mechanism cannot work.

4. State-owned enterprises cannot survive long under competition, and competition eventually leads to the privatization or collapse of state-owned enterprises.

One limitation of this chapter is that I have not discussed the political institutions of market socialism. One can argue that state-owned firms might behave differently under different political regimes and that the Chinese experience might not be applicable in general. In particular, political democracy might make state ownership work better. However, I deeply believe that my overall arguments hold, whatever the political system might be. Of course, only history will tell us the truth.

4. The Anti-Competition Nature of the Anti-Monopoly Law

On August 1, 2008, China's Anti-Monopoly Law will be implemented. It is an important piece of legislation. About 10 years ago, I participated in this law's legislative discussions. For various reasons, I did not continue with this project. Not until now have we seen such a law proposed. Truthfully, I am not optimistic about its prospects. Regardless of whether one is discussing the foundation of the economics on which the law is built or the actual effect it will have, both are cause for concern.

The Three Definitions of the Firm

To explain my viewpoint, I first need to introduce a few definitions related to enterprises and markets and to enterprise functions in economic theory:

1. Enterprises are a function of production. That is, enterprises are viewed as a unit that has resource inputs and product outputs. Correspondingly, we can understand the market as a static mechanism that allocates resources through price competition. That definition is the most mainstream viewpoint found in economic textbooks.

2. Enterprises are a function of innovation. That is, enterprises are viewed as a specialized organization for creating new technology, new products, new markets, new business models, and new methods of production. Correspondingly, markets can be understood as a dynamic process that achieves economic growth through innovation.[1]

3. Third, enterprises are bearers of reputation.[2] That is, the market is a cooperative system with division of labor and specialization

as characteristics, and enterprises are the reputation foundation that sustains that system. The existence and the operation of enterprises establish responsibility in the market economy and promote broader cooperation between strangers.

The Anti-Monopoly Law was built on the first definition of enterprises. Here, enterprises are viewed as only production units, but the market environment they face (such as consumer demand, technology levels, etc.) is a given. The only function of enterprises is to maximize profits through price and to maximize social efficiency through production choices. Under that analytical framework, people believe that the more enterprises there are, the fiercer competition will be, thus causing higher efficiency, which will be more beneficial to society. Conversely, if a market is occupied by just a few enterprises, it will turn into a so-called oligarch monopoly, which is bad for society. The standard of measurement for monopolies is the degree of concentration in market share. It appears that the higher the market concentration, the more serious the monopoly. Therefore, the Anti-Monopoly Law was designed with the hope of limiting the concentration of market share among individual enterprises.

Consequently, the Anti-Monopoly Law opposes big enterprises and their growth. However, we actually see that the signs of economic development—such as new products, wage increases, and growth of society's wealth—are in large part brought about by big enterprises. Thus, we could say that the Anti-Monopoly Law ideal does not conform to the real state of the economy. It is an obvious contradiction with the growing number of enterprises emerging during economic development.

Oligarchy Competition That Is Beneficial to Society

To explain the contradiction in the Anti-Monopoly Law, we must find a new inspiration in the history of economic thought. Well-known economist Joseph Schumpeter[3] had a very important exposition. He believed that enterprises are a type of tool for innovation and that economic growth is a dynamic process. In the process he called "creative destruction," new products replace old products, and new production methods replace old production methods. That process is the essential feature of economic development. For example, in the past, young people listened to music on their Walkman portable cassette players. However, when the digital MP3 players emerged, the Walkman disappeared from the market. One could say that MP3 manufacturers' new products "destroyed" the old products.

Taking Schumpeter's theory about innovation as a starting point, I tend to believe that oligarchy competition is the most suitable market structure for innovation. In a so-called perfect competition market structure, it is hard to sustain true innovation and to ensure the research and development investments that innovation relies on. The "perfect" competition market structure is not perfect at all. The ferocity of competition is not decided by the number of producers in an industry.

Traditional agriculture has many farmers, but they focus little on competition. In contrast, when markets are led by a small number of enterprises such as automobiles, electronics, and software, enterprises always feel threatened by competition. Bill Gates often says, "Microsoft is only 18 months from death." In the software industry, innovation is vitally important. Although Microsoft is a leader in the software industry, if it does not work hard, a competitor will quickly replace it. Similar to Microsoft, as soon as an enterprise becomes an industry leader, innovation becomes an institutionalized and routine process. Innovation becomes something enterprises consider continuously.

A well-operating market is often led by a few brand-name enterprises, and large enterprises function to preserve market order. They not only must be responsible for the actions of their own employees, but also must take joint liability for the behavior of their suppliers. For example, if the employees of a food and beverage company make a mistake that injures the health of its customers, the company must take responsibility. If the upstream suppliers of a car manufacturer provide defective parts, the enterprise must also take responsibility should an accident occur. Only then can trust be established in the market, so consumers can purchase merchandise with confidence. Establishing trust is difficult in a final product market that was formed by a large number of unknown small enterprises.

The theoretical foundation of the Anti-Monopoly Law contains an implied premise: when the market share in an industry is more concentrated, there will be fewer products, so prices will be higher. Many examples from industry demonstrate that circumstances are precisely the opposite. Rapid growth in production and dramatic decreases in prices normally go together with increases in market concentration.[4] The automobile, computer, and cell phone industries are examples. If a market bears the weight of too many enterprises, even if it is a so-called perfect competition market, production increases and price decreases do not normally occur. That point is often overlooked.

Freedom of Entry: The True Boundary Between Monopoly and Competition

To summarize, if we define enterprises as a tool for innovation or as a bearer of reputation and not just as a production unit, the theoretical economic foundation on which the Anti-Monopoly Law relies no longer exists. Economists do not like monopolies, but traditional economic theory has yet to propose a good definition of monopolies and nonmonopolies, which is regrettable. Actually, if we think carefully about the issue, monopolies truly become a problem only when government restrictions limit free entry and thus damage the foundation of market competition. Without government protections, all monopolies would have no substance.[5]

In that respect, economics should take a lesson from management studies. Management scholars emphasize that if an enterprise wants to succeed, it must create value for consumers. Creating value for consumers is the only path to survival. If an enterprise cannot create value for consumers according to the traditional textbook meaning and instead tries to squeeze customers at will, it will "get a taste of its own medicine." We can accept that the market will use competition to eliminate noninnovative enterprises and enterprises that try to earn money by squeezing customers.

In the computer chip market—from the point of view of traditional economic theory—Intel is a high-level monopolistic enterprise. However, over the past 30 years, how much has the speed of Intel chips increased? How much has the price declined? Both Intel and Microsoft must spare no effort to increase innovation, decrease costs, and increase production. Otherwise, their competitors will catch up with them.

If the government decided to limit entry to an industry to 1,000 enterprises—which is enough dispersion with regard to the economics definition—what would happen? I believe the most likely outcome would be that technological progress would slow, service awareness would decline, and the long-term price pattern would remain unchanged. Therefore, the only true measurement of competition is freedom of market entry.

In China, petroleum, telecommunications, and other industries are often criticized for low quality and high prices. The real issue is that the government has not opened those industries, and only a select number of enterprises are allowed to enter the market. For China's telecommunications and oil enterprises to better serve society, the only effective method is to remove restrictions on entry into those industries. Then, even if no new enterprises enter the industry immediately, the incumbent enterprises will work hard to cater to consumers because of the threat of potential competition. If they do not, only the Department of Economic Management can supervise them, tell them how to set prices, and tell them how to improve service, but the core problem will still exist.

A year from now (2008), the Anti-Monopoly Law will be implemented, but I am not optimistic. The enterprise behavior directed at and limited by the Anti-Monopoly Law is actually part of market innovation and the reputation mechanism, which are the essence of market competition. As for breaking up government-protected industries, the law is almost useless. Therefore, I am concerned that a law aimed at opposing monopolies will ultimately become a tool to oppose market competition. And that is something we must guard against.

5. Liberalize Commercial Activity

Since Adam Smith, economists have clearly recognized that the prosperity of a country or territory is decided largely by the legislative and regulatory environment faced by entrepreneurs who are starting and operating a business. A freer commercial environment encourages more entrepreneurs to invest in startups, thus providing more employment opportunities. It also encourages entrepreneurs to continuously innovate, thus promoting increases in productivity and wage levels.

For a long time, economists had only qualitative characterizations of the commercial environment—a view that has changed only recently. Starting in 2003, the World Bank and the International Finance Corporation undertook an unprecedented project to rank the commercial environment of 170 countries and territories. A series of quantitative standards for government rules and enforcement levels were used as measurements. They included all the regulatory and bureaucratic processes that a business must undergo from start to dissolution, as well as the effects those rules have on business, especially local small and medium-sized enterprises. The *Doing Business Report* could be considered the most authoritative guide on the investment environment for entrepreneurs in different countries and territories. Since its publication, it has had a large effect in many countries and has promoted government policy reforms.

Doing Business 2007: How to Reform was formally published on September 6, 2006. The World Bank and the International Finance Corporation held a press conference in Beijing on September 14. I was invited to speak at that press conference. As a Chinese reader of the report, I was both gratified and concerned when it first came out. Gratification came from the fact that over the past year, China placed fourth globally for business environment reforms and placed first in East Asia. Its overall business ranking increased 15 places. China earned that ranking by overhauling many legal codes and institutions. According to the report, China quickened the business registration process, strengthened investor protections, simplified trading across borders, and even opened consumer credit bureaus. All of those measures play a positive role in commercial activity and economic development.

I was concerned because even with that much progress, the overall score for China's commercial environment was still near the bottom: China placed 93rd out of 170 countries and territories, much lower than the average. China ranked 128th in "starting a business," 153rd in "dealing with licenses," 101st in "getting credit," and 168th in "paying taxes."

Thirteen steps are required to register a Chinese business to operate legally. The process takes 35 days and costs 9.3 percent of the annual per capita income. The minimum starting capital is 213.1 percent of the average per capita income. In contrast, that process takes only two days in Australia and Canada. Many countries and economic systems (such as the United States and Hong Kong) have no minimum capital thresholds. The tax burden on Chinese businesses is also the heaviest. A medium-sized Chinese enterprise must make 44 tax payments a year, spend 872 hours preparing them, and pay a total tax rate of 77.1 percent. Those three metrics are all much higher than the average level in East Asia.

It must be noted that China's survey sample was Shanghai. The commercial environment in most regions in China is much worse than in Shanghai. Also, the *Doing Business Report* makes certain assumptions: (a) an entrepreneur can get information at any time; (b) all government departments and nongovernmental organizations carry out their duties efficiently; and (c) there is no corruption.

The report demonstrates that even though China has been successful over the past 27 years of reform in building market economy institutions, the Chinese economy is still highly controlled. Chinese entrepreneurs experience irrational sanctions when starting and operating a business. Actually, I believe that many of the measures used by the government to manage the economy under central planning have been preserved in the name of regulation. The main administrative measure used by government departments to control economic activity is the system of examination and approval. When businesses do anything, they must interact with government bureaucrats, thereby unnecessarily wasting time and money.

Over the past few years, with China joining the World Trade Organization, over half of the examination and approval programs have been tidied up by the central and local governments. However, a quantitative reduction has not produced a related qualitative change. Some unimportant examination and approval bodies have been scrapped, but many "high-rent" examination and approval bodies remain. For example, in some important industries, businesses do not have true investment autonomy. Even private business investment still requires government approval.

In February 2005, the State Council proclaimed the "36 provisions" to encourage and promote private business development. It aimed to create equal provisions for private businesses to enter the market and to liberalize the commercial environment. Most of the provisions were not actually implemented. Some examination and approval bodies that had already been scrapped were reintroduced in the name of industrial policy and macroeconomic adjustment. In some important industries, "overcapacity" has become an excuse to inhibit private business. During macroeconomic adjustments, banks will not even execute loan contracts, causing some private businesses to have difficulty operating.

Government limitations on commercial activity are perhaps founded on good intentions, such as protecting the consumer, ensuring the safety of workers, reducing pollution, and so on. The World Bank analysis of 170 countries and territories proves that the result of government controls often conflicts with their original intention. For example, analysis of the data shows that excessive market entry requirements absolutely do not improve product quality, ensure worker safety, or reduce pollution.[1] They only suppress private investment, thus pushing more people into the informal economy, which, in turn, increases consumer prices and fosters corruption. Those countries with the most serious environmental pollution are often the very countries with the most limitations on market entry.

Now we need to discuss the relationship between government regulation and corruption. Just as *Doing Business 2007* points out, in different countries, excessive market entry procedures and corruption are always interrelated. That relationship is especially the case in developing countries, where every procedure is a "point of engagement," thus an opportunity for bribery. One can easily understand why those countries with the worst commercial environments are also the very countries with the worst corruption problems.

During the process of reform in China, the wealth-creating activities of entrepreneurs and the rent-seeking behavior of government officials are often mixed together. The reason is that in countries with a market economy, citizens and businesses have the right to engage in legitimate commercial activities, whereas in China the government has monopolized those activities. Examples include government permission to start a business or to engage in investment activity. Individuals and businesses must resort to bribery to redeem their rights to engage in normal economic activity that they should have had to begin with.

Limits on the principle of free commerce often also injure the interests of the ordinary laborer. For example, minimum capital requirements discriminate against the poor. They deprive the poor of the opportunity to start a business, and they put employees at a disadvantage in negotiating wages. Another direct impairment on the interests of laborers is the government's excessive intervention in the hiring system. In the World Bank report, the employment system is 1 of the 10 major indicators used to measure the commercial environment. The report's analysis of countries' standards for employment systems shows that countries with the most restrictions on employment are also the countries with the highest unemployment rates. The strictest interventions in the labor market cause many unpleasant side effects, such as (a) reduced employment opportunities, (b) lengthened unemployment time, (c) deteriorated personnel skills, (d) reduced research and development, and (e) smaller corporate scales. Some regulations that appear to protect the interests of labor actually harm labor. The report references a very enlightening example: In Venezuela, employees fear being promoted. The reason is a law that was recently passed prohibiting businesses from laying off personnel with wages lower than 1.5 times the minimum wage. Smart employers have found a way to circumvent the law. When they want to lay off an employee, they first promote that employee so that the new wage is more than 1.5 times the minimum wage. Thus, they can then legally lay off that employee.

At a time when China is still very far from reaching a true market economy, public opinion is already filled with high levels of mistrust toward the market. That mistrust has caused the introduction of some anti-market policies. I hope that the *Doing Business Report 2007* can strengthen our confidence in continued reform. The market is not perfect, but it is still the most effective means of solving the problems we face. If our regulations could give commercial activity more freedom, even reaching a level above the world average, then more people would engage in entrepreneurial and innovative activities, our growth would be more sustainable, more people would find employment opportunities and sources of income, our government would be cleaner, and our society would be more harmonious!

6. Good Policy and Bad Policy

Government is an organization that sets policy. Each person's decisions, behavior, and level of welfare are all affected by policy. Some government policies are good, and some are bad. That judgment is acceptable to everyone. However, people may differ in what they judge as a good or bad policy.

We often hear others say that a policy was good, but enforcement was poor. So if a policy is considered good, but its enforcement is always bad, where does the problem truly lie? What standard can we use to judge a policy?

How Economists Judge Policy

Usually, people and economists differ in how they judge policies. Ordinary people often judge a policy by the objective it pursues or whether it is virtuous or evil. Even if different people have different standards of virtue and evil, most people's standards can easily coincide with regard to policy objectives. For example, when the government proposes a policy aimed at reducing the gap between rich and poor, to bring about common prosperity, everyone agrees that it is a good policy. Other good policies include increasing wages to increase the people's livelihood, increasing welfare to build a harmonious society, increasing employment opportunities, protecting the disadvantaged, controlling consumer prices and housing prices, protecting the ecosystem, and reducing pollution.

How do economists evaluate policy? An economist's influence on the social value of a policy objective is exactly the same as that of the average person—the preference of just one citizen. The first standard that economists use when evaluating a policy is whether or not its results are the same as or conflict with the policy's objective. When economists regard a policy as bad, they do not mean that they, as individuals, dislike the objective of the policymakers. For example, when economists regard minimum-wage policies and policies that restrict employment liberty as bad policies, they do not mean that the interests of labor should not be protected. Rather, they believe those policies are bad because economic theory and experience have proved that such policies reduce employment opportunities and increase unemployment, especially for young people. The best method for protecting the interests of laborers is competition among employers. The enormous increase in the wages of nannies in China over the past few years proves that point.

Another example of economists' judging policy objectives and their results is high taxes. Economists regard high taxes as bad because they suppress people's incentive to work, because they are disadvantageous to starting a business and innovation, and because they obstruct economic development. Economists regard using expansionary policy to stimulate the economy as bad because it hides the mistaken investment decisions of entrepreneurs, leads to distortions of industry structures, and ultimately leads to an economic recession or even a serious crisis. Economists regard the planned economy as bad, not because of its objective, but because it is completely unworkable.

The second standard that economists use to evaluate a policy is whether or not a lower-cost, higher-efficiency alternative exists. For example, Beijing Municipality is trying to control the number of vehicles on its streets. It is currently using a lottery system in which 20,000 new license plates are issued each month. The issue here is would using an auction or district toll collection system be better? The lottery system cannot allocate a limited number of vehicles to the people and enterprises that need them most. Such a drawback would necessarily limit the flow of talent and capital, which would be disadvantageous to Beijing's economic development and which would perhaps lead to corruption. Therefore, the lottery system is not a good policy.

The third standard that economists use to evaluate a policy is whether or not it is compatible with "consumer sovereignty." Economist Ludwig von Mises proposed this standard. A basic principle of the market economy is that the consumer is the true "boss." The consumer should determine whether a type of product has value and the amount it is worth. The entrepreneur must certainly make decisions on the basis of the projected spending decisions of consumers. As a result, it is hard to say that the government's industrial policies are good policies. The reason is they do not encourage entrepreneurs to understand consumer preferences and do not use those preferences to make investment policies and production decisions according to consumer demand. Instead, industrial policies encourage entrepreneurs to make investment and production decisions on the basis of the preferences of government officials. Therefore, it is not a good policy.

Policies That Limit Free Competition Are Not Good Policies

Next, I would like to discuss why a policy's objective can be good even if its results are not optimal and often conflict with its objective. Using the terminology of economics, the policy does not satisfy the incentive compatibility constraint. All stakeholders in society have personal interests, preferences, and private information. When they pursue their own interests, they are actively and rationally "using" policy, not "enforcing" policy.

Our decisionmakers assume that people influenced by policy are impelled by it. As long as a policy exists, people will act according to the policymakers' intentions. The minimum-wage law, for example, is aimed at protecting low-income laborers. Enterprises that obey the law will, of course, implement it, but they can still legally reduce the number of workers. The government cannot force enterprises to employ a certain number of people. If a company originally employed 1,000 people, but now employs only 500 people, then ultimately, those who are injured the most are precisely the low-income classes that the law was trying to protect. Those who could find employment before the minimum-wage law was implemented now cannot find work. Setting policy that satisfies the incentive compatibility constraint requires the government to grasp a lot of information, but the government cannot actually grasp all the information necessary to set policy, even if it does have the power to set policy.

One of my basic conclusions is that laissez faire—or policy that does not require forced government intervention—is the best policy. From this perspective, any policy that limits entrepreneurial spirit or inhibits business creation and innovation is not a good policy. Economic growth relies on entrepreneurial judgment, risk taking, and innovation, so any policy that suppresses the spirit of entrepreneurial innovation is definitely not a good policy. Any policy that limits free competition or maintains government and state-sector monopolies is not a good policy. That conclusion is especially the case for many policies in China that limit private enterprises from entering certain industries.

Here, I want to emphasize that the logic of the market that I speak of—where each person must first make others happy to make oneself happy—has free competition as a prerequisite. Without competition, one does not need to make others happy in order to make oneself happy, just like the state sector. Free competition is key to the operation of the logic of the market. There is an old a saying, "For the workman to get rich, what he builds must fall down." The premise of this saying is that the workman has no competition. With competition, if an enterprise produces shoddy products, it will have no customers. Any policy that enlarges or strengthens state-owned enterprises is not a good policy. Most state-owned enterprises consume value rather than create it. Much of the profit they earn comes from government subsidies, or what economics calls transfers of consumer surplus.

Any policy that leads entrepreneurs to rent-seek is not a good policy. Industrial policies lead to entrepreneurial rent-seeking. Many people, including some Americans, praise China's industrial policies. Actually, China's industrial policies have never been very successful. The premise of industrial policy is that government officials understand the future direction of development, including changes in consumer preferences and technological trends, better than entrepreneurs do. That assumption is baseless. Government officials are no more farsighted, or impartial, than are entrepreneurs. Actually, industrial policy often turns into rent-seeking policy. In other words, when government officials use industrial policy to distribute funds, entrepreneurs devise ways to establish relationships with the government and write approvable proposals in order to receive subsidies. For the new energy policy, some entrepreneurs applied for tens of million, or even hundreds of millions, yuan in government subsidies. After receiving the money, they did not actually enter the new energy industry.

Any policy that increases the government's ability to control—including control of budgets, resources, and land—is not really a good policy. When the government uses administrative means to control prices, including housing prices, it is also not using good policy. Government control cannot truly solve the problem. Instead, it disrupts the market.

Any policy that is erratic is not a good policy. An entrepreneur makes his decisions on the basis of forecasts. The variableness of policy will necessarily lead to disruptions of entrepreneurial forecasts, short-term investments, looting of resources, and atrophy of innovation. It will cause entrepreneurs not to care about their reputation, thereby leading to abuse and fraud.

Why Bad Policy Is Prevalent

We need to ask why so many bad policies have emerged. I believe there are two broad reasons: ignorance and interests. First, policies grounded in ignorance or mistaken information are ubiquitous. For example, ignorance and mistaken information led to bad policy at the beginning of the planned economy. The objective of the planned economy is very noble. But because we are ignorant, we did not know how an economy truly operated. We thought government officials could grasp all the necessary information to implement an effective resource allocation plan. We thought each person had the incentive to enforce the plan implemented by government.

From those facts, we can understand why many politicians and government officials often dislike economics, that is, true economics—people are not willing to admit that they are stupid! Of course, ignorance is not limited to average people and government officials. It also applies to intellectuals, including economists. During the 1940s and 1950s, a not-so-small number of "economists" were loyal followers of the planned economy, including even some neoliberal economists.

The second reason for the spread of bad policy is vested interests. Bad policies that arise from vested interests—or policies set for one's own interests—are also ubiquitous. Trade protectionist policies are a classic example. Because some enterprises and workers are threatened by competition, they use various means to persuade the government to limit trade freedom to protect their own interests. Of course, pursuing one's own interests is not a problem as long as personal happiness is attained by first creating value for others according to market rules. The bad policies that arise from the vested interests to which I refer are the policies whose results do not lead to attaining profit by creating value for others; instead, they sacrifice other people's interests in order to attain income. Therefore, they are bad policies. Trade protectionism makes the majority of consumers subsidize a small number of producers (and the workers who are employed by those enterprises).

A more troubling matter is that bad policies resulting from both ignorance and interests are complementary and mutually support- ive. In many cases, vested interests are cloaked in grandiose theory. Trade protectionism is often done in the name of protecting national industry. On the one hand, because private interests are off-limits for discussion, the vested interests have an incentive to find theoretical support that will protect those interests. On the other hand, scholars who supply erroneous information are always happy to service that market. Take, for example, the family planning policy. We have diffi- culty adjusting that policy for two reasons: First, "ignorance" makes us look at population totals, not the population structure. We know only that more people mean more of a burden rather than a larger market. Second, the family planning "army" has become a vested interest. However, the only opposition to adjusting the family plan- ning policy is in the name of "national interests." The new Labor Contract Law has similar issues.

Keynesian policy is also the merger of ignorance and interests. Keynesianism was originally a theory that researched short-term economic fluctuations (even though it was incorrect). Now, it has become a theory for economic development and transition. Many of the theoretical foundations for China's implementing the 12th Five-Year Plan were merely a Keynesian formula. According to that formula, economic growth comes from the "troika" of consumption, investment, and net exports. The more money government spends, the faster gross domestic product (GDP) grows. We initially cre- ated GDP for consumption, whereas now we create consumption for GDP. Originally, investment was intended to increase efficiency and to increase future production, but now investment is intended to increase aggregate demand and current GDP, with no relation to ef- ficiency. Originally, trade was intended to increase the level of hap- piness for the whole world, thus benefiting all nations in the world- wide division of labor. Now, trade increases GDP only if exports are larger than imports, which gives trade protection a theoretical basis. It is truly ridiculous.

What drives interest in Keynesian policy? Why do politicians, entrepreneurs, economists, and the public like Keynesianism? Politicians like Keynesianism for two reasons. First, Keynesian policy allows government to spend large amounts of money, and spending money is something government officials like to do. Second, politicians often focus on short-term objectives only. We know that under the current democratic system, politicians consider only the affairs within their own political term, unlike in the past when the emperor had to consider the state of the nation under his sons and grandsons. Keynesianism provides an excuse for the government to pursue its short-term interests.

Entrepreneurs like Keynesianism because many of them do not want to suffer the consequences of their mistakes. They hope the government will lower interest rates and issue more currency to rescue them from the brink of bankruptcy. Entrepreneurs always like a loose monetary policy, never a strict monetary policy.

Economists like Keynesianism because it provides many employment opportunities for Keynesian economists. It turns the government into an enormous market for the consumption of policy economics.

The public likes Keynesianism because the public likes a free lunch. The public thinks that using credit to increase wages and welfare costs the government nothing. Keynesianism tells people that the market failed, so the government must correct the market's failures. It suits the tastes of the masses!

Reform Calls for Leadership

From here, we can examine China's future. China's future—and the kinds of policies we have—will be determined to a large degree by our ideals, what we believe in and do not believe in. If we believe in the market economy, our future will be bright. Otherwise, if we continue to question the market, to distrust the entrepreneurial spirit, and to be enamored with government intervention, our prospects will be bleak. Stated simply, can ideals overcome interests? During the first 10 years of reform, ideals overcame interests. Our beliefs, even though they were implemented with resistance, allowed reform to move forward. Today, interests are basically over-coming ideals. Very few people are discussing ideals.

Almost all policies are intended to protect and increase the self-interests of various sectors. If that objective cannot be changed, then we cannot be too optimistic about the future. Why? Vested interests are extremely strong. Many vested interests act in the name of na-tional interests or state interests. Vested interests can use nationalist emotions to realize their own objectives. In China, nationalism has deep roots. As soon as the banner of nationalism is raised, ideals are unnecessary. Concealed behind that banner are vested interests, which are holding the ordinary people hostage. Principles have be-come fragile because principles are often grasped by a small group of people without political power.

Reform calls for leadership! We need great leaders. Great leaders are different from average people because they see further, prefer principles, and have more ideals. Great leaders are more willing to sacrifice their interests for their ideals. In the 1980s, we had many cadres with ideals who competed with one another to accomplish reforms. Now, people are competing to accomplish nothing because doing nothing is safer. The public is willing to accept principles only when it has no other choice. Only during a crisis is the public willing to seek a great leader like Deng Xiaoping. Perhaps our future reform will appear only after a true crisis occurs. Of course, no one wants the country to suffer a crisis, but history has proved that maybe it is the only path to reform. We can only wait.

7. The Market and Morality

The basic assumption of economics and religious ethics is that people are self-centered. The greatest difference between the logic of religion and the logic of the market is that religion attempts to change people's hearts, whereas the market changes people's actions. Action for the benefit of others leads to personal happiness.

Why People Are Self-Centered

People make mistakes or misbehave for two reasons. The first reason is ignorance. Knowledge is limited, and people might not understand the difference between good and bad. They try to do good, yet the result is bad. The second reason is shamelessness. When people know that doing something is bad and will injure others, they still do it for their own benefit. For example, in the widely followed food safety issue, throughout the entire linked process, many people contributed to the problem. Some were ignorant, and some were shameless. In reality, the two are hard to separate. Ignorance can also be said to be the root of many shameless actions. Those actions manifest themselves as a lack of wisdom. The result is that clever people are duped by their own cleverness. However, every human mistake should not simply be considered shameless. That point is extremely important.

With regard to the market economy, scholars, including economists, must maintain that the market itself does not change human nature. The market has never tried to change human nature, and guardians of the market have never considered using the market to change human nature. Instead, precisely because human nature cannot be changed, the market economy exists, which is also the reason the market economy is necessary: It causes human actions to better conform to the requirements of virtue.

Broadly speaking, human nature means that almost all people are self-centered. People are not necessarily selfish, but they are self-centered. Aristotle and Confucius, as well as Adam Smith, thought the same.

Adam Smith believed that sympathy is universal. Even "the greatest ruffian, the most hardened violator of the laws of society, is not altogether without it."[1] But all sympathy revolves around the self. The extent of sympathy is related to both physical distance and biological distance. People can feel sympathy for others only when they can put themselves in another's position, making possible the ideal "Do unto others as you would have others do unto you." We have more sympathy for the loss of a relative than for the loss of someone thousands of miles away. Seeing the death of a monkey is harder than seeing the death of an ant. The reason is that monkeys are more similar to people than ants. Perhaps people have more sympathy for ants than for plants. Animals are closer to humans in appearance and biology than plants. Therefore, sympathy is built on a self-centered foundation.

Even altruism is self-centered. People who sacrifice self-interest for their acquaintances outnumber those who sacrifice self-interest for strangers. Many people willingly give up a little to help the world, but few people willingly make the ultimate sacrifice to save others. Adam Smith addressed that subject in *The Theory of Moral Sentiments*.[2] My understanding of Confucianism's system of ethics is that it is also built on a self-centered foundation. Confucian ethics contains orders. They start with family members and expand to the tribe, then to the nation, because it is self-centered. Patriotism is also self-centered; otherwise, why can someone not love another country?

In reality, all religions assume that people are self-centered. No difference exists between that assumption and the basic assumption of economics. With regard to assumptions about human nature, regardless of whether one is discussing scientific, religious, ancient, modern, Chinese, or foreign assumptions, they are all the same. If Adam Smith had not assumed that people were self-centered, he would not have written either *The Theory of Moral Sentiments* or *The Wealth of Nations*. Similarly, if Confucius had not assumed that people were self-centered, we would not have the Confucian system of morality. It is precisely because of the issues that humanity's self-centered nature possibly generates that it needs to be guided, thus leading to religion. There is internal debate in Confucianism about vice and virtue in human nature. Hobbes and Locke, two great Western philosophers, described two different natural states of human action. Their difference is not important, but their basic assumption was that people are self-centered. Everything they advocated expounded on that assumption.

The Logic of the Market and the Logic of Robbery

Self-centeredness creates a problem: People are self-centered, but every person's survival depends on cooperation with others and the assistance of others. How can self-centered humans attain mutual cooperation? In other words, how can self-interested nature benefit others instead of harming them?

Everyone wants to be happy and continuously pursues a better life. Attaining that goal can be summed up by two methods. The first is to make oneself happy by making others unhappy, thus harming others to benefit oneself. I call this method "the logic of robbery." The second is to make oneself happy by making others happy. I call this method "the logic of the market." More precisely, the logic of the market is actually the logic of religion. All religions teach people to accumulate merit by doing good deeds, which brings about happiness for the self by benefiting others. The philosopher Laozi said, "The more [the Confucian gentleman] gives to others, the more does he have himself." Buddhism advocates realizing "emptiness" to reach the boundary of "nonself," thus "relieving all living creatures from torment" and bringing about happiness for the self. Of course, reaching the nonself requires asceticism. The nonself is not innate. If it were innate, there would be no need for asceticism, and religion would not exist. Speaking from this aspect, the biggest difference between the logic of religion and the logic of the market is that religion requires people to change their nature before they can behave virtuously, whereas the logic of the market does not want to change people's nature. Instead, it tries to regulate people's actions so that a self-interested nature is realized by benefiting others.

The last time I went to Yuci in Shanxi Province, I saw an antithetical couplet written on the government office building of the ancient county. It went something like this:

Of one hundred virtuous deeds, respect for parents is of the highest importance. This is judged by the mind, not actions. If it was judged by actions, the poor could not respect their parents.

Of ten thousand evil deeds, licentiousness is the worst of all vices. This is judged by actions, not the mind. If it was judged by the mind, no one on earth could be perfect.

What does that verse mean? Virtue is judged by the mind, but vice is judged by actions. Whether or not a person is filial is not judged by how much money he gives to his parents, the house he builds, or the car he buys. If that were the case, poor children could never be filial. Judging whether or not someone is evil cannot be determined by individual thoughts; instead, it depends on the evilness of personal actions. Morality regulates actions, not the mind! And that distinction is the basic difference between the logic of religion and the logic of the market. The market does not require people to change the nature of their minds, only their actions. The market requires a person to satisfy the needs of others in order to realize a self-interested motive. Speaking from that perspective, the market itself is the highest form of ethics. It stops people from harming others. A person's increase in wealth or status must be built on a foundation of creating happiness for others, or wealth creation for society. That is my understanding of the logic of the market.

The logic of the market is not opposed to ethics and religion. That which is truly opposed to the logic of the market is the logic of robbery. The logic of robbery is everywhere. Perhaps the logic of robbery starts from an extremely virtuous standpoint. That was the case when the planned economy was implemented. Many governments often use the logic of robbery. They do not bring happiness to others, but they still attain happiness for themselves. Of course, in the real market economy, those two logics coexist. Some people earn money not because they brought happiness to others, but instead because they brought unhappiness to others. However, that is not the essence of the logic of the market.

In the long term, if people can continuously make money, they can do so because they rely on honest dealings, not swindles. The historian Sima Qian once said: "The longer a government clerk is honest, the more wealthy he becomes. Wealth converges on honest merchants." Governments can harm the happiness of ordinary people for decades, such as by expropriating peasant land or forcing farmers to sell their products to the government at below market prices. It is impossible for businesses to do the same in the free market. Therefore, I believe the market system best conforms to morality. However, just as we err in our understanding of many issues, we also have misunderstandings about the market.

Perhaps prejudices about the market are related to emotions. Simply put, the market gives every person the opportunity to get rich, as long as value is created for others. Those who provide services to the most people make the most money in a healthy market economy. A nanny can service only one person or one family, so there is little money to be made as a nanny. Producing iPads and iPhones can service tens of millions, so there is much more money to be made. The market compensates people according to the number of people served. The more happiness they bring to others, the more money they can make; or the less happiness they bring to others, the less money they can make. That is the logic of the market.

Sometimes under the same circumstances, one person makes money and another does not, causing dissatisfaction to the latter. That dissatisfaction is related to a special characteristic of human nature. We often attribute success to personal intelligence and ability, but failure is always the fault of others. We often view ourselves as noble and others as contemptible. People who do not make a lot of money often assert that the reason is not because they do not have the ability to make a lot of money; rather, it is because their moral standards are too high and because they are unwilling to cheat others.[3] They believe that people who can earn such large amounts of money are blackhearted. That belief is self-comfort. In reality, those who criticize others for a lack of moral standards are often the ones with the lowest moral standards. Those who require others to be selfless are perhaps the greediest. They love to occupy the moral high ground, thereby misleading others while seeking personal gain. When one says that another is too greedy, one is often showing resentment toward another's high prices, with the hope of making a purchase at a lower price. From the seller's perspective, that price is too low to buy something so valuable. If such a situation is viewed only from the moral and ethical perspective, perhaps there will be paradoxical assessments.

With regard to the relationship between the market and morality, some clarification is needed about the misunderstandings that have always existed. Everyone agrees that causing oneself to be happy by making others happy conforms to morality. However, I believe that convincing people of that fact is not enough. We must rely on the institutions of the free market and free competition. Without free competition, only government monopolies exist—meaning that only a few people can engage in certain activities—and that is the logic of robbery. State-owned banks make so much money because they rely partly on the logic of robbery. Depositors earn 2 percent or 3 percent on deposits, but banks loan the money out for 5 percent or 6 percent. With such a large gap in interest rates, even an idiot could make money. State banks' profits are high partly because they exploit savers, not because they create value. And exploitation is anti-market. The government's intervention in the market is too heavy.

In the microview, each person has a pair of visible hands that can be used to achieve personal goals. In the macroview, the market has a pair of invisible hands. That pair of invisible hands monitors the visible hands so they cannot engage in wrongdoing. Thus, the invisible hands help others. If on the macrolevel, there is another pair of visible hands, the market may be powerless to prevent those visible hands from harming others.

Morality Can Only Appear in the Market

The previous text does not mean to negate the pursuit of religion or ethics. They are similar to the market in that they cause people to act virtuously. The difference is, religion and ethics consider issues of the mind, whereas the market considers issues of actions.

According to Adam Smith, in a competitive market, a person pursuing personal interest is not bad. His is not evil behavior; instead, pursuing personal interest leads to more benefit for society than does directly pursuing social interests, and it is better. That was the greatness of Adam Smith. He saw what the average person did not see, and what he saw was definitely reality. When we look at the results of central planning, it is hard to say that the original intentions were bad, but central planning resulted in disaster.

Actually, Adam Smith's basic ideas were proposed by Chinese historian Sima Qian 2,000 years ago. Perhaps Sima Qian was the world's earliest steadfast free-market proponent. He clearly stated that people's pursuit of happiness cannot be changed, nor can they be convinced otherwise. He said, "The best is to allow others to follow their pursuits; ... they can be led to their pursuits or can be taught or regulated, but the worst is to fight against their pursuits." Nature should be allowed to take its course. The government does not need to make so many plans, to issue so many industrial policies, or to mobilize people to do this or that.

The Chinese philosopher Laozi, who lived a few hundred years before Sima Qian, was humanity's first classical liberal. He recognized the appropriateness of people's pursuit of happiness. He understood the danger that government intervention posed to human happiness. However, he did not understand the subtleties of the market, so he taught that restricting one's desires was the path to happiness. In contrast with Laozi, Sima Qian recognized that restricting one's desires was not the best way to pursue happiness. He believed that the market economy could turn people's self-interested desires into actions that benefit others. Labor could be divided among agriculture, industry, commerce, mining, and fishing, "with everyone encouraged to pursue their own business and enjoy what they do." When "everyone works hard according to their abilities," wealth is like water in that it flows from high points to low points. It comes without being called and leaves without being asked. "A rich country and rich families" are a natural matter. Sima Qian also recognized that wealth is the foundation of morals because "courtesy is understood after the grain room is full. Honor and disgrace are known when food and clothing are adequate." Moreover, "courtesy exists when there is abundance, but discarded when there is nothing."

We must recognize that people are ignorant. People pursue their own self-interests, but some are farsighted, and some are near-sighted. The disparity between people is not a difference in human nature; it is a difference in vision. Confucianism teaches that gentlemen are farsighted, and small men are near-sighted, which is the biggest difference between people.

Another characteristic of the market economy is that only those who compete with long-term interests in mind can truly make money, which is why people in the market economy care for their reputations. Take a bottle of water as an example. We do not know who produced it, nor do we know the owner of the business. But we can drink it without concern because the profit system functions to turn self-interested desires into actions that benefit others. I do not believe a contradiction exists between ethics, religion, or philosophy and the market. There is simply a difference in the perspective from which issues are considered. The difference between fields of study is not a difference in objects of study, but a difference in study methods. The route to the objective is different. People are ignorant, so education is important. It must make people understand their long-term interests so that they do not sacrifice their long-term interests for short-term interests.

A point to emphasize is that altruism cannot resolve conflicts between people. For example, one person is willing to sell an object for Y 2, but another insists on paying Y 5 for the same object. The seller then reduces the price to 50 cents, but the buyer offers Y 20. Such a transaction cannot happen when the seller has too much goodwill toward the buyer. The market is built on a self-centered foundation, so negotiation is possible, allowing for equilibrium of interests. If everyone were a fervent (Confucian) gentleman, transaction prices could not be determined.

The market economy needs a moral foundation, but those morals can appear and be found only in the market. Conversely, morals must be built on the foundation of the market economy. Virtuous intentions can lead to both good and bad behavior. We need a system that requires people to satisfy others' interests before satisfying their own self-interests. Education is secondary. Education does not instill morals in someone; it makes people understand reason. I often ask business circles to explain what an enterprise is. What are the true features of the competitiveness of an enterprise? Those features are name and reputation. Because we are inherently shortsighted, we need a good system, as well as good theoretical research, to make us see further. There is basis for that opinion: In countries with relatively developed market economies, the people have the highest moral levels. An untrustworthy enterprise cannot survive. In contrast, the countries with undeveloped market economies—with the most government intervention—have the most fraud.

Of course, I do not disagree that spiritual cultivation is important. Spiritual cultivation itself is a necessity of self-interest because a person's happiness in large part relies on other people's approval.

We hope to be better than others and to be respected by others, so we need a good reputation. Those needs also have a self-interested foundation. People's morals and compassion come from being self-centered. In Adam Smith's words, the best way to persuade someone to be virtuous is to tell him his own interest lies in virtue, not that others need it. If someone does not care about himself, how can he care about others?

The Biggest Failure of Chinese Education: Shamelessness

As pointed out earlier, a basic problem faced by humanity is that each person is self-centered and that some people are shameless, but cooperation with others is necessary. How the two aspects of self-centered versus cooperation can be unified is a question all philosophical, ethical, and market theories hope to resolve. I deeply believe that the market economy itself is the most effective way to resolve that contradiction and challenge.

To reiterate, human history contains two major logics: the logic of robbery and the logic of the market. War between nations is the logic of robbery. Free trade and exchanges are the logic of the market. I believe these two logics will coexist in the future.

We hope that we can use the logic of the market to resolve international relations. We should rely on free trade, not on subjugation or weapons, to resolve issues. Fortunately, humanity has the ability to learn. For example, during World War II, Japan and Germany attempted to use the logic of robbery to become prosperous and strong, but they failed. After World War II, Japan and Germany relied on the production of automobiles and electronics to rebuild their economies. They relied on the logic of the market. The progress of humanity has been a continuous transition to the logic of the market. When we sit down to negotiate with Americans, we focus on what is good for the United States, and Americans focus on what is good for China. That is the brilliance of humanity.

Too many misunderstandings exist between scholars who research ethics and those who study the market. Many human conflicts come from misunderstandings or are caused by ignorance. To reconcile disagreements and misunderstandings, scholars of ethics and economists should unite because their goal is the same. In the future, research on ethics and the market should be unified. Actually, economics was a part of ethics during the Middle Ages in the West. As an economist, I have never denied the importance of ethics. Institutions are frameworks that also require ethics.

If society does not pay attention to the structure of institutions, without respect for human rights or property rights, and if it relies only on preaching, everyone will become a hypocrite. What is Chinese education's biggest failure? It is not suppressing the innovation of young people or destroying their curiosity. The biggest failure is turning people into hypocrites, making everyone shameless. Why? Because we have not built a proper system of private property rights. Those who say they serve the people often do nothing to serve the people.

In the West, not a single enterprise displays a sign saying honesty is important. There is no need because honesty is automatic. That is the market. Without the logic of the market, without basic market principles, we have only illusory preaching. In the end, the deeds do not match the words.

In earlier days, when a student lost a pencil sharpener in school, the teacher would line up the students to see whose face turned red. The student with the red face most likely took the pencil sharpener. Today, no one's face would turn red because the logic of the market has been negated, and society has become so hypocritical and full of lies. That reality grieves me. When ethics are emphasized, the point should be remembered; otherwise, our constructive contribution to society will be small.

Universal Values Are Necessary—and Possible

Values are a code of conduct we have commonly acknowledged. The goal is to resolve our conflicts and restrain our behavior. Different countries and territories naturally have different values and behavioral codes. With globalization, the values and codes of some areas will be preserved, but some basic rules must be universal. For example, requiring everyone to drive on the same side of the road will dramatically reduce accidents. China drives on the right, and the United Kingdom drives on the left. But if the Chinese and the British drive on the same road, there must be a universal code. Originally, each European country had different traffic regulations. Napoleon's integration of the continent of Europe led to the unification of traffic regulations.[4]

In the era of globalization, commonly respected global rules are necessary. Currently, some people overemphasize the uniqueness of Chinese values. According to the logic of the preceding section, perhaps China's uniqueness comes from ignorance or perhaps it comes from shamelessness. Opposing universal values may not be good for humanity itself. Without universal values, how can humans interact? For example, trade between different countries must take place according to market rules. Every person's rights must be respected. The system of private property should be universally recognized. One person cannot steal another's property, nor can another be forced to buy someone's products. We can arrive at a fair price only through negotiation.

From the perspective of equilibrium interests, having a common code is vital. Not recognizing universal values equates to saying a unified traffic code is unnecessary. The result will perhaps be conflict—or even something more tragic. Of course, universal values do not mean simply forcing one party's codes on another party. The formation of codes is perhaps the result of mutual compromise.

Language is another example. If each country wants to continue speaking its own language, no one will be able to interact. Language has evolved over several thousand years. The artificial language Esperanto was created more than 100 years ago, but it never became mainstream. Perhaps an artificial language is as unworkable as the planned economy. Communication first requires a common language; which language to use is secondary. The specific language that will be used may relate to history. English became the international language of business and academia for many reasons, one of which is that the United States became a superpower. Today, the number of foreigners learning Chinese is growing because China is on the rise. Perhaps some Chinese values will also become universal values. That Confucianism, Daoism, and other traditional philosophies are now taken more seriously all over the world proves this point. If we do not recognize universal values, Chinese culture will never become global, so China will never rise!

Universal values are possible. When the rising sea level separated land masses, today's different cultures were formed. Because all humanity has a common ancestor, cultural conflict should not be in our genes.

Moreover, many human conflicts of interest have been exaggerated. Some of the exaggerations come from ignorance and some from shamelessness. Some philosophers trace human conflicts back to disproportionate class conflicts, so ultimately, everything will be a struggle. We should recognize that the conflicts of interest between the working class and capitalists are fewer than we think. Many conflicts of interest happen among workers rather than between the working class and the capitalists. Americans who oppose Chinese exports come mainly from the American working class, not the American capitalists. Entrepreneurs lobby the U.S. government on China's behalf, not on the behalf of American workers, because the conflict between the Chinese working class and the American working class is larger than the conflict between the Chinese working class and the American capitalists. The former conflict has been inflated by our ignorance. China's conflicts with the United States, Southeast Asia, and Japan are much smaller than we believe. The ideas instilled in us by misconceptions have caused us to exaggerate conflicts. Now with a more global economy and enhanced technology, it is completely possible to communicate more, especially if the rise of China simplifies the formation of universal values. I basically believe that overemphasizing China's uniqueness is not in the interest of China or the Chinese people.

If everyone acted according to the logic of the market—attaining happiness by devising ways to create value for others or to bring about wealth for other nations or peoples—global conflicts would lessen. Free trade is extremely important. When I lecture in the United States, I recommend two books to American politicians. One is Adam Smith's *The Wealth of Nations*, for its free trade theories; the other is Laozi's *Tao Te Ching*. Laozi taught us that to be a world leader, we cannot be arrogant or domineering; we need to be mindful and tolerant. That lesson is especially important in leading people of other cultures! Islamic culture may be different from ours, but human nature is the same. Muslims too cherish peace; the issue is we must truly understand them.

In summary, universal values are (a) necessary and (b) possible. For that reason, I believe humanity's future is still bright. If we do not acknowledge that point, our only choice is to walk down the path of the logic of robbery. Then, the world would not have a peaceful future, only a day of reckoning.

PART TWO

THE LOGIC OF CHINA'S REFORM

8. Rational Thinking on China's Reforms

How to Think Rationally

In current debates about China's economic reforms, emotional outbursts are more common than rational thinking. Intuition has suppressed logical analysis. Popular sentiments have their uses to a community, but just having emotions is not enough. We must learn to reason, because relying on emotional outbursts cannot solve the problems we face.

What is "reason"? My understanding is that reason includes at least four aspects. First, reason requires us to detach ourselves from our own status, identity, and interests when evaluating the merits and drawbacks of a reform or policy. We must learn to consider other positions. An old Chinese proverb says, "Consider others when deciding fairness." For example, if one is a farmer, a worker, a poor person, or a rich person, one cannot consider the interests of only the farmers, the workers, the poor, or the rich. That meaning is actually the essence of John Rawls's book *A Theory of Justice*. In it, Rawls requires us to use a "veil of ignorance" to view issues.[1] We cannot pigeonhole something from the start and then make judgments based only on our own interests. If that were not the case, democracy would turn into tyranny of the majority. Of course, in reality, when every new policy is implemented, each person is in a special position, so if change interferes with that person's interests, complete detachment is very difficult. That reality is precisely why we must emphasize the importance of reason. At least, scholars must detach themselves; otherwise, the independence of scholars is improbable.

Second, reason requires us to consider the feasibility of a policy when we evaluate its merits and drawbacks. We also must compare that policy with any feasible alternatives. We cannot just use completely infeasible goals as reasons to oppose a policy.

If we use discussions of income distribution as an example, we can imagine a society formed by two people with three possible situations: A, B, and C. In situation A, each person receives 100 units. In situation B, one person receives 120 units, and the other person receives 180 units. In situation C, each receives 150 units. However, assume situation B is the social arrangement. Now, if all three situations are feasible, the best social arrangement should be situation C. However, if situation C is infeasible, we cannot use it to criticize situation B. If the feasibility of each choice is not considered, and if we absolutely want both people's incomes to be equal, we must go with situation A, but both people suffer a loss. Of course, if all of society's values are biased toward equal distribution over income differences, changing from situation B to situation A is acceptable. But we absolutely cannot pursue infeasible situation C as our goal because it would be irrational. In the current discussions related to reform, some people completely disregard the compatibility of a policy with people's incentives. They are bewitched by practices suitable only for a utopian society. Their solutions to the problems faced during reform are worse than useless.

Third, reason requires us to combine reality, principles, empirical evidence, and logical analysis. We cannot replace reality with emotion or use intuition to replace logical inference. Intuition is important for our understanding of certain phenomena, but it is often not enough. Without a meticulous logical analysis, and without the theoretical instruction of science, conclusions inferred through intuition may be incorrect. For example, intuition perhaps tells us that the state's use of administrative means to suppress the price of medication would benefit patients. Reality suggests otherwise. After the price is forced down, many effective domestic drugs would disappear from the market, so patients would have no choice but to pay more for imported medication.

Intuition perhaps tells us that state-owned enterprises improve the income gap and solve the employment issue. Substantial evidence and many theoretical analyses prove that, on average, areas with more state-owned enterprises have larger income gaps and worse employment prospects. Currently, some government departments yield to public opinion and often introduce policies without any empirical analysis or statistical backing. The results are counterproductive because not only do they harm the people's interests, but also they harm the government's image. The public has a right to vent its emotions, but scholars must reason. They cannot allow the public's emotions to control them. Government policy must also be reasonable; it cannot be held prisoner by public emotion. When one researches real issues, case analysis is very important, but case analysis must be combined with logical analysis. Using isolated cases to promote a general theory conflicts with the spirit of science.

Fourth, reason requires us to have a forward-looking spirit when implementing a new policy. That approach means—with certain historical factors in mind—incentivizing everyone to make the pie bigger to produce a win–win outcome for everyone's interests and for society as a whole. To be looking backward is to entangle ourselves in historical grudges. In this respect, Deng Xiaoping, an older-generation reformer, set a good example for us in his attitude toward dealing with Sino-Japanese relations. If we still hold a grudge against Japan for its invasion of China during World War II, without considering the best option for China's future, then we should not develop trade or economic relations with Japan; we should just boycott Japanese goods. Boycotting Japanese goods would be a lose–lose situation that would in no way benefit China. Of course, history should not be forgotten, but the point of not forgetting the past is to make a better future. If we do not care about our future and only keep history in mind to seek temporary psychological balance without any real significance, we are behaving irrationally.

We must also have a "forward-looking" spirit when dealing with the problems that exist in the process of Chinese economic reform. The issues that arose in China's Reform and Opening are unique. We have many irrational laws that do not conform to the spirit of reform. Many rational actions are simultaneously illegal. Many of the business world's activities comply with the fundamentals of reform—and are encouraged at every level of government—but they may not comply with the legislation originally set at each level of government. Today, clearly determining what is legal and what is illegal is very difficult. The latest economic analysis and experiences of some countries (or regions) show that illegal behavior formed because of unique historical conditions can be ended only by unique measures, such as a special amnesty. Such measures would rescue the entire society from the trap of illegality and would lay the foundation for a strong public order. If we are only backward looking (entangling ourselves in the past), people will perhaps seek some emotional balance, but all of society will be stuck in a long-term imbalance. Such an imbalance would benefit neither the country's economic development nor ordinary people. Hong Kong is an excellent example. Before the Independent Commission Against Corruption was formed, the Hong Kong Police Force was very corrupt. Without special amnesty for previous corruption, the Hong Kong Police Force could not have cleaned up as quickly, and Hong Kong would have had a difficult time developing to its current level. When individuals are entangled in the good and bad of the past, they are their own victim.

Three Constraints on China's Reforms

From the beginning, China's economic reforms faced three important constraints: (a) power structure restraints, (b) ideological restraints, and (c) knowledge restraints. Those three constraints greatly influenced the progress of reform.

Power Structure Restraints

Under the command economy, the power to allocate resources was concentrated in the government. Private citizens not only had no property rights, but also did not even have the basic right to choose their occupations. Reform is really a matter of transferring the power to allocate resources from the government to private citizens and of replacing bureaucrats with entrepreneurs who make economic decisions. However, reform itself means the government must implement that power transfer. In other words, the government is the object of reform, but it is simultaneously the formulator and executor of the reform proposal. Naturally, some bureaucrats will resist any reform measures, either directly or indirectly. They will always attempt to use their power to manipulate reform and to engage in rent-seeking. When they do, some powers held by government under the command economy will often be preserved under the name of "reform" or will appear in a new form (such as "industrial management" or "macroadjustment"). Therefore, after 20 years of reform, the most powerful government bureau under the command economy is still the most powerful government bureau today.

High-level government leaders have been the main driving force of China's reforms. Those who participated in the reforms of the 1980s, however, all clearly remember that the reformers then had very limited authority over central government bureaucrats. There was insufficient authority to completely implement reform measures because China's power structure was divided. Not only was power divided among the leaders at the top, but also different levels of government all had different scopes of power. Basically, every department had the power to set policy, and all had their own form of protection. Therefore, the establishment of main policy not only requires high-level leaders to reach an agreement among themselves, but also requires the many interlocking government departments to have a positive attitude toward cooperation. Using modern economic theory as an example, a reform proposal can satisfy only the participation constraint and incentive compatibility constraint of the related government departments when it can be implemented. Because bureaucrats have various interests, no proposal can satisfy everyone. Reformers have no choice but to compromise often in exchange for bureaucratic support. Bureaucrats always attempt to use their powers to manipulate reform in accordance with their interests. Therefore, very bold reform measures will often, in the end, become perfunctory and overly cautious and will even be abandoned halfway, which is the main context in which the reformist economists in the mid- to late-1990s called for "new authoritarian government."

In the 1980s, the State Commission for Restructuring was an important driving force for reform. Because the Commission for Restructuring was a new department, it had no vested interests under the command economy. It was resolute toward reform and could form an important constraint on existing government departments. After the 1990s, the Commission for Restructuring's power was weakened significantly, and it existed in name only. Ultimately, even its name was abolished. Its important constraints on bureaus with vested interests were removed. Each department could set "reform proposals." From then on, "deepening reform" easily became an excuse for some departments to reseize power.

Ideological Restraints

Ideological restraints have had an important influence on China's process of reform and have produced several results. First, reformers cannot propose visible, clear reform goals. Many reform measures were implemented with unclear names and untenable arguments. As examples of untenable arguments, one might say there is no contradiction between the market and socialism or that capitalist reforms perfect the socialist system and are the initial stages of socialism. Thus, reformers often have no choice but to "signal left and turn right," even "turning off their lights and driving in the dark." Naturally, the probability of an accident increases drastically.

Second, ideological restraints have caused different people to have completely different or even conflicting interpretations of reform measures. Lower-level executing departments are unsure of what to do, so they take a wait-and-see approach, thus delaying reform. Ideological restraints also increase the room for rent-seeking activities in government departments.

Third, ideological restraints have placed reformers in a fragile position politically. Even today, those people who still promote "leftist" viewpoints are the safest politically. People who promote reform are often attacked by the "left." For political safety, some reformers are completely hogtied, not daring to boldly go forward, thus delaying a golden opportunity for reform. Some opportunists often use "political correctness" to seek personal gain and have imperceptibly expanded the anti-reformist sphere of influence.

Fourth, ideological constraints removed the formation of reform policy from public discussion. Because no benefit is derived from communal discussion, risks are increased during the process of implementation. Such is especially the case when ideological restraints make it difficult for social scientists in fields outside of economics to participate in discussions about reform and to contribute their wisdom. As a result, some of them have been imperceptibly pushed into the camp of reform critics. In the past, we used "no debate" to avoid disputes, but perhaps that method was suitable only in the era of forceful leaders.

Fifth, ideological restraints have made it difficult for other supporting reforms to keep pace with economic reform, thus increasing risks.

A classic example of ideological restraints on Chinese reform is state-owned enterprise reform. Without ideological restraints, we could publicly discuss how to reform state-owned enterprises, and no one would hit anyone else with an ideological "club." All opinions could be put on the table and would ultimately produce a state-owned enterprise reform proposal with a goal and steps for implementation. State-owned assets could be sold at better prices, so asset erosion could be reduced significantly. But because of ideological restraints, local governments can often implement state-owned enterprise reform only surreptitiously. Thus, there is no way to avoid some misconduct.

It should be noted that during the whole process of reform, reformers and the academic world constantly attempt to break down traditional ideological restraints on reform using "theoretical innovation." Examples include "preliminary stage of socialism theory," "socialism with Chinese characteristics," and the "Three Represents." Now, it appears that we must have more bold theoretical innovation to further break through ideological restraints on reform.

Knowledge Restraints

Chinese reform also faces another important restraint: the restraint of knowledge. Designing a transformation plan from a command economy to a market economy is not easy. China does not have a market economy tradition. The vast majority of people lack a personal opinion about the market economy. For a long time, even reform leaders and economists were unclear about how the market mechanism actually operates. Although today's economists can learn some theories about market economies from textbooks, many have no actual experience. The older generation of economists could use Marxist political economy to respond to questions of why reform must happen, but they were ineffective in explaining how reform should be implemented.

In the mid-1980s, young economists emerged. They had fewer ideological conventions and restrictions and instead pursued more utilitarian issues. Therefore, they did not mind being labeled as "capitalist" or "socialist"; they single-mindedly researched how the economy operated. They made a huge contribution to the reform plans after 1984; some of them even participated directly in the design of those plans. Yet, many of those young economists were idealistic and powerless to influence the bureaucratic system in power.

Scientific knowledge is necessary for setting reform plans, but it is not sufficient. The reason no one knows how to reform is because reform is a process of "learning by doing," just as many economists say it is. The interdependence of the different parts of reform can appear only successively. Because no one knows how to reform, "crossing the river by feeling the stones" is the only choice. The experimental characteristics of Chinese economic reforms reflect that point. Not all the consequences of special reforms can be anticipated. Some after-the-fact reversals are necessary. Local governments were allowed to take the initiative on reform, partly because the central government did not know which step to take next. A lack of knowledge about the market economy caused unavoidable lapses in the reform process. Of course, reform has been implemented to date, thereby demonstrating that our knowledge related to the market economy has increased significantly. However, the government must come up with better reform proposals to avoid new lapses.

I would also like to point out that the three restraints on China's reforms are mutually reinforcing. For example, knowledge constraints give the bureaucrats who are holding power under the old system more room to manipulate reform according to their own interests. They can use the excuse that "economists do not understand reality" or "reform measures are infeasible" to oppose some reform proposals or to cause a proposal to lose form in implementation. Ideological restraints can prevent economists and other social scientists from having a way to boldly explore issues and can cause them difficulty with ideological innovation. Lack of knowledge that leads to lapses in the process of reform further strengthens ideological restraints, and so on.

Compensation Issues during Reform

Under any system, patterns of established interests will form, and a privileged class will exist. Regardless of whether a reform or a revolution occurs, both involve an adjustment in the pattern of established interests. The essence of a revolution differs from the method it uses to adjust relationships of interest.

A so-called revolution strips one group of wealth or power through violence and force, and it transfers that wealth or power to another group. During a revolution, some people will suffer, and some will benefit. Therefore, revolution is not a Pareto improvement (where no one is worse off, but at least one person benefits). Even if those who benefit are the majority, and those impaired are the minority, the revolution will not necessarily increase a society's total wealth. Therefore, revolution is not even a Kaldor-Hicks improvement (where those who are benefited gain more than those who are impaired lose). For example, China's Land Revolution in the 1950s confiscated all the landowners' land without compensation and allocated it to peasants. Speaking from the viewpoint of population ratio, those who were impaired were the minority, and those who were benefited were the vast majority. The land area did not increase, however, so it is hard to state clearly whether or not society's total wealth increased.

Reform differs from revolution in that reform does not take wealth from one group without compensation and transfer it to another group. Instead, it recognizes the status quo formed by members of society under the original system. It increases the total wealth of society through a rearrangement of rights and assets to incentivize everyone. Such reform is a Pareto improvement.

Revolution strips the establishment of its interests, but reform must respect the vested interests formed under the original system. It does not matter whether those kinds of vested interests are established by law or have been recognized over time. In other words, reform should not cause anyone to be worse off than they were under the original system. Accordingly, if a specific reform measure will increase the total wealth of society but will simultaneously impair the interest of a portion of society, those who are benefited have a responsibility to compensate ("buy out") those who would otherwise be impaired, or else it cannot be called a reform. This principle also means that the prerequisite for reform is to increase the total wealth of society. If society's total wealth does not increase, those impaired cannot receive compensation.

Respecting vested interests and supplying compensation to privileged classes that are impaired during reform are issues we should not shy away from. Otherwise, we cannot rationalize the many compensation (or buyout) measures in the process of reform. For example, under the command economy, urbanites were a privileged class compared with villagers, and workers were a privileged class compared with peasants. Therefore, when the government increased the price of agricultural products, it also had to give nonstaple food subsidies to urbanites. When the price of agricultural production materials increased, the government did not subsidize peasants because peasants were not a vested interest in the command economy. Similarly, when migrant workers are laid off, the business does not have to buy them out for their length of service or to provide unemployment benefits. When state-owned enterprise employees are laid off, the business must buy them out for their length of service and must pay them unemployment benefits. The reason is we must respect the vested interests of workers formed under the command economy.

The only special interest of peasants that the country recognizes is land-use rights, so peasants must be compensated when land is requisitioned. New vested interests will appear under some institutions during the process of reform. If some people are expected to be impaired when changing those institutions, perhaps compensation should be considered. Stockownership reform is a classic example. Its purpose was to turn nontradable shares into tradable ones. Nontradable shares were held either by government and state-owned enterprises or by private controlling shareholders. Owners of nontradable shares must give bonus shares to owners of tradable shares, such as at a ratio of 3 to 10 or 2 to 10. The reason is to respect the vested interests of owners of tradable shares that were formed when nontradable shares could not be traded, which thus buys out their support for stockownership reform.

Compensation for the vested interests of government officials is a very sensitive issue, and people generally do not dare mention it. That reluctance has a certain rationality because some of those officials are policymakers, so they have considerable bargaining power. The result of avoiding this issue is "hidden subsidies" (including corruption and favoritism). Hidden subsidies are a large cost to society. Many criticized the reform proposal of turning government cars for senior officials into private cars with government subsidies. But according to the experiences of countries such as Japan, it saved a relatively large amount of money. The money wasted by government officials' "being reimbursed for what they spend" is far more than what they can actually enjoy. So, the net value for society would be enormous even if the government spends Y 1 trillion in compensation in exchange for laying off 10 million public employees.

In discussing this topic, I am not saying that all compensation is rational or fair. Some compensation is actually too little (such as compensation for the requisition of peasant land), and some is excessive. Perhaps differences in compensation have to do with bargaining power, or perhaps they have to do with asymmetric information. It is a technical issue and requires more research on related aspects. However, respect for the patterns of established interests formed under the original system and some type of rational compensation for those whose interests are impaired during the reform process are basic principles of reform.

Because of historical traditions, some Chinese people are accustomed to understanding reform while using revolutionary concepts. Their understanding of reform is that it simply strips others of their interests, which is incorrect.

Here, it is necessary to separate absolute interests from relative interests. So-called absolute interests are the absolute amounts of income, wealth, and privilege held by the people involved. So-called relative interests are the relative positions of a person's income, wealth, and privilege in relation to other members of society. Imagine a society with two members, A and B. Under the original system, A had 100 units of wealth, and B had 150 units of wealth. If under the new system, A's wealth became 200 units, and B's wealth became 300 units, we could say each person's absolute interests increased once, but their relative interests have not changed. If in a new system, each person's wealth became 200 units, we could say that each person's absolute interests increased, but A's relative interests increased while B's relative interests decreased.

The respect and compensation of "vested interests" discussed earlier are absolute vested interests, not relative vested interests. In the examples, even if A's relative interests are impaired, there should be no compensation. One of the reasons relative interest cannot be compensated for is that it is too subjective and hard to measure. Another reason is that the goal of reform is to build a society trending toward equality of opportunity, not to form a new privileged class. If impairments of relative interests all need compensation, then there is no point in changing the old system, because the goal of equality of opportunity runs counter to the goal of reform. If we speak of China's situation from the view point of relative interests, then—under the command economy—government officials had the highest status, followed by the workers, and then the peasants. Reform naturally causes the original highest-status group to have the largest drop in relative interests. If that change is not the case, reform cannot be called a success.

Another important point is that compensation for those impaired in the process of reform needs to be a one-time deal. If it is unending, a new system cannot form.

How to Eradicate Poverty and Reduce the Income Gap through Economic Development

During discussions related to Chinese economic reform, the phrase "efficiency first, with consideration for fairness" has been questioned. Because "fairness" is an ideal that requires a value judgment, scholars who emphasize efficiency seem to have lost their sense of moral justice. Actually, fairness could be understood as "equality of opportunity"; it could also be understood as "equality of results." With equality of opportunity, fairness and efficiency are not a contradiction because only a free economy with equality of opportunity can achieve the most optimal allocation of resources. A better wording of the phrase would be "equality of opportunity first, with consideration for equality of results." If fairness refers to "equality of results," efficiency and fairness are to a certain extent a contradiction, but there is nothing wrong with "efficiency first, with consideration for fairness." Even according to John Rawls's *A Theory of Justice*, equality of opportunity is more in line with social justice than with equality of results.[2]

Of course, any society must pay attention to the relationship between efficiency and income distribution. To say that economists do not pay attention to equality demonstrates a lack of common sense about economics. Economists prove only that focusing solely on income equality will possibly impair efficiency. As to the point most suitable to tradeoff between efficiency and equality, that suitability is decided by society's value judgment, because economics has not provided a conclusion. Statistical analysis by experts about income distribution shows that since reform, the Gini coefficient has expanded. How much of that increase is reasonable and how much is unreasonable—or whether or not China has reached the limit between efficiency and equality (where improving equality can come only from impairing efficiency)—awaits further analysis.

Not only should we focus on the relative income gap, but also we should focus more on the absolute living standards of the poor. I would like to point out here that the viewpoint that pursuing efficiency and economic growth will certainly impair the poor and increase the income gap is baseless. In 1978, China's population in absolute poverty was 250 million, but poverty has decreased to 2.6 million today. If there had been no economic growth brought about by efficiency gains, that reduction would have been impossible. My analysis of 31 provinces, municipalities, and autonomous regions found that, on average, the higher an area's per capita gross domestic product and economic growth, the lower that area's absolute poverty ratio and Gini coefficient. Therefore, borrowing a phrase from Deng Xiaoping, "[D]evelopment is the best way to resolve the poverty issue and reduce the income gap."

China's absolute poverty exists mostly in rural areas. The main reason for the increase in the Gini coefficient is the relatively slow growth of rural incomes. Without the government's policies to increase the competitiveness of businesses as a way to reduce the income gap, millions of rural laborers cannot transition to urban employment. Without such policies, not only would the absolute poverty issue remain unresolved, but also it would not reduce the income gap.

Development levels among China's regions differ greatly. Statistics show that most provinces have Gini coefficients of below 0.4, which is lower than the national average. According to the research of foreign scholars, 30 percent to 50 percent of the increase in China's Gini coefficient comes from increased regional differences.[3] Therefore, from the viewpoint of reducing disparities in income distribution, reducing regional differences should be our objective. However, we must recognize that interregional differences are to a large extent institutional differences and differences in entrepreneur contingents. The relatively backward regions are basically all regions with the slowest institutional reforms, the worst environments for starting a business, and the state-owned enterprise–led economies. Professor Zhiwu Chen of Yale University has conducted research using multinational sources to show that relying on central government transfer payments cannot solve regional differences. On the contrary, countries with the highest proportions of government spending are, on average, precisely the countries with the largest regional differences.[4]

Some people believe that expansion in the income gap is mainly caused by development of private enterprises, so the way to reduce the income gap is to develop state-owned enterprises. My analysis of 31 provinces, municipalities, and autonomous regions showed that, generally speaking, the higher the proportion of urban workers in the state-owned sector, the higher that area's Gini coefficient. Thus, we cannot use the development of state-owned enterprises as a way to resolve the income gap issue. In reality, the large-scale layoffs of urban workers in the 1990s were caused by the inefficiency of state-owned enterprises.

In any country, the government must use certain transfer payments to reduce the income gap, but the government's method of transfer payment must be suitable and must be meticulously designed. We undoubtedly cannot assume that increasing government spending will necessarily narrow the income gap. On the contrary, statistics show that, generally speaking, regions with higher government expenditures as a proportion of gross domestic product also have higher Gini coefficients.

We should not view "letting some people get rich first" as opposing "common prosperity." Even more so, we should not view common prosperity as being the same as equal allocation of wealth. Without differences, common prosperity would be impossible. Nobel Prize–winning economist James Mirrlees's research from 35 years ago shows that the biggest obstacle that governments face when collecting taxes is the inability to get information on an individual's ability.[5] Because of information limitations, no policy can attain equality of results. If income taxes are too high, people with high ability could feign low ability by reducing their work. Similarly, even if incomes are equal monetarily, it would be impossible for people with different abilities to enjoy the same quality of life.

If we really care about poor people, we should give priority to the equality of opportunity (and also to efficiency), for example, giving more educational opportunities to the poor. Recent research by Nobel Prize–winning economist James Heckman and other scholars has shown that in China, education level has already become the main factor for determining a family's income level.[6] A university student from a rural area could help his family escape from poverty. Regrettably, in recent discussions on institutional reforms in education, public opinion has focused all its attention on tuition increases and the burden they put on the poor. The public has ignored the issue of increased admissions providing more educational opportunities for common people. In 1978, Chinese universities accepted 400,000 students. In 2005, Chinese universities admitted more than 5 million students, an increase of 1,250 percent. I believe—even speaking for lower-income classes—that higher tuition with more opportunities to attend university is better than low tuition and no opportunity to attend university. Of course, the government and society have a responsibility to help resolve the tuition problems of poor students. Furthermore, to increase education funds, the government must increase government expenditures. But without large-scale taxes on private enterprises, where will government revenue come from?

Income Distribution Issues and Globalization

Many issues related to China's reform must now be placed against the backdrop of economic globalization before they can be discussed. For example, the government's income distribution policies cannot sacrifice the international competitiveness of Chinese companies. Otherwise, when China's businesses collapse, the biggest losers are still the common people.

The expansion of China's income gap is related to the globalization of the economy. Salaried top managers in foreign-invested enterprises or private companies possibly have annual salaries of more than Y 1 million, but the annual earnings of common workers in the manufacturing industries still have not reached Y 10,000. Such a wide income gap was not common during the process of development in other countries. Why does China have such a large gap?

With economic globalization, there is a divergence in the market of different qualities of labor. Stated simply, higher-skilled labor (such as software developers or high-level managers) is more mobile and has a larger market area. Low-skilled labor has less mobility and a smaller market area (limited to the domestic market). Compared with income levels in developed countries, the gap between higher-skilled labor in China and in the West is much smaller than the gap for low-skilled labor. For example, the wages of Chinese manufacturing workers are one-fortieth of American manufacturing wages, but the salaries of high-level, white-collar Chinese professionals who work for foreign-invested enterprises are one-third to one-half, or even more, of the same level of white-collar professionals in the United States. We can imagine how much smaller the gap between higher-skilled and lower-skilled labor would be without globalization.

Thus, we face a difficult issue. If we use taxes to suppress the incomes of high-skilled labor, that effort will cause a large-scale brain drain, and Chinese businesses would be unable to internationalize. If the wages of low-skilled labor increase too much, Chinese businesses will lose their cost advantage, many businesses will fold, and foreign enterprises will move elsewhere. Private entrepreneurs and high-skilled talent can immigrate, but the average worker can only return home, so ultimately, the latter suffers a greater loss.

I do not mean to say that we cannot do anything to improve the conditions of common workers. Nor am I saying that wages should not increase with advances in business productivity. I am saying that we cannot omit the backdrop of globalization when discussing China's income distribution issue. The survival of national enterprises and the country's economic development are preconditions for solving the poverty issue, and they are the constraints when setting income distribution policies.

The challenges to income distribution policies brought about by economic globalization are not faced only by China. Many developing countries also face similar challenges. The research of Professor Xavier Sala-i-Martin at Columbia University shows that between 1990 and 1998, mainly because of a reduction in intercountry income differences (most of it coming from increases in Chinese incomes), the degree of income inequality worldwide has decreased, but the degree of income inequality within countries has increased.[7] I suppose having those two phenomena occur simultaneously is related to economic globalization. On the one hand, globalization increased domestic income gaps; on the other hand, it reduced the gap between developed countries and China. When we weigh the pros and cons, the pros outweigh the cons.

The Source of Corruption: The Government's Monopoly on Resource Allocation

We must admit that a part of the income gap is caused by corruption, and that fact is intolerable.

Corruption also existed under the command economy. Since reform, however, people feel as though corruption is worse that it was originally. I think there are two reasons. One reason is that invisible nonmonetary corruption (such as "exchanges" for promotions) has become visible monetary corruption. People have a harder time accepting monetary corruption than material corruption. The second reason is that actual corruption *has* increased.

A mathematical equation I once used to analyze actual corruption showed that the increase in actual corruption has a few origins: (a) with the increase in the degree to which the Chinese economy has monetized, the economic value of power has increased; (b) the complexity of economic relations has caused supervision to become increasingly more difficult; (c) the growth in market opportunity has raised government officials' "preserved utility" (the utility they would receive if they were forced out of the government as punishment for corruption); (d) the severity of punishment has been reduced (e.g., the amount embezzled to receive the death penalty was increased significantly); and (e) the formal salaries of government officials are relatively low.

Those five factors are all related to power. Power is the root of corruption; other aspects are its symptoms. Anti-corruption measures must address both the symptoms and the root, but direct action would eradicate the root. Thus, direct action would reduce the power of government officials. Some have proposed "high salaries to buy honesty," which makes a bit of sense. But where the power of government officials is excessive, high salaries cannot encourage honesty. If officials' salaries are too high, the public will object. The key issue here is that government departments in China have monopolized many rights that belong to private citizens and businesses in other countries with a market economy. Examples include starting a business and engaging in investment activities, both of which require government approval. Individuals and businesses have no option but to "buy out" by means of corruption rights to engage in normal economic activity that they should have had to begin with.

In connection with the current anti-corruption measures that cure only the symptoms without curing the cause, I stated in 1994 that if we do not change the fundamentals of our government-controlled economic system and reduce the government's administrative approval authorities, corruption of private goods (according to the textbook definition, without exclusiveness) is instead a "second-best" choice. My meaning is that to stop corruption we must eradicate its root, not cure its symptoms. Stressing anti-corruption measures without wanting to reduce government power is self-deception. Not only can it not succeed—or even if it does succeed in the short term—but also it comes with the price of immense damage to society.

A prerequisite for high economic growth without corruption is the abolition of the government's monopoly over the power to allocate resources. Some say that I am defending corruption, but they actually misunderstand my views. Penetrating discussion of issues is the responsibility of scholars. In 1999, at the High-Level Forum on Chinese Development, I said, "Government control needs to be given up just as drugs need to be given up," and "If government examination and approvals were abolished, corruption could be reduced by at least 50 percent." That message greatly affected the proceeding system of examination and approvals reform. Ten thousand good wishes cannot match one effective action!

We must admit that in China's process of reform, the value-creating activities of entrepreneurs are often mixed together with the rent-seeking behavior of government bureaucrats. Accordingly, some people's negative views of entrepreneurs gain sympathy in society. However, we must understand that those views were caused by the system in which the government monopolizes resource allocation, and that issue must be resolved by reform. When value creation and rent-seeking are mixed, people easily see one without seeing the other. We next need to lessen the opportunities for rent-seeking and even ultimately to eradicate them. Then, the only way for entrepreneurs to make money will be to create wealth for society.

In that regard, we need to understand the source of "rent." Stated simply, all rent comes from monopoly. Conversely, with monopoly, there is rent. Resources such as land and mines are natural monopolies. The simplest way to resolve rent-seeking is to partition property rights. Once property rights are defined, people will not rent-seek. If property rights are not defined, people will struggle for rent, which will lead to a waste of resources. Rent-seeking is so widespread in urban land and mining resources because property rights are not defined and because transaction methods are not standard.

Another type of monopoly is created by government regulation. We can call it administrative monopoly or statutory monopoly. Examples include the number of telecommunication licenses or the government approval needed by individuals to start a business. Those administrative monopolies bring about administrative monopoly rent. The process of rent-seeking breaks up "legal" monopolies by illegal methods (including bribery). During that process, rent-seeking and value creation are mixed together. Rent-seeking partly recovers the creation of value, which is a conclusion well-known among economists. The solution to this problem is to abolish monopolies. Where monopolies cannot be abolished, methods such as "public bidding" will increase transaction transparency, thereby reducing rent-seeking activities.

When discussing rent-seeking, we must discuss state-owned enterprises. I believe that the state-owned enterprise sector is the largest hive of rent-seeking activity. It could even be called "rent dissipating," because it has monopolized most resources without creating much value. State-owned enterprises are "full-membership rent-seekers." Not only are the rent-seekers the heads of government departments and related businesses, but also ordinary workers enjoy monopolistic rent. Petroleum companies, power companies, and telecommunications companies all pay their employees much higher wages than do their counterparts in competitive industries. That is proof of full-membership rent-seeking in monopolistic industries.

The "profit" made by the state-owned enterprises that rely on monopolies is not paid in taxes or dividends to the government, but subsidies from the government make up for any losses. Government subsidies for state-owned enterprises are actually "bribes" to a small group of people using taxpayer money. Those government subsidies are also a type of corruption, similar to buying votes in an election.

Only when the scope of government power is reduced to public areas, such as protecting public order or providing public goods, could we possibly use "high salaries to buy honesty." Only then can the phenomenon of corruption be eradicated.

The Problem of Mixing Up Academics and Policy

During the current discussion related to China's reform, some public opinion has confused the academic viewpoint of scholars with promotion of policy. That confusion not only is harmful to the real development of scholarship but also is harmful to setting and improving policy.

The duty of scholars is to "seek truth" by understanding issues clearly and stating them more plainly. Academic viewpoints are presented as if–then statements. They discuss the cause-and-effect relationship between objects. Take, for example, this statement: "If we do not reduce the power of government, then corruption is unavoidable." Such an academic viewpoint does not show approval for corruption; on the contrary, it hopes that people can clearly recognize the source of corruption and thus find an effective method to counter it.

Scholars and politicians are different. True scholars say only what they believe is correct, but politicians say what others want to hear or what is "politically correct." Therefore, the public should not use the same standards to criticize both politicians and scholars.

Perhaps different scholars propose different academic viewpoints. The authenticity of different academic viewpoints can be determined through academic debate, but the debate will probably never end. The correctness of an academic viewpoint cannot be determined by a vote. The theories that the majority approves of are not necessarily correct; otherwise, we could not have science nor would we need it. When scholars discuss issues, they must use academic standards and logic, without grandstanding.

Scholars, of course, can also advocate policies they support. In that respect, they are equals with the masses. Their only advantage in influencing policy is their theoretical persuasion, not their individual value judgments. True scholars often have a deep faith in their beliefs after thoughtful and strict argumentation. With regard to the consequences of policy, they often see further than the average person (that is, the value of theory). They pay attention to their own long-term reputation, and they hope their viewpoints can pass the test of time. Unless they are pandering to public opinion, the policies that they advocate may or may not be the same as the majority's view.

Policy and scholarship are different because policy can be voted on. Policymaking is the mixture of science and politics. Before making policy, surveys are conducted, data are collected, experts are consulted, and feasibility is determined; thus, it could be called a scientific process. When the type of policy is finally chosen, it has certainly undergone a political process, no matter what kind of political system a country has. Some important policies can be determined by vote in democratic countries or by an individual in autocratic countries; no matter which system is used, it is totally political. Therefore, it is rare to have a policy set completely on the basis of the theories advocated by a school of thought.

No matter the kind of political process used for setting policy, we must recognize that almost no policy can satisfy all interest groups; thus, whatever the policy, someone will oppose it. We must also understand that the majority's choices will not necessarily be in the long-term interests of the majority. (The Taiwanese election of Chen Shui-bian is an example.) We must prevent the majority from becoming the prisoner of a minority interest group, and we must also prevent the "tyranny of the majority," because each one of us may at some time, in some way, be a member of the minority. Therefore, we must learn to think rationally!

9. China's Gradual Reform: A Historical Perspective

Almost all former socialist countries are marching toward a market economy. "Big Bang" and "gradualism" have been identified as the two polar-case approaches of the transition. Roughly speaking, the eastern European countries and the former Soviet Union have taken more or less a Big Bang approach, whereas China has taken a gradual approach.[1] In 1990, when the architects of the Big Bang drafted their blueprint for massive privatization and price liberalization, China's 12-year-old gradual reform was under heavy attack from both Chinese economists and their Western counterparts.[2] Surprisingly, just two years later, fashions reversed, even though the reform in China almost stagnated during this period (until early 1992). Now, China's gradual reform is widely described as a success.

Many papers have discussed the comparative advantages or disadvantages of gradualism vis-à-vis the Big Bang in transforming a socialist system into a market economy. Although the research is inconclusive, most economists attribute performance differences between China and the eastern European countries and the former Soviet Union to their different reform approaches.[3] The key point of the proponents of gradualism is that gradual reform can split and spread transitional costs over a long period and is thus more feasible, both politically and economically.

The existing studies of transition have been almost exclusively conducted either from an economic perspective or from a social-choice theoretical approach.[4] Few studies have been done from a historical perspective. Much of the debate has focused on how the reform should proceed, ignoring how it has already proceeded. The contribution of this chapter is that it provides a historical perspective of China's gradual reform. Its purpose is to show how economic reforms have proceeded in China so far, rather than to argue about which reform approach is superior. The chapter explains why China has adopted the gradualist approach and how China's gradual reform has been successful.

The chapter is organized as follows. It first describes some stylized facts of Chinese reform followed by an analysis of the underlying reasons that have led China to gradualism. It then discusses how China's gradual reform became a success. Our analysis shows that much of the success of Chinese economic reform is attributed (a) to those policies and factors that have been heavily criticized by many economists and (b) to some policies and factors that were actually implemented by the "conservatives."

China's Gradual Reform: Stylized Facts

China's economic reform has been identified by many economists as "gradualism" when compared with Russia's Big Bang approach. But there is no theoretical definition that captures even the major features of the Chinese economic reform process.[5] That fact reflects the complexity of the reform. In this section, instead of considering theoretical definitions of gradualism and Big Bang, we summarize the major stylized facts of China's gradual reforms.

Chinese economic reforms have not been conducted according to a well-defined and time-consistent objective model. That analysis does not necessarily mean that Chinese reform has been objectiveless. Rather, the objective model of the reform has been continuously readjusted during the reform process, from "planned economy with some market adjustment," to "socialist planned commodity economy," to "socialist market economy."[6] Furthermore, even the market-oriented direction has not proceeded uniformly. Frequent reversals have occurred. In addition, different people had different understandings of the same objective model, which made the objective model more ambiguous.

Chinese economic reforms have not been following a well-designed blueprint. That finding does not mean that China has not drawn up a blueprint. On the contrary, up until 1988, the State Commission for Restructuring the Economic Systems (SCRES) had drawn up 14 blueprints.[7] The first blueprint was created as early as December 1979.[8] An overall plan of reforms was also drawn in 1981 at the request of Premier Zhao Ziyang.[9] Two Big Bang–type blueprints were created in 1986 and 1988, respectively. However, none of the 14 blueprints were implemented, either because they were not politically and economically feasible or because they were technically unimplementable. Gradualism does not mean that a blueprint is not needed. If a well-designed reform program is implemented step by step, it is still gradualism. But China's gradualism is not such a case. For that reason, it might be more appropriate to call it "piecemeal" reform rather than gradualism.

Chinese economic reforms have followed an easy-to-hard sequence. Most economists agree that some intertemporal interdependence exists between different components of reforms; in particular, implementation of some components may be preconditioned by implementing others. For example, Wu and Liu argue that price liberalization should precede enterprise reform; whereas Newbery argues that the breakup of monopolies should precede price liberalization.[10] A wrong sequence may be worse than no reform, because implementing some programs may block other more fundamental reforms. Although it might be too early to determine whether China has followed an optimal sequence, it is clear that China has followed an easy-to-hard sequence.[11] The easy-to-hard sequence may not necessarily differ from an optimal sequence, because the easiest reform might just be the precondition for the hardest. Nonetheless, China did not choose the easy-to-hard sequence because it is optimal. If it proves optimal, that is fortunate. In fact, many leading Chinese reform economists criticized the easy-to-hard sequence for being shortsighted.[12]

Chinese economic reforms have been progressing through a dual-track system. The dual-track system was first introduced in the price reform. Under this system, most products have two prices: the planned quotas are allocated at the plan prices and the above-plan products are transacted at market prices. Most (state-owned) enterprises acquire inputs and sell outputs through both the planned and market channels.[13] The dual-track system is also used in most other reform areas, including foreign exchange, labor reform, housing reform, social security reform, and ownership reform. As a result, the entire Chinese economy evolved into a dual-track economy.[14] The dual track is the most important characteristic of China's gradual reform, and it encompasses most other features of the reform. The key point of the dual-track system is not the coexistence of the plan track and the market track, but the fact that the market track was introduced at margin and parallel to the plan track. For example, market transactions were created not by cutting but by delimiting the planned allocations; the nonstate sector was created not by denationalizing or privatizing the state-sector but by freeing the entry of new enterprises.[15] Recognizing that difference is crucial for understanding the dual-track system.

Chinese economic reforms have not stripped any major interest groups of their vested interests; it has just changed the ways with which vested interests are materialized. One of the major features of the dual-track system is respect for the status quo of all agents formulated under the old planning system. That is the reason it emerged spontaneously from the very beginning of reform and with little resistance. For many economists, the economic reform cannot be a Pareto improvement, because there must be some people who are worse off.[16] In particular, government bureaucrats are assumed to be the major losers, because the reform will reduce or eliminate most of their privileges and rent-seeking opportunities.[17] If that is true, the reform's success depends heavily on how to mitigate powerful bureaucrats' resistance. The dual-track system seems to have served this purpose very well. Moreover, the dual-track system actually makes bureaucrats better off, rather than worse off, because they now have better opportunities and more efficient ways to enjoy economic rents. That is why more and more government bureaucrats have switched to supporting reform as it has proceeded[18]—although they steer the reform course following their interests.[19]

Chinese economic reforms have been dominated by local governments. It might be more appropriate to say that the entire reform has been a combination of top-to-bottom and bottom-to-top processes.[20] Local government dominance is an important feature of the reform. Many reform programs have been initiated by local governments— and even by the grass roots—and then recognized and adopted as national policies by the central government.[21] Much of the planning system was dismantled by local governments. Moreover, many local governments have been far ahead of their national leaders in reforming the economy. That finding does not necessarily mean that local governments' activities were against the central leaders' will. In fact, it was Premier Zhao Ziyang's reform strategy to use local governments to fight against more conservative bureaucrats in the central ministries.[22] As pointed out by Zhengfu Shi,[23] decentralization of reform governance was a feature of the central leaders' style of governing the reform.

Chinese economic reforms have exhibited great regional variations. This fact is related to the previous section and is also a mirror of the evolutionary process in a spatial dimension. Some regions have been running far ahead of other regions. In the late 1980s, some coastal areas, such as Guangdong Province, became quasi-market economies, whereas most inland areas were still planning dominant. The spatial picture of reform is similar to the spatial picture of economic development.

China's economic reform has been an experimental process. It is hard to find a single reform program that has been implemented without first undergoing experimentation. Reform experiments have been either region based (typically city based), sector based, or even firm based. Typically, a particular reform program is first tried in selected regions, sectors, or enterprises. If successful, it is implemented in other regions, sectors, or enterprises; if it fails, the program is discontinued. Experimentation is used not only for single reform programs but also for "comprehensive reform programs."[24] From time to time, the SCRES selected some experimental cities for a comprehensive reform.

Chinese economic reforms have been an evolutionary process, which has proceeded in a "stop–go cycle." The evolutionary process means that many small and halfhearted reform measurers accumulate into a radical change over time.[25] This feature applies not only to the whole reform program but also to almost all single-reform packages, including agricultural reform, price reform, enterprise reform, ownership reform, macrocontrol system reform, and even housing reform. The "dual-track system" as an evolutionary approach exists everywhere. No single area of reform has been implemented with one stroke. For example, the price reform began in 1979 and is still under way. The reforms of state-owned enterprises have been at the top of the agenda for a long time, but they are far from being completed.

The stop–go cycle refers to a reform push usually being followed by a setback, which will, in turn, be followed by another push. In a push period, some important and even radical reform measures are implemented, whereas in a setback period, part of those measures are withdrawn. Because, in most cycles, the pullbacks are fewer than the forward measures,[26] changes have accumulated gradually. As a result, the entire economic system has been moving toward a market system. Reform cycles have been related to political cycles. In the push period, "reformists" are active, and "conservatives" remain silent, whereas in the setback period, the situation reverses. The correlation is obvious, but causality between reform cycles and political cycles is not unambiguous.[27]

Random Walk: How China Adopted Gradualism

The Chinese economic reform process looks more or less like a random walk. Deng Xiaoping's strategy was to "take one step and look for the next" and "grope for stones to cross the river." This random walk had worried both the leaders in charge of reforms as well as the reform-minded economists, because both economic and political problems had been accumulating rapidly. As early as 1981, then Premier Zhao Ziyang pointed out, in his report to the People's Congress: "These reforms (implemented so far) are still partial and exploratory in nature, and our work has suffered from certain incongruities and from lack of coordination. The task before us is to sum up our experience in these reforms and, after careful investigation, study, and repeated scientific confirmation, to draw up as soon as possible an overall plan for reforming the economy and carry it out step by step."[28]

Criticism of "groping for stones to cross the river" among academics accelerated in 1985,[29] which led to two aborted Big Bang–type blueprints, in 1986 and 1988, respectively. As Nolan[30] observes: "[What] most economists of China have put forward is that its industrial performance in the 1980s would have been much better if it had followed the path of a rapid transition to a market economy. A larger body of informed opinion both inside and outside the country considered that—in the early 1980s—China's policymakers should have liberalized industrial prices, eliminated the industrial material balance planning system, opened the industrial market to international competition (the surest guardian against monopoly), and rapidly privatized state industry." All those considerations show that China's gradualism has not been a rigorously designed strategy of reform. In other words, China did not "adopt" a gradualist strategy purposely,[31] although it has "become" gradualist. Nevertheless, the observed stylized facts of China's gradual reforms are not accidental. They are the consequences of certain underlying reasons. In this section, we shall analyze those underlying reasons and show how China became gradualist.

No time to wait. China's economic reform began after the Cultural Revolution, which had ended in economic chaos. Agriculture had stagnated for a decade with more than 25 percent of the 800 million rural people living below the poverty line, according to Chinese standards. Discontent was mounting in the countryside, and peasant uprisings were everywhere. In the urban areas, the planning system was out of order, many industrial production units did not produce at all, and many factory workers did not work. Shortages were everywhere, and most necessities—such as foodstuffs, matches, and toilet paper—were rationed. Millions of "young intellectuals" returned from the countryside and were searching for jobs. The widespread dissatisfaction periodically erupted into major strikes and street protests in many industrial cities.

Under such circumstances, the leadership's first priority was survival. Reform became the only way to survive, although there was no consensus on how to reform. With no consensus, the leaders had no time to design a reform blueprint using rigorous cost–benefit considerations before implementing any effective measures. The urgent issue of the moment was to restore the production order by giving peasants incentives to produce and workers incentives to work. Pragmatism was the only acceptable philosophy. Any measures that could move the economy were welcome, no matter what their long-term effects. Not surprisingly, the household-contract responsibility system in agriculture, which was initiated by some local peasants, was recognized and adopted nationally by the central government, although the leaders viewed it as expediency.

The industrial reform began with *fangquan rangli* (downshifting decision rights and leaving profit to the firm) and performance-based bonuses, even before the problems of measuring performance were solved.[32] Another example is that nonstate-owned enterprises and private businesses in urban areas in the early 1980s were encouraged initially not to reform the urban economy but to create jobs for millions of job seekers who could not be absorbed by state-owned enterprises. There was no time to wait for a well-designed blueprint and then to implement it step by step.

Nobody knows where to go. The frequently changing objective model was not only one major feature of China's reforms but also one of the major reasons for China's gradualism. China had been groping for stones to cross the river partly because no one had any idea where the opposite bank was.[33] As Gang Fan[34] correctly pointed out, the Chinese—neither the leadership nor the majority of people (including economists)—had no clear idea about where to go at the beginning of economic reform in the late 1970s. All they knew was that the conventional centrally planned system did not work well, and some changes were needed. Most households and individuals did not totally lose faith in the old system. The "elites" still believed at that time that if they got a chance to run the economy, they could solve the problems better than other socialist countries. The failure of the economy was attributed mainly to the ceaseless political movements, not to the defects of the basic structure of the system itself. The dominant objective of reform at the early stage was "to perfect the socialist planned economy" by improving planning methods with "input–output analysis" and computers, and by introducing some market elements at margin, rather than to change the entire system. In fact, until early 1984, the Soviet Union's planning system was still a model for the Chinese.[35] All those factors ruled out the possibility that China could set up a radical program at the beginning of reform.

Nobody knows how to reform. Even if China knew the direction in which to take reform, it still faced the problem of how to reform. Designing a blueprint for transforming a planned economy into a market economy is not easy. Neither Chinese leaders nor Chinese economists clearly understood how the market mechanism works. Economists learned some principles of the market economy from textbooks, but they had no experience. Older-generation economists had been preoccupied with Marxist economics. They had theories on why reform must be undertaken, but they were incapable of answering the question of how the reform should be accomplished. Consequently, young economists were mobilized in the mid-1980s.[36]

Young economists were less ideological and more pragmatic, which gave them the advantage to concentrate on studying how economic systems work rather than on whether a particular institution is capitalist or socialist. They made great contributions to designing a series of post-1984 reform programs, and they even directly drew up the blueprints. However, many of them were idealists. They were incapable of dealing with the bureaucrats who were in charge of implementing reforms. Modern economics is a necessary—but not sufficient—condition for one to draw up a blueprint for reforms.[37] Nobody knew how to reform partly because reform, by its nature, is a learn-by-doing process (as many economists pointed out) and because the interdependence between different reform components was yet to be revealed.[38] Given that nobody knew how to reform, groping for stones to cross the river was the only choice China could take. The experimental feature of China's reforms partly reflects this problem. Reform cycles are also related to this problem. When not all consequences of a particular reform program are known *ex ante*, some *ex post* reversals are inevitable. Local governments were granted autonomy to reform partly because the central government did not know how.

Nobody has authority to implement a well-designed reform program. Even if economists were able to design a reform blueprint, implementation of such a blueprint required a strong reform-minded authority. Advocates of the idea of a complete blueprint reform assumed (implicitly) that such an authority exists, but their assumption was unrealistic. Lack of reform-minded authority was one of the major reasons that several comprehensive reform blueprints failed in the 1980s. The Chinese structure of authority is fragmented. Authority is split not just between top leaders but also between different levels of bureaucrats. Under such a structure, major policy initiatives require not only a consensus among the top leaders but also the active cooperation of many bureaucratic units that have vested interests to block or manipulate any policies that are not in their interests.

In modern economics terminology, a reform blueprint is implementable only if it satisfies concerned bureaucrats' participation constraints and incentive compatibility constraints. Because bureaucrats' interests are diverse, such a blueprint is impossible to design. Bureaucrats always make the best use of their positions to steer the reform course following their own interests, which often transforms bold initiatives into modest programs. As a result, as pointed out by Kang Chen, "[T]he types of reform proposed, the attempted reforms that failed, and the elements of reforms implemented were all a result of the complex of political forces within the centrally planned system, rather than simply a matter of choice between abstract economic models."[39]

For instance, in 1981, Premier Zhao Ziyang, China's reform-minded leader until 1989, intended to take advantages of the favorable macroeconomic environment after the rectification policy to implement an "overall" reform package with the price reform as its major component. However, this reform plan was never put in effect because of opposition from various sources.[40] Instead, a marginal reform—which allowed enterprises to sell their above-quota products at "floating prices" within a range of up to 20 percent higher or lower than the fixed prices—was carried out.[41] By delegating partial reform autonomy to local governments through various ways, such as "experimental cities" and "open cities," the central ministries' economic power was indirectly undermined, which otherwise could not be done. That finding partially explains why Chinese economic reform has been so local-government dominant. However, the local-government dominance not only undermined the ministries' power but also led to some reform-minded economists' arguing that China needed "new authoritarianism."[42]

Nobody is willing to take a big risk. Under the Chinese political, social, and economic structure, reform is a big venture, which involves both economic and political risks. In applying Karl Marx's words mechanically, failure would destroy not only the reform but also the reformers themselves.[43] That fear makes all the leaders very cautious in making their reform decisions. Many proposed reform projects have been delayed or even canceled simply because their perceived risks were too great. That lack of action was particularly true in the case of price reform.

Under the old system, pricing was a major tool for the government to collect revenues and to redistribute national income among different sectors, regions, and classes of people (particularly between rural and urban citizens). In some sense, price reform is reform of the whole economic system, including wages, subsidies, and taxation. Price reform involves two major risks. The first is inflation, which directly affects people's living standards as well as income distribution.[44] A strong resistance against the price reform came from ordinary people. The second risk was the government budget problem.

The two are interrelated. To mitigate ordinary people's resistance to price reform, compensation must be made through various subsidies, which implies a large budget deficit, which, in turn, further increases inflationary pressure. Theoretically, the price reform can also bring revenues to the government through improvements in efficiency. However, the increase in expenditure is certain and immediate, but the increase in revenues is uncertain and takes time. Simple computation has always showed that government revenue would decrease with the price reform. Even at the very beginning of reform, both the leadership and economists realized that the price reform was crucial and agreed that it must be done, but fears of inflation and the budget deficit continuously delayed price reform.[45]

The risk-averse attitudes of reformers have contributed to many other features of Chinese economic reforms, including the "easy-to-hard sequence," the reform's experimental nature, and the local-government dominance. The easy-to-hard sequence is simply a consequence of aversion to risks.[46] Reform experiments can greatly reduce the risks of any particular reform program. By letting local governments try to reform, the central government not only can diversify the risks of national-level reforms but also can disassociate itself from a particular failure—at least in the short run.

It takes time for people to get used to a market economy. Economic reforms not only change the system but also change people and their habits, value judgments, and behavior. The socialist planned economy was a quiet life under which everything seemed "fixed." Decision rights were concentrated in the hands of a small group of people, so the majority of people did not need to make many choices for themselves. Even for those who were decisionmakers, most of their work was routine because the environment was stable. There was little need for initiative, creativity, and innovation.

People who have lived for decades under such a system have difficulty in adjusting to a market economy where everyone needs to make his own choices in the face of an uncertain environment. It takes time for them to learn how to deal with price fluctuation, uncertainty, multiple choices, and competition. An entrepreneurial class is crucial for the efficiency of a market economy. It takes time for an entrepreneurial class to emerge. Much of the reform's delays can be attributed to ordinary people's reluctance to be in an uncertain environment and to managers' incapability to maneuver in a market. Although two-digit inflation is not a big problem today, and the government dared to free all foodstuff prices in 1993, 10 years ago raising the price of a box of matches from 2 cents to 3 cents was a political problem.[47] Enlarging autonomy of enterprises has been one major objective of state-owned enterprise reform. But at the early stage, many managers did not like autonomy because they were used to carrying out the decisions of their superiors rather than making decisions by themselves.

How China's Gradual Reform Became a Success

Murphy, Shleifer, and Vishny[48] convincingly argue that partial reform is fraught with pitfalls. They show that when some resources—but not all—are allowed to move into the private sector and when state prices remain distorted, the result may significantly disrupt the state sector. Why has a "significant disruption" not happened in China? The following analysis shows that much of the success of the Chinese economic reform can be attributed to those policies or factors that many economists had heavily criticized. Some of those policies were actually implemented by "conservatives." In some sense, China's economic reform has been a process of "lucky shots."

The 1981 Rectification Policy and the 1989–1990 Austerity Policy

In the late 1970s and early 1980s, China faced two tasks: (a) reforming an irrational economic system and (b) rectifying a distorted production structure. From the policy agenda point of view, those two tasks were assumed to conflict with each other in the short run. So the problem in the first stage of reform was to determine which should receive a higher priority, reform or rectification?[49]

In 1980, the government decided to delay reform during two years of rectification. However, with regard to consequences, the reform was not actually delayed by the rectification. On the contrary, the first big market expansion of industrial production in the 1980s was a consequence of the rectification policy. When the government shifted the priority of planned resource allocation from heavy industry to light industry, excess capacity existed in both industries. In heavy industry, materials such as steel products became oversupplied. The machinery sector was particularly hurt because many planned orders were canceled. In light industry, traditional consumer goods such as watches and sewing machines were also overproduced after facing chronic shortages. The excess supplies generated strong pressure for price reductions and competition. At the beginning, the government tried to control the situation by using planning mechanisms, including adjusting prices and limiting production. But the problem was so serious that the government eventually gave up.

For many enterprises, finding markets for their products became the only way to survive. Thus, the rectification policy created the first industrial products market. The watch industry is a good example. As Byrd and Tidrick[50] document, from 1980 to 1983, the government reduced official watch prices three times. The total reduction was more than 20 percent of the original price. Nevertheless, the producers still exceeded the production limits issued by the planning authority. Commercial departments accepted only those watches that were easy to sell at planned prices. The producers had to mobilize their workers to sell the rest on the street at, of course, market prices. The planned prices for watches gradually disappeared. It is worth noting that the rectification created not only consumer goods markets but also producer goods markets. In 1980, direct sales outside the state plan accounted for 46 percent of total sales by enterprises under the First Ministry of Machinery Industry, as well as 33 percent of sales by all machinery producers.[51] Although planned prices were not officially abolished, most machinery products were, in fact, sold at market prices by 1983.

The 1989–1990 austerity policy is another example that shows how the consequences of a policy might differ from its original purpose. There was no consensus among economists about the austerity policy—partly because the policy was initiated and implemented by "conservatives." For many economists, the policy was the biggest reversal of the reform process. One of the major purposes of the policy was to crack down on rural enterprises and to increase the dominance of state enterprises in the economy.

Initially, the policy seemed to have followed its makers' will. Many rural enterprises went bankrupt. From 1988 to 1990, the number of rural enterprises fell by 377,600, and employment fell by 2.8 million.[52] However, the situation soon showed that the policy hurt the state-owned enterprises much harder than rural enterprises, although few state enterprises went bankrupt. From 1988 to 1990, the after-tax profit of the state industrial sector decreased by 56.5 percent, the total loss increased 3.3 times, and the proportion of loss makers in all state-owned enterprises increased from 10.9 percent to

27.6 percent.[53] In the first half of 1990, industrial output grew by 0.9 percent, whereas the state industrial sector's growth rate was negative. By the end of 1991, the total output value of rural enterprises accounted for 30.83 percent of total industrial output value,[54] compared with 24 percent in 1988. More important, two years after the austerity policy, rural enterprises for the first time obtained real legitimacy ("birth certificates") in the mind of the central government.

Budgetary Contracting System between Adjacent Levels of Government

The budgetary contracting system was first introduced in 1980, renewed in 1984 with some modifications, and fully institutionalized in 1988.[55] Under such a system, lower-level governments have an obligation to hand over a fixed amount or a fixed proportion of their revenues to higher-level governments; they can keep the remainder for themselves. It was no longer possible to make arbitrary transfers of surpluses between different levels of government or other governments at similar levels. Many leading reform-minded Chinese economists heavily attacked the system because "it promoted regional protectionism, segmented the integrated market, and increased local governments' administrative interventions into enterprises."[56] In fact, the system was first introduced partly to stabilize the central government's budget revenue, rather than to implement market reforms.[57] However, analysis shows that this policy might have been the most important single contributor to the marketization of the Chinese economy in the 1980s.

First, this system actually splits the whole Chinese economy into many small public economies. It is equivalent to delimiting the property rights among different levels of government, such that each local community becomes a "conglomerate," and each level of government becomes the real residual claimant of its own public economy.[58] As I argued, such a split-up improves both monitoring incentives and work incentives of local bureaucrats and the firms in their localities.[59] Because local governments are much closer to their "agents" (the people), firms face more pressure to deliver residual profits to the local government. Furthermore, local governments cannot finance their spending by printing money; their budget constraint is much stricter than the central government's constraint. The budgetary contracting system boosted the rapid development of rural enterprises, which are now the major engine of economic growth in China.

Second, the system has forced local governments to compete with one another in markets and has helped to marketize the whole economy. Although a local government may still use planning mechanisms to control local enterprises, it can do business with other local governments only by bargaining. The bargaining process between different local governments made the central planning system progressively more difficult to implement, and it eventually forced the planning system to evolve into a dual-track system, which was then converging into a single market system.[60] The critics seem to have underestimated the force of the principles of the market mechanism: competition and the survival of the fittest. As the size of each community shrinks and the number of communities increases, competition becomes more intense. Because the competitiveness of each public economy depends on its efficiency compared with its counterparts, the local government is eventually forced to grant more autonomy to its firms (if we assume that assigning the decision rights to the firms is more efficient).[61]

The competition mechanism also works vertically. For example, when the provincial government–controlled firms are challenged by the more efficient rural enterprises, the provincial government has to respond constructively if it still wants to receive some revenue from its firms. Truly, all government bureaucrats are greedy for rent, and they resist giving up their power, if possible. But without monopoly, their rent can be guaranteed only by improving the efficiency of the firms (to a great extent depending on overall competition). Local protection may work for a short time. But anti-protection forces are perhaps more powerful. The more efficient firms and more efficient regions are always trying to break the barriers of their neighbors. Local protection also directly contributed to the marketization of the whole economy. It forced those firms and regions—those that the central government had protected for a long time and had supplied with underpriced raw materials—to enter the market.[62] Having 30 planned economies is, of course, not the goal of the reform. But we are sure that if the Chinese economy were split into 2,181 or 55,800 mini planned economies,[63] each of them would soon either evolve into a private economy or decay, and the entire Chinese economy would be an integrated market economy on the basis of private property rights.

The Lag of the State-Owned Enterprise Reform

The state-owned enterprise reform has been the focus of China's economic reforms. It strained most reformers' energy and intelligence. Although the overall performance of state-owned enterprises has greatly improved through various reform measures (i.e., expansion of autonomy, profit retention, and the contract responsibility system), the achievements are far from the desired objectives. Even though the government put forth tremendous effort and attained some success, many economists argue that the state-owned enterprise reform has been a failure.

After 15 years of reform, the government has not yet found an effective proposal for state-owned enterprises.[64] However, if one views the state-owned enterprise reform in the context of the entire economic reform process, one may find that the lag of the state-owned enterprise reform might not be as bad as many assumed. Wei and Peng[65] find that the development of the nonstate sector was negatively dependent on the reform of the state sector in the initial stage of reform. In other words, the faster that state-owned enterprises were reformed, the more difficult it was for the nonstate-owned economy to develop.

We argue that the state sector's main contribution to the reform is that it has provided a "social security service" for the reform program. First, under the traditional planning system, the enterprise is not only a job provider but also an insurer for workers. Doing business in the market is risky because businesses may fail. To induce an individual worker to leave a state-owned enterprise to find a job in the market or to set up his or her own business, that person must be paid a premium. The Chinese experience shows that "unpaid leave" with a state-owned enterprise can greatly reduce an individual worker's risk in moving into the market because the person's status quo is not affected.

Second, the existence of the unreformed state sector can also reduce labor costs for the nonstate sector, which surely promotes the latter's development. The full labor cost of an employee must include daily living expenses as well as housing, medical insurance, and so on. When an individual working for a nonstate enterprise (e.g., a joint venture) can stay in an apartment provided by his previous state employer or a family member's employer, the nonstate employer needs to pay only living expenses, which are much lower than the full labor cost. The situation is precisely that in China where, because joint ventures do not need to provide housing as the state sector does, they can afford to pay higher nominal wages to attract high-quality employees. This example shows a kind of "implicit privatization" in the sense that the state sector subsidizes the private sector. If one thinks that privatization is the right direction for reform, one should be happy with this implicit privatization.

Third, at the macrolevel, a mass privatization—or allowing the state sector to fire redundant workers—would create massive unemployment. Although it might be justified by economic efficiency, imposing such layoffs incurs too much political and social costs. Keeping unemployment within the state sector can provide much more favorable political and social conditions for the nonstate sector to expand and for the entire economic reform to go smoothly.[66] Compared with a market economy where social insurance accounts for a significant proportion of gross national product, China's state-owned enterprises' losses may not be as high as many assumed. That assumption does not mean that the state-owned enterprise reform should be postponed indefinitely. Rather, privatization of the state sector is always necessary, but it would be more feasible and smoother after a large nonstate sector has emerged.

The Development of Rural Enterprises

The contributions of rural enterprises to both economic growth and marketization have been widely appreciated today.[67] We must emphasize that rural enterprises' far-reaching effects on the reform process were hardly recognized until the late 1980s. Development of rural enterprises was initially promoted by local governments partly to absorb the surplus labor force released from the rural sector. Initially, the central government accommodated rural enterprise development only to complement the state sector but never encouraged it. Even many reform-minded economists were very critical of rural enterprises because of "their small-scale, high consumption of resources, and pollution of the environment."[68] As the rural enterprise sector became a threat to the state sector, the central government tried to crack down on it. But it was too late. As was pointed out, rural enterprises obtained real legitimacy with the central government only very recently. The failure of the 1989–1990 austerity policy was attributed mainly to the local governments' resistance to rural enterprises' efficiency.

High Growth of the Economy

The relationship between economic growth and economic reform during the reform period has been a hot topic among Chinese economists. The dominant argument in the 1980s was that during the reform period, the growth rate should be set lower to create a "good environment" for reforms, because high growth would inevitably generate inflationary pressure, which would make it impossible to implement reform policies.[69] This argument shares the same spirit with the Big Bang advocates' argument for stabilization. It was also occasionally supported by practice. However, Chinese experiences show that fast economic growth per se might facilitate rather than obstruct reforms. The reason is that marketizing a growing economy is much easier than marketizing a stagnate economy, given the rigidity of economic relationships.

As Zhigang Wang[70] argues, China's dual-track system has been converging in a market track mainly because the expansion of the market track resulted in economic growth, rather than because of the shrinking of the planned track in absolute volume. For example, although the total volume of centrally allocated steel increased by 14.9 percent from 1979 to 1988 and because the total steel supply increased by 89.25 percent, the ratio of centrally allocated steel to total steel dropped from 77 percent in 1979 to 46.8 percent in 1988. (Theoretically, as long as the market track grows faster than the planned track, the dual-track system will eventually converge in a market economy.) Similarly, fast expansion of the nonstate sector has also resulted from high economic growth rather than from a decrease in the state sector. From 1978 to 1990, gross industrial output increased by 195 percent, whereas that of the state sector increased by 142 percent, and the collective sector increased by 617 percent. As a result, the share of the state sector was reduced from 77.63 percent to 54.6 percent. In some sense, the Chinese economy has "grown" out of planning and "grown" out of public ownership. Growth itself is a vehicle for reform.

Summary

The Chinese evolutionary reform itself demonstrates how powerful the "invisible hand" is in creating institutions. We expect that the reform process will continue with its own logic. Economists can draw a clear lesson from the Chinese experience. Marketizaton of a planned economy is an evolutionary process with interactions among all self-interested agents. Although social elites might be able to design a planned economy, nobody can design a market economy. The reason is that, by its nature, the market economy is created by all the people involved (including politicians) through their self-interested activities under the governance of an invisible hand.

The Chinese leaders did not intend to bring a market economy to China when they launched their reform program. Instead, their purpose was just to "perfect" the existing public ownership–based planned economy by improving people's incentives. However, the reform created its own path to a market economy. Policies that encourage and tolerate people's self-interested actions also encourage and tolerate people's institutional innovations. When peasants, workers, and bureaucrats are allowed to pursue their self-interests, the defects of the old system are revealed, demands for further changes are created, and new institutions will emerge sooner or later. The distinction between a good economic system and a bad economic system is not the absence of theft in a good system and the presence of theft in a bad system; rather, in a good system, people have freedom and incentives to protect their assets from being stolen, whereas they have no such freedom and incentives in a bad system.

10. Property Rights Reform, the Rise of Entrepreneurs, and China's Economic Development

China's economic miracle of the past three decades can be attributed to the reallocation of entrepreneurial talents from the government and agricultural sectors to business activities. That change is unprecedented in the past 2,000 years of Chinese history. When entrepreneurial talents switched to business activities, they created wealth, and the economy boomed. Those entrepreneurs can be separated into three groups: (a) peasant-background entrepreneurs, (b) official-background entrepreneurs, and (c) returnee entrepreneurs and engineer-background entrepreneurs. They have emerged sequentially and have successively led three decades of economic growth.

The success of the Chinese economy arose from a gradual replacement of position-based rights with property-based rights that has triggered the reallocation of entrepreneurial talents. We also argue that when position-based rights and property-based rights coexist, then value creation and rent-seeking can be complementary. Therefore, one should not be puzzled by the coexistence of rapid economic growth and pervasive corruption in China. If one is to improve the efficiency of allocating entrepreneurial talents and efforts, it is important to further reduce the domain of position-based rights and to build a better-defined—and protected—property rights system.

Introduction

When China started its economic transition, it was unimaginable that an economic miracle would occur in China within only 30 years. In 1980, Deng Xiaoping set the goal of quadrupling China's total national income by the year 2000. Indeed, many people, including government officials and economists, thought Deng Xiaoping was too ambitious and unrealistic. However, China's economy has developed even faster than Deng Xiaoping's goal.

In the past three decades, China's per capita gross domestic product (GDP) doubled faster than every 10 years and reached US$2,500 by 2007. China had risen to the fourth-largest economy in the world by 2005, up from 10th in 1978. It was also the third-largest international trade country by 2004, up from 27th in 1978.[1] In 2006, China surpassed Japan to become the largest foreign currency holder. In 2007, 5 of the top 10 largest companies listed by market value were from China. The debate about the exchange rate of the Chinese currency has become an international political and economic issue.

Many outside observers have been puzzled: how could the Chinese economy have been so successful, given that the government still controls large amounts of resources and that property rights are vaguely defined?

My simple answer is that China's fast economic development has resulted from the gradual introduction of markets and the replacement of position-based rights with property-based rights (to be defined later). History has shown that the market mechanism is the best engine for economic growth and can create economic miracles such as China. In fact, China's economic development is fundamentally the same as some economic development in Western countries—such as Great Britain during the Industrial Revolution, the United States in the late 19th and early 20th centuries, and some East Asian countries such as Japan and South Korea after World War II. Once market forces are introduced and the right incentives are set up for people to pursue wealth, the miracle of growth will follow sooner or later. So the best way to understand such economic development is to understand how markets operate.

What is the market economy? A simple explanation is "the market economy is equal to freely established prices plus entrepreneurship."[2] Freely set prices provide signals as well as incentives for resource allocation, and entrepreneurs may act in advance of known prices and decide what to produce and how to produce it under uncertainty.[3] Entrepreneurs are not just price takers but also price makers. In fact, in an uncertain world—as is always the case in a market economy—the most important decision is "discovering the relevant prices,"[4] that is, foreseeing the price that customers are willing to pay and the products or services they are willing to buy, as well as the costs of production. Profit pursuit and survival drive entrepreneurs to organize enterprises efficiently and to innovate new products, new production technologies, new business models, and new organizations. It is through entrepreneurial initiatives that an economy grows and thrives.[5]

This explanation provides guidance for understanding China's transition from a planned economy to a market economy. The key to the success of Chinese economic reform is liberalization of prices through a dual-track system: the rise of entrepreneurs through the development of nonstate sectors and the privatization of the state sector. Under the planning regime, prices were set by the government, and those prices played little role in developing new resource allocations. Both production and investment decisions were made by officials according to their "social goals," instead of by entrepreneurs for profits. Since the beginning of reform, prices have been gradually freed and have become major signals for redirecting resource allocations. Thus, entrepreneurs have gradually replaced bureaucrats as economic decisionmakers—although the government still holds considerable control rights even today.

History shows the importance of liberalizing prices. Looking at the world, we find that the wealth gap between countries is, in general, very different from the resource gap. In fact, many developed countries that use liberalized pricing systems have relatively limited natural resources, whereas many underdeveloped countries have abundant natural resources.

Entrepreneurial talents are one of the most important factors of economic development.[6] There are two basic facts about the distribution of entrepreneurial talents. First, although entrepreneurs are a phenomenon of the market economy, entrepreneurial talents have always existed. However, before the Industrial Revolution, those talents were engaged mainly in the military, political struggles, and government service rather than in productive activities as in Western countries today. Second, although everyone may have some decisionmaking ability, only a relatively small segment of the population can be said to be entrepreneurial. Entrepreneurial talents are scarce resources in every society.

Although endowments of entrepreneurial talents are important for economic development, even more important is the allocation of entrepreneurial talents among different uses. As Baumol[7] argues,

159

although the supply of entrepreneurial talents varies among societies, the productive contribution of the society's entrepreneurial activities varies much more because of their participation in productive activities, such as innovations in contrast to largely unproductive (even destructive) activities.[8]

I believe Baumol's proposition provides a powerful explanation for China's astonishing economic growth in the past three decades. The economic reform has brought about many changes. However, in my view, the most important change is the movement of entrepreneurial talents from the government and agricultural sectors to the business and industrial sectors. That change is unprecedented in China's history of the past 2,000 years. Most entrepreneurs now create value instead of simply distributing income and resources, which is the main reason Chinese wealth and income have grown so rapidly.

Behind the rise of entrepreneurship is a change in property rights, where we define "property rights" as "an incentive and accountability system to link one's action to one's expectations of return."[9] When property rights are well-defined and protected by law and social norms, everyone is fully accountable and responsible for his or her own behavior. When property rights are not well-defined, both prices and incentives will be distorted, and entrepreneurs will be less than fully productive.[10]

We must recognize that in reality, property rights are generally vaguely defined. There is no economy where all property rights are completely well-defined. However, vagueness of property rights differs from country to country and from time to time. The distribution of property rights is not a dichotomy but a continuum between complete vagueness and complete clarity. Correctness of price signals and incentives of entrepreneurs are positively correlated to clarity of property rights. Prices and incentives tend to converge as clarity of property rights gradually increases. An economy can grow as long as the vagueness of property rights decreases. It does not need to wait until property rights have been clearly defined.

That point is crucial for understanding the growth of the Chinese economy in the past three decades. The success of China provides neither conflict with the property rights theory developed by Armen Alchian,[11] among others, nor does it require support for free-ownership theories. In China, property rights are still not well-defined and protected, and firm ownership is still vague, compared with most developed economies. However, progress in China's economic development is occurring because China has been moving increasingly toward a private property–based economy from a position-based rights economy. Property rights have become less vague and better protected in the past three decades. The success of rural reform in the late 1970s and early 1980s, for example, has its source in contracting out the use of land to rural households. The resulting property rights are much better defined under the household-contract responsibility system than under the collective commune system.

In urban settings, under the planned economy, almost all economic rights were position based, and nonpublic businesses were completely illegal. During the reform, the government has taken several steps to grant legal status to the private sector. Sole proprietorships were legalized in 1982. Privately owned enterprises eventually obtained legal status in 1988 after a long debate. Protection of private property rights was explicitly written into the new constitution in 2004, and those institutional changes have greatly promoted the rise of business entrepreneurship and the related economic growth. By the end of the 1990s, most rural enterprises and small and medium-sized state enterprises were fully or partially privatized. Without those legal steps for implementing private property rights, entrepreneurs would not have emerged, and China would not have been so successful in its economic development. In fact, the Chinese economy almost stagnated from 1989 to 1990.

Of course, China still has a long way to go in building a well-defined property rights system, which is essential for sustainable economic development in the future. My view is that the Western-developed property rights theory is a powerful tool for understanding Chinese economic development. China's economic reform has been like watching a movie. If we reach the correct conclusion, we should grasp the entire story, not just focus on one part.

Even though my main conclusion is that the best explanation for China's economic development is the gradual liberalization of the economy and the establishment of property rights, thereby causing a reallocation of entrepreneurial talents, I also recognize that economic development and entrepreneur reallocation formed bilateral casual relations and mutual strengthening. On the one hand, the rise of entrepreneurs has promoted economic development. On the other hand, the development of the Chinese economy has provided further business opportunities and has attracted more entrepreneurial talents to start and to expand businesses, which, in turn, has promoted further development of the economy. It is thus a virtuous cycle that continuously injects vitality into the Chinese economy, causing it to succeed.

The Importance of Entrepreneurial Talent Allocation

When we look at an economy, one of the most important questions we need to ask is this: What do the most talented people do? In particular, do they work for the government, or do they run commercial businesses?

As Murphy, Shleifer and Vishny argue, people with general talents can succeed in many occupations, such as entrepreneurs, government officials, lawyers, speculators, and professors. Such success is unlikely among people with specialized talents in music, arts, or sports.[12] The ablest people choose occupations that will exhibit the greatest (or most promising) returns to their ability. Both entrepreneurs and government officials are occupations in which having marginally greater talent leads to a higher payoff. Thus, those two occupations compete for the same entrepreneurial talents in the population, and countries differ in their occupational allocations of entrepreneurial talents.[13]

Regardless of location, entrepreneurs rationally select careers that have the greatest individual returns, but the distribution of entrepreneurial talents differs between countries. In developed countries, such as Germany, Great Britain, and the United States, the best entrepreneurial people tend to move toward businesses, whereas in underdeveloped countries, such as most Latin American and African countries, the best entrepreneurial people work in the government or the military. Over time, when more entrepreneurial people switch to government jobs, economic growth slows down and even stagnates. Thus, we may conclude that the allocation of entrepreneurial talents between governments and businesses is one of the most important determinants—even if not the only determinant—of developing an economy. The reason some countries are undeveloped is not because they lack entrepreneurial resources; it is because their entrepreneurial talents have been allocated to the government or to other nonproductive sectors.

Where does that effect come from? Basically, when entrepreneurial people enter business, they create economic value and wealth through productive ways, such as more efficient use of resources, cost reduction, and technological innovations. In contrast, when they work in government, they mainly engage in redistributing income and, at worst, even destroy existing economic wealth and production through largely unproductive—and often destructive—rent-seeking or even illegal activities.[14]

That difference is rooted in the fundamental differences between the ways government and businesses collect revenues. The government exists first to provide public services, which may also be valuable for society. For example, without government protection of property rights and provision of public infrastructure, it would be next to impossible for private entrepreneurs to be productive. For that reason, we are willing to have government. However, the nature of public services requires the government to charge for its services through taxes, not through pricing as a business does. Taxes are legally compulsory, not voluntary, payments, which means that the government can collect revenues even without producing anything of value for society. We have no way of guaranteeing that the services provided by government are comparable in value to the taxes collected by government. In fact, once the government can legitimately collect taxes, government officials generally have incentives to oversupply some services, much beyond the social optimal level, and to undersupply other services—when it serves their personal interests. Typically, citizens must "buy" some imposed services and may be overcharged by the government.

The expansion of government is in the interest of officials because their power and even their compensation are increased accordingly.[15] The size of government is determined by the amount of taxes it can collect, not by the consent of the citizenry. Additionally, talented people in government can innovate new ways to impose services and levy taxes. That innovation means that when entrepreneurial people run the government, society may suffer more than when ordinary people run the government. In addition, when politicians compete for power, they may consume social resources without providing compensating social benefits.

In contrast, business entrepreneurs get revenues from buyers through pricing, and the price is a voluntary payment. No buyer would willingly pay a price for a good or service that is more than its value to him or her. Even customers of a monopolistic firm will not pay more for its goods and services than its value to them. In a competitive market, competition between firms creates consumer surplus (equal to the total value of a good or service to the individual consumer minus the price paid), and those who provide the highest consumer surplus will survive and thrive. In summary, when entrepreneurial talents run businesses, they create value and wealth for society.

The allocation of entrepreneurial talents is an important contributor to economic growth because it determines technological progress. Over the long term, economic growth can be sustained only through continued technological innovation. The rate of innovation determines the growth rate. Innovation is the basic duty of entrepreneurs in commercial enterprises.[16] As Murphy, Shleifer, and Vishny argue, technological progress determines the ability of the ablest entrepreneurs.[17] When the ablest people in a population choose to be entrepreneurs or go into business, the business that they engage in must have the fastest relative technological increase. Productivity and income growth will also increase. In comparison, when the ablest people in a population choose to be government officials, their abilities are used mainly for rent-seeking activities, not for increasing the possibility of technological progress. Thus, the economy stagnates. The difference in technological progress between countries is determined by differences in entrepreneurial talents in commercial sectors.

The allocation of entrepreneurial talents also affects the productivity of other production factors, particularly labor and capital. The productivity of labor and capital is, to a large extent, dependent on the ability of the entrepreneur. Production workers produce more of whatever they produce when they are employed by a high-ability entrepreneur than by a low-ability entrepreneur.[18] Similarly, productivity of capital is also positively related to the ability of the entrepreneur. So it is not strange that total factor productivity tends to be much lower in countries where the talented people work in government than where the talented people run businesses. Furthermore, given that the wage of a production worker is determined by that person's marginal productivity, labor income will be lower in the former countries than in the latter. When talented people run businesses, households have good investment opportunities and thus have greater incentives to save for investment. In other words, the allocation of entrepreneurial talents also determines income distribution and capital accumulation. Less-developed countries are short of capital partly because their entrepreneurial talents are misallocated into the government.

The allocation of entrepreneurial talents between government and business also affects the size and distribution of firms. The size of a firm tends to increase with the ability of the entrepreneur. High-ability entrepreneurs tend to run large firms, and low-ability entrepreneurs tend to run small firms.[19] That fact is a basic reason that return on entrepreneurial talents is graduated. At the country level, the average size of firms will be smaller in countries where the ablest people run the government, leaving relatively low-ability people to run businesses. Unless the government issues monopoly rights, firm concentration will be relatively lower in countries where the ablest are in government. Because economies of scope are caused by economies of scale, countries with the ablest people in government are not very competitive in the international market.

Although the link between the allocation of entrepreneurial talents and economic growth is logical, a few studies have provided evidence to show that rent-seeking activities have a negative effect on growth.[20] Cross-regional variations in the talent allocation in China serve as direct evidence supporting the link. In Figure 10.1, the horizontal (or X) axis measures the percentage of government officials in the population of each province, and the vertical (or Y) axis measures the GDP growth index. We find that the trend is down: GDP has grown more slowly for provinces with higher percentages of government officials. Investigations also show that in regions where government positions are more attractive, the growth rate is lower.

Incentive Changes in China: From Position-Based Rights to Property-Based Rights

Given the characteristics of graduated returns for the performance of government officials and entrepreneurs, if they all have the choice to become entrepreneurs, what attracts them to do so? The answer is the relative compensation that society provides government officials and entrepreneurs who have the same level of abilities.[21] Compensation is not limited to economic return; it also includes social status

Figure 10.1
GOVERNMENT EMPLOYEES IN THE POPULATION AND THE PER CAPITA
GDP INDEX

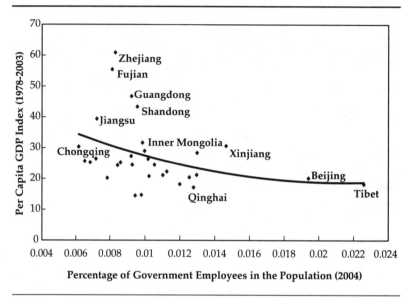

Percentage of Government Employees in the Population (2004)

SOURCE: *China Statistical Yearbook,* 2004.

and other benefits (such as control over people and resources). Economic return and social status can be correlated both negatively and positively. When they are negatively correlated, individual preferences for economic return and social status play an important role. Generally speaking, when government officials earn more "total" compensation than do entrepreneurs, the able choose to be government officials; otherwise, they would choose to be entrepreneurs.

There are many determinants of the relative rewards of government officials and entrepreneurs, including the property rights system, regulation of businesses, the size and discretionary power of government, the size of markets, and so on.[22] The protection of private property rights can be among the most important. Being an entrepreneur is more attractive when private property rights are well-defined and protected and when the government cannot easily confiscate private property and profits. Being a government official is more attractive when the government holds considerable discretionary powers and when doing business is heavily constrained by regulations so that rent-seeking opportunities are substantial. If the size of government is larger relative to the size of markets, private entrepreneurship is less attractive.

Ancient China was characterized by the fact that the government was open, whereas the market was restricted. The overall incentive system was strongly biased against businesses and in favor of government sectors.[23] Through imperial examinations, it was possible, at least theoretically, for anyone to become a government official with wealth, power, and prestige. In contrast, business activities were discouraged by both legal institutions and social norms, and businesspeople ranked lowest in social status. As a result, the most talented people were attracted to government for rent-seeking activities, rather than value creation in business. That misallocation of talents still exists under planned economic regimes. However, even during China's planned economy, some entrepreneurial talents were located in rural areas because of urban residency control.

Today, the reallocation of entrepreneurial talents to business sectors from the government and the agricultural sectors has taken place in China since the beginning of the reform. With gradual liberalization of price and decontrol of the economy, the relative attractiveness to talents has changed increasingly in favor of business. I summarize such change as the transition from position-based rights to property-based rights.

A fundamental issue is the distribution of control rights over resources, wealth, products, people, and actions. The rights that a person has will determine that individual's consumption, freedom, power, and happiness. Rights can be distributed in the population by law, administration, contracts, and social norms, as well as other factors such as private information and personal relations.

Regardless of what element decides the distribution, all rights must rely on some deep-rooted source. Among the sources of rights, position and property are the two most important. When rights depend on a special position in the social structure, we say that rights are position based. When rights depend on special property (seen and unseen), we say that rights are property based. For example, in a rank-structured enterprise in the market economy, most rights are based on position (decided by contract). Major decisionmaking power is held by the CEO, and other rights are held by department managers and those in other positions.

When rights are determined by power, an individual's rights come from his position. If someone wants to have any special rights, that person must first attain the position that those special rights depend on. Without that position, there are no rights to be had. As soon as that person loses the position, he or she loses the related rights. When rights are property based, an individual's rights come from possession of property. If someone wants to have any special rights that depend on a type of property, he or she must first attain that type of property. Without that property, there are no rights to be had. As soon as the person loses that property, he or she also loses the rights that depend on that property.

One important distinction between property-based rights and position-based rights is that the former can be better defined than the latter. Property-based rights are normally clearly defined and protected by law and social norms, and they have relatively strict boundaries. Disputes over property-based rights can be addressed through legal processes. By contrast, position-based rights are generally only loosely defined and are subject to frequent administrative changes. A holder of position-based rights often has discretionary power to change the boundary of rights—and even to create new positions. When a dispute occurs, in most cases, the only way to solve it is through an administrative process that is itself also position based. Therefore, rent-seeking activities stem from position-based rights.

Another characteristic of position-based rights is that they have term limits and are not marketable. They can be used by the rights holder only while in office and cannot be legally sold when the holder leaves office. Consequently, position-based rights are often abused. The incumbent holder has a short-term horizon. Unlike property owners, position holders tend to maximize their personal value for the rights of their term of office, not the discounted present value of long-term earnings. Like property, a position may also be transferred from one person to another from time to time. The difference is that whereas the transfer of property is governed by contracts and voluntarily conducted, the transfer of a position is governed by administration and is not necessarily voluntary, and the loser of a position cannot get market-based compensation from the position gainer. In other words, positions can be transferred using administrative means, but they cannot be transacted legally. Buying and selling position-based rights are often considered forms of corruption because, unlike transfers of property, they are not part of the wealth creation process.

A third difference is that the number of positions is more limited than property in the following sense.[24] In most cases, the number of positions with particular rights tends to be fixed: When a person gains a position, another person loses that position. Or when a new position is created, the rights attached to other positions or properties may be diluted. In contrast, properties can increase through production and innovation almost without limit. For example, the production of a new car does not mean the loss of value of another property. In fact, in a society where property rights are well protected, the way to gain new property is to create it or to create another property for exchange. For that reason, competition for property-based rights creates value, whereas competition for positions often redistributes value.

That conceptualization of position-based rights and property-based rights is very important for understanding the nature of a state-owned economy.[25] The rights in the state-owned (or "publicly" owned) economy are often misunderstood as belonging to the whole populace, but that ownership is not the case. In the public and private economies, rights can be owned and exercised only by individual owners.[26] The essential difference is that in the publicly owned economy, rights derive from position, but in the privately owned economy, rights derive from property, or at least that is the case initially.[27]

In a public economy like pre-reform China, the government owns all means of production. The economy is organized and operated through a mega-administrative system. The administrative system is hierarchically structured, usually with many positions at different levels. All positions are top-down ranked, with the central agent at the top. The rights attached to a position determine not only its occupier's decisionmaking authority but also the individual's personal income, perks, control benefits, and prestige. Examples of position-dependent personal benefits include whether an official can use a car and, if so, the type of car as well as whether a telephone is installed in the person's home or office. Under such a system, bureaucratic position is widely considered a standard of almost everything.[28]

In China's pre-reform regime, individuals owned no property, except some basic living materials that, in most cases, were also derived from a particular position. Private commerce was illegal. Anyone engaged in market activity risked punishment, humiliation, or even prison.[29] Given that no rights were established on the basis of property, the only way someone could get any rights over property and improve his or her living standard was to enter the government or a quasi-government agency and become a bureaucrat.[30]

Those who had no opportunity to work with the government and the state sector—such as peasants in rural areas and the urban jobless—could live only at subsistence levels. State-owned enterprises were positioned lower and had fewer rights attached than central government departments of the same administrative rank. Hence, working in a government department was more attractive than working in a state enterprise. So bureaucratic careers were the best choice not only for entrepreneurial talents but also for all other people, regardless of their ability. That is one of the reasons the government in China became so large.

Government positions can also be very competitive. Abler people are on average more successful in their bureaucratic careers than are less able people. They climb the ladder to higher positions faster. However, in most cases they do so, not because they create more value and wealth for society with their higher ability, but because they are more skillful at politics. Competition for entering the government and for promotion can be very intense. The higher the position is, the fiercer the competition. The difference is that in a competitive market, success is determined by productivity, whereas in the government, success depends on political performance, personal connections, and even "damage-ability" to others, rather than economic performance. I use the term "damage-ability" to refer to injuring competitors through extortion, damaged work accomplishments, and even bodily harm.[31] Troublemakers are often better off than value makers. When many compete for fewer higher positions, the best way to get one of those positions is often to pull down rivals. The game of promotion becomes a game of damaging each other. Thus, much talent, time, and energy are used in unproductive and even destructive ways. One way to restrict power struggles is to use seniority-based systems in promotion so that no one has an incentive to harm others and manipulate information. However, seniority-based systems also lead to a situation in which no one has an incentive to do anything good, because under such a system, the most secure way to be promoted is to make no mistakes, rather than to perform better.

Given that superiors make promotion decisions for their subordinates, and a superior's utility is unrelated to a subordinate's economic performance, it is crucial for the subordinate to have a good relationship (*guanxi*) with the superior, rather than to perform well. Because an official may move from one position to another, the *guanxi* needs to be networked. Building and maintaining a relationship network are important tasks for officials, which can be socially costly. However, such a network gives the able an advantage.

In China, the government is less constrained by law. Government officials often create new positions and expand the boundary of rights for rent-seeking, which is similar to erecting more and more tollbooths on a road.[32] Also, quite often, position-based rights are duplicated and overlap across departments, while different departments may compete for rights. All of those activities can consume resources and destroy value.

Since the economic reforms of 1978 gradually reintroduced and expanded property-based positions, they have coexisted with traditional position-based rights. The reintroduction of property-based rights has occurred gradually. They were first reintroduced on the local level and then became national policy changes. Next, the highest-level reformers addressed them, and they were finally recognized by the constitution and other laws.

Rural areas pioneered the reintroduction of property-based rights. When the household-contract responsibility system was implemented in rural areas, the peasants were allowed to have rights to assigned land and to own their products and means of production, such as livestock and tractors. They were also allowed to sell their products in markets. In other words, they were able to improve their lives through their productivity, even though they had no opportunity to enter the government. The agricultural reform also promoted the development of nonstate industries (which will be discussed in the next section).

In urban areas, property-based rights were reintroduced mainly under the pressure of unemployment. When 17 million "educated youths" returned from rural areas after the Cultural Revolution, it was impossible for the government to provide them with jobs in the state sector. With implicit encouragement—and even explicit encouragement of some government leaders at both local and central levels—self-employed businesses emerged spontaneously in 1978. The ideological and legal controversies over self-employment were settled in June 1981 by the Sixth Plenary Session of the 11th Congress of the Chinese Communist Party, which stated that "the self-employment economy within a certain extent is a necessary supplement to the public economy." That statement gave urbanites the legal right to self-employment and property ownership to attain wealth. The policy to "guide, encourage, promote, and support the self-employed economy" was implemented.

The self-employed economy attained legal status after the constitution was revised in 1982. After Deng Xiaoping said, "Let some people get rich first," making a fortune through work became a type of honor or was at least not as shameful as before. According to the 1985 survey by the Economic System Reform Institute of China, self-employed people were ranked in the top 10 occupations in economic status (wealth status), although their social status was ranked only eighth. In contrast, government officials were ranked seventh in economic status, although their social status was still ranked at the top (not counting "university student" as an occupation).[33]

Similar to sole proprietorships, the legalization of private enterprises in China was also an evolutionary process. They spontaneously arose mostly in the countryside and small cities in the early 1980s. They were encouraged by various policies of central and local reformers. In October 1987, the 13th Central Committee of the Communist Party of China formally recognized private enterprises as a "complement" to the "socialist economy." In the spring of 1988, the Seventh National People's Congress legalized them by revising the constitution. After a long debate, provisions to protect private property were written into the constitution in 2004. They were reaffirmed by the Property Law.

The establishment of a property-based rights system involves a long evolutionary process, with some temporary reversions. It is not a once-and-for-all solution. China is no exception. Even the constitutional adoption of protection for private property rights is not an endpoint of the process. Legalization of property rights is necessary, but it is insufficient. How to implement laws and whether citizens respect laws are at least equally, if not more, important. Property rights need support from cultural and social norms. China still has a long way to go to establish a well-protected property rights system. However, one must recognize that China has moved far in that direction.

Although position-based rights are still pervasive in China today, the gradual emergence of property-based rights in the past three decades has changed incentive systems dramatically, particularly for talented people. Entering the government is no longer the only way for someone to have control and a quality life. Having a private business is also an option. Wealth and money speak powerfully. By being successful at business, one can manage people and property, become rich and prestigious, and enjoy extras such as a big house, luxury car, and international travel, which had previously been available to only a small group of senior government officials. In fact, today many entrepreneurs live better than many officials do, prompting many officials to become very jealous of entrepreneurs. It is precisely that change in incentives that attracted increasingly more entrepreneurial talents into the private sector, thereby implementing a reallocation of entrepreneurial talents. Without reallocation of entrepreneurial talent, China could not possibly have created such an economic miracle in such a short time. That reallocation will be discussed in more detail later.

The occupational choice of university graduates may be a good indirect indicator of the relative attractiveness of business and the government. Figure 10.2 illustrates the job placement trend for undergraduates at Peking University between the government and business sectors. After 1997, the percentage of students entering the business sectors surpassed the percentage of students going into the government and academic institutions. Since I began serving as the dean of Peking University's Guanghua School of Management in 2006, students have rarely chosen to work in government. They are the best and brightest of China's youth. Their career choices strongly indicate that the relative attractiveness of commerce has obviously increased.

The educational background of private entrepreneurs can also serve as an indicator of changes in the relative attractiveness of the government and business sectors in the past two decades. Figure 10.3 shows changes in the percentages of entrepreneurs with

Figure 10.2
PEKING UNIVERSITY STUDENT JOB PLACEMENT

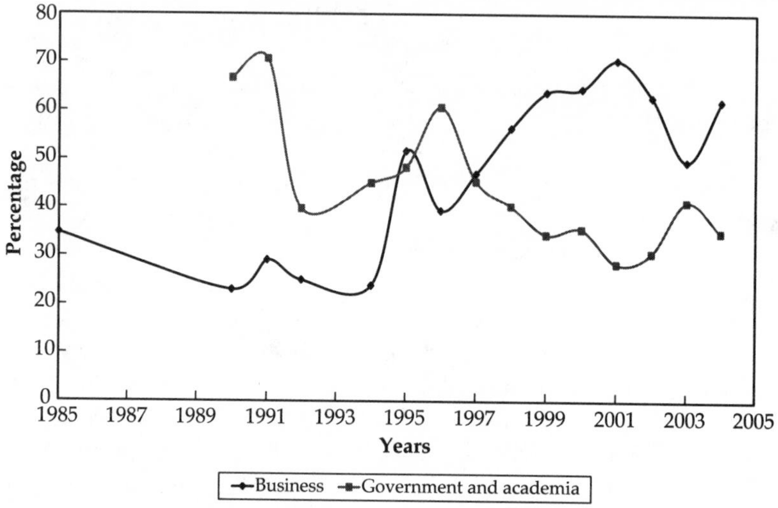

SOURCE: Peking University Student Office.

a high school education or less and those with a college education or more, respectively. Note that the percentage of entrepreneurs with college and above has increased from 17.1 percent in the 1993 survey to 49.3 percent in the 2006 survey. Figure 10.3 shows that highly educated people are increasingly moving into the private sector.

The Three Dominant Groups of Entrepreneurs in China

The rise of business entrepreneurs in the past three decades has been one of the most important changes brought about by the economic reform. Three dominant types of business entrepreneurs have emerged sequentially as the reform has progressed. Because the three categories of entrepreneurs mostly followed the process of reform successively, we can call them the three generations of dominant entrepreneurs.

Figure 10.3
EDUCATION BACKGROUNDS OF PRIVATE BUSINESS OWNERS

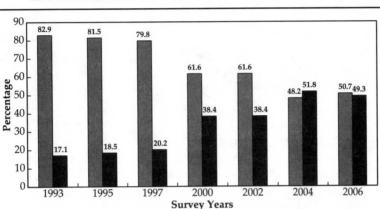

SOURCE: All-China Federation of Industry and Commerce, *Zhongguo Siying Qiye Daxing Diaocha* (1993–2006), China Federation of Industry and Commerce Press, 2007.

The first generation (1978–1988) comprises the peasant-background entrepreneurs, resulting from the rural reform of the late 1970s and early 1980s. The second generation (1989–1999) encompasses the bureaucrat-background entrepreneurs. Ironically, the birth of the second generation was triggered by the political event on June 4, 1989, and was accelerated by Deng Xiaoping's Southern Tour in 1992. The third generation (2000–2009) comprises returnee and engineer-background entrepreneurs who emerged mainly around the turn of the 21st century. The three generations of Chinese entrepreneurs generally differ (a) in their educational backgrounds; (b) in the businesses they start; and (c) by firm ownership and governance, by financing, and, in particular, by their connections to government. However, they are now merging into a joint force for growth.

Looking at the economic development of China, we find that the driving sectors differ from one decade to another. Roughly speaking, the economic growth of the first decade was driven mainly by manufacturing; that of the second decade by the financial, real estate, and other service sectors; and that of the third decade by high-tech industry. The three types of dominant entrepreneurs have led sequentially.

The Rise of the Peasant-Background Entrepreneur in the First Decade

Before China began its economic transition 30 years ago, the endowments of entrepreneurial talents were allocated in two sectors—the countryside and the government. Given that the government was the best choice of occupation for talented people under the planned economy, how could significant entrepreneurial talents have been clustered in the rural areas?

The answer is that China had implemented a strict urban residency control system (*hukou zhidu*) since the late 1950s. Under that system, the government and the state sector were closed to rural people. Those who were born in rural areas were identified as rural citizens outside the state sector, and they had to stay in rural sectors as commune peasants for a lifetime, regardless of their talents. Given that they had neither the option to enter the business sector nor the option to enter the government and state sectors, the best that talented rural people could do was to become leaders of their home villages—with somewhat more privileges than their fellow peasants. Those who had no such opportunity might conduct some type of business in the black or gray markets. Those people risked being punished for their illegal business activities and, indeed, some of them were jailed.

As the household-contract responsibility system was implemented and as rural markets were gradually liberalized, peasants obtained some freedom to do business, whereas village leaders lost their traditional control over the villagers. As a result, many entrepreneurial village leaders chose to start so-called rural enterprises. Meanwhile, those with entrepreneurial talents—who were once suppressed or even jailed for conducting illegal businesses—restarted their entrepreneurial activities either through their own private businesses or by being appointed to run rural enterprises.

Given that the rural population was so large, the supply of entrepreneurial talents was also very large. It was, therefore, natural that rural enterprises and rural private enterprises developed quickly in many areas (see Figure 10.4). By 1985, the number of rural enterprises had reached 12.2 million—up by 700 percent from 1978.

Figure 10.4
THE DEVELOPMENT OF TOWN AND VILLAGE ENTERPRISES

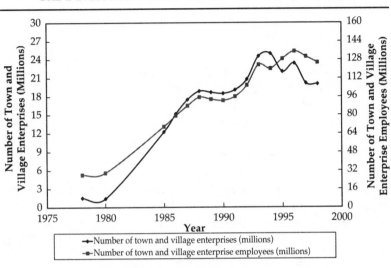

SOURCE: *China Statistical Yearbook,* 1999.

By 1990, the number of rural enterprises reached 18.5 million, more than 10 times the number in 1984, and the number of employees of rural enterprises was more than 92 million. The rural enterprises and rural private enterprises were engaged primarily in manufacturing, transportation, and commerce, and they were the major driving force for economic growth in China during the 1980s. The development of rural enterprises also helped commercialize the entire economy, because rural enterprises functioned outside the planning regime.

It should be pointed out that throughout the 1980s, entrepreneurship was ranked very low in social and political status, and government work was still the most attractive occupation for all Chinese people. Furthermore, conducting private businesses was politically risky. However, given that the government was inaccessible to rural people, becoming an entrepreneur was the best choice for rural entrepreneurial talents. If we assume that government positions had opened up to people from the countryside before reform, then all entrepreneurial talents in society would have been drawn into the government. Thus, there might not have been a rise in entrepreneurs in the 1980s, and the speed of economic growth might have been much lower. Moreover, residency restrictions preserved the "embers" of entrepreneurs for China's economic reforms.

Rural enterprises were the dominant ownership form of the non-state sector in the 1980s. Because most rural enterprises were legally owned by towns and villages, their property rights were, therefore, vaguely defined. Some observers argued that rural enterprises posed a challenge to property rights theories. Some economists tried to reconcile the performance of rural enterprises with standard property rights theory by introducing a cultural dimension of cooperation;[34] others even used the success of rural enterprises to defend public ownership. My view is different. I see no contradiction between the success of rural enterprises and the theory of property rights. First, although rural enterprises were publicly owned, their legal owners were much fewer than the "owners" of typical state-owned enterprises. Given that few private firms existed before the late 1980s, that form of ownership was the most efficient among all types of public ownership.[35] I predicted that once private ownership was legal, rural enterprises would lose their competitiveness unless they were privatized.

Second, although rural enterprises were legally owned by the local public, many of them were actually founded and controlled by entrepreneurs or quasi-entrepreneurs with bureaucratic backgrounds (mainly village heads), making them so-called red-cap firms. They were registered as local public firms mainly because private firms were illegal or were discriminated against by both government policies and ideology.[36] More important, from the viewpoint of the firm's behavior, many of their founder-managers believed that they had a high probability of being able to buy out their firms one day. After all, property rights are nothing but a kind of expectation for controlling, using, and transferring property for private benefits.

Observation suggests that Chinese practitioners did indeed follow the standard property rights theory—although not consciously. After private firms obtained legal status in 1988—particularly after Deng Xiaoping's Southern Tour in 1992—the development of private firms soon overshadowed rural enterprises. Many local governments began to privatize their rural enterprises in various forms, such as by taking off "red caps," joint-stock corporatizations, or by simply selling out.

For instance, in Zibo City, Shandong Province, private shareholders owned 30 percent of the rural enterprises by 1992. Their ownership rose to 70 percent by 1995. By 1996, about one-third of the rural enterprises had been privatized in Nanhai City in Guangdong Province. By the first half of 1997, more than 60 percent of the township enterprises in Shenyang, the capital of Liaoning Province, became joint-stock companies or joint-stock cooperatives. By the end of 1997, 50 percent or more of rural enterprises had been privatized in provinces such as Guangdong, Shandong, Zhejiang, and even Liaoning, a relatively backward and politically conservative region.[37] The rural enterprises of southern Jiangsu were once widely recognized as role models of local public ownership—the so-called *Sunan* model—which some outside observers used as the best example to challenge the theory of property rights. Ironically, for those outside observers, by the first half of 1997, 90 percent of the rural enterprises with assets under Y 5 million had been privatized in Jiangsu.[38] In 2000, the *China Statistical Yearbook* ceased publishing the number of rural enterprises.

Although there were no systematic statistics, both casual observation and careful case studies show that most rural enterprises were privatized into the hands of their founder-managers (in some cases, with a few shares owned by their employees). That change occurred in Jiangsu Province.[39] By 2001, regarding the number of registered private firms, Jiangsu was ranked first among all 31 provincial regions.[40] The actual situation applied well to entrepreneurs' expectations, proving the explanatory power of property rights theory.

Guanqiu Lu and his Wanxiang Company might be a typical example of how a peasant-background entrepreneur founded a rural enterprise that was eventually privatized into his ownership.[41] Lu was born in 1945 to a peasant family in Xiaoshan County, Zhejiang Province. In 1969, he started the Agricultural Machine Repair Factory with Y 4,000. Although he raised the startup capital, the factory was registered as being owned by a town (then called "the commune"). In 1983, when policies became flexible, Lu signed a four-year management contract with the town government under the household-contract responsibility system using trees on his assigned land as collateral—trees appraised at Y 20,000. The business was renamed the Wanxiang Factory, and it produced mainly car and truck components.

In the first year, Lu overfulfilled the contracted target by a wide margin. According to the contract, he was supposed to receive a bonus of Y 87,000. However, after someone reported him to the State Council, he took just 10 percent of the bonus and returned the remainder to the factory. In the following three years, he overfulfilled the target every year. In 1988, when private firms received legal status, he turned back half of the factory's net assets to the town government and privatized the factory under his ownership through a management buyout. Thus, Wanxiang was transferred from a rural enterprise to a private firm. Lu is now widely recognized as one of the most successful peasant-background entrepreneurs in China. Under his leadership, Wanxiang Company has grown to be one of the largest private companies in China with investments in diversified industries. Now, the company is managed by Lu's son, who graduated from an American university.

When we talk about the rise of entrepreneurship in the first decade of reform, we should also mention the millions of self-employed businesspeople in urban areas. The reason they chose self-employment was very similar to that of peasant-background entrepreneurs. They started their self-employed businesses because they had no available job opportunities in the government and state sectors, so they had to create their own "rice bowls." They also had no higher education. For that reason, they might also be classified as peasant-background entrepreneurs although they held urban citizenships. Some self-employed businesses were de facto private firms without registration.[42] Some grew to be very large firms. Figure 10.5 shows the fast increase in self-employed people in urban areas from 1978 to 2004.

The Bureaucrat-Background Entrepreneurs in the Second Decade

In the 1980s, while millions of entrepreneurial peasants started their businesses, very few government officials with entrepreneurial talents became entrepreneurs. After private firms were legalized in 1988, the situation changed. Some low-ranking entrepreneurial officials at local levels began to choose private business. The boom of bureaucrat-background entrepreneurs—particularly those who held positions in county-level governments—was further triggered by two important

Figure 10.5
NUMBER OF SELF-EMPLOYED INDIVIDUALS IN URBAN AREAS

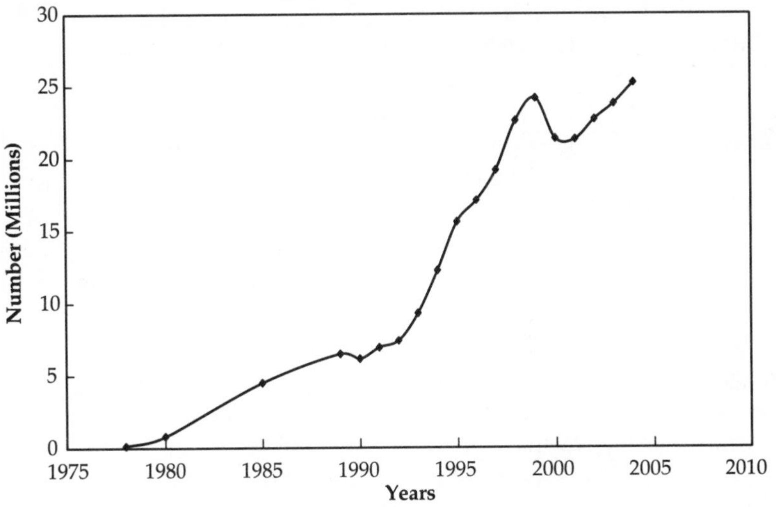

SOURCE: *China Statistical Yearbook*, 2005.

events: (a) the political event in 1989 and (b) Deng Xiaoping's Southern Tour in 1992. In October 1992, "building a socialist market economy" was officially accepted as the legitimate goal of reform by the 14th Congress of the Communist Party of China. Various liberalization policies followed to promote private or, more generally, nonstate economic activities, and registration of private firms became easier. Making a fortune became celebrated.

At that point, it was obvious that switching to private businesses was the best choice for politically depressed entrepreneurial officials. Although they had little hope of being promoted in the government, they thought they might become rich by transitioning to private business (so-called *xia hai*). According to the Ministry of Personnel, in 1992 alone, 120,000 officials quit the government and began their own private businesses. In addition, about 10 million officials and quasi-officials took unpaid leave to start businesses, and thousands of professors, college students, and engineers joined them.[43] The success of those businesses induced even more entrepreneurial bureaucrats into business enterprises.[44]

In contrast to the peasant-background entrepreneurs and self-employed businesspeople in urban settings, the bureaucrat-background entrepreneurs were all well-educated and held university degrees. They had very broad perspectives on economic issues and a good sense of what China needed most at that time. Some of them traveled abroad during their bureaucratic careers and so had knowledge of capitalist economies and how they operated. These entrepreneurs also had better connections to their old colleagues in government who controlled key resources.

More important, when they started their businesses, private firms were legal, which gave them a big advantage over the peasant-background entrepreneurs. Their firms were truly privately owned. Businesses they started were all high value added, such as financial services, real estate companies, consultancies, and even high-tech firms. Those sectors were underdeveloped at the time and were, therefore, very profitable. Thus, in a few years, those bureaucrat-background entrepreneurs accumulated a fortune, which might have taken a typical peasant-background entrepreneur decades to accumulate.

Lun Feng and his partners exemplify how a typical bureaucrat-background entrepreneur did his business. He was my classmate at Northwestern University of China from 1978 to 1981. His political ambition was revealed even during his undergraduate years. He applied to become a Communist Party member immediately after entering the university. After graduation, he continued studying for his master's degree at the Central Party School, which provided ideological training for rising senior government officials.[45] After graduating from the party school, he joined the State Commission for Economic Restructuring and was soon appointed to found a reform institute for the Hainan Provincial Government. After 1989, he lost his government position and found a temporary job that paid daily wages in the private company Nande Group (founded by Qizhong Mu, who was jailed during the 1980s for conducting private business and was jailed again in the late 1990s for fraud).

Since his life was so miserable at the time, I felt compelled to let Feng's family move into my apartment in 1990 when I went to Oxford. In 1992, encouraged by Deng Xiaoping's Southern Tour, Feng, together with five close friends from different government organizations, founded a private company called Vantone in Hainan Province. They made their first fortune by doing residential land trading. By 1994, Vantone had investments in several regions, including Beijing, Xi'an, Nanning, and Shenzhen. Its businesses were also diversified in several industries, including finance, retail, and pharmaceuticals, apart from its core business in real estate. Feng developed the Vantone Center in Beijing, the then highest-priced commercial office building, and pioneered that type of high-price real estate.

In 1995, three of his partners left Vantone and founded their own companies.[46] Vantone survived under Feng's leadership and has continued its development through several restructurings. Today, it is one of the dominant players in China's real estate market and is listed on the Hong Kong Stock Exchange. Recently, Vantone joined the development of the new Twin Towers in New York City. Lun Feng is now widely recognized as one of the most influential opinion leaders in the business community and his recently published book *Growing Up in the Wilderness* is a best seller.

Although the rise of rural enterprises in the first decade of the reform was mainly attributed to the peasant-background entrepreneurs, the development of the urban private sector in the second decade of the reform was driven by bureaucrat-background entrepreneurs. Figure 10.6 shows the changes in employment in urban private enterprises. The number of employees of urban private firms increased dramatically by 1,750 percent within 10 years, going from 570,000 in 1990 to 10.53 million in 1999.

The bureaucrat-background entrepreneurs played a crucial role in creating new sectors and in the privatization of the Chinese economy. They capitalized then dead assets, such as urban land, and securitized many other assets, such as fixed assets of state-owned enterprises. Once urban land became tradable, it was more efficiently allocated. The housing market flourished,[47] and the car industry and the service sector followed. Suddenly, while the economy of China boomed, local government budgets increased sharply, and infrastructure—particularly transportation—improved dramatically.[48] The better allocation of resources and efficiency gains drove sustained economic

Figure 10.6
NUMBER OF PRIVATE ENTERPRISE EMPLOYEES
IN URBAN AREAS

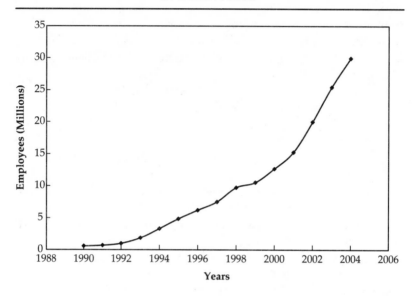

SOURCE: *China Statistical Yearbook*, 2005.

growth. It is no exaggeration to say that bureaucrat-background entrepreneurs were the major driving force for the high economic growth of the 1990s, even though they did not engage in manufacturing.

When discussing bureaucrat-background entrepreneurs, we should not overlook the fact that many state-owned enterprise managers also turned themselves into private or quasi-private entrepreneurs. Under the state-ownership system, managers are defined as government officials. They are ranked according to administrative divisions and are compensated accordingly. Their positions are determined by the government and are transferred between the government and state-owned enterprises. During the process of privatization, many small and medium-sized state-owned enterprises were bought by their managers. According to the All-China Federation of Industry and Commerce's 2002 survey of 3,257 private enterprises, 25.7 percent

(837 companies) were privatized state-owned or collective enterprises. Of those, 60.6 percent were bought by managers.[49] I have included the manager-background entrepreneurs with the bureaucrat-background entrepreneurs.

The Returnee and Engineer-Background Entrepreneurs in the Third Decade

By the turn of the century, private enterprises had emerged as the dominant ownership type of the newly established firms in China. For example, from 2000 to 2001, the number of private firms increased by 15.1 percent from 1,761,769 to 2,028,548. However, during the same period, the total number of firms of all ownership types was reduced by 4.1 percent, from 7,316,000 to 7,063,000 because of downsizing the state-owned and collective-owned economy. By 2005, the number of private firms reached 4,300,916, accounting for 53.4 percent of the total, and outnumbered the combination of state-owned, collective-owned, and foreign direct investment firms.[50]

Unlike the 1980s and most of the 1990s, the most influential newly established private enterprises in the next decade were founded by returnee Chinese scholars and engineer-background entrepreneurs. The rise of the returnee and engineer-background entrepreneurs was triggered mainly by two factors: (a) the Internet boom and (b) China's joining the World Trade Organization in 2001. From 1978 to 1998, more than 300,000 young Chinese went to more than 100 foreign countries—84 percent for continuing education and 10 percent for employment.[51] Until 1998, fewer than one-third returned to China, and the other two-thirds worked abroad. However, since 1998, the Internet boom has occurred, and the business environment has improved greatly. After China joined the World Trade Organization in 2001, increasingly more overseas Chinese students have returned to their homeland. From 1999 to 2003, nearly 80,000 overseas students returned to China. In 2000 alone, 15,000 returned from the United States. Those newly returned Chinese are nicknamed "sea turtles."

Even though their reasons for returning to China were numerous, many of those students were attracted by the opportunity to start their own businesses, particularly in high-tech industries. From the late 1990s, many local governments adopted favorable tax, finance, and land-use policies and established incubators in order to attract students returning from overseas to start businesses in high-tech industries. Beijing, Shanghai, Guangzhou, and Shenzhen were the four major regions for returning entrepreneurs. For example, in Zhongguancun Science Park of Beijing, which is called China's Silicon Valley, the number of high-tech firms founded by returning students rose from only 251 in 1999 to 1,838 by 2003, accounting for 15 percent of firms in the whole park area. The returnee entrepreneurs had strong technical backgrounds in their chosen industries—38 percent had doctorates, 45 percent had master's degrees, and 57 percent owned patents. Many of them had work experience in the U.S. Silicon Valley. In Shanghai alone, more than 2,700 firms had been founded by returnee entrepreneurs by November 2003. According to a government survey in 2003, nearly 500 out of 3,000 returnee students founded their own companies in Shenzhen.[52]

The Internet boom attracted not only returnee entrepreneurs but also many domestic entrepreneurial engineers into private businesses. The engineers had very solid educations in technology, were very innovative, and had a good sense of market demands. Once demand appeared and the environment became favorable, they jumped into businesses. The first boom of this group of entrepreneurs emerged as early as the mid-1980s in the Zhongguancun area of Beijing. The next decade was the golden age for the engineer-background entrepreneurs.[53]

It is no exaggeration to claim that it was the returnees and engineer-background entrepreneurs who brought the Internet to China and more generally bolstered China's new economy. The leading Internet and high-tech companies were all founded by either returnees or engineer-background entrepreneurs.[54] The leading consulting companies, such as Horizon Consultancy and Sinotrust-Adfaith; the leading film maker HY Brother; and the leading private equity and venture capital companies, such as Hina Group and Softbank China, were also founded by returnee entrepreneurs.

Unlike the peasant-background entrepreneurs, who started with few financial resources, and the bureaucrat-background entrepreneurs, who started businesses with bank loans, the returnee and engineer-background entrepreneurs in the past decade often started their businesses with foreign venture capital. Thus, many of them were not very cash constrained. Their property rights were also clearly defined from the beginning, and many successful companies of that kind were also listed on either domestic or overseas stock exchanges.

Yanhong Li might be a typical returnee entrepreneur. Li received his bachelor's degree in information management from Peking University in 1991. He then went to the State University of New York at Buffalo. There, he studied computer science and received a master's degree. Afterward, he worked as a consultant with Dow Jones, as a financial information system designer with the *Wall Street Journal*, and as a senior engineer with Infoseek, for a total of eight years. During that time, he invented ESP (embedded server pages) technology and the Go.Com search engine. He was granted a patent for a quality-based, page-ranking technology. Drawing on his work experience, he even published a Chinese book titled *Business War in Silicon Valley* in 1998. In the book, he asked whether it was too late to start a business. He convinced himself that he could not afford to wait any longer. Then he decided to return to China and start his company.

In late 1999, he and his friend Yong Li cofounded Baidu in Beijing, with an investment of US$1.2 million from an American venture capitalist. Baidu soon developed the Chinese search engine and marketed it. In October 2000, Baidu received an additional US$10 million from four venture capital funds: DFJ, IDG, Integrity Partners, and Peninsula Capital. In 2004, Baidu overtook Yahoo! and Google to become the largest search engine in China. In August 2005, Baidu listed its initial public offering on NASDAQ. In 2006, Baidu's market share rose to 66 percent. That same year, Li was selected as one of the top 10 people in the Chinese economy by CCTV. In 2006, *Business Week* listed him among the best global business leaders.

So far, I have described the emergence of the three dominant types of entrepreneurs in China as a sequential process. However, some overlap existed. Even in the early 1980s, a few talented people quit the state sector and founded their own businesses.[55] However, my basic model of entrepreneurship emergence is consistent with reality.

Supporting my argument is the listing of the top 500 richest people in China by publisher Rupert Hoogewerf.[56] I searched online and consulted privately to verify the backgrounds of China's top 200 richest people. The results are summarized by group in Table 10.1:[57] (a) peasants and self-employed; (b) government and state-owned sector employees; (c) overseas returnees and engineers; and (d) residents of Hong Kong, Macao, Singapore, and Australia.

Table 10.1
BACKGROUNDS OF CHINA'S 200 WEALTHIEST PEOPLE

Year Started Business	Peasants and Self-Employed	Government and State-Owned Sector	Overseas Returnees and Engineers	Residents of Hong Kong, Macau, Singapore, and Australia	Total
1978–1987	42 (55.2%)	21 (27.6%)	0 (0%)	13 (17.1%)	76 (100%)
1988–1997	14 (15.7%)	64 (71.9%)	5 (5.6%)	6 (6.7%)	89 (100%)
1998–2007	0 (0%)	4 (44.4%)	5 (55.6%)	0 (0%)	9 (100%)

SOURCE: Author's calculations.

Note that the second category includes not just those who worked in government departments and state-owned enterprises; it also includes those who had lifetime employment status in quasi-governmental institutions, such as universities, schools, and state-run research organizations. They are included because under the planned economy regime, they held "iron rice bowls,"[58] were officially identified as "public servants," and were paid by the government according to their respective positions. They were very privileged compared with the peasants and the employees of the nonstate sectors.

It should also be noted that many in the fourth category had peasant backgrounds. They obtained citizenship in Hong Kong, Macao, Singapore, and Australia through either illegal or legal immigration. The table shows that the founding years of firms by (a) peasant turned entrepreneur, (b) official turned entrepreneur, and (c) overseas returnee, were, respectively, concentrated in (a) the first decade from 1978 to 1987, (b) the second decade from 1988 to 1997, and (c) the third decade from 1998 to 2007. It is interesting to note that of the nine wealthiest people who started businesses after 1998, none were peasants. The explanation is twofold: First, the wealthiest people in the past 10 years came mainly from high technology and finance. Peasant entrepreneurs do not have the advantage in those fields. Second, in contrast with the period before 1990, the rural able people have had better opportunities for receiving a higher education since the mid-1990s. The rural youth that have not had higher education rarely have entrepreneurial ability.

Another available data set is the Large-Scale Survey of Private Enterprises by the All-China Federation of Industry and Commerce. The survey has been conducted biennially since 1993. The latest available survey was done in 2006.[59] The total sample was 3,837 private firms from which Table 10.2 provides information of occupational backgrounds immediately before founding. The table shows that the percentage of different occupational backgrounds varies with the founding time of the surveyed firms. The general trend is clear up to 2000. Roughly speaking, the percentage of peasants, workers, low-level staff members, and self-employed people before founding their private firms has a declining trend (from 54.4 percent pre-1991 to 42.9 percent between 1996 and 2000), whereas the percentage of government officials and cadres has a rising trend (from 5.9 percent pre-1991 to 12.3 percent between 1996 and 2000).

Table 10.2
EMPLOYMENT BACKGROUNDS OF PRIVATE OWNERS BEFORE STARTING A BUSINESS

| | Before 1991 | Year Business Was Started | | |
		1992–1995	1996–2000	After 2001
Peasant, Worker, or Low-Level Employee	30.2	26.7	24.7	26.1
Self-Employed	24.2	20	18.2	21.3
Government Employee or Village Cadre	5.9	10.6	12.3	9.7
State- or Collective-Owned Enterprise Manager	22	18.8	23.9	22.3
State- or Collective-Owned Enterprise Sales Personnel or Engineer	12.3	18	15.1	13.6
Soldiers	3.4	4	3.7	3.6
Resignees and Unemployed	2.1	1.9	2.1	3.5
	100.1	100	100	100.1

SOURCE: Author's calculations.

The rise of private entrepreneurs (plus foreign-invested firms, which are not discussed in this chapter) has fundamentally changed the ownership structure of the Chinese economy. (See Figures 10.7 and 10.8.) As shown in Figure 10.7, the state sector proportion (including state-owned and state-controlled enterprises) as represented by total industrial output value declined from 80.7 percent in 1978 to 28.2 percent in 1999; in the same period, the nonstate sector rose from 19.3 percent to 71.8 percent. Even if small nonstate firms are excluded, the proportion of the state sector dropped to 31.2 percent in 2006, and the nonstate sector rose to 68.8 percent.[60] In urban employment, the state sector declined from 78.3 percent in 1978 to 22.7 percent in 2006; at the same period, the nonstate sector increased from 21.7 percent to 77.3 percent. Overall, China has transformed itself from a state ownership–dominant economy to a nonstate ownership–dominant economy through its three-decade reform.

Figure 10.7
PROPORTIONS OF STATE AND NONSTATE SECTOR INDUSTRIAL
OUTPUT AND VALUE ADDED

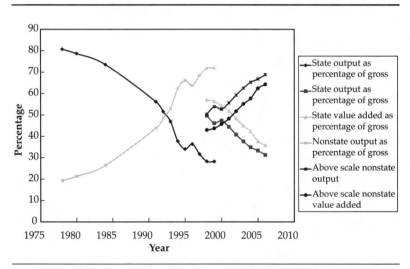

SOURCE: *China Statistical Yearbook,* 1996, 1997, 2000, 2005, and 2007.

Figure 10.8
CHANGES IN PROPORTIONS OF STATE AND NONSTATE
SECTOR URBAN EMPLOYMENT

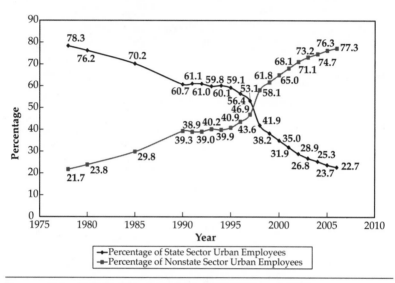

SOURCE: *China Statistical Yearbook*, 1996, 2000, 2005, and 2007.

Value Creation and Rent-Seeking Activities

In the previous section, I showed that when entrepreneurial talents work in the government, their activities are not productive because of rent-seeking. When they engage in private commercial activities, they create value and wealth. That sharp contrast is a bit of an exaggeration. On the one hand, as I mentioned in note 14, when one local economy competes with other local economies, government officials with entrepreneurial abilities can be productive. On the other hand, if the incentive mechanism is distorted by legal and administrative functions that benefit rent-seeking, perhaps entrepreneurial activity will not be productive.[61]

That fact is irrefutable when discussing China's economic transition because during the transition, position-based rights and property-based rights coexist. Even though the latter has gradually expanded, the former is still ubiquitous, and its rate of decrease is still insufficient. After 30 years of reform, the government still controls sizable production resources, such as commercial real estate, petroleum reserves, large-scale coal mines, and bank loans. It even has considerable discretion over business registration, market entry, large-scale investment decisions, employment contracts, and even price controls on some competitive commodities.

Overall, China's is a seriously controlled economy. According to the World Bank's report *Doing Business 2006*, China ranked 93rd out of 175 surveyed economic systems, lower than the average. For example, registering a new business takes 35 days and 13 procedures, and costs 9.3 percent of the average person's income. On average, a medium-sized enterprise must pay taxes 44 times, equal to 77.1 percent of profits, and must expend 872 work hours. China's detailed ranking is 128th in starting a business, 153rd in dealing with licenses, 101st in getting credit, and 160th in paying taxes. In such a controlled environment, rent-seeking and making connections with the government not only are attractive to entrepreneurs but also are, in many cases, necessary.

The coexistence of position-based rights and property-based rights led to rampant corruption between government officials and entrepreneurs in trading power for money. For that reason, the public often criticizes Chinese entrepreneurs. Although we should not ignore this fact, I would like to argue that, overall, entrepreneurs over the past 30 years have surpassed rent-seeking with value creation. Even though some entrepreneurs perhaps relied mainly on rent-seeking activities to make their fortunes, the vast majority made their fortunes through their productive contributions to society. Otherwise, we have no way to explain why China's economy has grown so fast, or why the quality of life for Chinese people has improved so quickly.

In addition, I would like to argue that in a highly controlled economy like China's, not engaging in some rent-seeking activity makes value creation impossible. Let me provide an example to explain this point. In 1980s China, much of the main production materials were rationed according to state planning, and prices were set by the government. The planning policy at the time did not allow nonstate-owned enterprises to have access to any scarce production materials, such as steel, petroleum, cement, and lumber.

If that policy had been strictly enforced, rural enterprises would not have arisen, but they are now commonly believed to have been the driving force of economic growth at the time. However, because rural enterprises were more efficient than state-owned enterprises, they were motivated to use any means, even illegal means, that might allow them to purchase those production materials. In fact, they bribed the government officials who controlled the rationing of materials and the managers of state-owned enterprises who could sell some rationed materials on the black market. The official price of iron at the time was Y 600. Imagine that the production rate at state-owned enterprises and rural enterprises was Y 800 and Y 1,200, respectively (the estimated difference in production rates is not an exaggeration because the black-market price at the time was about Y 1,200). If rural enterprises had to pay government officials Y 200 in bribes, the value to society was Y 400 higher than without bribery.

Without bribes, no government official would have a motive to allow a rural enterprise to buy the necessary production inputs, so the efficiency of resource allocation would be much lower.

In transitioning China, many corrupt practices have similar efficiency-increasing traits. My general recommendation is that when we discuss whether corrupt practices have a positive or negative function for economic growth, we must first be clear about the type of economy we are discussing. If the government is constrained to the realm of protecting property and providing public services, corruption is more likely to harm economic growth. However, if the government intrudes into the private realm—such as holding monopoly rights to engage in commercial activities, financing, and setting private contracts—then exchanging bribes for private rights will perhaps increase efficiency, even if it involves rent-seeking and redistribution of the national income. Indeed, bribery is a means to redeem those private rights that the government has legally, but irrationally, seized. Therefore, people should not be perplexed when rapid economic growth and rampant corruption coexist in reform era China.

Chinese entrepreneurs often play a part in illegal activities. Many people have been punished, but many others still have not been. Here, I would like to argue that many so-called illegal practices actually create wealth for society. The reason is that many laws set under the planned economy were irrational from the social perspective. Changes in the legal system have lagged behind the progress of reform. For example, when the household-contract responsibility system had already been widely implemented, the commune system was the only production ownership form sanctioned as legal under the constitution at the time.[62] Before 1988, private enterprises were illegal. Without entrepreneurs engaged in some illegal activities, private enterprises would not have arisen, and there would have been no economic growth.

A way to discuss this issue is to look at commercial activity in two dimensions: rationality and legality. With regard to rationality, an activity either creates value or destroys value.[63] With regard to legality, an activity is either legal or illegal. Thus, we have four types of activities: (a) value creating and legal, (b) value creating and illegal, (c) value destroying and legal, and (d) value destroying and illegal. (See Table 10.3.)

In an ideal world, all value-creating activities should be legalized, and all legal activities should create value. Thus, there would be only two types of activities: (a) value creating and legal and (d) value destroying and illegal. In an ideal world, respect for the law benefits society the most, and any illegal activity harms society the most. In reality, no economy is perfect. Some type a and type d activities inevitably will exist. Nonetheless, in Western developed countries, types a and d are more dominant than types b and c. In that kind of economy, because in most situations rational judgment is blurry, respect for the law perhaps is the most advantageous option for entrepreneurs. However, such is not the case in China. During China's transition period, types b and c were relatively more dominant than types a and d most of the time. Therefore, many illegal activities will create the value expected by society. Prohibiting all illegal activities will perhaps cause society's efficiency to decrease. From the

Table 10.3
LEGALITY AND RATIONALITY OF ECONOMIC BEHAVIOR

		Legality	
		Legal	Illegal
Rationality	Creates Value	I. Creates value and is legal	II. Creates value and is illegal.
	Destroys Value	III. Destroys value and is legal.	IV. Destroys value and is illegal.

SOURCE: Author's compilation.

195

perspective of social welfare, blaming entrepreneurs for all illegal activities is unfair. Many entrepreneurs deserve respect for taking on personal legal risks to increase social welfare.

Chinese entrepreneurs spend a large—indeed, excessive—amount of time and energy engaged in some other activities that, although legal in China, would lead to lowered efficiency in societies with better protections for property rights. The two basic functions of entrepreneurs are to handle uncertainty[64] and to implement innovation.[65]

In a broad sense, there is little difference between Chinese entrepreneurs and their Western counterparts in similar industries. However, let us first separate uncertainty into market uncertainty (i.e., technological changes and demand fluctuations) and policy uncertainty. Second, let us separate innovation into technological innovation (essentially meaning innovation as defined by Schumpeter) and institutional innovation (i.e., setting innovative institutional arrangements to meet legal but inefficient demands, such as a privately owned enterprise being registered as a legal collective enterprise and then being privatized). The result is that we then will discover—as summarized next—that there is a big difference between Chinese entrepreneurs and their Western counterparts.

Businesspeople in Western developed countries focus mainly on market uncertainty and technological innovation. By comparison, policy is not transparent in China, and it fluctuates. The legal system is inefficient and even absurd. Therefore, Chinese entrepreneurs focus mainly on policy uncertainty and institutional innovation. A focus on market uncertainty and technological innovation is relatively limited. (See Table 10.4.)

Table 10.4
ENTREPRENEURIAL UNCERTAINTY AND INNOVATION

		Uncertainty	
		Market Uncertainty	Policy Uncertainty
Innovation	Technological Innovation	Western Enterprises	
	Institutional Innovation		Chinese Enterprises

SOURCE: Author's compilation.

196

That news is both good and bad. The bad news is that by focusing mainly on policy uncertainty and institutional innovation, Chinese entrepreneurs are disadvantaged in the international market. When Western companies are busy creating more value for consumers and increasing competitiveness by better understanding consumer preferences and inventing lower-cost new products, Chinese companies are preoccupied with other matters that are of no benefit to their direct competitiveness in the market.[66] The market evaluates goods and services, not how hard their provider must work.

Now for the good news. By focusing mainly on policy uncertainty and institutional innovation, Chinese entrepreneurs have tremendous potential to improve their competitiveness. If government policy becomes more transparent and stable and if irrational legal and policy obstacles to commerce were eliminated, then Chinese entrepreneurs' focus could be better allocated to directly productive activities, thus allowing Chinese companies to be more competitive.

Conclusion

History shows that the economic development of a nation depends on the efficient allocation of entrepreneurial talents much more than on the endowment of those talents per se.[67] Talented people can work either in government or in business. When they work in business, they create value for society; when they work in government, they are engaged mainly in redistributive or less productive activities. In China's long history, the talented people were generally concentrated in the government. In this chapter, I argued that the economic miracle of China in the past three decades is attributable to the reallocation of the entrepreneurial talents from the government, state sector, and agricultural sector to business activities. That change is unprecedented in the past 2,000 years of Chinese history.

The reallocation of entrepreneurial talents has been triggered and accelerated by the evolutionary transition from position-based rights to property-based rights. Under the planned economic regime, all rights were position based, and obtaining a government position was the best choice for entrepreneurial talents. When property-based rights were introduced and expanded, the incentive system changed increasingly in favor of doing businesses. The talented people began to move to productive businesses and the economy took off.

I also identified three dominant groups of Chinese entrepreneurs who have risen roughly sequentially as the market-oriented reform has unfolded: (a) peasant-background entrepreneurs, (b) official-background entrepreneurs, and (c) returnee and engineer-background entrepreneurs. The three dominant groups of Chinese entrepreneurs differ in their education, the businesses they started, the ownership and governance, and the methods of financing. They sequentially became the leading sectors of China's economic growth in the past three decades, and now they are merging into a joint growth force.

The position-based rights and property-based rights have coexisted during the reform period. Economic activities are heavily regulated even now. Thus, inevitably, to do business in China, one has to deal with government relations. Good government relations are very important for business success. Accordingly, entrepreneurial activities in China have been a combination of value creation and rent-seeking activities. Rent-seeking is partly responsible for the negative image of entrepreneurs. However, we must recognize that under a controlled economy, much value creation can come about only because of rent-seeking activities. Indeed, some of the most important reformers were Chinese entrepreneurs. They used rent-seeking or even bribery to aid in liberating economic resources from government control. For example, without rural enterprises using bribery to obtain key supplies, price liberalization would have been delayed tremendously. In other words, in a controlled economy like China's, value creation and rent-seeking are complements, not surrogates.

The foregoing analysis has very important policy implications. If one is to improve the efficiency of the allocation of entrepreneurial talents and efforts, it is imperative to further reduce the domain of position-based rights and to build a better-defined and protected property rights system. If the Chinese government is willing to give up its control over substantial resources, to privatize the state sector further, and to continue its deregulation of the business environment, the productivity of Chinese entrepreneurs will improve further. Perhaps China will have another 30-year golden era of growth. That possibility, however, exceeds the scope of this book. To achieve that goal, substantial political reform is needed. And it is hoped that future political reform will shift more entrepreneurial activities from rent-seeking to value creation.

11. China's State-Owned Enterprise Reform: A Corporate Governance Perspective

State-owned enterprise (SOE) reform has been on the top of China's economic reform agenda since 1984. Is China's SOE reform a success or a failure? The answer is almost evenly distributed among economists. One argument—mainly from foreign economists concerned with China ("outsiders")—is that the reform has been quite successful in improving total factor productivity (TFP). Another argument comes from the research of influential economists.[1] According to their studies, the annual increase in TFP has been 2 percent to 4 percent since 1979, much higher than in the pre-reform period.[2] According to that finding, some economists even argue that private property rights may not be necessary for efficiency.

But most Chinese economists ("insiders") think that the reform has been unsuccessful, at least in the profitability of SOEs. It is widely reported (and most people believe) that one-third of SOEs take explicit losses, another one-third take implicit losses, and only one-third are slightly profitable.

Why are the viewpoints so divergent? One possible explanation is that the outsiders use econometric models to draw their conclusions, whereas the insiders base their judgments on their daily experience and intuition. When aggregated data are used to analyze the performance of the reform, it is quite possible to ignore some important phenomena. Conversely, when intuitive judgment is used, one might see the trees but not the forest. The second possible explanation might be psychological. Chinese economists are "forward looking"; they compare today's situation with the ideal model in their minds, and they are unhappy whenever they find undesirable gaps between reality and ideality. In contrast, foreign economists are "backward looking," comparing today's situation with the past. They are happy whenever they find that today is better than yesterday.

Certainly, that explanation cannot be the whole story. The most important question is, what criteria should one use in evaluating the SOE reform? For China's SOEs, both TFP and profitability are heavily distorted indictors (but TFP is better than profit). In my view, the proper criterion should be "qualitative." "Corporate governance" is such a candidate. Corporate governance is a concept characterizing the contractual relation between different members of the firm. It is structured for solving the two basic problems inherent within the firm: (a) the incentive problem—that is, how to motivate all participants of the firm to contribute to the firm's output, given that output is a collective outcome and individual contribution is hard to measure—and (b) the management selection problem—that is, what kind of mechanism can ensure that only the most entrepreneurial people are employed to fill the management position, given that entrepreneurial ability is hard to observe?

From the point of view of corporate governance, my basic argument is that China's SOE reform has been relatively successful in solving the short-term managerial incentive problem, but more important, it has been unsuccessful in solving the management selection mechanism and the long-term managerial incentive problem. Specifically, the variety of reform measures adopted since 1978 (basically the management contracting system) has provided the incumbent managers of SOEs with moderate incentives to make short-term profits, but the authority of selecting management is still held by the Communist Party's personnel departments and the industrial bureaucracy, which have inadequate incentives—and also lack the information—to find and to appoint entrepreneurial people for managerial positions. The fundamental reason is that bureaucrats, unlike their capitalist counterparts, do not assume risks for their selections.[3] For that reason, managerial tenure depends little on the performance of the enterprise, which, in turn, eliminates the manager's long-term incentives to run the enterprise efficiently. In addition, state-owned banks have neither the incentive nor the ability to enforce debt contracts. To solve the management selection problem and the long-term managerial incentive problem, the authority of selecting management must be transferred from bureaucrats to capitalists. Such a move calls for the privatization of both state enterprises and state banks.

This chapter is organized into three sections. The first section provides a theoretical framework of corporate governance and discusses how management is selected and disciplined by shareholders and debt holders in the capitalist firm. The second section discusses how successful or unsuccessful China's SOE reform has been in solving both the managerial incentive problem and the management selection problem. I provide a number of explanations for why neither the management contract system nor state-dominated corporatization can achieve their assumed goals, as well as why bankruptcy has failed to play an effective role in disciplining SOE managers, from a corporate governance perspective. The third section points to new developments in SOE reform—that is, ongoing privatization of state-owned enterprises.

Analytical Framework: What Does Corporate Governance Do in a Capitalist Firm?

The Origin of the Classical Capitalist Firm and Capital-Hiring-Labor

The best way to understand the problems facing SOEs is to begin with the origin of the capitalist firm and its contractual structure.

The firm is a collaboration of different participants (factor owners). From the point of view of function, all participants can be grouped into three types: (a) the marketing member, (b) the producing members, and (c) the capitalists. The marketing member decides "what to do and how do it"[4] or "how to discover the relative prices,"[5] the producing members execute those decisions by physically transforming inputs into outputs, and the capitalists finance decisions made by the marketing member.

Because of alienability of physical capital, the capitalists may not stand by their capital and therefore can be "outside members." In contrast, both the marketing member and the producing members are always "inside members." A necessary condition for a capitalist to be an insider is that he or she also works either as the marketing member or as a producing member. In other words, an inside capitalist must perform dual functions. For obvious reasons, I often refer to the marketing member as the "decisionmaker" and the rights to undertake marketing as "decision rights."

The importance of marketing comes from the uncertainty facing the firm.[6] In fact, without uncertainty, the firm would be unnecessary. Uncertainty makes marketing or decisionmaking play the dominant role in determining the return of the firm. The firm is more likely to go bankrupt when it produces a "wrong" product at a low cost than when it produces a "right" one at a high cost. Ability to make decisions is commonly referred to as "entrepreneurial ability." Although everyone may possess some entrepreneurial ability, individuals obviously differ in their entrepreneurial ability. This dissimilarity is so not just because different people face different costs of collecting and processing information but primarily because entrepreneurial ability greatly depends on the individual's "alertness" (Israel M. Kirzner), "imagination" (George L. S. Shackle), and "judgment" (Mark Casson). All those personal characteristics are at least partially *innate* and *uneducable*. The optimum requires that marketing or decision rights should be assigned to the person who has the highest entrepreneurial ability. However, the problem is that, unlike capital, entrepreneurial ability is not easy to observe. Given that constraint, for the firm to survive and to be profitable, there must be a mechanism to ensure that only a sufficiently (if not the most) qualified person will be the marketing member. That is the "management selection problem."

The dominance of the marketing member does not mean that the producing members and capitalists are irrelevant or unimportant. The return to the firm is a joint stochastic outcome of actions and services supplied by all members. Because of uncertainty and teamwork, it is impossible to reward all members with fixed contractual payments corresponding to their respective contributions to the total return.[7] And that lack of certainty creates an incentive problem: some party may take an action (e.g., shirking) that benefits himself or herself but that costs others. To deal with this problem, the firm must have a mechanism that will make each member as responsible for personal actions as possible. That is the "incentive problem."

Those two problems are interrelated because the return to the firm is jointly determined by both ability and actions. The observed organizational structure of the capitalist firm can be understood as an optimal response to those two problems.[8] Briefly speaking, the two problems are solved by assigning a *principalship*. Here, "principalship" is defined by residual claimancy and control rights. As the term suggests, the residual claim is an entitlement to claim the residual (total return minus contractual payments). Control rights, roughly speaking, refer to the rights of selecting and monitoring other agents.[9]

From the incentive point of view, the residual claim should be assigned to the marketing member, not only because the marketing member plays the dominant role in determining the residual, but also because that specific member's behavior is more difficult to monitor than that of others (asymmetry of monitoring).[10] The dominance role implies that the loss of the marketing member's incentive is more costly than that of any other members' incentives: therefore, it pays to sacrifice the latter for the former. The asymmetry of monitoring implies that assigning the residual to the marketing member will incur much less "aggregated" incentive losses.[11] The two factors together ensure that when the marketing member is the residual claimant, the welfare loss is lower than when the producing members are the residual claimants. Thus, the marketing member becomes the "entrepreneur," and the producing members become "workers."[12]

However, given that entrepreneurial ability is not easily observable, free choice of occupation implies that many unqualified people would claim to be entrepreneurial. The reason is as follows: Because of the limited liability (more generally, the nonnegative consumption) constraint, the low-bound net residual—and, therefore, the net expected return of being an entrepreneur instead of being a worker—is higher when one's personal wealth is low rather than high. That finding implies that someone with lower personal wealth is more likely to overreport his entrepreneurial ability than is someone with high personal wealth. In other words, insofar as entrepreneurial ability is concerned, the rich are more likely to be honest and credible when they choose to be entrepreneurs.

Priority in being the entrepreneur is given to capitalists because the choice of the rich is more informative than the choice of the poor in the sense of signaling entrepreneurial ability. That priority legitimizes the institutional characteristics of the classical capitalist firm: an entrepreneur is also a capitalist, and the residual becomes profit of capital. Thus, the observed capital-hiring-labor can be understood as the "self-selection" mechanism of entrepreneurship. Under such a mechanism, only those high-ability, would-be entrepreneurs can become actual entrepreneurs.

The Origin of the Joint Stock Company and Functions of Corporate Governance

The preceding discussion shows that the function of capital-hiring-labor is to exclude inferior candidates from entrepreneurship. However, the capital constraint is double-edged. Because the distribution of ability and the distribution of personal wealth in the population are in effect the same, liquidity constraints also exclude those with high ability but minimal assets from being entrepreneurs. Conversely, the capital owned by high-ability people earns its factor price plus a pure profit (rent) from signaling, whereas the capital owned by low-ability people can earn only its factor price because they are unable to signal. The implication is that a profitable opportunity exists for collaboration between high-ability, low-capital people and low-ability, high-capital people. Although a rich person with low ability cannot make a profit by marketing directly, he may increase his return by using his capital to signal someone else's ability, if he knows some high-ability people (e.g., his relatives), or if searching for high ability is not too costly.

Moreover, a high-ability person can increase his return if he can convince the rich that he is really good at marketing. Furthermore, the incentive for each party to search for the other is an increasing function of their respective recourses (ability or wealth), because the more personal wealth (or entrepreneurial ability) one has, the more rent one can earn, if searching is successful. As a result, they become *joint* entrepreneurs: the high-ability person is called the manager by doing the marketing, and the rich are called claim holders (shareholders or debt holders by claiming the residual and taking the responsibility for selecting the qualified manager). That is the origin and nature of a joint-stock company.

A joint-stock company as a collaboration between ability and wealth creates several agency-type problems, however. First, because of imperfect observation as well as the time-consuming process of uncovering ability, a capitalist inevitably makes some mistakes in selecting a manager. Someone who initially appears to have high ability may prove to be a "lemon" as the collaboration proceeds! If that happens, the capitalist should be given a chance to correct his mistake (of course, correcting the mistake can only minimize, not eliminate, the cost of the mistake; otherwise nobody cares about mistakes). The mistake can also occur the other way: a high-ability manager may be blamed for being a lemon by the capitalist's misjudgment. Because firing a manager usually conveys a problem with ability, the high-ability manager will be unfairly harmed. There should be a mechanism to protect the manager from such mistreatment.

Second, because of the major importance and poor monitoring ability of managerial activities, there is a serious incentive problem on the manager side. That finding suggests that managers should be motivated by some effective incentive mechanism. Third, when the capitalist is an outside member of the firm, capital itself is more vulnerable to abuse.[13] In addition, the revenue may not be verifiable for outsiders so that it might be consumed as perks or invested in unprofitable projects by the manager rather than paid out to investors. Because abuse of capital and misuse of revenue can benefit the manager in various ways, it is necessary for the capitalist to have some voice regarding the use of funds.

Fourth, when capital demand is high, investors will be diversified. That diversification creates an incentive problem of monitoring on the capitalist side because the cost of monitoring is concentrated, whereas the benefit of monitoring is spread. There should be some mechanism to mitigate this free-rider problem. Corporate governance is assumed to be such a mechanism to address all the agency problems within a joint-stock company. It governs relationships between different factor owners of the firm—in particular, between capitalists and managers through allocation of residual claim and control rights by both explicit and implicit contracts.[14]

What is an efficient corporate governance system? Economists have reached the following conclusions:

First and most fundamental, the residual claim and the control rights should be matched as well as possible; that is, whoever has claim to the residual and assumes risks should also have rights to control. Conversely, whoever has rights to control should assume risks. Frank Knight might be the first economist arguing for such a match.[15] More recently, Harris and Raviv argue that the claim residual should match the rights to control (voting rights), because otherwise "cheap voting rights" would lead to unqualified people being more likely to take over control of the firm.[16] Dewatripont and Tirole argue that residual claim is an incentive scheme for controlling parties to take appropriate action.[17] Of course, a full match of residual claim and control rights is impossible; otherwise, there would be no agency problem.

Second, managerial compensation should be more closely linked to the firm's performance, rather than fixed by contract. In other words, the manager should assume some risks! That argument has been well discussed in the literature of principal-agent theory.[18] In fact, this argument can be taken as a corollary of the first argument because, by his functioning as the marketing member, the manager holds "natural" control rights of business decisions and, therefore, must be motivated by residual sharing, given that his actions are difficult to monitor and to contract for. In particular, to motivate the manager to improve the long-term productivity of the firm—not just to increase total sales revenue and current profits—managerial compensation should be tied more strongly to long-term stock price performance. In particular, it is desirable for the manager to hold a considerable stake in the firm as an inside owner, because only by so doing can the manager's interests be more concurrent with the outside shareholder's interests.[19]

Third, as discussed earlier, the authority of selecting and monitoring management should be assigned to capitalists.[20] This argument can also be taken as a corollary of the first argument, because, by nature, capitalists are inevitably the eventual risk bearers. Only they have adequate incentives to select good managers, dismiss bad managers, and monitor managerial performance.

Fourth, the optimal corporate governance should be characterized by a state-contingent control structure; that is, the control rights should be contingent on the state of nature such that different claim holders control the firm in different states.[21] The reasoning is that in a world of incomplete contracts, only state-contingent control can best generate (partial) manager–claim holder congruence. In particular, Dewatripont and Tirole argue that (a) because of contractual incompleteness, monetary incentive schemes based on firm profitability are not sufficient to discipline managers, and endowing outsiders with control rights is desirable because they can take actions managers like (or dislike) after good (or bad) firm performance; (b) the firm's outsiders must be given incentive schemes in the form of securities to intervene appropriately in the firm; (c) the firm's managers should be rewarded by low outsider interference when performing well, and they should be punished by substantial outside involvement when performing poorly; and, therefore, (d) under some conditions, control should be given to equity holders when the firm does well and to debt holders in harsher times because the equity holders are more passive than are the debt holders about intervening in the firm.[22]

Fifth, to mitigate the free-rider problem of investors, one should prefer concentration of ownership with large investors.[23] When control rights are concentrated in the hands of a small number of investors with a collectively large cash flow stake, concerted actions by investors are much easier than when control rights, such as votes, are split among many of them. Concentration can take several distinct forms, including large shareholders, takeovers, and large creditors. A substantial minority shareholder has the incentive to collect information and to monitor the management, therefore avoiding the free-rider problem. That person also has enough voting control to put pressure on the management in some cases—or even to oust the management through a proxy fight or a takeover.[24] Large shareholders thus address the agency problem in that they have both a general interest in maximization and enough control over the assets of the firm to have their interests respected. Similarly, by combining substantial cash flow rights with the ability to interfere in the major decisions of the firm, large creditors can also discipline the management more effectively through their contingent control rights than can small creditors.[25]

Capital Structure and the Bankruptcy Mechanism

Both in theory and in practice, capital structure is one of the most important aspects of corporate governance. Efficiency and effectiveness of a corporate governance system rely greatly on capital structure, because shareholders and debt holders differ in both control rights and cash flows. They are "state-contingent owners" of the firm in different states. When the firm is solvent, shareholders are owners: they claim residual and control management, whereas debt holders are only contractual return claimants. However, when the firm is insolvent, debt holders take over control of the firm from shareholders. Because the switching point of control is determined by capital structure and because shareholders and debt holders exercise their respective control rights differently, capital structure has important implications for managerial behavior. The optimal capital structure is one that can most effectively solve both the managerial incentive problem and the management selection problem.

It is widely recognized that board of director control ("voting with hands") and the stock market ("voting with feet") are two major mechanisms through which shareholders exercise their control rights to deal with managerial agency problems. They are complementary but also substitutable. On the one hand, the decision to replace the incumbent by "voting with hands" is generally made according to the score from "voting with feet." On the other hand, an efficient stock market surely makes direct control less important. That is analogous to frequent police patrols making the prisons less crowded! In reality, which mechanism is more important depends on the level of development of stock markets as well as the concentration of shareholding. For instance, in the United States and Britain where stock markets are well developed and ownership is very diversified, takeover through stock markets plays a more active role than in Germany and Japan where stock markets are less developed and ownership is more concentrated.[26]

Although shareholders have the ultimate control over the manager when the firm is solvent, the control rights shift to debt holders when the firm becomes insolvent. The rationale for that shift is that in the latter case debt holders become de facto residual claimants and thus are better motivated to make adequate decisions. In general, debt holders' control is harsher for the manager than is shareholders' control, because the incumbent is more likely to lose his job in the case of debt holders' control than in the case of shareholders' control. For that reason, debt can serve better to discipline the manager.[27]

Because of the collective action problem of debt holders, debt holders' control is usually conducted and governed through a legally provided bankruptcy procedure.[28] Most bankruptcy laws in developed economies offer two options for debtholders' control of the insolvent firm: liquidation or reorganization. Liquidation means, in most cases, that the firm is dissolved, and its assets are sold piecemeal; sometimes, however, the firm is sold as a going concern. Whichever occurs, the proceeds of the sale are divided among debt holders according to fixed priority rules determined by law (usually, secured debt first, then various priority claims, followed by unsecured debts, then subordinate debts, and finally equity), and the incumbent manager loses his job.

Reorganization is a process through which the claim holders negotiate on whether and how to restructure the debtor firm's liabilities and assets, possibly with the objective of maintaining the company as a going concern. The restructuring of liabilities typically entails the exchange of debt for equity, extension of maturity, reductions in principal and interest, and injection of new capital. Asset restructuring may involve divesting unproductive units, eliminating unprofitable product lines, introducing new managerial practices, changing marketing orientations, and adopting more appropriate production technologies. Reorganization of the insolvent firm may also involve replacing the management team. But in general, the probability that the incumbent keeps his job is higher with reorganization than with liquidation. For that reason, liquidation is harsher for the manager than reorganization.

The choice between liquidation and reorganization often depends on the concentration of debt holders because of the transaction cost problem. If debts are more concentrated in the hands of a few large debt holders (such as banks), reorganization is more likely to occur; otherwise, liquidation is more likely.

Bankruptcy can result from the manager's incompetence, from managerial slack, or from some exogenous shock beyond the manager's control. No matter the reason, in many cases, the firm is worth more as a going concern after reorganization than if it is sold piecemeal. Thus, *ex post* efficiency might call for retaining the incumbent management of a bankrupt company. However, if one anticipates that approach, management might have little incentive to avoid bankruptcy, and an incompetent manager might not be replaced promptly, given that the exact reason for bankruptcy is not easy to identify. The optimal bankruptcy procedure must balance between realizing *ex post* efficiency and *ex ante* disciplining management.[29]

Although our discussion of the creditor's control has focused on bankruptcy, debt financing can mitigate the managerial agency problem in various other ways. For instance, debts (a) force the manager to pay out funds to investors rather than to himself or herself, (b) force the sale of unproductive assets, and (c) limit the manager's ability to make unprofitable—but power-enhancing—investments.[30] By triggering the investigation when debtors default on debt payments or when the firm needs to refinance overdue debts, debt contracts help reveal information about the firm so that investors can better monitor and discipline the manager.[31]

It should be pointed out that the capital market and bankruptcy are mechanisms not only for disciplining management but also for constraining capitalists' behavior. For instance, transferability of shares ensures that the capitalist can easily correct mistakes in judging the manager's ability, while inability to withdraw real capital can protect the high-ability manager from unfair harm by an individual shareholder's misplaced blame. The market valuation of stocks considers not only the performance of the manager, but also the performance of the shareholders. The replacement of management is often preceded by the replacement of the shareholders; the shareholders are harmed before the manager. Similarly, debt contracts, on the one hand, restrain the debt holders from intervening in management in good times and, on the other hand, punish the debt holders for lending to the wrong people (entrepreneurs or managers) and for financing the wrong projects. After all, the capitalists are the ones who take responsibility for selecting and disciplining managers. If they do not pay for their careless mistakes, who will?

Summary

In this section, I have presented an analytical framework of what corporate governance does in a capitalist firm. I argued that corporate governance is a mechanism that is assumed to address both the managerial incentive problem and the management selection problem through the allocation of residual claim and control rights. In particular, capitalists' control is crucial for selecting the most entrepreneurial people for managerial positions, as well as for motivating and disciplining managers because, as "natural" risk bearers, only they have adequate incentives to select good managers, replace bad managers, and monitor managerial performance (either as shareholders or as debt holders).

Given that the existing literature almost exclusively focuses on the managerial incentive problem and the role of capitalists in disciplining management, I have emphasized that the management selection problem and the function played by capitalists in selecting high-ability management might be more important for efficient corporate governance of the firm. After all, everyone can be motivated to work hard by proper incentive schemes, but only a small fraction of the population is qualified for entrepreneurship and management. From the point of view of resource allocation efficiency, a hard-working but less competent manager is definitely worse than a highly competent but more discretionary manager. In the next section, we will apply that framework to analyze SOE reform in China.

Evaluation of the State-Owned Enterprise Reform in China

Introduction: Are Most Serious Agency Problems of SOEs on the Side of Government Bureaucrats?

The most distinct feature of SOEs in relation to capitalist firms is that, by definition, the role of principal in state-owned enterprises is played by the "state" (government) rather than by natural capitalists: it is the government that appoints, motivates, and disciplines managers and that finances firms' projects. That feature has substantial implications for the enterprises' corporate governance. First, it implies that the investor in the firm is a total outsider and that inside ownership does not exist. Because the owner is far from the management team and the manager has no stake in the firm, the agency problem of SOEs on the management side is potentially far more serious than that of any capitalist firm where the CEO normally holds a considerable stake and is, therefore, an inside owner.

Second, because the state (or government) is a pseudoplayer rather than a physical entity, principalship of the state has to be delegated to and exercised by government bureaucrats through a hierarchical structure.[32] Bureaucrats hold the de facto extremely concentrated control rights of the firm under the name of the state, but they are not residual claimants (at least in a legal sense) because the residual belongs to the state; that is, control rights are separated from residual claim in the first place. Moreover, those bureaucrats typically have goals that are different from social welfare and that are dictated by their own political and economic interests. That situation creates another agency problem: how to motivate and monitor bureaucrats in order for them to behave like capitalists in selecting, disciplining, and motivating management. In any realistic sense, this second agency problem is far more serious than the first.[33] For that reason, many Chinese economists have concluded that the problem of SOEs is mainly that of the principal rather than that of agents.[34]

During the pre-reform period (before 1979), both the residual claim and control rights of state-owned enterprises in China were almost completely held by the governments (in most cases, at the central and provincial levels). The entire economy of the state sector was organized like one giant company with almost all decisions for production, investments, and employment centrally planned.[35] Revenue and cost budgets were also centralized by the state treasurer. The so-called enterprise was nothing but a production plant. The enterprise had a director but no "manager" in the sense of business decisions; the director (normally the party secretary) was nothing more than a special worker, whose main task was to coordinate and supervise ordinary workers in implementing the government-made production plan, rather than marketing. All inside members of the enterprise were compensated through a centrally set hierarchical wage–fringe benefit system, which was little related to firm performance. If anyone had incentives to improve the economy, it was the central government leaders and top bureaucrats because they were virtually the partial residual claimants (both politically and economically, as well as legally and illegally).[36]

The benefit of central planning was that the agency problem of managerial theft and expropriation of funds at the firm level was tightly restricted because management had little freedom to make discretionary decisions. However, the cost was the loss of both resource allocation efficiency and managerial incentives to improve production efficiency and technology efficiency, which also caused a serious agency problem of bureaucrats.[37]

The Chinese SOE reform first introduced in 1979 can be characterized as a continuously evolving process of shifting decision rights and residual claims from the government to the firm level. The reform started with no intention of abolishing state ownership. Rather, it was intended to improve efficiency within state ownership. Nevertheless, reform has been directed by a doctrine that potentially conflicts with the conventional doctrine of state ownership. I call this new doctrine the "reform doctrine," according to which, both the decision rights and the residual claim should be shifted to the inside members of the firm (i.e., the manager and workers).

The argument for shifting the decision rights to the manager of the firm draws on the assumption that decisions made at the firm level are more efficient than decisions made at the central agent level because of the information and communication problem. The theoretical legitimacy of this assumption dates back to Hayek, whereas Chinese economists' argument draws mainly on the observed poor performance of the traditional centralized planning system. The argument for shifting the residual claim to inside members of the firm focuses on incentive considerations. Although the modern theory of incentives was introduced into China much later, the pre-reform Chinese experience seems sufficient for both Chinese economists and reform-minded leaders to understand how essential the incentive system is for economic performance, although it has come much later for them to understand that the incentive system depends primarily on property rights and ownership structure.

The reform doctrine can be summarized by a popular official slogan: "The goal of the reform is to make the firm independent, autonomous, and responsible for the profits and losses." If that doctrine were fully implemented, state ownership would no longer exist in any economic sense; the government would be left as nothing more than a bondholder. However, for a long time, economists and practitioners have not thoroughly recognized the inconsistency between the reform doctrine and state ownership. As a result, they are puzzled by the fact that, on the one hand, bureaucrats still enjoy considerable administrative intervention in the firm even after more than a decade of reform, and, on the other hand, the economy suffers from managerial insider control.[38]

In practice, shifting decision rights and residual claim has been conducted through various policies. In the early stage of reform, the basic policy was *fangquan rangli* (granting autonomy and sharing profit). From 1986 to the early 1990s, the dominant policy was the management contract system. In 1994, the state-dominated corporatization of SOEs was officially adopted as a substitute for the management contract system. In the remaining part of this section, I will analyze the effect of the management contract system (analysis applies to the policy of *fangquan rangli*) and then will give a personal view of corporatization policy. Finally, I will discuss why changes in the financial structure of SOEs and bankruptcy have failed to play a role in disciplining managers. As pointed out in this chapter's introduction, from a corporate governance perspective, my basic argument is that China's SEO reform has been relatively successful in solving the short-term incentive problem, but it has failed to solve the long-term managerial incentive problem and the management selection problem. Those two problems cannot be solved without a fundamental change of ownership.

How Has the Management Contract System Improved the Short-Term Managerial Incentive?

The management contract system evolved from, and was viewed as a remedy for, the early and loosely defined administrative policy of *fangquan rangli* because, as often claimed, *fangquan rangli* granted managers autonomy but failed to bond them with responsibility. It is not easy to identify where and when the first contract came into existence. We do know that the management contract system was initiated by local governments, and it spread nationwide after 1987 following the State Council's "Decisions on Deepening Enterprise Reform and Invigorating Enterprises" announced in December 1986. By 1989, a large majority of SOEs had adopted the management contract system.[39]

The management contract system has various names in China: the profit (or loss) contracts, the factory management responsibility system, the asset responsibility system, and the system of leasing contracts. The basic content of the management contact system was to set profit-sharing rules and to delimit decision rights through contracts negotiated by the firm and the group of government agencies (normally including the line department and financial department; sometimes contracts are signed directly between management and mayors). The contract normally lasted for three to four years. The details of contracts varied across enterprises, regions, and industrial sectors.

The following are commonly identified as typical contract forms: (a) the increasing profit remittance contract (*shangjiao lirun dizheng baogan*), which involves base profit remittance plus a preset annual increasing rate; (b) the fixed-profit remittance contract (*shangjiao lirun dinge baogan*), in which the firm retains all extra profit after fulfilling the fixed remittance target; (c) the base profit remittance with above-target profit sharing (*shangjiao lirun jishu baogan, chaoe fencheng*); (d) the loss reduction (or fixed subsidy) contract for loss

214

makers (*kuishun qiyi jiankui/butie baogan*); (e) the enterprise management responsibility contract (*qiyi jingying zerenzhi*), which normally sets the total profit target and profit growth rate; (f) the asset responsibility contract (*zhichan jingying zerenzhi*), in which the main targets are asset preservation and enhancing; and (g) the profit and tax guarantee contract (*liangbao yigua zhonghe chengbao*), in which total wages are linked to the realized profit and tax).

Typically, all contracts contain indicators of profit and tax target, use of retained profits, debt repayments, asset appreciation, product and technology innovation, product quality improvement, and enterprise rating. In some cases, contracts also include output target, product cost target, and even fulfillment of the state plan. However, in most cases, only profit targets are weakly enforceable, and other terms can be taken only as references. It should also be pointed out that in many cases, the contracts differ only in name rather than in content.[40]

From that description, we see that the management contract system deals mainly with residual sharing. Under the management contract system, the firm obtains a considerable residual share of current profits. According to a survey conducted by the Institute of Economics at the China Academy of Social Science, marginal profit retention rates steadily increased over the 1980s, rising from a mean (across firms) of 24 percent in 1980 to a mean of 63 percent in 1989 (see Figure 11.1).[41] However, it should be pointed out that only a tiny fraction of the retained profit legally accrues to the management team.

From the viewpoint of decision rights, the management contract system has an *enabling feature* in the sense that management's autonomy is restricted by government intervention mainly from other sources rather than from the contract per se. Although suffering from considerable administrative intervention—through the management contract system, together with other reform policies, such as price liberalization and output plan reduction—managers have gradually obtained considerable decision rights. Table 11.1 presents details of the realization of managerial decision rights.[42]

From the viewpoint of incentives, although suffering from the renegotiation problem and the ratchet effect, the management contract system does provide relatively strong incentives for managers to make short-term profits. As I argued in early articles,[43] under the management contract system, two kinds of incentives work for managers: (a) formal and explicit and (b) informal and implicit. The

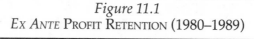

Figure 11.1
EX ANTE PROFIT RETENTION (1980–1989)

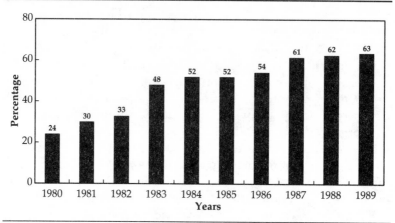

SOURCE: Theodore Groves, Hong Yongmiao, John McMillan, and Barry Naughton, "Autonomy and Incentives in Chinese State Enterprises," *Quarterly Journal of Economics* 109, no. 1 (1994): 202–6.

formal and explicit incentive comes from the fact that managers (and workers) can legally claim part of the residual according to the signed contract. Granting autonomy of business decisions makes the manager a natural holder of some control rights. By granting the manager a partial residual, the residual claim and control right can be better matched at the firm level. Such better matching certainly better motivates the manager to make profits.[44]

However, given that ownership is absent, and the manager has little stake in the firm, managerial autonomy has also generated various agency-type problems, including profit diversion and asset stripping. Those agency problems are often referred to as "insider control" problems.[45] Such problems arise partly because the government has inadequate information for monitoring the firm but, more important, because the bureaucrats concerned have no incentive to do otherwise. In many cases, managers collude with bureaucrats in cheating the state.

Nevertheless, in contrast to the conventional wisdom that managerial discretion is harmful to firm performance, I argue that, in

Table 11.1
REALIZATION OF ENTERPRISE AUTONOMY (PERCENTAGE)

Decision Rights	1993	1994	1995
Production decisions	88.7	94.0	97.3
Pricing decisions	75.9	73.6	85.4
Sale decisions	88.5	90.5	95.9
Purchase decisions	90.9	95.0	97.8
Export and import decisions	15.3	25.8	41.3
Investment decisions	38.9	61.2	72.8
Use of retained funds	63.7	73.8	88.3
Disposal of assets	29.4	46.6	68.2
Joint ventures and mergers	23.3	39.7	59.7
Hiring and firing of labor	43.5	61.0	74.8
Personnel decisions	53.7	73.3	74.8
Wages and bonuses	70.2	86.0	93.1
Internal organization design	79.3	90.5	94.4
Refusal of proration	7.0	10.3	17.4

SOURCE: Survey results of 2,752 managers by China Entrepreneurs Survey System, quoted from *Almanac of China's Economy 1996*.
NOTE: The sample consists of 72.9 percent state-owned enterprises, 12.8 percent collective enterprises, 7.4 percent joint ventures, and 6.9 percent other enterprises (including private). Therefore, the indicators overestimate the realization of autonomy for state-owned enterprises.

SOEs—at least in Chinese SOEs—insider control might do more good than harm. Given that there is no natural owner to motivate the manager and that the residual that managers can legally claim is tiny,[46] how can those most important but least monitorable people be motivated to work harder? It is the illegal expropriation of profits that motivates them to work harder. In other words, given the *ex ante* inefficient ownership structure, the insider control can be an *ex post* efficient remedy. It can be a Pareto improvement because, unlike in a capitalist firm, nobody is made worse off, but management becomes better off. Thus, I call it the "informal and implicit incentive."[47]

The informal and implicit incentive exists because, by manipulating accounts ("hiding profit") and stripping assets, managers can illegally but safely claim more virtual residual than specified in the contract. Hiding profits and stripping assets are possible because managers possess more autonomy in decisionmaking, making it very hard for the state to have judicial and administrative checks on their behavior. Although managers cannot freely pocket the money, they have many ways to spend it. The pervasive phenomena of drinking foreign wines, feasting, and indulging in karaoke, prostitution, and gambling that we see among managers are all reflections of a de facto claim to the residual.

Typical forms of hiding profits and stripping assets include (a) setting up independent or so-called subsidiary companies with little government control,[48] (b) making investment in and transferring profit through sales or purchasing prices to those companies, (c) putting all perks into costs calculations, (d) diverting profits to private or quasi-private accounts (*xiao jinku*), (e) inviting relatives and friends to banquets and holidays, and (f) purchasing luxury cars. All those tactics might be called implicit privatization. As a result, the correlation between personal benefit and total "real" profit is much stronger than official statistics show and the formal contract allows.

Casual observation suggests that managers of better-performing firms have a much more luxurious life than do those of poor performers. This strong correlation has greatly improved managerial incentive to make profits, although it has negative effects as well. I bet that without implicit privatization, Chinese SOEs on the whole would have performed much worse.[49]

"Delivering good news" was a dominant strategy in pre-reform China. But now the fashion has changed. Today, China's SOEs have strong incentives to deliver "bad news." Although some loss makers still overreport, most state enterprises underreport profits, because reported profits belong to the state, whereas hidden profits accrue to management.[50] Underreporting can partially explain why the statistically reported profit index of the SOEs is so discouraging. It suggests that the actual financial situation of SOEs is much better than statistics show. If that were not the case, one could hardly understand why both goods and service markets are so bullish in China.

Using accounting profits to judge the performance of Chinese SOEs is very misleading. After all, when the firm manager can manipulate accounting statements, accounting profits are nothing more than a ledger number. Apart from underreporting profits, profits fall for three more reasons. The first is competition between the non-state and the state sectors, as well as among the SOEs, which has destroyed monopoly profit.[51] In this sense, the fall in profit is good news because it signals more efficient allocation of resources.

The second reason is the change in financial structure. The debt–asset ratio of all industrial SOEs was raised from 18.7 percent in 1980 to about 67.9 percent in 1994.[52] That change converted the previous profits into financial costs. The third reason is "profit-tax conversion," which also converted profits into costs (taxes). Therefore, profits are a very misleading indicator for SOE performance.

Those theoretical predictions are consistent with recent empirical studies. For instance, Hayashi and Wada find that, in a sample of 796 SOEs from 1991 to 1995, the ratio of production costs to sales changed little, but both administrative costs and financial costs increased by large amounts.[53] Their finding suggests that profits of SOEs are eroded mainly by administrative costs and financial costs. I speculate that much of the increase in administrative costs comes from management's expropriation of real profits.[54]

However, although the reform has improved management's incentive to make current profits, the long-term incentive problem has yet to be solved. Casual observation suggests that managers of SOEs prefer to distribute retained profits to employees or to invest in quick revenue-generating projects, rather than investing in long-term productivity-enhancing projects and research and development.[55] In many cases, abnormal short-term profits are made at the great expense of long-term productivity.[56] Asset stripping is also harmful to long-term growth. The problem becomes particularly serious as managers approach retirement age.[57]

The reason for management myopia is that, because no personal capital is at stake, the manager's enjoyment of benefits from the firm cannot stretch beyond his tenure. Managers are very uncertain of whether they will still hold the position even the next year.[58] Their tenure with the firm primarily depends on bureaucratic preferences that are little related to firm performance.

Let us now address the management selection problem. Although I argue that the reform has greatly improved the short-term managerial incentive mechanism, a fundamental problem has not been solved for Chinese SOEs, that is, selection of high-ability managers. The reason is that SOE managers are appointed by government bureaucrats rather than by capitalists.[59] That fact has important implications.

First, because of the adverse selection problem, selecting good managers is hard work. It requires that selectors must have adequate incentives to learn about candidates' abilities and to install high-quality candidates. Adverse selection is most serious in China because, with no personal stake to signal ability, too many people pretend that they are qualified for management. But worse is that bureaucrats, unlike capitalists, have the right to select, but they do not bear the consequences of their selections. That fact implies that not only would-be managers but also bureaucrats themselves have the adverse selection problem. They have no adequate incentive to search for good managers; even if they know some candidates are capable, they still lack adequate incentive to appoint them. Observation suggests that bureaucrats too often base their selections on personal connections (*guanxi*) rather than on merits. Appointing friendly managers is the most effective way for bureaucrats to rent-seek.[60]

Second, in contrast to the capitalist firm where the manager tries to become a capitalist, SOE managers too often try for promotion to bureaucrats. They do so because as long as bureaucrats appoint managers, the bureaucrats are always in the superior position, and promotion to bureaucrat is a manager's best reward. As a result, SOE managers behave more like professional bureaucrats than professional managers. For managers, the firm is nothing more than a springboard for becoming bureaucrats. That attitude induces managers to care only for short-term and easily measured performance, and it also explains why many "excellent" firms fail once their managers are promoted to government.

Third, with bureaucrats selecting management, good performers are just as likely to be removed as bad performers, if not more. For that reason, once a firm becomes highly profitable, bureaucrats have every incentive to collect rents by replacing the incumbent with their preference. Thus, the best way for the incumbents to secure their position is to make sure the firm is not too good and not too bad.[61]

Empirical investigations strongly support the preceding theoretical arguments. A survey by the China Entrepreneurs Survey System found that 67.3 percent of the managers pay their "first concern" to their bureaucratic superiors' evaluations.[62] Since 1987, the Chinese Entrepreneur Association has conducted the nationwide "Excellent Entrepreneurs (Managers) Assessment," and every year, 20 SOE managers are selected as Golden Globe Winners. According to *China Entrepreneur Magazine*,[63] by the end of 1997, only 4 of the first 20 winners were still managing at their original enterprises. Among the other 16, 3 had been promoted to government, 5 had retired at the normal age, 4 had been dismissed, 1 had escaped to the Philippines after diverting assets, and 1 had died from illness. The 159 winners (up to 1995) followed a roughly similar pattern. Those still in the position are very worried about their future. This phenomenon of "good managers are short-lived" has attracted much attention among academics and managers.[64]

I do not deny that the quality of SOE managers has made some progress compared with the pre-reform period. From the early 1980s, the government tried to strengthen managerial quality by setting some "hard criteria," such as education level and age, for management qualification.[65] As a result, the average education level of SOE managers has increased.[66] In addition, competition has also made the managers more market oriented in making their production decisions. However, as we all know, managerial capability is far beyond being measured by any hard indictors, let alone that, in China, even hard indicators can be manipulated.[67] It is most important to provide selectors with good incentives to find good managers case by case; otherwise, even the hard criteria can be misused to exclude good managers (as in the example cited in note 61).

Can the State-Dominated Corporatization Solve the Management Selection Problem?

The management contract system–dominated reform has revealed that state-owned enterprises are confronted with a fundamental dilemma. On the one hand, when the government controls the enterprises, managers have no incentive and little autonomy to make efficient decisions. On the other hand, when the government loses its control, the insiders' control generates enormous agency problems. This dilemma makes it impossible to separate governments from enterprise business in any practical sense. Even worse, with this dilemma, bureaucrats enjoy considerable administrative freedom to intervene in the management for their own interests rather than the state's interest. The state sector has evolved into one characterized by insider control under administrative intervention.[68]

Having recognized that this fundamental dilemma could not be solved by the management contract system in a traditional way, some economists proposed the "state shareholding system" as an alternative as early as 1984. The assumption was that the dilemma is rooted in integration of the owner-government with the regulator-government. Therefore, as long as the owner-government was separated from the regulator-government—so that the only role for the owner-government was that of stockholder—all the problems could be solved.[69]

The basic framework of the state shareholding system can be described as a multitiered network structure. On the top is a national state asset management committee (NSAMC), established by the People's Congress or the State Council; the NSAMC is delegated by the state as the owner of all state-owned enterprises. Below the NSAMC, a number of state asset holding companies (SAHCs) are set up as acting stockholders, each of which holds the stocks of the SOEs and appoints board members and supervisors to the SOEs. Then, the stocks of the SOEs can be traded on stock markets. Within this multitiered structure, SOEs become legal entities with full managerial autonomy over business decisions and corporate assets, and the SAHCs can discipline the managers through both "voting with hands" and "voting with feet," just like in a Western-style market economy.

In practice, many local governments, including Shanghai, Shenzhen, and Beijing, have established such multitiered networks within their jurisdictions in the past few years. In all three cases, SAHCs were typically formed either from transforming the original line departments or from upgrading the giant SOEs. In a few cases, SAHCs are completely newly organized entities.[70] Figure 11.2 describes Shanghai's multitiered state asset management system.

Although a systematic implementation of the state shareholding system as described has been delayed at the national level (and may never be implemented), the state-dominated corporatization of individual SOEs has been widespread. The experiment began as early

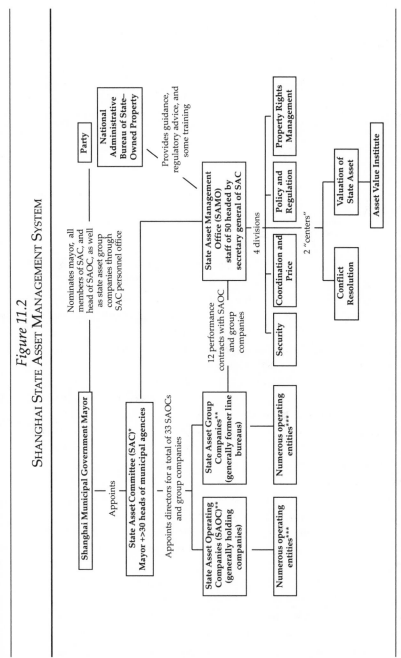

Figure 11.2
SHANGHAI STATE ASSET MANAGEMENT SYSTEM

SOURCE: *China's Management of Enterprise Assets: The State as Shareholder* (Washington: World Bank, 1997).
NOTE: The "operating entities "claim the 14 rights against the holding company group level.
*In Shanghai, 60 percent of its state assets of Shanghai are under this SAC, whereas 30 percent are under management of identical structures at the district level. The remaining assets are not allocated to either.
**Functions include administration of sector, management and operations, and performance supervision. Each SAOC and group is organized vertically on a sector basis.
***Entities at the operating level total more than 15,000.

as 1984. By the end of 1991, there were about 3,220 so-called joint stock experiment companies.[71] In 1991, two local stock exchanges were established in Shanghai and Shenzhen, both of which were later endorsed by the central governments and have now become national stock exchanges. In 1993, the Company Law was enacted, and then the "modern enterprise system" was officially adopted by the Chinese Communist Party Congress as the organizational mode of SOEs. In 1995, the State Council selected 100 large SOEs for corporatization experiments. As of 1996, approximately 5,800 industrial SOEs had been corporatized, some of which are listed on the stock exchanges.[72]

Can the state shareholding system solve the problems of SOEs as assumed? My answer is no. My overall criticism of that approach is that one cannot make a zebra from a black horse simply by painting white stripes on its back.

First, the state shareholding system cannot solve the management selection problem. The reason is that the officers of the NSAMC and SAHCs are still bureaucrats, not capitalists. No matter whether you call them shareholders or managing directors, bureaucrats are bureaucrats, and you cannot turn them into capitalists simply by renaming them. They have rights to select boards of directors and managers of SOEs, but they assume no risk from their selections. Therefore, voting rights in their hands are typical "cheap voting rights."[73] Therefore, they still have no good incentives to find and appoint good managers, and those "lemons" can still easily occupy the management positions by bribing officers of the NSAMC and SAHCs.

We have seen that, although the managers of corporatized SOEs (including those listed companies) are appointed formally by the board of directors, all appointment decisions are still made by the line governments and the Communist Party's personnel departments, let alone that all board members are from government departments or other SOEs. As a result, there has been little fundamental change in corporate governance.

Most Chinese economists agree that it is important to have a managerial labor market, but few realize that markets for managers are essentially capital markets. The key question is this: who is purchasing the services of managers? If government officials are the buyers, then managers have to please government officials, and professional managers will not emerge.

Second, the state shareholding system still cannot separate the government from enterprises. As I pointed out earlier, the proposal of the state shareholding system is made on the assumption that the core nonseparation of the government and enterprises lies in the integration of government as regulator and government as asset owner. Some argue that as long as the regulator is separate from the asset owner—let the State Assets Management Committee represent asset owners and the State Council represent the government—the government will be separated from the enterprises accordingly. Such thinking is very naive. Any owner has to supervise management through control rights. The state as a stockholder (and in most cases the *only* stockholder) will naturally intervene.

The key problem is how to determine the boundary of such intervention. The prevailing theory contains a misconception: a very well-defined division of rights seems to exist among stockholders, the board of directors, and management, and thus everyone clearly knows who should do what. That conclusion is definitely untrue. Of course, part of the relationship among the three parties is well-defined, but much of it is not. Control rights have a public domain in which the tacit understanding determines who should move one step forward and who should move one step back. For instance, according to the Company Law and the corporate charter, the shareholders meeting has the power to make decisions on "important issues." But what constitutes an important issue is moot. Should we call an issue important when a sum of US$5 million or US$10 million is involved in a transaction? For true stockholders or board members who bear the risk of transactions, their decision of whether to intervene depends on how much trust they have in the manager. If they trust the manager, they will not intervene even if the manager is doing something that fundamentally alters the enterprise. If they do not trust the manager, even if the manager is doing something trivial, they may still intervene.

The problem is that the tacit understanding between a real stockholder and management in dealing with the public domain of control rights cannot be duplicated between a state stockholder and the management of SOEs. It is more likely that something important to a real stockholder would be viewed by the state stockholder as trivial, whereas something trivial to a real stockholder would be viewed by the state stockholder as important. The reason is the government official acting as a state stockholder bears no risk. The other possibility is that managers can bribe state stockholders to make them totally cease their intervention. Thus, we will likely constantly shift between excessive administrative intervention and insider control without reaching any real tacit agreement to solve the problem of separating the government from enterprises.

It seems that managers of corporatized SOEs complain more about bureaucratic intervention than they did before. Once the bureaucrats became legal "bosses," they have had legitimate control rights to intervene in the firm. The managers frequently echo that *popo jia laoban* (the government plus the boss) has made the situation worse rather than better.[74]

Third, state shareholding cannot protect state assets from being expropriated by the management. As a stockholder, the state is a legal residual claimant. However, it may not have effective ways to collect residuals. How much residual the state can collect depends not only on the incentives for management to make a profit but also on the firm's financial statement. Because of the problems of hidden actions and hidden information, the state as a residual claimant has to monitor the enterprise if it wants to obtain any residual. The effectiveness of monitoring is determined by two factors: information and incentives.

The modern theory of the firm has proved that monitoring by stockholders requires information that is difficult and costly to obtain. The information collection is often dependent on incentives. How much information you obtain is determined to a large extent on how much incentive you have to collect it. Even dispersed shareholders of a capitalist company often lack adequate incentive to collect information. Given that officers of the NSAMC and of SAHCs are only agents of the state and are not ultimate residual claimants, their incentives to collect information is limited. Moreover, it is very tempting for them to collude with management in expropriating the state assets. Consequently, even if the actual profit is high, the state may be unable to collect it, just as has happened thus far.

In sum, I argue that the state shareholding system as currently proposed and practiced cannot solve the agency problems of state-owned enterprises both on the management side and on the bureaucrat side. The state is not qualified to be a stockholder; at most, it can serve only as a debt holder that comes into control only when the enterprises are insolvent. Because the rights of debt holders are clearer and because violations or abuse of those rights are easier to verify in court, management can be better protected from administrative interventions by bureaucrats, and state assets can be better protected from expropriation by managers. I believe that only when the state is deprived of equity ownership of enterprises can the problems be partially solved.[75]

Why Has Bankruptcy Not Played a Role in Disciplining Management?

Chinese economic reform has made fundamental changes in the corporate finance of state enterprises. In the pre-reform period, state-owned enterprises were almost completely financed through the state budget with few debts. Since the reform, debt finance has gradually taken over budget (equity) finance.[76] The average debt–asset ratio of all industrial SOEs has increased from 18.7 percent in 1980 to 67.9 percent in 1994.[77] The ratio is still rising. In particular, there are many "zero-equity firms." The high debt–asset ratio has resulted for two main reasons: (a) as the distribution of national income has changed, households have overtaken the state as the major source of investment capital, and (b) because direct financing markets are very tightly restricted and underdeveloped, the state banks have become the only channel of funds flowing from households to enterprises.[78]

As a result of debt financing, many SOEs are at the brink of bankruptcy at any time. Although China enacted the Bankruptcy Law in 1986 (which became effective in late 1988), in the early 1990s, few bankruptcy cases were filed compared with tens of thousands of financially distressed firms. Since 1994, bankruptcy cases have dramatically increased, following the central government's initiation of an experimental "capital structure optimization" and specific favored policies designed to enforce the Bankruptcy Law.[79] From 1994 to 1996, 6,753 bankruptcy cases were filed.[80] In addition, there have been many out-of-court resolutions.

Theoretically, when enterprises become insolvent, creditors will take control, and the threat of bankruptcy can discipline the management. Nevertheless, that is not the case in China. Rather, bankruptcy has been widely used by enterprises and local governments as a way to write off debts instead of disciplining managers.[81] After undergoing bankruptcy procedures—either through reorganization or through liquidation—most incumbent managers still run the firms as going concerns; probably the only major difference is that considerable debts have been canceled (and in some cases, the enterprises are renamed). For that reason, managers are more than willing to file for bankruptcy. In contrast, state-owned banks as dominant debt holders have been very passive in dealing with distressed firms. Typically, when debtor firms default, creditor banks passively accommodate them by taking such actions as extending the payment period for loans and capitalizing unpaid interest rather than by pursuing their claims through bankruptcy or other active means. Indeed, banks have filed very few bankruptcies.[82]

Why has bankruptcy not played a role in disciplining managers? There are several reasons. The first is that the debt between state banks and state enterprises is not a real debt in a legal sense. In a legal sense, a debt is a contract between the debtor and the creditor. When the debtor borrows from the creditor, the debtor fully understands that he has an obligation to repay the debt on time; otherwise he will face a bankruptcy penalty. Conversely, the creditor fully realizes that there is some risk of default by the debtor. The terms of the contract are negotiated between the debtor and the creditor and must take into account all those considerations. Bankruptcy is a procedure of enforcing the debt contract.

However, in China, debts between the banks and the SOEs are very different. In the 1980s, when a SOE borrowed from a state bank, the SOE manager viewed the loan as just a new way to get funds from the government, and he had little sense that the borrowed money would have to be repaid. The bank viewed the loan as just an allocation of funds to the state firm on behalf of the government, and it had little sense of the risk of possible default. In fact, a large number of bank loans were decided by the government through an administrative procedure, rather than being negotiated between the firm and the bank. In this sense, "debts" of SOEs were more like equity than debts. The only difference between debts and budget funds was a change to items on the balance sheets.

Not until the 1990s—when debts had accumulated to a point where the state banks were burdened with enormous overdue bad debts and when both SOEs and state-owned banks became relatively independent entities with their own interests—was bank money recognized as being different from budget funds. For that reason, I call the SOEs' debts "the *ex post* debts."[83] Because of this *ex post* nature, bankruptcy of SOEs is more like bargaining over the terms of new debt contracts rather than enforcing the existing debt contracts.

The second reason, which is related to the first, is that in many cases, the incumbent managers of SOEs are not the right people to blame for default because much of the bad debt did not result from their decisions. Many SOEs are overly capital intensive, and a large part of the firms' assets are nonperforming. But investment decisions that were debt financed were made by government bureaucrats rather than by managers. When debts are due and investments have failed, the decisionmakers have already gone or are in higher government positions.

Even if investment decisions were correct, bad debts have accumulated through several generations of managers, some of whom have either retired or moved to the government line departments—or even to banks. It is almost impossible to trace who was responsible for what part of the problem. The incumbents have every reason for arguing that they were not at fault. Indeed, many incumbents attribute poor performance to bad debts, rather than the other way around. They argue that too many nonperforming assets are useless but bear interest and that if there were no such assets on the books, their firms would be profitable.[84] There is no good reason to reject their argument. Rather, the government has widely accepted the argument as guidance for policymaking.

The third reason is that the managers of state-owned banks care about the accounting figures rather than about the real value of the bank asset; their careers and private benefits (like perks) all depend only on the accounting figures. They have every incentive to cover up rather than to signal nonperforming claims. If nonperforming debts appear, they may be replaced, and bonuses may be reduced. In contrast, by engaging in accounting tricks to disguise nonperforming debts, the bank can overstate its profits and may, therefore, maintain the ability to pay higher employee bonuses and to continue a level of loan quotas that would be impossible at lower reported profit levels.

Casual observation and empirical studies suggest that the managers of state-owned banks quite often record their bad loans as accounts receivable, roll over loans with new lending, and write their overdue interest payments as increases in the outstanding principal.[85] Although incumbent bank managers may know that bad debts will eventually show up, the best situation for them is for those debts to appear during their successor's tenure rather than during their own. That may be why state-owned banks are so passive in solving the bad-debt problem of SOEs.

The fourth reason is that the bankruptcy procedure is dominated by local governments.[86] In China, the state-owned banks are owned by the central government, whereas most SOEs are owned by local governments. With decentralization, local governments have obtained considerable autonomy and self-interests. They have every incentive to use the bank's passivity to write off the debts of the firms they control, even if those debts are recoverable. Although the Bankruptcy Law requires that reorganization and liquidation schemes be discussed and approved at creditors' meetings with a simple majority of creditors and an amount of unsecured debt claim, in practice, local judges and bank branch managers can hardly go against the local government's decisions, because the local government virtually determines their careers and welfare.

It is very hard and costly for the central authorities and the bank's headquarters to verify the true financial state of a firm. Even worse, some central government agencies (such as the State Economic and Trade Commission and the State Commission for Restructuring the Economic System) are biased in favor of debtors because their delegated task is to "invigorate state-owned enterprises" rather than to "take care of state-owned banks."[87]

Many other plausible reasons exist for why debts have failed to play a positive role in disciplining management, such as the government's concern for potential social unrest should bankrupt firms release too many redundant workers. However, from the preceding analysis, we see that the fundamental reason is that both enterprises and banks are owned by the state and controlled by bureaucrats rather than by capitalists. For debts to play a role, ownership of the debtor must be differentiated from ownership of the creditor, the debtor must hold responsibility for its performance, and the creditor must have incentives to enforce the debt contract. Those requirements can be achieved only when both the firm and the bank are privatized.

Conclusion: Privatization Is the Only Way Out

In this chapter, I have argued that Chinese state enterprise reform has been relatively successful in solving the short-term managerial incentive problem through both its formal, explicit incentive system and its informal, implicit incentive system. However, it has failed to solve the long-term managerial incentive problem and the management selection problem. An incumbent manager may have incentives to make short-term profits, but at present, no mechanism exists to ensure that only qualified people can be selected for management. The fundamental reason is that bureaucrats rather than capitalists still select the managers of SOEs.

Because the bureaucrats have the authority to select managers but do not bear the consequences for their selections, they have no proper incentives to find and appoint high-ability people. Moreover, because good performance does not guarantee the incumbent manager's longevity with the enterprise, the manager does not have long-term incentives. If one is to ensure that only high-ability people will become professional managers, authority for selecting management should be transferred from bureaucrats to capitalists. Such a move calls for the privatization of the SOEs. Fortunately, China is well on the way in this regard.

Although Chinese economic reform began with no intention to privatize, in the past two decades—particularly since the early 1990s—both explicit privatization and implicit privatization have accelerated in China. In 1978, at the beginning of the reform, 78 percent of total industrial output came from SOEs. By 1995, the SOEs' share had shrunk to only one-third.[88] A recent survey estimates that more than 70 percent of small SOEs have been fully or partially privatized in Shandong and a few other provinces.[89] The privatization process has further accelerated since the Chinese Communist Party's 15th Congress. Today, many large and medium-sized SOEs selected by local governments are listed for sale.

Although I have argued that the state shareholding system cannot solve the management selection problem, I have recognized that corporatization of SOEs combined with their being publicly traded on stock exchanges can serve as a first step toward privatization—if it is followed by the proper transfer of state shares into private hands.[90]

Interestingly, observation suggests that the major players behind the ongoing privatization process are local governments at various levels. Although not all local governments are undertaking explicit and wholesale privatization programs, almost all local governments are considering privatization of their enterprises in one way or another. The question is this: what motivates local governments to privatize the enterprises under their control?

Li, Li, and Zhang argue that the ongoing privatization in China is a consequence of the cross-regional competition that has followed the decentralization policy introduced at the early stage of reform.[91] Their argument is as follows: When cross-regional competition is sufficiently intense in the product market, each region has to cut production costs significantly in order to maintain a minimum market share for survival. Given that the managers' efforts are hidden, to induce the managers to reduce costs enough, local governments may have to grant the managers total or partial residual shares. In general, more intense product competition triggers a higher degree of privatization. It is in the local bureaucrats' interest to give up more residual shares of profits to managers because the induced "incentive effect" more likely dominates the "distribution effect" as competition intensifies.[92]

The debt crisis of state-owned enterprises can also provide a force for privatization. Given that most state-owned enterprises cannot continue operating with the existing debt burden, new equity funds need to be injected. However, the state has no funds to inject. The only way to solve the overindebtedness problem is to introduce new, nonstate shareholders, that is, to privatize.

Observation also suggests that privatization of SOEs has been and will continue to be a process of "capitalization" of (some) incumbent bureaucrats and managers (and even some workers). As the reform proceeds, incumbent bureaucrats find it more and more difficult to capture rents in their current positions because of the disappearance of monopolistic profits and managerial discretion. Experience teaches them that they can do much better by doing business directly with their remaining political capital of "connections" (before it fully depreciates). They need to make up their minds to *xia hai* (go into business). By doing so, they lose little because the rents they used to enjoy can be embedded into profits that may legally accrue to them in various forms. They have no risk to bear because startup capital comes from the state (initially, the firm is "owned" by the state).

Before leaving the government, they will grant full autonomy to the firms with which they will work. They will appoint themselves as chairmen or chairwomen of the board, as directors, or as executives. Once they pocket some profits, they will buy into the firms. They can do so quietly because once the firms are corporatized, the firms can easily be sold piecemeal instead of as an entirety.

That process may be further accelerated by the ongoing government restructuring launched by the new prime minister, Zhu Rongji. In addition, the central government may have to sell its stocks because of its budget deficit. The SOEs will gradually evolve into private joint-stock companies. At this stage, it is possible for the government to become a bondholder whom private shareholders can protect. Once incumbent bureaucrats become capitalists, they will have incentives to select high-ability people for management; they themselves will voluntarily step down if unqualified. The separation of government from enterprises will be achieved accordingly.

To conclude, it should be pointed out that although privatization of state-owned enterprises is very encouraging and promising, privatization of the state banks is yet to come. There may be good reasons for delaying the privatization of state banks. However, unless banks are privatized, they cannot be expected to play a constructive role in corporate governance of enterprises. The reason is that only private banks can have adequate incentives to select good managers and good projects for financing, and to enforce debt contracts through the bankruptcy mechanism.

As long as banks are owned by the state and run by bureaucrats— and thus the state remains the ultimate rescuer of failing concerns—enterprises, even privately owned, cannot be financially well disciplined by the banks. Thus, the fundamental problems of moral hazard and adverse selection cannot be solved as well as in a capitalist firm. China should learn this lesson not only from its own experience but also from that of Korea and other countries.[93]

12. China's Price Reform

The Chinese economic reform that started in 1978 can be understood as a transition process from central planning to the market economy. The basic difference between the centrally planned economy and the market economy is the price formation mechanism and its function. Under central planning, prices are set by the government and serve only as an accounting tool. In the market economy, price is determined by the relationship between supply and demand, and it adjusts resource allocation. The liberalization of prices—or the transformation of government-set prices to market-set prices—is commonly believed to be the most important step in the process of economic transformation, as well as the most difficult. Without successful price system reforms, reforms of the entire economic system cannot possibly succeed.

Similar to other socialist planned economies, the prices of almost all products and factors of production were set by the government in pre-reform China. Businesses did not have the right to set prices, and the government rarely adjusted prices in relation to supply and demand. Since reform, China has successfully loosened price controls on the vast majority of products. Reform in the factors of the production market has also made important progress.[1] Figures 12.1–12.3 describe the breakdown of retail goods, agricultural goods, and production materials set by the government, guided by the government, and set by the market as a proportion of transaction amounts over time.

In 1978, the government set prices for 97 percent of retail goods, 92.2 percent of agricultural goods, and 100 percent of production materials. In 1993, after 15 years of reform, government-set prices (including government-guided prices) in each of those categories decreased to 6.2 percent, 12.5 percent, and 18.9 percent, respectively. In 2004, market-set prices further increased to 95.3 percent, 96.5 percent, and 87.8 percent, respectively, so government-set prices each decreased to 4.7 percent, 3.3 percent, and 12.5 percent, respectively.

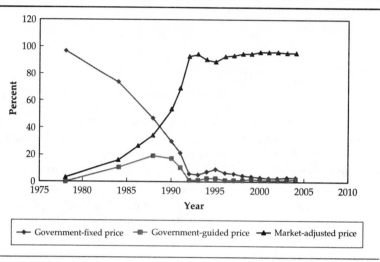

Figure 12.1
THE CHANGES IN THE PRICE FORMATION MECHANISM OF RETAIL PRODUCTS

SOURCE: Cheng Zhiping, *30-Year Price Reform (1977–2006)* (Beijing: China Market Press, 2006), p. 163.

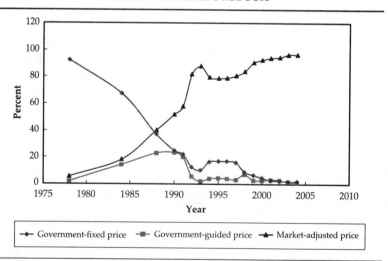

Figure 12.2
THE CHANGES IN THE PRICE FORMATION MECHANISM
OF AGRICULTURAL PRODUCTS

SOURCE: Cheng Zhiping, *30-Year Price Reform (1977–2006)* (Beijing: China Market Press, 2006), p. 163.

Figure 12.3
THE CHANGES IN THE PRICE FORMATION MECHANISM
OF PRODUCTION MATERIALS

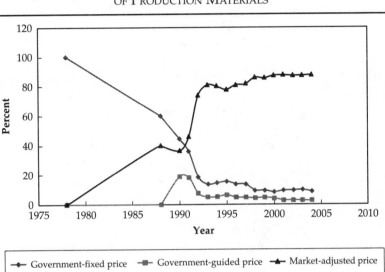

SOURCE: Cheng Zhiping, *30-Year Price Reform (1977–2006)* (Beijing: China Market Press, 2006), p. 163.

We could say that the process of liberalization in product prices has basically been completed.

In contrast with the former Soviet Union and eastern European socialist countries, China's price liberalization did not go through a one-time "shock" in which all price controls were abolished. China implemented incremental reforms in price controls through the "dual-track system." That so-called dual-track price, narrowly speaking, refers to the same product having a government price (listed price) and a market price simultaneously. Planned production is distributed according to the listed price, but off-plan production is sold according to the market price that is freely set by supply and demand. Broadly speaking, it also includes the government's controlling the price of some products while liberalizing the price of some other products.[2]

The dual-track system is a gradual transformation from the planned economy to the market economy. During this gradual process, government-set prices continually decrease as a proportion

237

of total transactions, whereas market prices continually increase in proportion. After many price adjustments and price liberalizations, the two are merged, implementing a single market price system.

The success of the Chinese price reform is attributable to its continuous and long process of liberalizing prices and building a market price mechanism. It improved resource allocation efficiency and promoted rapid economic growth without causing hyperinflation. In the 28 years between 1978 and 2006, China's real gross domestic product increased 1,234 percent, or an annualized rate of growth exceeding 9.7 percent. At the same time, the consumer price index increased only 371 percent, or an annualized rate of 5.7 percent.[3]

By comparison, between 1991 and 2000, Russia's overall industrial price index increased 15,140 times, while the consumer price index increased 9,297 times.[4] Perhaps the reason China incrementally built the market price mechanism using the dual-track system, instead of abolishing price controls all at once, has many aspects to it. One very important reason is that for a long time at the beginning of reform, the Chinese government absolutely did not have a market economy as a goal for reform. There also was no meticulous reform proposal. During the process of reform, the orientation of reform policies was argued about continuously.[5]

Actually, the early stages of reform only expanded the autonomy of large enterprises and adjusted irrational prices to incentivize producers. Market measures were introduced to improve and perfect state planning; they were not intended to replace the centrally planned economy. Any viewpoints that promoted the market economy were criticized. The leadership recognized the importance of the market mechanism but only as a "necessary complement" to planning, because planning could not possibly manage everything well. The market certainly was not the main mechanism for resource allocation.

Mainstream economists admonished the government to respect "the law of value" when making plans and setting policy, but they did not believe the government should abolish price controls on main industrial products and allow supply and demand to set prices. Under that condition, all price reform measures put into effect by the government were primarily price adjustments with the premise of not damaging overall economic planning. Naturally, liberalizing prices could not possibly be a basic policy choice. Price reform became the key to reforming the entire economic system only after the Third Plenary Session of the 12th Central Committee of the Communist Party of China in October 1984 set "the planned commodity economy" as the goal of reform. A transition to the market price system could then be put on the agenda.

At that time, high levels of government adopted the suggestions of some economists to transform the planned price system into the market price system by the dual-track price. That became the official policy for industrial product price reform.[6] The government accepted the dual-track system for reform for two reasons. First, the irrational price system had already become a stumbling block to reform, so it had to be eliminated. The traditional method of government proposals to adjust irrational prices was a slippery slope and was hard to implement. The government was worried that sharp adjustments in prices would lead to serious inflation and government deficits.

Second, because of the development of township and village enterprises and the expansion of state-owned enterprise autonomy, nonplanned products and production were a considerable portion of society's total output at the time. Government-set prices were increasingly difficult to administer. Most nonplanned products were not transacted in accordance with government-set prices. Instead, they were exchanged at black market or gray market prices. In other words, exchange activity in the market already existed; it was just illegal.

The dual-track price reform legalized the spontaneous dual-track price that already existed. The moved became the movers. It was easy to start, and the risk was small, so the government adopted it. Thus, the dual-track system price was formally implemented in the entire production materials sector in 1985. The dual-track system price caused the monetizing of existing corruption, creating a huge amount of "bureaucratic profiteering." It also caused the administration of planning targets to be increasingly more difficult, which aroused common dissatisfaction in society.

By 1988, the dual-track system price had already received intense criticism. In light of that criticism, the leadership in government decided on the "price gauntlet" to merge two tracks into one. The vast majority of prices would be completely liberalized and transferred to the market track. A small amount of important raw materials was bought back at higher prices to return to the centrally planned track.

Their market price was canceled. After a wave of panic buying and inflationary pressures, there was no option but to abandon the price gauntlet plan and to continue the dual-track price system.

After the political disturbances in 1989, the direction of reform changed. Central planning regained its foothold. Market reforms were questioned, and the government resumed price controls in the name of administrative consolidations. Even though the government could not possibly get rid of the market track completely, further liberalizing prices was not an option.

Deng Xiaoping's 1992 Southern Tour redetermined the direction of market reforms. The 14th Chinese Communist Party National Representatives Congress established "the socialist market economy" as the goal of reform. The pace of market economy reforms increased, and the government loosened controls on the vast majority of industrial production materials. By 1993, dual-track pricing had basically merged into the single-track market price. The structural reforms of China's product prices had basically been completed. From the preceding discussion, we can see that the success of China's price reforms was possibly just a meandering process.

The Planned Price Structure and Price Disruptions

Before 1978, China implemented a Stalinist centrally planned economic system. Production, transportation, distribution, and consumption were all organized by government planning. The production of industrial goods was essentially monopolized by state-owned enterprises. Enterprises received raw materials and other inputs and organized production according to planned targets. Products were sold to government commercial or materials sectors. Essentially, no decision authority existed in the areas of personnel, finance, materials, supply, production, or sales.

By comparison, the power to set and adjust almost all prices was controlled by the government's price management departments, but it had nothing to do with supply and demand. The government's power to set prices was concentrated in the Central Price Department. Price departments in local governments had very limited scope to set or adjust prices. Enterprises had no authority to set prices. Moreover, as soon as any product's price was set, it was rarely adjusted.

In the agricultural sector, China implemented the collective production system in the people's communes. Every year, the government
issued the purchase plan for main agricultural products. Except for
the goods consumed by farmers, their produce had to be sold to the
government at government-set prices. It could not be sold on the
market. All residential products and materials used for agricultural
production were also provided by state-owned commercial sectors at
government-set prices.

In the market economy, prices are signals so that limited resources
realize efficient allocation. Under China's planned economy, prices
were not used as signals to adjust resource allocation. Instead, prices
were used as tools to realize the state's industrialization strategy,
to accumulate capital, to redistribute income, and to perform economic calculation. So when the government set prices, it did not consider supply and demand, only how to benefit the planners' "social
objectives." Even if the government wanted to consider supply and
demand, there are millions of products, so the government has no
way of obtaining enough information. Thus, the purposeful and in-
advertent results of the government's setting prices are sustained
and serious distortions in the relative price system.

People commonly believe that China's pre-reform price distortions had the following features.

First, prices on agricultural goods were relatively low, and prices
on industrial goods were relatively high. Chinese economists call
that price distortion between industrial and agricultural goods the
"scissors gap." Gauging the scissors gap between industrial and
agricultural goods prices is not easy, but the estimates of some economists can provide us with a valuable reference. Using 1977 as an
example, if the fair value of an industrial laborer's output was worth
three times that of an agricultural laborer's output, then agricultural
goods were 29.4 percent lower than the fair price, and industrial
goods were 14.2 percent higher than the fair price.[7] If the fair value
of an industrial laborer's output was worth twice the value of an
agricultural laborer's output, then agricultural goods prices were
41.1 percent lower than the fair price, and industrial goods prices
were 28.5 percent higher than the fair price.[8]

The government purposefully distorted prices of industrial goods
with the goal of accumulating capital to realize the state's industrialization strategy. After the Chinese Communist Party seized power

in 1949, the Chinese government drew up aggressive and ambitious industrialization plans. According to the economic theories of the time, the key to realizing industrialization was capital accumulation. Given that 80 percent of China's population was involved in agriculture, farmers primarily provided the capital accumulation needed by industrialization. Because the agrarian population was large and spread out, it would be difficult for the government to collect revenue from farmers through taxes. A workable solution was to artificially suppress the price of agricultural products. Collecting taxes through prices turned "obvious taking" into "secret taking." According to the estimates of some economists, between 1950 and 1978, the state used the price scissor gap to get more than Y 523.9 billion in revenue from farmers. That figure is 1.4 times the original value of the fixed assets owned by the state-owned industrial sectors with independent accounts in 1978.[9]

Second, in the industrial sectors, raw materials and basic infrastructure prices were low, and processed industrial goods prices were high. The huge differences in capital-return margins of different industries mirror that price distortion. Figure 12.4 shows the capital-return margin of China's state-owned industrial sectors in 1978. State-owned industrial enterprises on average had a 12.3 percent return on capital but with huge differences between industries.

Overall, the return on capital for processing industries was much higher than for mining and raw materials industries. The main reason was the serious irrationality of relative prices. Except for the petroleum industry, the return on capital for the mining and raw materials industries did not surpass 5 percent, but the return on capital for all processing industries exceeded 38 percent, and the watch industry had a return on capital of 61.1 percent. The petroleum industry's return on capital was high mainly because of the high profits of oil products. The price of crude oil was relatively much lower, even though no rent (resource prices) was deducted from profit. Even if we do not take resource prices into account, there was almost no profit in the coal industry. Actually, the price of raw coal was even lower than the average production cost, and the entire industry was losing money in 1978.

The internal price distortions of the industrial sector were partly on purpose and were partly caused by a rigid price management

Figure 12.4
RETURN ON CAPITAL OF STATE-OWNED ENTERPRISES IN 1979

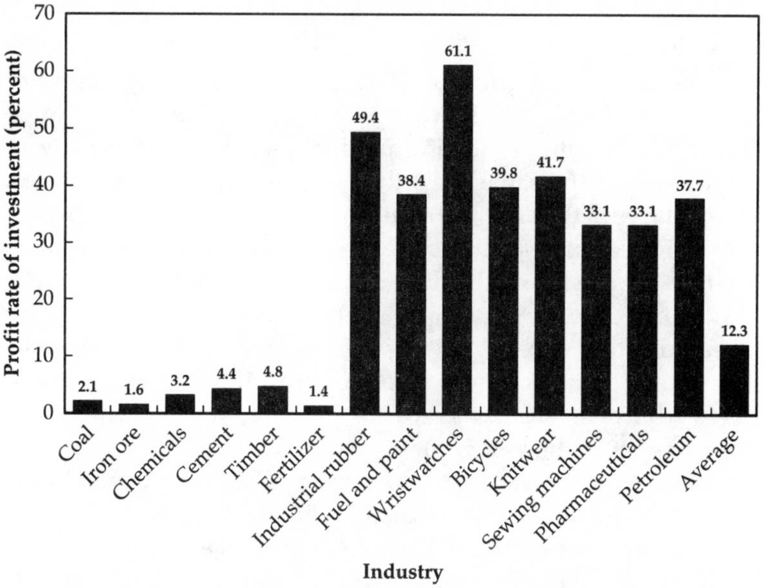

SOURCE: Zhang Zhuoyuan, "Jiage tizhi gaige," *Zhongguo gaige yu fazhan baogao: 1978–1994, Zhongguo de daolu* (Beijing: Zhongguo Caizheng Jingji Chubanshe, 1995).

system. Purposeful price distortions refer to China's central planners' understanding of "industrialization" to mean the development of processing industries. Setting high prices on production goods was beneficial to local initiatives in developing processing industries. Perhaps the government knew raw materials were relatively simple, so production targets were easy to hit.

Processed goods are more complex, so prices need to guarantee the completion of central plans. An important reason the government set prices of raw materials industries so low is that it did not consider the cost of capital or the resource price. In addition, the management system was rigid; the planned price could not possibly adjust with the relative change in the rate of production. It was inevitable that price distortions would become more serious by the day.

243

For example, between 1952 and 1977, the labor productivity of the machinery industry increased three times, and that of the chemical industry increased four times, but the coal industry's labor productivity increased only 12 percent. Those industries' prices were still maintained at the level set in the First Five-Year Plan.[10]

Third, the main agricultural sideline products had disorderly prices; even retail prices were lower than procurement prices. Although agricultural sideline products were priced well below equilibrium, at the same time, the government implemented low-wage policies in the cities, so there was no choice but to set the retail price of agricultural sideline products for urban residents lower. The government subsidized the price differences and operation losses.

After 1978, the purchase price of agricultural sideline goods was increased, but the retail price was not, so government expenditures on agricultural sideline product subsidies increased, causing a heavy burden. The subsidies for grain, cotton, and oil are examples. In 1978, the government spent Y 1.114 billion on subsidies for those products, or close to 1 percent of that year's expenditures. By 1983, those products were costing the government Y 20.167 billion, which was 14.3 percent of the entire government budget at the time.[11]

Fourth, there were price distortions between different varieties of the same product; those price distortions did not reflect quality differences. Such distortions are the inevitable result of the government's setting prices, because the pricing department of the government absolutely has no way to obtain enough information on every type of product's varieties to set a rational price. It would have a hard time knowing how consumers would evaluate quality differences between products.

Because of the rigid guiding ideology of government price setting and the price formation system, centrally planned prices basically did not respond to supply and demand. However, every economic actor is rational, so supply and demand will certainly respond to price. For example, the result of low agricultural sideline products is farmers' having no incentive to produce. If demand for agricultural sideline products is higher than the long-term supply, the government has no option but to implement rationing. It can be said that the main goal of agricultural product price reform was the same as the household-contract responsibility system, which was to adjust the incentives for farmers to produce agriculture sideline products. After the purchase price of agricultural sideline products is increased, retail price reform is also required; otherwise, the government's budget cannot bear it over the long term.

Speaking just of the industrial sector, we see that price distortion made it very hard to implement the system as it was intended. Even though it was basically monopolized by state-owned sectors before reform—and the government had production targets for each region, industry, and enterprise—in situations where prices were seriously distorted, it was hard to strictly carry out planning targets even if they were correct. Everyone had the initiative to develop relatively high-priced processing industries, but they had no initiative to develop relatively low-priced raw materials industries. Consequently, the processing industry had overcapacity, but the production capability of raw materials was seriously lacking. In the Chinese economy, the former was called "the long line," and the latter was called "the short line." The government had no option but to adjust the structure of industry every few years to suppress the long line and to bolster the short line.

During China's economic liberalization reforms, the government decided to give state-owned enterprises a certain amount of production autonomy, and it allowed a certain proportion of profits to be left with the enterprise as an incentive. And with the rise of rural enterprises after agricultural reforms, central planning became harder to implement. The problems caused by price distortions were laid bare. Enterprises were willing to produce goods with relatively high prices, not goods with relatively low prices. Because relative prices between variants—even of the same product, such as steel—were irrational, enterprises were willing to produce more variants with relatively high prices, but not those with relatively low prices. Consequently, even if the overall production plan was carried out, the supply of different variants was in a state of serious disequilibrium. Some variants had excess capacity, and some did not meet demand requirements.

Another example is the glass industry. Enterprises were willing to produce thin glass but not thick glass, because price was determined by the area or size not by the thickness. With an irrational price, the profits of enterprises did not reflect the real social value they created, thus forming the so-called imbalance between bitter and sweet.

The government also had no way to implement a serious economic assessment of the enterprises. Precisely in such a situation, the original price system was unsustainable, so industrial price reform was put on the table.

Gradual Implementation of Price Liberalization through the Dual-Track System

As previously described, China's economic reforms started between 1978 and 1984. The centrally planned economy was considered to be a rational economic system; its fundamentals were not questioned. At the time, mainstream economists and the government leaders supervising the reforms all recognized that state planning could not manage all aspects of economic life. The areas that planning could not manage well needed market adjustment, but the main part of the economy, namely, the industrial sector, needed to implement a planning system.

The guiding ideology of reform at the time was "rely mainly on economic planning, while making market adjustments subsidiary." In other words, the market was only a "complement" to state planning. This guiding ideology reflected a few points about price reform. The prices of primary products, especially the prices of main industrial products, must be decided by the government not by the demand and supply of the market. Prices were irrational because the government did not respect "the law of value" when setting prices, not because the price formation mechanism was irrational. The main method to resolve price distortions was to adjust the planned price, not to liberalize price controls and to let market supply and demand determine price. The steps of price reform must be split up and implemented according to "the ease or difficulty of each product," and they should not be done in one stroke.

Of course, during China's planned economy, even though the government had strict plans for the purchase and sale of agricultural subsidiary products, the agricultural sector was always in another category and was not included in the main part of the planned economy. The government could not possibly incorporate the actions of 800 million farmers into economic planning.

From the beginning of reform, high-level government leaders recognized that only the price mechanism could incentivize the farmers to resolve China's agricultural problems, especially the grain problem. In December 1978, the Third Plenary Session of the 11th Communist Party of China Central Committee decided: "In the summer of 1979, the state monopoly purchase price of grain will be increased 20 percent, and above-quota purchase prices will have a foundation 50 percent higher than that. Agricultural sideline products such as cotton, oilseed, sugar, livestock, aquatic products, lumber products, etc., also need to be progressively increased in price according to circumstances."

According to the decision of the Third Plenary Session, in the summer of 1979, the government increased the purchase price of 18 agricultural sideline products, with an average increase of 25 percent.[12] At the end of 1979, the government accordingly increased the sales price of eight types of main nonstaple foodstuffs (not including grain) for urban residents, with an average increase of about 30 percent. So that urban residents would not be affected by the price increase, the government issued subsidies for nonstaple foods at the same time.[13]

When prices were increased, the government also opened up the free market for agricultural sideline products. After farmers completed their obligations to the state at the set purchase price, they were allowed to sell their surplus on the free market. Urban residents could use government ration cards to buy products at the list price from state-owned grain stores and nonstaple foodstuff stores. They could also go to the free market and buy the agricultural sideline products. Thus, agricultural sideline products transitioned to the dual-track system.[14] Prices increased, but the supply of products quickly became abundant, which was to everyone's benefit.

From the start of reform, a very popular viewpoint was that the planned economy of the past was unsuccessful because the government controlled too much; it tried to control things it could not control or could not control well. Before 1978, the government also set the prices of merchandise, such as soap, laundry powder, toilet paper, and kettles. Of course, those goods came in countless varieties. The central planning bureau knew that it could not control that much merchandise, so the prices were often controlled by the price department of local governments. Government control of merchandise resulted in supply not meeting demand; consequently, many cities instituted a rationing system.

After Reform and Opening, economists almost unanimously believed that such merchandise had little effect on people's quality of life. So regardless of the overall condition of central planning, the government could not control the prices of such merchandise well, and prices should be adjusted by the market. The bureaucrats in charge of the economy also almost unanimously recognized that viewpoint. Thus, local governments liberated merchandise prices one after another.

For example, in Wuhan, in 1980, the Second Light Industrial System (the industrial department that produced merchandise) selected 71 types of merchandise that did not have a major influence on people to try floating prices. In 1982, market adjustment was implemented for 176 products. In May 1983, another 200 product prices were liberalized. At the same time, 49 second-class industrial articles with big differences in quality and fast changes in supply and demand were floated.[15] With regard to the entire country, by 1984, the prices of merchandise had basically been completely liberalized. After prices were liberalized, the market quickly became prosperous without causing popular discontent.

Even though there was agreement about implementing market adjustments for agricultural sideline products and small industrial products, the government's ability to set prices for major industrial products was not questioned during the early part of reform. Instead, such price setting was considered a matter of course. Reforms expanding the autonomy of state-owned enterprises and the ensuing reforms in agriculture that led to the rise of rural enterprises challenged the government's ability to set prices.

After 1979, the government successively implemented a reform policy that expanded the autonomy of enterprises. Enterprises could decide their own products and output beyond the government's directive. The enterprise itself needed to sell those products off plan, as well as to procure for itself the raw materials and inputs needed for those products. The government would not guarantee supply, but the government set the price of both products and inputs. In other words, the dual-track system was implemented for the production of state-owned enterprises, but the price was still single track.

Stimulated by retained profits and a system of bonuses, some high-priced, high-profit goods became oversupplied. Low-priced, low-profit (or even loss-making) production materials were in huge demand, but enterprises had no incentive to produce—or they were not even willing to finish planned production—so those products became seriously undersupplied. Thus, the Chinese economy went from a pre-reform state in which shortages were common to a state in which shortages and oversupply existed simultaneously. Irrational prices also brought about a serious income distribution problem. Because the earning differences among enterprises resulted mainly from prices, not effort, when profitable enterprises used retained earnings to issue bonuses to their workers, unprofitable enterprises used bank loans to issue bonuses. The government could let it slide but only out of fairness. That circumstance made it difficult for the government to effectively implement its macroeconomic policy.

The high-level leadership in government quickly realized that not resolving the price issue was unacceptable. If the price issue was not resolved, not only would the government have difficulty in implementing its production plans, but also it would have no way to evaluate the success or failure of an enterprise. If enterprise reform could not advance, it could even cause serious social issues.[16] The government still thought it best to use administrative measures to adjust prices and resolve the price issue, not to liberate prices.

An adjustment proposal was needed to adjust prices. To establish a workable price adjustment proposal, the State Council established the State Council Price Research Center on July 7, 1981. Senior economist Muqiao Xue led the center. He assembled more than 50 professionals, scholars, and cadres from the central government departments, provinces, cities, autonomous regions, and universities. They used modern methods to conduct theoretical price calculations, such as input–output tables and computer programs.[17] Because the price equations were too complex and because too many variables were involved, the Price Research Center was never able to produce a price reform proposal that was acceptable to high-level policymakers. In reality, it was just a utopian plan.

Without an overall price adjustment proposal, the government— on the one hand—used "tax substitution" to alleviate the profit disparity between enterprises caused by irrational prices[18] and—on the other hand—tried to resolve the price issue by making price adjustments to one product at a time. The latter method was called "achieving breakthrough with single soldiers." In reality, even though the government recognized the necessity of resolving the issue of irrational prices, when it came to setting policy, the government often hesitated and had difficulty being decisive. The reason was that for undersupplied products, the government feared that raising prices would cause inflation and social discontent. Prices should be raised, but the government did not dare to. For oversupplied products, the government feared that lowering prices would reduce government revenue. (The profit of state-owned enterprises was calculated using production values, not sales revenue.) It should have lowered prices, but it was unwilling to do so. The government was often more willing to issue vouchers than to increase prices, and it was more willing to limit outputs than to lower prices. Therefore, only in extreme cases, when it had absolutely no recourse, would the government consent to adjust prices.

A good example is the 1983 adjustment of textile prices. In the 1960s, China began producing polyester fibers. At that time, the price was set relatively high. With the increase in production, the cost decreased dramatically, but the price was not adjusted downward. Because the price was high, profits were also high, so localities had huge incentives to produce polyester fabric. By 1980 and 1981, annual production had reached 900 million meters, but annual sales had reached only 200 million meters. There were huge backlogs. Conversely, because the purchase price of cotton had been raised five times between 1963 and 1980, whereas the price of cotton yarn and cotton cloth had not—or the price was even less than the production cost—the government spent Y 4.6 billion on subsidies for cotton used in textiles just in 1982. Cotton yarn and cotton cloth were severely undersupplied. That is to say, the price of polyester textiles should have been decreased, and the price of cotton cloth increased. The government did not dare to make that decision for a long time.

Only by 1982, when the imbalance between the production and consumption of textile goods became intense, did the problem become "imperative to solve" (in the words of the State Council). The State Price Bureau repeatedly researched proposals; then, another four months were spent in repeated discussions among high-level leaders. Finally, Deng Xiaoping acknowledged the proposal. On January 21, 1983, the government issued the textile price adjustment proposal. It is believed to be the most successful price adjustment.[19]

An important special characteristic of China's price system reform was that when prices were irrational, if the government did not adopt measures on its own, market forces would push forward spontaneous price reforms. When the government worried about reductions in revenue and so was unwilling to lower prices or when the price was not lowered enough or when oversupplied products had high planned prices, enterprises often broke government restrictions because of market pressure. After enterprises reduced prices, the government could ultimately only accept the prices as fact. According to the Chinese phrase, the matter was settled by leaving it unsettled.

The watch industry is an excellent example. Because prices were high and profit margins were wide, watch factories were set up everywhere, resulting in serious oversupply. According to Byrd and Tidrick,[20] from 1980 to 1983, the government reduced the planned price of watches three times, even though it would have preferred not to. In total, the planned price was even less than a 20 percent decrease in price, so it was far from the equilibrium price. The factories' output was much higher than the government-set production target. The commercial departments purchased only those watches that were easy to sell at planned prices. The only option that the factories had was to allow workers to sell the watches on the street for market prices. Thus, the planned purchase price of watches progressively disappeared.

Another example is the machinery industry. Starting in 1980, the economic structure was adjusted. After fixed-asset investment was reduced, the government significantly decreased production targets for the industry. That year, the nonplanned direct sales of an enterprise under the First Machinery Industry Ministry were worth 46 percent of total sales, and machinery produced for market sales was worth 33 percent.[21] By 1983, although the planned price had not been abolished—and the official message was to rectify the market order, thereby requiring enterprises to enforce the planned price—the majority of machine products were sold at market prices. That was spontaneous price reform.

The hardest part of price reform was pricing for production materials, especially raw materials. Because the planned price was low, demand was enormous, but enterprises had no incentive to increase production. Steel, coal, cement, wood, and so on were in a long-term state of undersupply. The price of production needed to be increased. Even though the government increased prices for coal, pig iron, and steel in April 1979 by 30.5 percent, 30 percent, and 20 percent, respectively, the shortage issue was far from resolved.[22]

Production materials are inputs for most enterprises, so reforms to increase the price of inputs would cause costs to increase for the user. That approach would probably increase linked prices, which was what the government feared. If price reforms for production materials led to inflation, the government would have to subsidize residents. Whether or not the government could bear that financial burden required earnest calculation. The results of those calculations needed to persuade all participating policymakers, which was not easy. Therefore, a comprehensive proposal to adjust the prices of production materials was never presented.

Although the government's price reform proposal was never presented, spontaneous price reform was always at work. The reason is that with the expansion of enterprise autonomy and the development of rural enterprises, an increasingly larger portion of products was not controlled by state planning, regardless of whether it was the sale of merchandise or the procurement of inputs. According to the Chinese Economic System Reform Research Institute's 1985 survey of 429 state-owned industrial enterprises, in 1984, 32.1 percent of products on average (as a percentage of total sales) were sold by the enterprises themselves, and 16.4 percent of major raw materials on average were purchased on the market (the nonplanned supply). The proportion of enterprises with product self-sale rates and market purchasing rates exceeding 40 percent were 48.6 percent and 24 percent, respectively.[23] Those off-plan transactions in products and inputs could be carried out only with the consent of both the buyer and seller, so the planned price could not possibly be complied with.

Rural (township and village) enterprises were the main driving force of the spontaneous price reform. Agricultural reforms produced much surplus labor, and farmers had more freedom to be industrious. As a result, rural enterprises developed throughout the country, starting from the coast. By 1984, the number of rural enterprises reached 1.6 million, employed 38 million workers, and had total sales of Y 126 billion (which was equal to 26 percent of the sales of state-owned industrial enterprises).[24]

Rural enterprises were an unplanned outcome. From the beginning, they operated under market rules. Their establishment was not prearranged for, they did not use government money, they were not given production targets, and they were not provided raw materials. From the outset, the central government did not allow state-owned enterprises to provide rural enterprises with raw materials, nor were banks allowed to provide them with loans. But their products had a market, and they could make money, so they were willing to pay higher prices for raw materials.

When rural enterprises were willing to pay higher prices, the state-owned enterprises that produced raw materials were more willing to sell their above-target output to rural enterprises than they were to sell to the Materials Department at planned prices. Some state-owned enterprises that received planned quotas began to scalp their production targets on the market. Even state-owned materials departments started speculative buying and selling. Thus, black markets and gray markets were created for production materials. Rural enterprises even bribed state-owned enterprises in order to attain raw materials.

The same product had a two-track price: (a) the planned price and (b) the market price. The result was a spontaneous dual-track system. It could be said that from the first day rural enterprises appeared, an illegal dual-track system came into existence. On the one hand, manufacturers, driven by their own interests, wanted to reduce planned production targets or used all sorts of excuses not to fulfill planned production targets. On the other hand, the enterprises that received those goods looked to increase the planned production quota and falsely reported demand to the highest extent feasible. Setting and implementing planned production targets became increasingly difficult.[25]

China's local governments were also an important driving force of the spontaneous price reform. Starting in 1980, after the central government implemented fiscal sharing policies with local governments and after many state-owned enterprises were put under the management of local governments, those local governments became the consumers and producers of products. Local governments, in general, were unwilling to sell raw materials that were in great demand but short supply at planned prices to enterprises in other areas because they wanted to develop their own processing industries with higher earnings. Even though raw materials had planned supply targets, suppliers often required additional compensation to deliver their products.

Because planning could not be strictly enforced, to get raw materials, local governments established "production cooperation officers" to resolve supply issues by means of interregional "exchanges." The essence of those exchanges was to use planned prices as a pretext for using the market price. For example, in 1984, the list price of a bicycle produced by Shanghai was Y 120, but the market price was Y 200. The list price of one ton of steel produced by Liaoning was Y 600, but the market price was Y 1,000. If Shanghai wanted to buy one ton of steel from Liaoning at the list price, it had to provide Liaoning with five bicycles (Y 400 discount under the market price for steel / Y 80 discount under market price for bicycles = five bicycles per ton of steel). If the market price of a bicycle did not change, but the market price of one ton of steel increased to Y 1,200, then Shanghai needed 7.5 bicycles to exchange for one ton of steel (Y 600 discount under market price for steel / Y 80 discount under market price for bicycles = 7.5 bicycles per ton of steel). Similarly, Shanghai needed to trade hard-to-get products such as bicycles and Santana cars for Shanxi coal. Otherwise, even with planned production targets, planned supply could not be attained.

By 1984, market transactions for production materials were already well-developed. The actual transaction price was completely decided by supply and demand, even though that approach was illegal.[26] Market participants included rural enterprises, state-owned enterprises, all levels of government, and even a number of government trading companies that specialized in raw materials speculation. It could be said that finding an enterprise that did not participate in market transactions was almost impossible. Under the circumstances, the central government investigated and cracked down on illegal market transactions,[27] but it had no choice but to loosen price controls.

On May 20, 1984, the State Council put into effect a policy allowing the industrial production materials that were part of an enterprise's own sales (2 percent of planned products) and those that were above the production target to be priced higher by enterprises up to 20 percent of the state list price. Buyer and seller could negotiate a price within an allowed range. That rule was impossible to implement because the difference between the list price and the black-market price of most production materials was higher than 20 percent. Figure 12.5 shows the list and market price of steel in the Wuhan area in 1984 and 1985. From the figure, we can see that the market price was 60 percent to 128 percent higher than the planned price.

The government never proposed a price adjustment proposal for production materials, but it had no way to prohibit the illegal market

Figure 12.5
A COMPARISON OF PLANNED PRICES AND MARKET PRICES OF STEEL
IN THE WUHAN AREA

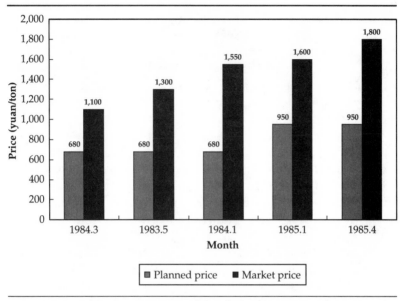

SOURCE: Wen Guifang, "Jiji de tuijin shengchan cailiao liutong he jiage gaige," *Chengben jiage ziliao* 4 (1985).

transactions that had spread over the entire country. It was precisely in that setting that at the end of 1984, the dual-track system became a policy choice that the leadership in government was willing to accept.[28] Policymakers were aware that "giving priority to liberalization" was more workable than "giving priority to adjustment" as a means to resolve the price issue. Incrementally liberalizing prices was easier than adjusting all prices, and the risk was also smaller. It was better to liberalize nonplanned activity and see the result than to remain immobile.

Not long after, on January 24, 1985, with approval of the State Council, the State Price Bureau and the State Materials Bureau formally implemented a policy that canceled the 20 percent price restriction. Enterprises could sell according to the local market price and could participate in market transactions.[29] From then on, off-plan production materials transacted according to market prices were no longer illegal, and the dual-track system became legal. The price reform that had long perplexed government had made a breakthrough.

After the dual-track price system had been implemented for production materials, "giving priority to liberalization" was applied to the price reforms of other products. In 1985, the government liberalized the purchase price of the vast majority of sideline agricultural products. The monopoly price of grain and oil was abolished, and the contract system for purchases was implemented. In 1986, the government liberalized the price of seven durable consumer goods, such as brand-name bicycles, refrigerators, and washing machines. In 1988, the government liberalized the price of 13 types of tobacco and alcohol.

Even though illegal and semi-illegal dual-track price systems existed before 1985, the legalization of the dual-track system caused corruption and the so-called chaotic economic order to become more serious. Because of the huge difference between the planned price and the market price, the money-and-power trade flourished. Some people with power or government connections obtained resources at the planned price and then sold them on the market. Huge profits came easily, causing fervent public discontent. Manufacturing enterprises were unwilling to sign contracts to supply planned products, and even if they did sign them, all kinds of excuses were used not to fulfill them. Surplus products were sold on the market as much as possible. Enterprises in need of materials often had to pay exorbitant "other fees" to get their rightful within-plan supplies. Executing the government plan became extremely difficult, if not impossible.[30]

During the First Plenary Session of the Seventh National People's Congress in March 1988, the dual-track system was the key issue. The people's representatives expressed their strongest concerns about the issue. Under those circumstances, Deng Xiaoping and other high-level government leaders believed that "short-term pain is better than long-term pain." They decided on the "price gauntlet," quickly merging the dual-track system into a single-track system.

After high-level leaders were determined to implement that policy, a series of price reform measures was proposed in April 1988. On April 5, the State Council sent out a notice stating that the price of pork, fresh eggs, sugar, and vegetables would be liberalized. "Implicit subsidies" (subsidies given to enterprises) for residential prices became "explicit subsidies" (subsidies given directly to workers). After May, the price of color TVs was allowed to float freely. In July, the State Council decided to liberalize the price of branded tobacco and alcohol starting on July 28.

After those prices were liberalized, there were serious price increases. The price of pork increased 50–60 percent, vegetables increased 31.7 percent, and 18-inch color televisions increased from Y 1,330 to Y 1,900. The price of some branded tobacco and alcohol increased more than tenfold.[31] The invisible inflation sustained by ration cards under price controls of the past became visible inflation manifested by prices. Thus, inflation expectations were common.

During a meeting of the Politburo of the Communist Party of China on August 15–17, 1988, the "Proposal for the Early Steps of Price and Wage Reform" was passed. It required that during the "price gauntlet," the military and the police needed to make precautionary preparations to guard against possible unforeseen circumstances during price reform. On the day the proposal was made public (August 19), a buying panic engulfed the entire country. Social stability was threatened. Under those circumstances, on August 30, the State Council met to stabilize prices. On September 26, the Third Plenary Session of the 13th Central Committee of the Communist Party of China decided to launch "administrative consolidation."[32] The price gauntlet was terminated.

The years between 1989 and 1991 have been called the three years of "administrative consolidation." During that time, the government did not follow the ideology formed in 1985 to further liberalize prices. Instead, it strengthened price controls and used administrative means to adjust the prices of some products. There was heated debate over whether reform should be considered socialist or capitalist, especially after the political disturbance caused by the "Tiananmen incident." The official mainstream media criticized the promotion of market reforms. The direction of reform changed. Rural enterprises were viewed as the prime suspects in destroying economic order, so they were suppressed. The government froze the prices of some products. Maximum prices were set on production materials that were originally liberalized and unplanned. All levels of government were forced to enforce those changes strictly. Important agricultural production materials, such as fertilizers, pesticides, and plastic sheeting, were monopolized. Durable consumer goods that had already been liberalized, such as refrigerators, washing machines, black-and-white televisions, and bicycles, now had an approval system for price increases. Color televisions were monopolized. Some markets, including the rice market, were closed.

After inflation was under control, the government also used administrative means to adjust the prices of five categories, or more than 20 types of products. That adjustment included appropriate increases in underpriced grain, cotton, and sugar, which had government-set purchase prices. The price of state-allocated coal was increased twice, the price of crude oil was increased three times, and the price of rail freight was increased twice. The price of passenger tickets for railways, waterways, and airways was increased. The monopoly sales price of grain and cooking oil, which had not been adjusted for 25 years, was increased.[33]

The year of transition for Chinese reform was 1992. Deng Xiaoping's Southern Tour redetermined the direction of China's market reforms. The 14th National Congress of the Communist Party of China established the "socialist market economy" as the goal of reform. The pace of market reforms was suddenly increased. Price reform measures returned to "giving priority to liberalization." The pace of price liberalization took its biggest stride in 1992. The prices of production materials were almost completely liberalized. The State Price Bureau revised and issued its Catalog of Central Price Controls. In it, the 47 categories, or 737 types, of heavy industry production materials and transportation prices in 1991 were reduced to 89 types, liberalizing close to 600 types at once. (Thirty-three types were set by the government, and 56 types were guided by the government.) The 40 types of agricultural products that were originally in the catalog were reduced to 10 types. (Six were set by the government, and four were guided by the government.) The 41 types of light industry merchandise were reduced to 9.[34]

At the end of 1992, 844 counties and cities had liberalized the price of foodstuffs. By 1993, except for the few industry prices that were set by the government, such as those for power, communications, and petroleum, the prices of the vast majority of production materials and residential materials were completely determined by the market. Those locales had completed the process from the dual-track price to a single market price. If calculated using transaction amounts, 93.8 percent of retail merchandise prices, 87.5 percent of agricultural product purchase prices, and 81.1 percent of production material ex-factory prices had been liberalized.

It could be said that, at that point, the liberalization of China's product market had basically been completed. During the 10th National People's Congress in 1997, the Standing Committee passed the Pricing Law. The law clarified the scope of government-guided prices and government-set prices as applied to (a) a small amount of merchandise vital to the development of the national economy and the quality of life, (b) a small number of scarce resources, (c) natural monopolies, (d) important public facilities, and (e) important services in the public interest. The main role of the government Department of Price Control changed from "setting prices" to "setting the rules and acting as judge."[35]

Lessons from China's Price Reform

Within about 15 years since it started economic reform, China had basically completed its price system reform. During the transition process from planned prices to market prices, the Chinese economy maintained relatively high growth without experiencing hyperinflation. In the 22 years between 1978 and 2000, China's per capita gross domestic product had an annual average growth of 8.3 percent, but the consumer price index increased on average 6.9 percent annually, so the former was 40.7 percent higher than the latter.[36] In my judgment, if any country can ensure that the real growth in incomes is higher than the increase in prices during reform, the possibility of inflation causing social chaos is not great. It could be said that China's price reform was an enormous success.

Not only can other countries draw lessons from China's experience with price reform, but also it is significant for our understanding of the evolution of economic systems.

Lesson 1: Know how to use the spontaneous power of the market. China's price liberalization was progressively completed through the dual-track system, but our analysis has shown that the dual-track system was not the result of the meticulous design of reforms. It arose spontaneously during the process of reform. The brilliance of the leaders of China's reforms laid in their taking the spontaneous dual-track price that existed and turned it into a conscious reform policy. In the early stages of reform, the high-level reformers attempted to implement an overall price reform proposal. They did not succeed, because countless market participants held supply-and-demand information. Such information could not possibly have been in the government's database or in the planners' minds.

The leadership of China's reform quickly realized the limits of their knowledge, so they resorted to "feeling the rocks while crossing the river." When the government had no way to develop a price reform proposal, enterprises with certain decisionmaking power and other market participants driven by their own interests spontaneously breached price controls. A market track was created alongside the planned track, and an outlet for reform was found. Even though the government tried to eliminate transactions at illegal prices, it ultimately realized that it was better to make the best of the situation and use it voluntarily than to attempt to stop it and fail. Thus, the spontaneous dual-track system became a conscious reform policy.

The failure of the "price gauntlet" in 1988 and the success of price reforms in 1992 show that even though the dual-track system had many drawbacks, the transition from centrally planned prices and market prices coexisting to a single market price required us to wait until conditions were ripe, rather than to act rashly.

Lesson 2: Make economic reform a Pareto improvement. The goal of price reform is to allow the market to adjust the allocation of resources, thus raising economic efficiency and increasing the total wealth of society (a "Kaldo-Hicks improvement"). If we could not have turned the process of price reform into a Pareto improvement, reform could have possibly resulted in a revolution.

Any system will produce vested interests. Those vested interests under a centrally planned system are government officials who have the power to allocate scarce resources and merchandise, as well as the enterprises and people that receive such goods at lower prices. For example, compared with rural residents, China's urban residents are the vested interests of centrally planned prices because they receive transfer payments from the low-priced merchandise with which they are supplied. When the prices of those materials and merchandise are raised, the vested interests are harmed. During the price reform, the Chinese government especially emphasized compensation to vested interests. For example, every time the retail price of agricultural sideline products was increased, the government would meticulously calculate the relative increase in price subsidies.

The dual-track system entered the market mechanism from the margin. On the one hand, it improved the efficiency of resource allocation and increased the total wealth of society. On the other hand, it used central-planning targets to protect the vested interests of those who received low-priced goods under the old system.[37] For that reason, the dual-track system's introduction was special, but it was not met with any strong resistance.

The government bureaucrats who were responsible for resource allocation are viewed as the biggest losers of reform because most of their power and rent-seeking behavior was reduced or eliminated. For the reform to succeed, the planners needed to consider how to lighten the resistance from powerful bureaucrats. The dual-track system resolved that issue. In some situations, the dual-track system improved the circumstances of bureaucrats, rather than making them worse. Now, they had better opportunities and more effective ways to receive economic benefits (such as using the difference between the centrally planned price and the market price to rent-seek). That point explains why increasingly more government departments began to support this kind of reform.

However, some government officials opposed the dual-track system because the centrally planned targets in their name had not been implemented. The objective of their opposition was to return to the centrally planned track, not to transition to the market track. That point also means that the transition from the dual-track system to the single market price cannot be made too rapidly. The reason the 1992 price liberalization was relatively smooth was because the original vested interests in government had a new avenue for benefiting themselves (such as using their powers to directly engage in commercial activities).

Lesson 3: Effectively control inflation. During the transition between central planning and market prices, inflation is unavoidable for two reasons. First, under central planning, product shortages are allocated by production targets and ration coupons. The production targets and ration coupons are a form of purchasing power, but because they are not "fiat currency," they are not reflected in the official price. In other words, the real price level under central planning is certainly higher than the nominal monetary price level. Invisible inflation exists. When production targets and ration coupons are abolished, the nominal price will increase, so invisible inflation will turn into visible inflation. The government provides price subsidies, which in effect use currency to replace production targets and ration coupons.

Even though real incomes have not decreased, people feel the price increases. Second, in theory, inflation is a monetary phenomenon; so as long as currency issues are limited, changes in relative prices will not cause the general price level to increase. Because of vested interests, it is very hard to allow prices that were set too high to fall. A workable solution is to adjust relative prices by increasing the money supply.

Figure 12.6 shows the change in China's retail price index since reform. From the figure, we can see that every time a price reform measure is enacted, a relatively large increase in the price level follows.

Even though inflation is unavoidable during price reform, it is important to control inflation at a level that consumers can accept. Consumers who have lived under central planning for a long time have a relatively low tolerance for inflation because they are accustomed to fixed prices. When the reform begins, an increase in the price of any product will lead to inflation expectations. Therefore, too many price reform measures cannot be implemented simultaneously, especially in the early stages of reform. The one

Figure 12.6
RETAIL PRICE INDEX (1978–2006)

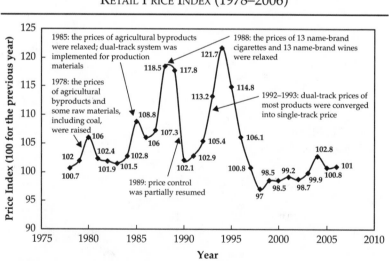

SOURCE: *China Statistical Yearbook*, 2007.

important reason China's price reform was gradual was because the government feared inflation. With the progress of reforms, consumers' tolerance for inflation also increased. In China's case, 6 percent inflation in 1980 was considered unacceptable. After 1985, 6 percent inflation was not considered a major problem. From that perspective, perhaps it is suitable to progress from a slow pace of price reform to a fast pace.

China's experience also shows that when relatively high inflation already exists in the economy, implementing price reform measures is unwise. The failure of the price gauntlet in 1988 offers a lesson. At the beginning of the year, there were obvious inflationary pressures. In February, the retail price index broke through 10 percent; in June, it increased to 16.5 percent; and in July, it further increased to 19.3 percent.[38] However, in August, the government still decided to "liberalize the vast majority of merchandise prices, allowing them to be adjusted by the market." That change led to serious panic buying, and price reform was suspended.

China's experience also shows that creating a relatively tight macroenvironment is helpful in the liberalization of price controls, even if it may come at the cost of economic growth speed. The time between 1989 and 1991 has been called the three years of "administrative consolidation." The government's main goal was to control inflation, which was bad for reform, and the rate of economic growth dropped significantly. If we look back on that period, contractionary policies actually created good conditions for the 1992 price liberalization. The consumer price index decreased from 17.8 percent in 1989 to 2.9 percent in 1991, and the difference between the centrally planned price and the market price of production materials decreased significantly. Consequently, the large-scale price liberalization in 1992 did not have a great effect on society. Without the contractionary policies, the price liberalization of 1992 may have been unworkable. We could call it a stroke of good luck.

Appendix to Chapter 12: Taking Price Reform as the Center of Systemic Economic Reform

Find the Mechanism for System Reform

The basic objectives of China's economic reform should be to place central planning on a foundation of the law of value.[1] To guarantee the normal operation of the economy, the market system should be implemented to establish a self-adjusting mechanism for the new planned economic system. The fundamental problem with the old system is that it lacked a mechanism to guarantee the normal operation of the economy. Even though our economic system is an organism, it has no way to sustain its own life; instead, it relies on constant doses of medication. There is no panacea in this world, and neither is there a living creature that can sustain itself forever on medication.

The goal of reform is to create a new mechanism. Many people have recognized this goal. Reform itself also needs a mechanism, but few have focused on that need. The experiences of previously implemented economic reforms have shown that how smoothly reform is implemented relies on whether or not a mechanism for reform can be found. Finding a mechanism involves providing an institution for the economic system. We should concentrate on finding a mechanism for reform and then use that mechanism to create other institutions.

We learned that lesson during our experiences with rural reforms. Rural reforms did wonders for the economy. The key lesson was that rural reform founded institutions to sustain itself. The appearance of household specialization, the development of the division of labor, the formation of new economic associations, the prosperity of the rural economy, the large-scale migration of labor, and the reorganization of production factors were not designed beforehand but were created by the reform mechanism. We cannot underestimate the power of the reform mechanism.

We have even tried to implement rural reforms in the urban areas but have not been very successful. There are various reasons for that lack of success, but an important one might be that we did not clearly recognize the importance of the mechanisms behind rural reform. We concentrated on the word "contract" without recognizing the more important word "liberalization." The household-contract responsibility system produced tremendous energy, but such energy can be fully used only after the market has been liberalized. If we had contracted without liberalization, peasants would have eaten a little better and would have been clothed a little better—ending starvation and relieving the discomfort of winter—but it would absolutely not have led the countryside into an era of historical transition, for example, from a natural economy to a commodity economy. Further, as long as the market is liberalized, the responsibility system is a self-evident requirement. Simply stated, liberalizing the market was a mechanism for rural reform.

Systemic reforms of urban industry are considerably more complex and challenging than are those of the countryside. That element has without question caused reform to be more arduous. The difficulty may be largely attributable to our lack of focus on finding a mechanism for reform, even though we organized large masses of people and consumed large amounts of resources trying to design an ideal new system. We have attempted to develop a comprehensive plan that encompasses the planning system, the public finance system, the materials system, the commercial system, the price system, the labor wage system, and the social welfare system, among others, but we have not prioritized researching a mechanism for reform itself. Our failure to present a satisfactory reform proposal seems inevitable because throughout the process, we concentrated our attention on people, not mechanisms. We have thought only about using people to change systems, and we never considered using systems to change systems. Although the spirit of hard work is laudable, it shows a lack of ingenuity. Of course, urban reform in practice has inspired people, but the source of that inspiration is embodied in the role that institutions play in reform. Unfortunately, many people are not consciously aware of that point.

In China, many researchers of urban reforms are often ignorant of the role of the economic system in the countryside. That lack of knowledge is an oversight. With the rise of the rural economy, villagers have begun to enter the cities. Agricultural labor resources have driven industry, and the countryside has started a wave of industrialization. The rural and urban economic systems are merging more by the day. The development of the commodity economy is an essential aspect of the rural economy, but the commodity economy requires a unified market. It cannot be limited to the countryside; it must encompass all of society. The rural economic system is developing with the use of an intrinsic mechanism, and it is engulfing the cities with an unstoppable momentum. If we fail to recognize that fact and discuss cities only as cities, while failing to find a mechanism for reform, the current urban economic system will be in danger of collapsing under pressure from the new systems, unless we smother rural reform at the outset.

China has already started to globalize. The modern world is economically competitive, and if we want to be successful, we must adapt to the rest of the world. If we do not adapt, we will be left behind. The successful operation of our economic system will largely determine whether or not we can adapt. The establishment of special economic zones and the opening of 14 large and medium-sized coastal cities have introduced a new type of operating mechanism within China's borders. That fact is important to consider as we implement urban systemic reforms.

It is imperative that we find a mechanism for economic reform; to do so, we must clearly understand the old system's basic rules of operation.

Consider the Old System's Basic Rules of Operation

Let us first discuss theoretical issues.

The basic contradiction of the social economy is that between supply and demand. The planned economy is a historical manifestation of that basic contradiction.

Under certain technological conditions, the resources needed to accommodate society's production are limited. A basic problem in economic activity is deciding what to produce, how much to produce, and what method of factor composition to use to implement production. Increased production of one type of product necessitates a relative decrease in another. So-called choice means to make comparisons between gains and losses and then to make a selection. We refer to this process as economic efficiency. Without choice, there is no economy. So-called economy means causing the objective function—that is, economic efficiency, under the constraint of limited resources—to be maximized during the selection process.

The result of choice is displayed by an entity such as the economic structure. The so-called economic structure refers to the state of industry distribution determined by certain factor structures (supply) and social demand structures. Thus, the contradiction between demand and supply is manifested in the economic structure. If a certain economic structure can sustain equilibrium between the supply and demand of various products, we call it an equilibrium structure, which is the basic definition of aggregate balance. It follows that aggregate balance and economic efficiency are inseparable twins. On the one hand, balance is the result of selection using efficiency as a standard; on the other hand, efficiency can be attained only under conditions of balance. The two can be separated only through theoretical thinking.

With regard to the form of material objects, resources and products are incomparable. Comparison is the premise of choice. Without comparison, there is no choice to speak of, and we must have a common language for comparison. That language should satisfy the following conditions: (a) it should truly reflect the degree of scarcity to guarantee that limited resources are used for the most efficient production, and (b) it should coordinate the relationship between various industries to guarantee equilibrium in the economic structure. The common language is price.

Accordingly, price is the standard of choice. Price is a tool that unifies economic efficiency and aggregate equilibrium. Its basic function is to coordinate supply and demand. Without price, we have no way to accept or reject numerous possible selections, and without economic efficiency, there is no aggregate equilibrium.

In actuality, technology is improving, and resource and social demand structures are changing. Thus, the process of economic development is actually the evolutionary process of the economic structure. Static equilibrium does not exist. Choice is a nonstop process, and coordination of the economic structure is also a nonstop process. Price is a standard of selection. Precisely because of its flexibility, price leads to production and consumption substitutions, which guarantee the economy's dynamic equilibrium. Unless a society is in an absolutely static state, price rigidity will cause the selection standard to work improperly, possibly causing the economic structure to lose its dynamic equilibrium.

In that regard, price is also a type of signal. It transmits information, guides resource allocation according to rational economic principles, guarantees the rationality of the economic structure's dynamic state, and maximizes economic efficiency.

Now let us discuss practical issues.

Under the old system, we tried to cast off the chains of price, but it continued to possess us like a specter, taking its ruthless revenge.

A rigid price system caused an irrational price structure, which, in turn, provided us with incorrect signals and wrong selection standards. The result was distortions in the economic structure, causing the inseparable twins—aggregate equilibrium and economic efficiency—to become enemies who perished together. Conflicts developed between macro and micro, between the plan and the market, between the concentrated and the dispersed, between the whole and the parts, between the long-term and the present, and between speed and efficiency. Thus, rivalries arose between the central government and local governments, between administration and the economy, between the state and the peasants, between workers and the peasants, between the cities and the countryside, and so on. It is precisely during such extreme contradictions that the economic system operates forcefully. Our understanding of China's economic issues should draw on that main thread.

First, incorrect price signals cause distorted economic calculations. Enterprises that try to achieve maximum efficiency by making choices based on those prices will necessarily destroy the macroeconomic planned equilibrium. Macroeconomic planning is determined by the "calculation price" in the planner's frame of mind, which is different from the real price transmitted to producers. It follows that one option would be to allow enterprises to make choices according to the principles of economic efficiency, thus destroying the planned equilibrium. The other option is to force enterprises to produce goods according to the plan, thereby depriving them of their right to make choices (and engage in economic activity). It must be one or the other. That is the basis behind the saying "Death from unification; chaos from liberalization." In this situation, we refer to "economic accounts" and "political accounts," or "low-level profit" and "high-level profit" as antithetical ideals. We view completion of plans as socialism and emphasis on profit making as capitalism. That view is attributable not so much to the subjective fabrications of theorists as it is to the objective requirement of practitioners to free themselves from a predicament.

Of course, absolute disregard for profit is unimaginable. The country needs savings, the people need a livelihood, the treasury cannot always finance deficit finance, and there must be things to waste before waste can occur. That observation brought about the notion of so-called adequate profit. The well-known Chinese economist Sun Yefang fiercely criticized this poorly articulated idea, not realizing that it contained a high degree of dialectical thinking. Precisely because it provided us with a theoretical basis, we were able to avoid government bankruptcy under the premise of completing plans.

Second, price distortions cause aggregate equilibrium to lose its objective basis, because the "calculation price" of the planner's imagination has no objective standard. We have no way to verify which products are undersupplied and which are oversupplied. Instead, plans are completely subjective. Temporary issues such as the long (oversupplied) and short lines (undersupplied) become permanent, and shortage and excess exist simultaneously. Even though we use aggregate equilibrium as the basic context of planning, the result would often be planned destruction of aggregate equilibrium.

Third, price distortions cause conflicts between material and value indicators, as well as between macroeconomic and microeconomic appraisals. For a distorted economic structure to reach forced equilibrium, planning must be done with physical objectives, and implementation must be guaranteed through administrative order. A top-down administrative system must control the economy, thus requiring enterprises to disregard efficiency and interests and to be restricted to an "iron rice bowl" or "commune cafeteria" system of allocation. Such restriction causes them to lack vitality and motivation and to stop caring about operational conditions and technological processes, ultimately impeding economic development.

Fourth, a distorted and rigid price system does not allow the economic system to evolve rationally, leading to a deformed economic structure. That deformed structure causes cyclical proportional dislocations in the national economy, with successive dislocations advancing the economy toward the verge of collapse.

In short, a rigid price system necessarily corresponds to a management system that has high levels of concentration, a priority for government order, and a disregard for the principles of material interest. It inevitably leads to inappropriate political intervention into the economy, eventually hampering its normal operation.

By acknowledging the regular operation of the old system and by correctly understanding the crux of the issue, we discovered that price system reform can work as a mechanism of systemic reform. We cannot untangle the knots of the old system without reforming the current price system. And when reform does not progress smoothly, we cannot attain the goal of "macroeconomic control, microeconomic vitality, control without death, and liberalization without chaos."

Before further discussing price system reform, let us discuss issues related to price adjustment.

Don't Pawn Off Our Treasures on Price Adjustment

The old price system was like a thermometer, except that it was filled with a nickel-iron alloy instead of mercury. Everyone now acknowledges that we need a new thermometer because the gauge on the old one did not accurately reflect the actual temperature.

That progress is encouraging because it shows that the specter is beginning to take its original form. What kind of thermometer should we use as a replacement?

The irrationality of the price system prevents the entire national economic system from progressing smoothly. Many people believe that the pressing issue of the day is to adjust prices so that there are no obstacles to systemic reform. Unfortunately, adjusting prices not only encounters economic difficulties but also involves big political risks. Consequently, proponents of price adjustments never dare to act.

I believe that price adjustments fail to resolve the root issue, and it makes little sense to simply replace the old iron-nickel thermometer with a new iron-nickel thermometer. We need a mercury thermometer.

Price adjustment is not price reform. The latter seeks to cure the maladies of the price system, whereas the former attempts only to address symptoms. The irrational price structure is a symptom, whereas the irrational price system is the root cause. The price problem arises from a rigid price structure in which the relationship between supply and demand has been severed. Prices have become mispriced. Within the confines of that system, even prices that were once rational will quickly become irrational unless the economy is absolutely static.

We tend to see fixed prices as an indicator of price stability, but that is a profound mistake. Price stability instead refers to the stability of the general price index. Without the stability of the general price index, changes in prices will not reflect real fluctuations in supply and demand and will thus hamper the function of prices. The goal of general price stability is to have a thermometer that accurately reflects the current temperature. Fixed prices are completely different. As soon as prices are fixed, they do not reflect supply and demand, thereby causing mispricing. Thus, fixed prices and price stability run counter to each other. Instead, the result of fixed prices is similar to that of inflation in that both cause prices to work improperly, although to different degrees and with different methods. Fixed prices are similar to an unchanging thermometer, whereas inflation is similar to a thermometer that changes erratically.

Using price adjustment as a means of resolving issues is inadvisable for a number of reasons.

First, prices represent a structure with infinite parameters. We cannot know the value of the parameters without knowing the supply-and-demand functions of every product. Instead, we know only that price changes cause a chain reaction, but we cannot know the specific degree of the chain reaction. If we believe that two products are priced too low now, it is possible that after we raise the price of the first product, we will discover that the price of the second is too high. If we raise the price of both products, the new prices may be even more irrational.

Second, an irrational price structure corresponds to an irrational economic structure. In an irrational economic structure, production prices that lead to even profit rates on capital differ from market prices that lead to supply-and-demand equilibrium. Setting prices according to production costs would result in market disequilibrium, whereas setting prices according to market equilibrium would result in uneven profit rates. Therefore, even if we calculate every price parameter, we still would not know how to set prices. Moreover, under the old system, data on costs and market demand were both incorrect because production and consumption did not reflect the choices made by economic actors. Even if they had choices, their choices would depend on irrational prices. And if we made adjustments according to those data, they would very likely be flawed. That approach is akin to allowing our enemies to lead us into war. The possibility of not failing is slight.

Third, the goal of price reform is to rationalize the economic structure. Economic structure rationalization involves a dynamic process of nonstop choice, whereas price adjustment is characterized by disconnected and discontinuous movement. By focusing on price adjustments, we assume that the economy is static. Attempting to use static methods to resolve dynamic problems not only fails to resolve the issue but also causes periodic oscillations in the economy. If the new price structure continues to be irrational, the economic structure will merely experience new distortions.

Fourth, price adjustment causes the government to spend money on compensation. Some people oppose price adjustment out of a fear of creating budget issues, which leads to further delays in resolving the price issue.

Fifth, the average person is extremely sensitive to price adjustment. Even minute price increases lead to complaints, without regard to possible benefits (such as corresponding decreases in the prices of other products). Even if everyone benefited from price adjustment, each individual would feel as though he or she suffered a loss, which would result in widespread cries of dissatisfaction. Therefore, the state loses double by spending additional money for increased discontent. There is no need to speak of political chaos erupting because increased animosity alone creates impediments to reform.

Sixth, if we bet our fortunes on price adjustment and it does not succeed, we will delay the opportunity to create a favorable path to reform.

Those arguments do not mean that I oppose any adjustment in prices. My key point is that price adjustment cannot solve the fundamental problem targeted. There is nothing wrong in a starving person having a snack before a banquet.

Can a Central Link Be Grasped in Price System Reform?

So-called reform of the price system refers to a planned loosening of price controls. It gradually forms a price structure that flexibly reflects the market supply-and-demand equilibrium. The function of prices will be fully brought into play in the economy.

Why does price system reform serve as the center of—and mechanism for—the entire systemic reform?

First, the general principle of systemic reform requires putting a priority on the planned economy, with supplemental market adjustments, macroeconomic control, and microeconomic flexibility. So-called macroeconomic control refers to the frequent, conscious maintenance of the general equilibrium of the national economy. That is the basic premise of the priority given to economic planning. So-called microeconomic flexibility allows enterprises to choose production and operational activities according to the principle of efficiency maximization. Once enterprises are given the right to make choices, there must be a rational price system in order to have "control without death and flexibility without chaos."

Second, the goal of systemic reform is to introduce the market mechanism into the planned economy. Price is the core of the market mechanism, and the price system reform process reflects its formation.

Third, the old planned system, materials supply system, commercial system, budget system, and wage system all corresponded to the old price system. Without changing the price system, other systems cannot fundamentally change. Additionally, as long as the price system is loosened, all market relationships will change, forcing other systems to loosen in tandem. Grasping the price system reform is analogous to controlling an ox by taking hold of its nose.

Fourth, price system reform will cause fundamental changes in the planning and control system. The priority of planning targets will transition from material objects and directives to values and guidance. The focus of planning will move to medium-term and long-term strategic planning and macroeconomic control. The state needs only to control macroeconomic variables—such as the aggregate supply and demand, the aggregate investment scope, the interest rate levels, the money supply, the range of wage growth, the general price levels, and so on—to guarantee planned proportional development of the national economy. Government does not need to directly control the production and operational activities of the enterprises, because the entire macroeconomy can be completely flexible.

Fifth, although the substitute tax payment system has already begun, a rational tax system can be built only on a rational price system. Implementing the substitution tax payment system while still suffering from irrational prices is comparable to using a harvester on uneven ground. Currently, we have no choice but to have diverse tax rates (different tax rates for different enterprises) to overcome rigid prices. Having diverse tax rates violates the economic laws of taxation. Diversified tax rates can turn into unified tax rates only if we move from rigid prices to flexible prices.

Sixth, price system reform will bring about a rational economic structure. A rational control system and economic structure will form simultaneously, and reform and adjustments will be unified.

Seventh, price rationalization will fully reveal interregional advantages, and a wave of competition will break up local protectionism. A rational division of labor will form among regions, and the full power of urban hubs will be realized.

Eighth, price structure reform will result in the merger of urban and rural economic systems. Their orderly operation under a common mechanism will form the new economic system.

The concrete method of price system reform can imitate price reform of agricultural sideline products, that is, implement a dual-track system in which old prices are directed by old methods and new prices by new methods. In the end, a completely new substitution price system would be established. Unlike price adjustment, price system reform is a continuous process. The issue is not whether the first step attains a rational price, but whether there is a trend toward one.

We could tentatively use a number of the following steps.

First, appraise list prices and set the scope of supply for list-price goods. The scope should be fixed at a base-year level and expanded no further. Supplier enterprises would be forced to guarantee supply at the old price, including product variety and quantity targets. All new products, as well as increased demand of old varieties, would not be supplied at a guaranteed list price. The price of unlimited supplies proves that the list price corresponds to the market equilibrium price, and, therefore, the list price would be automatically abolished.

Second, freeze list prices as well as the quantities of materials necessary for livelihood. Price policies could be strictly enforced to settle popular sentiments, and losses from those commodities could continue to be subsidized. Before formally transitioning to market prices, we could consider a suitable degree of price adjustment. However, the goal of price adjustment should be to create the conditions for reforming prices, rather than to block the path to price reform. The list price of some products enjoyed only by a small number of people should be discontinued.

Third, open negotiable price markets for all products. Those markets could be pioneer markets for discovering equilibrium prices. Individuals and enterprises should be allowed to trade commodities supplied at list prices, and the state should tax the profits from such trade by state-owned enterprises.

Fourth, designate the scope of unified prices, negotiable prices, and free-market prices. Rates for noncompetitive commodities, public goods, and labor should be uniformly set by the state. All other products should be left to negotiable or free-market prices on the basis of supply and demand.

Fifth, adjust prices for noncompetitive products by referring to the negotiable price market. The negotiable price market should be allowed to exist long term to act as a feedback mechanism for adjusting prices. The state should operate large-scale enterprises that produce such products.

Sixth, gradually liberalize all production materials markets with negotiable and free-market prices. Products with excessive disparities between list and market prices could be opened up step by step. Alternatively, preliminary adjustments could be followed before liberalization.

Seventh, once adjustments are made to the economic structure, market supply-and-demand relationships will change. List prices for some fixed-quantity supplies of consumer goods (such as textiles) may become insignificant, so list prices can automatically be canceled. Increasing personal incomes will obviously alter consumption patterns, and the list price of fixed-quantity supplies of consumer goods will gradually decrease as a proportion of aggregate household expenditures. In that way, suitable methods can be used to discontinue the list-price supply of consumer goods when the time is right. That approach will not increase discontent because wealthier people will not be sensitive to small losses.

Eighth, during the process of reform, the state should implement flexible market operations, buying goods when and where prices are low and selling them when and where they are high. In addition, it should encourage commercial enterprises and sole proprietors to do the same. Of course, the ultimate goal is to smooth price fluctuations. At the same time, effective measures should be implemented to curb monopolistic behavior that dominates or partitions the market.

In reality, price system reform has already begun, largely spontaneously. The management of various products on the market is currently quite chaotic, a symptom of the failings of the old price system. Attempting to use the old price management system to resolve the chaos will not succeed; in fact, I do not think that chaos is necessarily bad. The attitude we have toward system reform is key. If we can turn price system reform into a mechanism for overall reform by consciously using the many price phases that exist in the current market, the bad will become good. In fact, the chaos gives us an opportunity to get out of our predicament by creating favorable conditions for us to implement price system reform deliberately. That is to say, the early stages of price reform have already begun; the forward army has already advanced, and it is now time to exploit a victory.

For a long time, there has been a mainstream viewpoint that liberalized prices will necessarily drive up all prices. That view has no economic logic or backing in fact. It regards price as a completely subjective decision, as though sellers could ask for any price they want. If that viewpoint were correct, the 800 million peasants would have become millionaires long ago. In reality, price is determined by objective laws and is not something that people can change.

In the past, we used government authority to determine prices, but we could not eliminate market prices. It is even more naive to assume that a supplier could determine prices at will, though it is undeniable that the producers of some monopoly products could set prices according to the principle of profit maximization, which would be unfavorable to society's rational allocation of resources. It is precisely at this point that we advocate the state's setting unified price policies for that kind of product.

Will price reform cause general price increases? Our view is that it will not, as long as we implement the correct macroeconomic policies. The reasons are as follows: First, the general price level is determined by the ratio between the money supply and the supply of goods. Assuming that the speed of money circulation does not change, the price level will not increase as long as the growth rate of the money supply does not surpass the growth rate of goods. A chain reaction would change the price structure rather than the general price level.

Second, along with the rationalization of the price structure, products with excess supply will decrease in price. Products with excess demand will, on the one hand, experience a decrease in wasteful demand and, on the other hand, experience an increase in supply. Prices will not increase too much and will remain within the band of current list and market prices. In other words, the general price level will basically remain stable.

Third, the flow of factor inputs and finished goods will increase along with the rationalization of prices, thus forming a unified national market. The larger a market is, the more stable prices will be. That is the basic idea in economics. We should also acknowledge that list price is arbitrarily set, so using it to calculate the price level would not reflect the true price level. It makes no sense to use an untrue price level to measure the rationality of the price structure.

Do Not Let Budget Problems Scare Us Out of Our Wits

We know that the function of prices is to adjust supply and demand, as well as to rationally allocate resources. Under the old system, price, to a large degree, was used as a form of taxation (purchasing at low prices) and welfare (supplying at low prices or giving away). It was also a tool for wealth redistribution. We assigned too much responsibility to price and ultimately damaged its function. Now, we should let price focus on the work it was meant to do. What will take over the work that prices did in the past? That question brings us to budget issues.

We have no choice but to consider budget issues. Are they as dire as some have imagined? My answer is no. On the contrary, I believe that budget issues will fundamentally improve after the price system is reformed.

Let us first examine budget revenue.

First, the economic structure is severely distorted under the irrational price system. That distortion actually causes inefficient resource allocation so that aggregate production remains at the interior of the production frontier. That kind of growth in national income brought about by price reform is difficult to estimate but should not be ignored. Although it is just a notion, if we take a look at the development of the countryside over the past few years, we can easily see that it is extraordinarily scientific. If the total national income increases, budgetary sources also expand. As long as we reform the tax system in time, how can government revenue not increase?

Second, along with the abolishment of the "total egalitarianism" system brought about by the price system reform, the incentive for enterprises and employees to develop production and increase income will be greatly expanded. The income effect of that type of responsibility will be enormous. After raw materials and energy increase in price, the income of processing enterprises and energy-consuming enterprises will not necessarily experience a corresponding decline. Experience has already proved that point. If we have a sound tax system, how could enterprises increase income while governments experience decreased revenue?

Third, along with the price reform, a large number of enterprises whose input is greater than their output would be eliminated through competition. The government's casting off the burden of subsidies for losses would be the same as increasing government revenue.

Fourth, along with the increase in personal income, there would be an increase in idle capital in society. When residential savings rise sharply, the state could issue a suitable amount of public debt to accumulate a portion of that capital into its hands.

Fifth, rural areas can become a new budget source. When peasants become wealthier, they should pay more taxes to the state. Many wealthy peasants already anticipate owing taxes.

Generally speaking, we are optimistic about budget revenue.

Now, let us look at budget expenditures.

First, because the supply of list-price consumer goods is fixed, corresponding state expenditures will not increase significantly.

Second, after price reform, capital construction should be chosen according to efficiency standards. That approach can prevent certain mindless and duplicate construction projects from being implemented. Thus, construction expenditures for state production would be limited to key projects. Others would be entirely left to localities and enterprises. If the projects are wasteful, the state would not be responsible.

Third, by encouraging individuals and enterprises to invest in schools and by encouraging enterprises to cooperate with the government research institutes in joint research and development, the state's expenses for education and scientific research would not need to increase much.

Fourth, because the rural areas have developed, the state's agricultural assistance funding can be decreased. Peasants can handle many rural affairs, and localities can manage urban public works.

Overall, I believe that the basic balance between government revenues and expenses can be maintained during price reform. If the state still feels uneasy, it could set the revenue levels low and force localities and enterprises to pay appropriately. Currently, many enterprises and localities are not worried about paying more taxes; instead, they feel too restricted in conducting their business.

In addition, I believe that during reform, appropriate deficits are not necessarily bad. Enterprises have already proved that point over the past few years. Some advocates of deficit spending use Western countries as examples. Opponents believe that Western countries lack effective demand, whereas we lack supply, so that allowing deficits would add fuel to the fire. I believe that both viewpoints are oversimplified. We should acknowledge that our country is in a period of structural transformation. If deficits are beneficial to structural adjustments and favorably mobilize unused resources, the result would be to increase supply, not just demand.

At this point, experiencing some degree of structural inflation is unavoidable, but it is not necessarily related to budget deficits. Further, individual savings of urban and rural residents are increasing rapidly, but most of that capital is not used for investment, so there is nothing wrong with the state borrowing money from banks. If budget disequilibrium benefits the general economic equilibrium, deficit spending is worthwhile. We are just scaring ourselves by putting excessive emphasis on budget issues.

The assumption that government revenue and national income will increase together is not absolute. Government budget issues have two mandates. The first is to control the macroeconomy in order to rationally allocate resources. The second is to implement wealth redistribution. The former uses the principles of efficiency, and the latter uses the principles of equality. The amount of revenue that government should take from the national income should be limited to the requirements of the two mandates—and no more. Experience has taught us that excessive concentration of revenue in government is often harmful to rational resource allocation.

Learn the Obstacles to Systemic Reform

While reforming the economic system, we should pay special attention to the following obstacles.

First, China's economic system is still in the process of forming, and many operational functions are unsound. That situation not only hinders the market mechanism from coming into play but also causes certain difficulties for the planned economy. Among those issues are (a) the existence of large-scale, self-sufficient production; (b) the lack of resource mobility; (c) an undeveloped credit system; (d) an incomplete statistical system; (e) a lax tax administration; (f) a problem of ineffective information transmission; (g) an incomplete judicial system; and (h) a faint idea of the rule of law.

Macroeconomic control under the new system is a type of sensory control, but unsound operational functions cause many sectors of the economy to be "unresponsive." The "central nervous system" is not responding to information, so many economic measures fail to have the desired result.

Second, enterprises are not accustomed to the market because we lack a generation of entrepreneurs. In the past, we implemented the "state standard theory." Enterprises were the servants of administrative bodies and dealt with fulfilling production rather than making business decisions. In the current flexible market, enterprises must transition from production units to business operators; that is similar to asking a child who has never left home to live independently. There must be a period of adjustment.

Initially, it will be difficult to avoid certain issues, and that difficulty will increase the friction coefficient of reform. We should differentiate between the chaos caused by defects in the market and the chaos caused by enterprises' misunderstandings of the market mechanism. The defects of the market may need to be fixed by planning, whereas enterprise adjustment to the market can be resolved only by the market itself.

Entrepreneurs represent the soul of enterprises. The quality of an entrepreneur determines the quality of the enterprise. As enterprises transition, the function of entrepreneurs will become more important. In some ways, the coming era is the era of entrepreneurs. They must have the ability to (a) absorb information, (b) discover investment opportunities, (c) raise capital, (d) organize production, (e) implement technology, and (f) open new markets. Those capabilities require them to have a spirit for risk taking. The old system stifled the formation of that kind of entrepreneurial group. The majority of people leading our enterprises are "safety first" administrative bureaucrats, not entrepreneurs with the courage to explore. It is hard to imagine that a market mechanism inserted into a planned economy could operate smoothly without entrepreneurs. We can anticipate that if we have a batch of new-era entrepreneurs, systemic reform will be much smoother.

Third, economic management departments are not accustomed to the new system. Under the old system, high-level administration relied on direct orders to manage the economy. The new system requires economic management to fundamentally change both its guiding ideology and its specific methods. That change is no different from having a military command take over the management of a multinational corporation. Many of those who try to deal with economic affairs are "good at managing things to death, but bad at being flexible." Under the new system, they will be at their wits' end trying to "control without death and liberate without chaos."

Fourth, ordinary people's values have not yet adapted to the new system. In the past, we were accustomed to using moral standards to measure economic activity. We lumped together the economy and morality. History has already proven that morality's dominance over the economy will get us nowhere. However, reality also tells us that economic dominance will bring about moral disdain. The opinions toward the peasants who got rich first underscore that point. It looks as though people's maladjusted values are a serious obstacle to systemic reform.

13. Market Reforms and Income Distribution

When discussing the past 30 years of Chinese Reform and Opening, we must discuss income distribution. Actually, all systems, speaking from a certain perspective, are systems of income distribution. In other words, each system determines the method through which members of society attain income and wealth. Because income and wealth are objectives that people always pursue, the income distribution system is, in essence, an incentive system, a system for the creation of society's wealth. A systemic reform is also a reform of the income distribution system.

Before 1978, China implemented central planning. From the income distribution angle, it had two special characteristics: (a) its main goals were high national savings and egalitarian distribution, and (b) the government controlled all distribution. The government directly determined the preliminary distribution of income; there were no market or factor prices. At that time, when our incomes increased, we first needed to thank the government. Because the government distributed incomes, we thought all income came from the government.

In the market economy, the price of production factors and products are set by the supply and demand of the market. This price-setting process simultaneously determines resource allocation and income distribution. In other words, wealth creation and income distribution are determined at the same time. China's reform could be called a transformation from government-directed income distribution to market-directed income distribution. Today, the government still plays a major role in resource allocation, whereas the market plays a major role in income distribution. When combined, those two mechanisms led to the current income distribution issues with which so many people are dissatisfied.

The Basic Facts of Changes in Income Distribution since the Reform

In the early days of reform, our main goal was to introduce the incentive mechanism, while breaking down the "iron rice bowl" and egalitarianism. In the late 1970s and early 1980s, Chinese economists published numerous articles calling for "distribution according to labor." During the Cultural Revolution, we did not even accept "distribution according to labor." Today, income distribution is not an issue, but at that time, it was a big issue.

With the introduction of policies about enterprise profit sharing and individual bonuses, the income gap between employees of different enterprises began to expand. The nonstate-owned sector also began to develop. Some people got rich because they engaged in sole-proprietor commercial activities. Differences in individual incomes between industries and enterprises led to social contradictions.

Between 1984 and 1986, there were debates in society about income distribution, referred to as "red-eye disease." A popular saying at the time was "Pick up chopsticks and eat meat; put down chopsticks and curse" [referring to someone who benefits from a system while at the same time denounces that system. Trans.]. There was no Internet at that time, and the government controlled the media, so if we searched for reports on the debates about the unfairness of income distribution, we probably would not find much.

The government's method of dealing with the income gap was to implement the "bonus tax." Debates about income distribution continued until the Third Plenary Session of the 14th National Congress of the Communist Party of China in 1993. The Third Plenary Session formally established the principle of "priority for efficiency, with consideration for equality," which brought the debates to a close.

By the 15th National Congress of the Chinese Communist Party in 1997, not only was emphasis put on "distribution according to labor," but also "distribution according to production factors" was acknowledged. In his report to the 15th National Congress, General Secretary Jiang Zemin, said, "The combination of distribution according to labor and distribution according to production factors will incentivize capital, technology, and other production factors to participate in the distribution of earnings." That approach was the process through which our way of thinking about the entire income distribution reform changed.

Contributions from numerous economists helped establish some important guiding ideologies and policies during China's economic reform. Income distribution was something I paid close attention to. My early views were formed under the background of the red-eye disease. In early 1986, I published an article titled "Research on Income Distribution Policies in the New Era" in the first issue of *Management World* journal.[1] My article proposed three points: (a) "The basic objectives of new era income distribution policies can be summarized as giving priority to efficiency incentives, resource equilibrium, and capital accumulation as premises while considering fair distribution and price stability"; (b) "The basic direction of transitions in the income distribution mechanism should be to strengthen the function of the market distribution mechanism, weaken the role of government in distributing income, use the market mechanism to resolve the efficiency issue, and use the government mechanism to resolve the equality issue"; and (c) "The fundamental direction of wage reform should introduce the market mechanism as the decider of wages."

Looking back, I can see that those 30 years of reform produced some basic facts. The efficiency of the Chinese economy increased tremendously, and per capita gross domestic product (GDP) increased dramatically. Essentially, in fewer than 10 years, our per capita GDP doubled, which should be considered a miracle of human history. Over the past 200 years, the United States doubled its per capita GDP every 40 years. However, China is still lagging behind others, because we started to develop a market economy too late.

For the past 30 years of Reform and Opening, we developed very rapidly. As a result, China's absolute poverty issue has basically been resolved. If we examine the World Bank's statistics—regardless of whether one is using the old standard or the new standard—the proportion of the population in poverty is decreasing dramatically. The proportion of rural poverty as a percentage of the population, using the old standard, was 40.7 percent in 1980 and 4.8 percent in 2002. Using the new standard, those proportions are 75.7 percent and 12.5 percent, respectively. The poverty rate of the entire population, using the old standard, was 23 percent in 1981 and 3 percent in 2001. Using the new standard, those proportions are 52.8 percent and 7.8 percent, respectively.[2]

We will see that the decrease in the poverty rate, if separated by province, is notably related to each province's GDP growth. The regions with the fastest GDP growth had the most rapid decrease in the poverty rate. That fact confirms Deng Xiaoping's belief that "development is the top priority."

Of course, it is undeniable that at the same time per capita incomes and living standards of almost everyone were dramatically increasing, the income gap also widened. Regardless of whether we are discussing the rural or the urban areas, the Gini coefficient of current statistics has increased. Something everyone must pay attention to is that, according to the World Bank's calculations, China's national Gini coefficient was close to 0.45 in 2001.[3] If we calculate urban and rural numbers separately, the urban number is 0.37 and the rural number is 0.33. Both the rural and urban numbers are below 0.4. If we account for differences in living expenses, the Gini coefficient for the entire population does not reach 0.4. That statistical issue is caused by the dual-tier structure that Professor Yining Li of Peking University refers to.[4]

A new saying has arisen: "The fruits of reform should be shared by all." Were the fruits of our reform over the past 30 years shared by all? My personal answer is yes, but the degree was different. I believe that even though the income gap between people has increased, the degree of fairness of Chinese society has increased. When I speak of the degree of fairness, it includes equality of opportunity. An important measure of social fairness is income mobility or the change in different income groups. According to the research of Professors Niny Khor and John H. Pencavel at Stanford University, the income mobility of China has increased tremendously.[5]

If we separate urbanites into five groups according to income (high to low), we will see that of the people in the highest income group in 1990, only 43.9 percent were still in the highest income group in 1995, and 5 percent had dropped into the lowest income group. Of the people in the lowest income group in 1990, only 49.6 percent were still in the lowest income groups by 1995. The other 50.4 percent had escaped the lowest income group, and 2.1 percent of them entered the highest income group. That finding shows how equality of opportunity increased. An expansion of the income gap does not always mean the rich get richer and the poor get poorer. It is equally possible that some rich people get poorer, and some poor people get richer.

In the United States, of the urbanite people in the lowest income group in 1993, 70.4 percent were still in the lowest group in 1998. Of those in the highest income group in 1993, 50.1 percent were still in the highest income group in 1998. Those numbers are much higher than China's numbers, so China's income mobility is higher than that of the United States.

Five Paradoxes of Income Distribution

Now, there are increasingly more debates about income distribution, which is related to the way we evaluate the success of our reform. Is development still the top priority? Is the policy that "gives priority to efficiency, with consideration for equality" correct? Should we maintain our direction toward market reforms? To answer those important questions, we must address the perplexities of our analysis of interregional statistics.[6]

The first paradox is the relationship between GDP growth and the income gap. The increase in China's Gini coefficient accompanies the growth of income levels. Is the income gap the price to be paid for attaining GDP growth? After we examine interregional data, that conclusion does not seem to be the case.

In Figure 13.1, the x-axis is each province's per capita GDP, and the y-axis is each province's 2000 Gini coefficient. On average, the regions with the highest per capita GDP are also the regions with the narrowest income gap. That is also the case for the growth rate of GDP. On average, the regions with the highest per capita growth rates have the narrowest relative income gaps, especially in provinces such as Zhejiang, Fujian, and Guangdong. Those regions with relatively low income growth have the widest relative income gaps.

The second paradox is the relationship between the scale of the state-owned economy and the income gap. Because state-owned enterprises pay wages that are closer to the average labor production rate, the income gap between employees will be relatively narrow. Private enterprises compensate according to an individual's marginal production rate, so the income gap is relatively wide. A natural inference would be that the regions with the state-owned sector as a larger proportion of the economy should have the narrowest income gap. However, the numbers completely contradict our inference.

Figure 13.1
REGIONAL GDP INDEXES AND GINI COEFFICIENTS

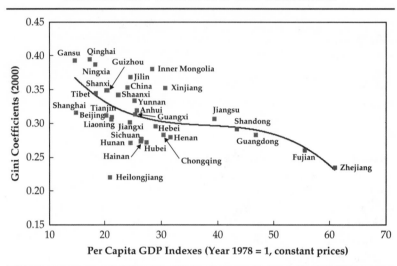

SOURCE: Data on Gini coefficients provided by Li Shi of Beijing Normal University. Other data were collected from the *China Statistical Yearbook*, 2004.

In Figure 13.2, the x-axis represents the proportion of a province's total workforce employed in the state-owned sector, and the y-axis represents that province's Gini coefficient. On average, the regions with the highest proportion of state-owned economic activity also have the highest income gaps.

The third paradox is the relationship between government expenditures and the income gap. The goal of government transfer payments is to reduce the income gap and to decrease the wide gap between rich and poor. In theory, the regions with government revenues as a higher percentage of GDP should have the narrowest income gap, but interregional data provide a completely different conclusion. In Figure 13.3, the x-axis represents government expenditures as a proportion of GDP, and the y-axis represents the Gini coefficient. The regions with the higher government expenditures as a proportion of GDP are the regions that have the higher Gini coefficients or, in other words, that have a wider income gap.

The fourth paradox is the relationship between profit and income distribution. Under the planned economy, the preliminary alloca-

Figure 13.2
REGIONAL STATE-OWNED ENTERPRISE EMPLOMENT RATIOS
AND GINI COEFFICIENTS

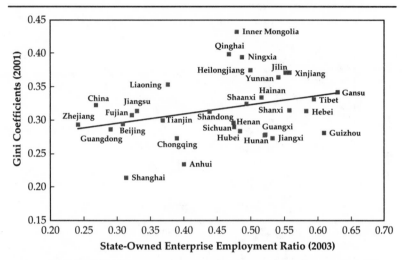

SOURCE: Data on Gini coefficients provided by Li Shi of Beijing Normal University. Other data were collected from the *China Statistical Yearbook*, 2004.

tion of income that an individual received came only from labor. In a market economy, not only are there earnings from labor, but also there are capital earnings and profits earned by entrepreneurs. After Reform and Opening, the source of individual income diversified, and profit even became some people's main source of income. We will naturally believe that if profits are a higher proportion of GDP, then the income gap of that society will naturally be slightly wider. However, we will see that interprovincial statistics do not support that conclusion.

I used data from the National Statistical Bureau to calculate earnings from labor, profits, production taxes, and depreciation as a proportion of each region's GDP. Overall, after I accounted for taxes and depreciation, earnings from labor constituted two-thirds of GDP, and profits constituted one-third.

The difference between regions is huge. Our first discovery is that areas with profits as a higher proportion of GDP also have the highest per capita incomes and the most rapid growth in incomes.

Figure 13.3
RATIO OF GOVERNMENT EXPENDITURES TO GINI COEFFICIENTS

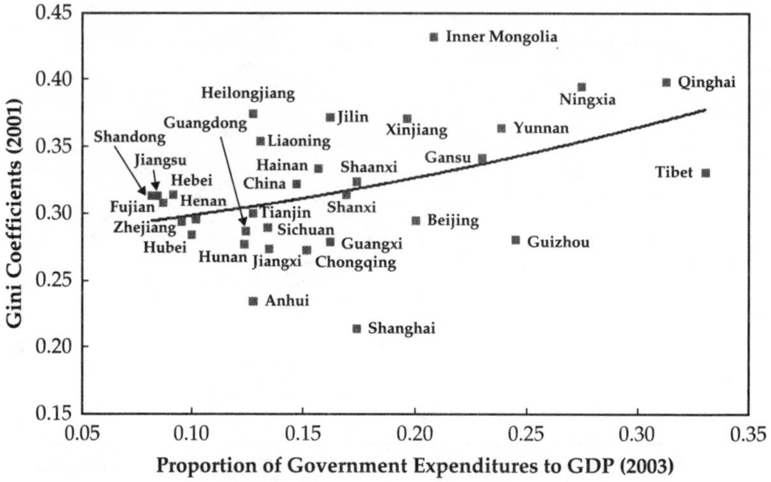

SOURCE: Data on Gini coefficients provided by Li Shi of Beijing Normal University. Other data were collected from the *China Statistical Yearbook*, 2004.

There is nothing strange about this point because profit stimulates investment and economic activity. The strange part is that, on average, the areas with the higher profits as a proportion of GDP have the narrower income gaps. The areas with the lower profits as a proportion of GDP have higher Gini coefficients (Figure 13.4).

The fifth paradox is the relationship between the degree to which an economy relies on the market and income distribution. If it is said that market openness increases the gap between the rich and poor, then the areas with lower degrees of market openness, as well as stronger roles for government, should have narrower income gaps. In reality, the opposite is true. Using Gang, Xiaolu, and Hengpeng's 2001 Provincial Market Openness Index[7] and Gini coefficient data on each province from the World Bank for the same year, we will discover an interesting phenomenon. On average, the regions with the highest degree of market openness have narrower income gaps, not wider ones (Figure 13.5).

290

Figure 13.4
PROFIT SHARE AND GINI INDEX

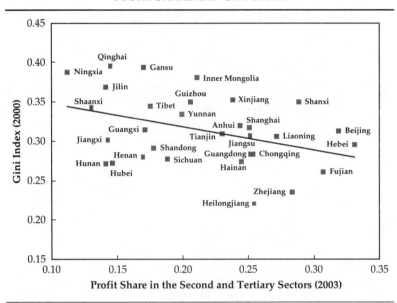

SOURCE: Data on Gini coefficients provided by Li Shi of Beijing Normal University. Other data were collected from the *China Statistical Yearbook,* 2004.

A Theoretical Explanation for the Five Paradoxes

How can we unravel the five paradoxes? Since the start of reform, the income gap and efficiency have increased together. The income gap is partially rational. A rational income gap is the price we must pay for economic growth and increases in efficiency. Perhaps it is also partially irrational. That is to say, we would not have to pay that price, and we could still maintain the same economic efficiency and income growth. Of course, whether or not we are willing to pursue that kind of efficiency and income growth is a value judgment. From an economics perspective, we care about whether or not our economy is on the efficient frontier between growth and the income gap.

Let me explain a basic theory. One of the contributions to economics made by Nobel prize–winning economist James Mirrlees is that asymmetric information on individual ability is the source of the

Figure 13.5
MARKETIZATION AND GINI COEFFICIENT (2001)

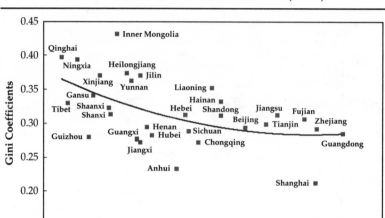

SOURCE: Data on Gini coefficients provided by Li Shi of Beijing Normal University. Marketization data are from Fan Gang, Wang Xiaolu, and Zhu Henpeng, *NERI Index of Marketization of China's Provinces 2006 Report* (Beijing Economic Science Press, 2007).

contradiction between efficiency and equality.[8] If the government knew each person's ability, it could assess taxes on or provide subsidies to each person with different abilities to implement any desired degree of income distribution. For example, during the same amount of work time, one person can create Y 200 of value, but another can create only Y 100 of value. The government needs to assess only Y 50 worth of taxes on the first person and then subsidize the second person for Y 50, so that they both can realize absolute equality.

However, because the government cannot know the ability of every person—under any system—then complete equality cannot be reached. Even if the government realistically had a way to make every person's monetary income the same, inequality would exist between people of different abilities. The reason is that to get the same income, those with high abilities need to spend relatively less time working and to spend more leisure time. Therefore, according to Mirrlees, attaining equality is impossible. Here, we have a contradiction between efficiency and equality, which information economics refers to as the contradiction between allocation efficiency and information rent. To attain higher resource allocation efficiency, higher-ability people must be allowed to receive more information rent (income). Conversely, to reduce the information rent of high achievers, the allocation efficiency of resources must be distorted.

Another important economic theory states that uncertainty influences income distribution. The higher the uncertainty, the wider the income gap will be. In 1921, University of Chicago professor Frank Knight[9] proved that profit comes from uncertainty. If society did not have uncertainty, there would be no profit in the economic sense (the part above the average rate of return on capital). If we speak from the perspective of economics, prices of the factors of production are costs. Profit is not the price of factors; profit is the part of an enterprise's revenues that surpasses costs. Without uncertainty, the result of competition would surely be that the price of a product would be completely absorbed by that product's factors of production (such as wages, interest, and rent). If that were the case, businesses would have no profits. Because of uncertainty, there is profit as surplus revenue, so there are entrepreneurs. This point is very important for our understanding of income gaps.

First, the role of an entrepreneur is to face uncertainty. Generally speaking, more uncertainty requires more able entrepreneurs and more profit. If an environment's uncertainty is extremely high, only those with extreme intelligence, above-average judgment, and courage will risk engaging in commercial activity. Such an individual is extremely rare in society, so he or she could earn extremely large profits.

Second, almost everyone is risk averse, and with uncertainty comes risk. For someone to take on risk, the person must be compensated for that risk. When uncertainty is greater, compensation for risk must be greater. In that way, even if everyone has the same expected income, their incomes will ultimately be different. Those with good luck will make money, and those with bad luck will lose money. The greater the uncertainty, the larger the income gap will be.

During the 30 years of China's Reform and Opening, the greatest uncertainty faced by those engaged in commercial activity was institutional uncertainty, policy uncertainty, and government behavior uncertainty. The source of such system uncertainty is government allocation of resources and the randomness of government behavior. To Chinese entrepreneurs, the hardest uncertainty to predict may not be market uncertainty or technological uncertainty, but the uncertainty of government policy and its implementation. With such uncertainty, just having normal entrepreneurial abilities may not be enough; political connections and background may be more important. Only those with government connections or those with government backgrounds risk doing business. Those without connections or those without backgrounds dare not risk doing business. Additionally, when the uncertainty of policy and government behavior is higher, the need for those connections and background is even greater.

In that way, we can provide a theoretical explanation for the five paradoxes that were discussed earlier. Even if institutional uncertainty is a common phenomenon, different regions of China have large differences in uncertainties about systemic environments, policy, and government behavior. The relationship between efficiency and income equality manifests itself differently in different regions. Furthermore, different regions have followed different development paths.

If the x-axis represents the GDP growth rate, and the y-axis represents the Gini coefficient, their relationship should be upward sloping, but the slope of each region is different. The regions with higher institutional uncertainty have steeper slopes. The reason is that in a region with a low degree of market openness and high policy uncertainty, doing business is much harder. Only a limited number of people will risk doing business, and most people will be unwilling to take the risk. Because competition is relatively nonintense, the risk takers can attain excess profits, even huge profits.

In a region with a high degree of market openness and relatively low institutional uncertainty, many entrepreneurs with ordinary ability or people without strong government connections can do business, so competition is intense, and profit rates are relatively low. In the regions with higher uncertainty, the number of private enterprises is small, the rate of economic growth is low, and aggregate profits are low, but profits are concentrated in the hands of a limited number of people, so the income gap is larger.

In a region with lower uncertainty, the number of private enterprises is larger, the rate of economic growth is high, and aggregate profits are high, but profits are spread relatively evenly. To attain the same rate of growth, the region with higher uncertainty must pay a higher price with regard to the income gap than does the region with lower uncertainty. The interregional statistics that we looked at earlier show that those regions with higher growth have more even income distributions. That downward-sloping line showing the relationship between growth rates and Gini coefficients is actually formed by different points on the upward-sloping lines of different regions (Figure 13.6).

How to Reduce the Unfair Gap in Income Distribution

If the previous conclusion is true, it has major implications for the next step in reform policies. Without harming GDP growth, how

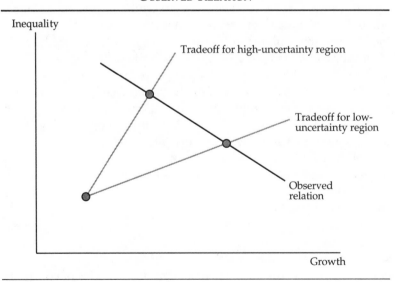

Figure 13.6.
TRADEOFF BETWEEN GROWTH AND INEQUALITY AND
OBSERVED RELATION

Inequality

Tradeoff for high-uncertainty region

Tradeoff for low-uncertainty region

Observed relation

Growth

do we reduce the income gap and unfair income distribution to the greatest extent? The key is to increase the degree of market openness in the economy to reduce the uncertainty caused by government behavior.

If the degree of market openness for all of China—or the way in which government behaves—could reach the level of Zhejiang Province, then we could sustain a high growth rate while decreasing income inequality to a large extent.

Similarly, political system reform has become very important. The most important political system reform would be to make all levels of government operate within the boundaries of the law. That change would reduce the uncertainty of government behavior and would build a true market economy. If the government acts according to prescribed procedures, both businesspeople and ordinary citizens can better predict government behavior and can be more certain about the consequences of their activities. Then, extremely high monopolistic profits and opportunities for a few people to earn a lot of money will be reduced significantly.

In that respect, an independent judiciary is key. Without judicial independence, a rule-of-law economy is impossible.

We also need to reduce government control over resources and the limits on entry into the market. If the government still allocates large amounts of resources, but we let the market determine individual income distribution, a large amount of resource prices in the form of profits will become the income of a limited number of people. That result will ensure an unfair income distribution. The government's control of resources not only harms efficiency but also harms fairness. The government's limits on market entry allow a limited number of people to do certain things, while prohibiting others from doing the same. It protects monopoly profit and leads to an expansion of the income gap. We should not assume that the relationship between efficiency and fairness is negatively correlated. If we continue systemic reform in the right direction, we will increase not only efficiency but also fairness.

Another important point is that government investment in education is a major way to decrease the income gap. Much recent research shows that an individual's income is more closely related to his level of education. The incomes of people with higher levels of education grow faster. If the government wants to help low-income groups, the best way is to raise their education level.

Compulsory education is without question the responsibility of government, and government should also increase investments in higher education. At the same time, competition should be introduced into higher education. Universities should be given more autonomy. They should be allowed to decide tuition costs, so they can collect relatively high tuition from high-income groups and provide full scholarships for students from low-income families. Our current circumstance is very strange. Low-quality universities have high tuition, so the tuition paid by students from low-income families is higher. Those third-tier universities with high tuitions are attended mostly by students from the countryside.

This chapter has shown that our use of transfer payments to reduce the income gap is unsuccessful. It is not as effective as relying on the market. We still need to maintain development as a top priority, especially in the era of globalization. To China, we cannot resolve the fairness issue without development. If we deter entrepreneurship, no one will be willing to do business, and the poverty issue will reappear.

I would like to raise a special point about the new Labor Contract Law. Some of its clauses could be fatal for China's future development. Perhaps that law's intention is good, in that it is meant to help low-income groups and workers. However, it could result in harming the very people it aims to help: those low-income groups, including migrant workers and some urban workers.

PART THREE

THE ORIGINS OF THE FINANCIAL CRISIS

14. Understanding the Crisis Is More Important than Reacting to It

The world is full of uncertainty. That old saying seems to have been forced on us today. In 2007, the Chinese Entrepreneur Confidence Index reached an eight-year high point. Even at the beginning of 2008, the index was the highest it had been in eight years. But by the end of the year, the entrepreneur confidence index had fallen to its lowest point in eight years, in fact much lower than at any other time during those past eight years. The confidence index for Chinese economists was similar. However, the survey data show that the downturn in confidence for economists appeared three months earlier than the downturn in confidence for entrepreneurs. Today, both Chinese entrepreneurs and economists have difficulty feeling as optimistic as they were a year and a half ago!

The change in entrepreneur confidence is really a sign of the times and reflects the change in the Chinese economic outlook. Over the past 12 months, the change in the Chinese Industrial Value-Added Index has had two main characteristics: (a) the growth rate has decreased rapidly, as though all businesses made mistakes simultaneously, and (b) the decrease in growth of heavy industry has become much larger than that of light industry. The fluctuations in the industries that generate production goods are much larger than in the industries that generate consumption goods. Those two characteristics are also the hallmarks of an economic recession. We should say that our economy has already entered hard times or is experiencing growth deterioration.

The change in China's economy is a microcosm of the change in the world economy, although our problems appeared a little later. Now, everyone is discussing when China's economy can get out of the trough. Where is the low point? Some people say it will be V-shaped, some say U-shaped, and others say it might be W-shaped. The most pessimistic view is that it will be L-shaped. But I believe that it is more important to understand why this worldwide economic decline occurred. There are probably different reasons for the decline. I believe the most fundamental issue is whether its source stems from market failure or government failure. In other words, is it a problem with the "invisible hand" or the "visible hand"? The different perceptions of and responses to what caused the current situation will lead to different policy choices. Policy choices are also related to the kind of economic structure China moves toward in the future, and they are similarly related to the future trend of economics.

Some people blame the current financial crisis on the market or believe it resulted from economic liberalization. After the crisis occurred, Keynesian policies of economic interference became very popular worldwide. Every country's government was implementing all kinds of policies to rescue the market, such as significant decreases in interest rates, large-scale expansions of bank credit, injections of capital into bankrupt financial institutions, uncontrolled increases in public works funding, consumption stimulus, increased supervision, takeovers of private companies, and countless other measures. However, reality and rational analysis show that it was not so much a failure of the market but a failure of government policy. It was not so much the greed of businesspeople but the errors of the bureaucrats that supervised monetary policy. The policies that governments are using to address the financial crisis are not solving the problem. They are only prolonging the crisis and making it worse. In my view, the crisis is an opportunity to resurrect the Austrian school of economics and to completely bury Keynesianism.

A Revisit of the Austrian School's Explanation of Depressions

Let us review the financial crisis that happened 80 years ago. Although that crisis occurred for reasons that differ from those of the current crisis—such as globalization and the rise of China, as well as other emerging markets—they have many similar characteristics. Before the 1929 crisis, technological innovation, productivity increases, and economic growth led to price stability and even price declines on the one hand. Everything seemed to be fine. On the other hand, continued bank credit expansion, excess liquidity, low interest rates, strong fixed-asset investment, and serious bubbles in the stock market and real estate seemed unsustainable. The long-term Japanese economic recession that started in the 1990s and the Asian

Financial Crisis at the end of the 1990s both had similar characteristics beforehand.

Did anyone predict the worldwide economic recession that began in 1929? Yes, two people did, and they were probably the only people, albeit, they did not predict the correct time. Those two people were Ludwig von Mises and Friedrich Hayek.[1] Both were leaders of the Austrian school of economics, and Hayek later received the Nobel Prize in Economics in 1974. They could predict the 1929 crisis because they had a full set of more rational business cycle theories.

According to their theories, the Federal Reserve implemented sustained expansionary monetary policies in the 1920s. Interest rates were set extremely low, and debt exposure was inflated. Ultimately, those two factors would result in a panic and then a depression. A depression occurs because interest rates that are too low will distort resource allocation signals. Entrepreneurs will begin to invest in projects that otherwise would not attract investment. That is especially true for capital-intensive industries, such as heavy industry or real estate, which are very sensitive to interest rates.

Stock market bubbles caused by excess liquidity will, in turn, foster a craze in fixed-asset investment, which causes the expansion of overinvestment. Greater investment demand leads to corresponding increases in the prices of commodities and in incomes. The cost of investing increases, which later proves that the original investment was unproductive. When the government can no longer continue the expansionary policies of the past, bubbles in equity and real estate collapse. Capital is now stuck in nonconvertible assets, such as factories and property. Capital is suddenly scarce, so investment projects are abandoned one after the other, thus causing a depression.

To Hayek and Mises, in any economy, a bust will follow artificial booms. Booms and busts are two sides of the same coin. Their theories tell us that to judge whether or not the economy is overheating, we cannot just look to see whether or not the price level is rising. We should look mainly at interest levels and credit expansion. Because there is a time gap between credit expansion and an increase in the price level, then while we were waiting for inflation to happen, the recession would have already arrived.

In contrast to Mises and Hayek, John Maynard Keynes believed that depressions were caused by a scarcity of effective demand. Excessive household savings cause scarcity of effective demand. When businesses are pessimistic about the future, they are unwilling to invest.

The 1929–1933 crisis created Keynesian economics. In the 1930s, either the Austrian school or Keynesianism could have become mainstream economics. However, the Austrian school was marginalized, and Keynesianism became mainstream. It ruled over the economics world for a few decades until people began to doubt it in the 1980s. Why was Keynesianism able to become mainstream? Simply put, Keynesianism provides an excellent theoretical basis for government intervention. When demand is scarce and the market has failed, the solution is for the government to intervene in the market, to increase demand, and therefore to lead the market out of recession.

The Austrian school believes that recessions are a necessary process for the market to self-adjust. They assist in easing the problems that exist in the economy. Government intervention can only make problems worse. In reality, if it were not for the Hoover administration's interventions (such as expanded public investments, limitations on income decreases, trade protectionism, etc.), that crisis would not have lasted as long as it did.[2]

For the above-listed reasons, governments love Keynesianism. Of course, many economists also like Keynesianism because if Keynesianism is correct, governments will create many employment opportunities for economists. If economists say that Austrian economics is correct, then government economists would have nothing to do. Austrian school economists advocate not intervening in the market because it will adjust itself. Economists are also an interest group, and Keynesianism serves their interests, which I believe is an important reason for its establishment.

With that background, let us look at Alan Greenspan's explanation of the economic crisis in the 1930s from his 1966 article "Gold and Economic Freedom."[3]

> When business . . . underwent a mild contraction . . . , the Federal Reserve created more paper reserves in the hope of forestalling any possible bank reserve shortage. . . . The "Fed" succeeded; . . . but it nearly destroyed the economies of the world in the process. The excess credit which the Fed pumped into the economy spilled over into the stock market—triggering a fantastic speculative boom. Belatedly, Federal Reserve officials attempted to sop up the excess

reserves and finally succeeded in braking the boom. But it was too late: by 1929, the speculative imbalances had become so overwhelming that the attempt precipitated a sharp retrenching and a consequent demoralizing of business confidence. As a result, the American economy collapsed.

Greenspan's explanation of the Great Depression written 40 years ago was exactly the same as Hayek's explanation 80 years ago. Regrettably, decades later, it is possible that Greenspan's behavior and the Fed's behavior that he criticized in those years were not much different.

The Source of This Global Financial Crisis

Let us reexamine the economic crisis we are currently facing. Did anyone foresee it? Actually, some people did. In 2006 or even earlier, scholarly investor Peter Schiff predicted that the subprime crisis would happen very quickly. He said that it would cause the U.S. economy to enter a period of depression. The same year, William White, chief economist of the Bank of International Settlements, wrote an article saying a global economic crisis was about to happen.[4] In addition, Krassimir Petrov, an economist at the Ludwig von Mises Institute in the United States, wrote an article comparing China's economy to the U.S. economy in the 1920s. He predicted that China would have a recession in 2008.[5]

Those three economists are considered either Austrian school economists or defenders of the Austrian school. Their theoretical framework for economic analysis comes from Hayek's business cycle theory. William White believes the theories of the Austrian school are most appropriate for analyzing current global economic issues. Of course, a few non–Austrian school scholars also made similar warnings.

In my view, according to all that the Austrian business cycle theory has stated clearly, there is little difference between the source of the current financial crisis and the 1929 crisis. The central bank started all the trouble. The Federal Reserve implemented sustained policies of low interest rates and credit expansion, which distorted market signals. On the one hand, the Fed misguided entrepreneurs into overinvesting in nonproductive capital goods. That overinvestment led to substantial increases in raw materials prices and wages and caused a stock market bubble. On the other hand, it also misguided consumers into increasing consumption and reducing savings. People who should not have borrowed money began to borrow, and people who should not have bought homes started buying homes. That situation led to a real estate bubble and unsustainably high consumption. Society's real resources did not increase.

When overinvestment and overconsumption turn into serious inflationary pressures (an increase in prices), the government (the Fed) has no choice but to stop monetary expansion and increase interest rates. (If the government continues to increase the money supply, it will lead to hyperinflation and a collapse of the monetary system.) At that time, towers built on sand began to collapse. Stock market and property bubbles evaporated. The original capital was sunk into nonconvertible fixed assets (such as factories and property). Capital became scarce, investment projects were abandoned one after another, bank loans were difficult to recall, credit contracted, and a recession began. The subprime crisis happened because the temptation of low interest rates and a housing bubble led people who should not borrow money to buy a house to borrow money to buy a house. That, however, was the fuse, not the source of the economic crisis.

After governments distort interest rate signals, the pricing mechanism will fail, regardless of whether we are discussing financial or real assets. For example, the price-to-earnings ratio of a stock is no longer a suitable gauge of the rationality of a stock price because profit itself is distorted. That distortion is totally the fault of the government and the monetary policies of the central bank. It has nothing to do with relaxed financial supervision. The highly leveraged U.S. economy is the result of the Fed's expansionary credit policies, not its source.

The reasoning for crises caused by credit expansion can be explained using Mises's metaphor for building a house. The person preparing to build a house owns the materials (such as bricks) but has only enough to build one small house. He incorrectly believes he can build a large house. So he begins laying the foundation according to his plans for a large house. Obviously, the sooner he discovers his mistake, the sooner he can adjust his plans without wasting too many resources and labor. If he uses up all of his resources before discovering his mistake, his only option is to demolish the half-built house and start over, suffering a serious loss in investments. Analogous to this example, the incorrect signals that caused the economic crisis came from the government—the Federal Reserve.

Another important cause of the crisis was the U.S. government's housing policies and debt guarantees for the real estate market. The Community Reinvestment Act passed by the U.S. Congress and the homeownership policies started by the Clinton administration seriously distorted prudent principles of business in residential lending.[6] Precisely because the U.S. government guaranteed Freddie Mac and Fannie Mae, China was willing to buy billions of dollars of U.S. debt on such generous terms. When the crisis happened, Freddie Mac and Fannie Mae owned about half of all residential mortgage debt. (Interestingly, the U.S. government established Fannie Mae during the Depression in the 1930s.) If the U.S. government had not made such a guarantee, China would not have loaned it money. After the government made its guarantee, lenders did not worry about borrowers' credit or their ability to repay. After being guaranteed, borrowers began to borrow money without worry. Government policy caused that morally hazardous behavior and was one of the main causes of the 1997 Asian Financial Crisis.

However, in another respect, the Asian crisis and the crisis in 1929 have one big difference: in 1929, China was a very small economy. We must incorporate that element into our understanding of today's economic crisis. Without understanding China's economy, we have no way of comprehending all the causes of today's crisis. Without understanding China's place in the world, we have no way of getting out of this crisis.

Internationally, some believe that China caused the crisis. The Chinese do not spend money, but they urge Americans to spend money. That viewpoint is, of course, incorrect. Similarly, we cannot blame the Asian Financial Crisis on U.S. creditors. However, the issues the commentators discuss are worth consideration, not just emotionally charged counterarguments.

China's trade surplus as a portion of gross domestic product (GDP) reached 7–8 percent. Foreign exchange reserves were $100 billion in 1996, $200 billion in 2001, $1 trillion in 2006, and $1.95 trillion in 2008. In the international economic system, what kind of effect will such a rapid increase in one country's foreign exchange have on the global economy? Assuming the crisis had happened five years earlier, would it have been as serious as today? I do not think so. If Americans had wanted to spend money, they could not have done so because no one would have provided it to them. If our financial system had been freer and had implemented foreign exchange rate liberalization, the renminbi's appreciation would have given Chinese businesses enough warning. Our entrepreneurs would have focused on increasing the quality of their products, not simply on using cheap labor and cheap resources to make exportable goods. We would not have had such a large imbalance of trade or such a large foreign exchange reserve. China's money supply would not have increased as fast, and investment scales would not have been as large. Even if the U.S. economy had problems, the difficulty we ourselves would have faced would not have been as large.

The economic crisis is certainly the result of multisided actions. Both lenders and borrowers have responsibility; without one there cannot be the other. However, the fundamental issue is to understand what led to those kinds of actions. Instead of saying that China's difficulties were caused by the U.S. financial system being too free, it is better to say that China's financial system is too unfree. No matter which aspect is being discussed, they are all mistakes related to the "visible hand."

Government Bailouts or Unhampered Adjustments?

When the economy has a problem, people often seek assistance from the government, which believes it is duty-bound to provide such assistance.

Can the government possibly use more debt and increased demand to rescue the economy from recession? I am skeptical. Why did the 1929 crisis last as long as it did? After the crisis started, the government interfered too much in the economy. Now, some people say President Franklin Roosevelt's 1933 New Deal policies saved the American economy. Actually, Roosevelt had few new policies; his New Deal had already been implemented by his predecessor, Herbert Hoover.[7] A large amount of evidence proves that large government investments in public infrastructure, tariff increases, and restrictions on wage adjustments were all put into effect before Roosevelt took office, and they all failed. According to the research of Austrian economists, it was precisely those government bailout measures that delayed the market's self-adjustment, causing the recession to last longer. The failure of Japanese bailout policies after 1990 also proves that point. Zero interest rate policies and large-scale public investment have certainly not brought Japan out of recession.[8]

Can our bailouts today succeed? I think they will have a short-term effect. However, the best method for solving the problem is market self-correction. Government bailouts probably delay market adjustment. For example, today's economy is like a drug addict. If a doctor gives the addict a prescription for morphine, the addiction will most likely become more serious. Even if overinvestment increases growth for a time, such growth will probably be short-lived, and the economy will fall again—most likely to a lower point.

Using real estate as an example, I support canceling all policies and regulations that increase transaction costs in the real estate market. Doing so will bring into play the functions of the market. Except for that effect, I do not support government rescue efforts. As long as transactions are unhampered, prices that need to fall should fall. The government should not intervene. If the government continuously looks for ways to support the market—for example, trying to keep the price of one square meter at Y 6,000 when it should be at Y 5,000—the government may be able to make it appear as if the price will not come down. However, if no one buys a house, then the real estate market cannot possibly develop. In contrast, if we let the price of one square meter suddenly fall to Y 5,000 or even to Y 3,000, the real estate market will recover very quickly. That reasoning also applies to all industries.

The government's rescue of bankrupt businesses not only disrupts the market's punishment mechanism and delays structural adjustment but also often causes small issues to develop into big issues. Governments are interested in solving only large problems, not small ones. Moreover, the government's rescue efforts reduce the business world's zeal for self-help. They cause more investment and more bad accounts. The more funds the government puts in, the scarcer funding becomes.

Currently, governments in all countries are using Keynesian policies to stimulate demand. In theory, that approach is very hard-headed. Because we believe the crisis was caused by American overconsumption and Chinese overinvestment, how can we possibly solve the problem by further stimulating consumption and investment?

Some people say that the Chinese only earn money but do not spend it; thus the savings rate is too high. However, over the past dozen or so years, Chinese household savings as a proportion of disposable income has declined. It decreased from more than 30 percent in 1996 to about 25 percent in 2000; since then, it has changed little. Chinese household savings as a proportion of GDP in 1996 was 20 percent, but in 2000, it was only 15 percent. In 2005, it was 16 percent, much lower than India's 22 percent.[9] Of course, China's savings rate is actually the world's highest; the main reason is that corporate and government savings are high, not the savings rate of households.

High corporate savings is partly rational and partly irrational. State-owned enterprises make such large investments because they believe that the money earned does not need to be issued as dividends or given to the government or households. The cost of capital is zero, or even less than zero (if unspent budgets must be returned); so unless it is all invested, it won't be useful at all. On the one hand are inefficient investments, and on the other hand are residents with no money to spend. That is China's reality.

The *China Statistical Yearbook* calculates separately the "contribution rate" of consumption, investment, and net exports to GDP growth. Some analysts often use that statistic, but some people find it very hard to comprehend. If we use that statistic to review the past 30 years, we will see that the "consumption contribution rate," "export contribution rate," and GDP growth are negatively correlated. Only the investment contribution rate and GDP growth are positively correlated. In other words, the higher the contribution rate is for consumption and exports, the lower GDP growth will be. The higher the contribution rate is for investment, the higher GDP growth will be. So, for GDP growth, should we stimulate consumption and exports or stimulate investment?

That issue proves that the demand economics of Keynesianism cannot provide us with answers to our problems. We need to know that production and supply, not demand, will promote economic growth. Supply creates demand; demand does not create supply. If stimulating demand could develop the economy, we would have early on entered a communist utopia!

During his 1992 Southern Tour, Deng Xiaoping did not tell us how to stimulate demand; yet afterward, the Chinese economy took off.

It took off because Deng Xiaoping increased the freedom of personal choice. Individuals had the opportunity to start a business and engage in trade. The economy began to grow naturally. That idea is still useful today. Therefore, we should do as the Austrian school advocates and use property rights and incentive scheme reforms to stimulate production, not stimulate demand by monetary policy or view savings as a sin. Such an approach is probably the best choice. The only method to allow residents to increase consumption is to increase incomes. If incomes increase, consumption will also naturally be higher.

Release Private Energy Early and Quickly

I would like to propose a few specific suggestions.

First, expand market reforms and liberate production: (a) monopolies need to be broken, (b) the market needs to be completely open to entry, (c) administrative approvals need to be reduced further, and (d) private enterprises need to freely and equally compete. Only after those market reforms are implemented can the vitality of the Chinese economy be released, thereby allowing entrepreneurs to be fully confident about the future. If we want to mess around with stimulating investment, we should mainly stimulate private business investment, not the ineffective investment of state-owned enterprises.

Second, expand reforms of the financial system, especially the foreign exchange market. If we had implemented foreign exchange reforms a few years earlier, perhaps the crisis would not have been as serious. Conversely, if we do not reform, getting out of the slump will be very difficult. Preparations for foreign exchange reform actually started in 1997, but the Asian Financial Crisis made us overly cautious. We believed foreign exchange reserves in hand meant safety, so we did not risk moving forward; we delayed foreign exchange reform for more than 10 years. In retrospect, excess foreign exchange reserves are just as harmful as shortages.

Third, promote labor market reforms. When one judges a policy's pluses and minuses, whether or not its goal is noble does not matter. What matters is its effectiveness. When we say a policy is bad, we mean that its effect and goal are not synonymous. China's Labor Contract Law is a classic example. The goal of the new Labor Contract

Law is to protect the interests of laborers. The law's principal victims are the average workers and migrant workers who are looking for work because the law has reduced employment opportunities. The Labor Contract Law's harm to the economy is not only its cost but also its damage to business culture.

Currently, businesses have increasingly more difficulty in managing people, and we are going back to the days when "doing is not as good as watching, and watching is not as good as making a mess out of it." Therefore, I recommend decisively ending the implementation of the part of the new Labor Contract Law that limits contract freedom, thus allowing freer labor contracts.

Fourth, transfer the state's wealth to the people. Economics studies the wealth of nations, not the wealth of states. Too much of China's wealth is concentrated in the hands of the state, not in the hands of the people. I think we could use the financial crisis to promote the transfer of wealth from the state to the people.

Primarily, we need to consider tax reductions, especially the value-added tax. The United Kingdom has already reduced its value-added tax to 15 percent; China needs to reduce its own. I do not promote discriminatory preferences or treatment because they will only lead to corruption and fraud. If we decide to lower taxes, all taxes should be lowered, including corporate and individual taxes. Reducing taxes is not a simple issue of redistributing incomes; it is an issue of mobilizing incentives to increase the total wealth of the nation. After lowering taxes, the government's revenues may actually increase.

Then, part of the shares of state-owned enterprises should be distributed to the people. Economists Zhiwu Chen, Guozhong Xie, and others have proposed similar suggestions, and I completely agree. The shares of publicly listed state-owned companies should be packaged up and a portion of those shares given to the people, thereby allowing the average person to participate in the distribution of capital gains. Currently, the central government controls between 70 percent and 80 percent of assets of public companies that are worth about Y 1.5 trillion. If 40 percent of those government-controlled assets were given to the people, they would amount to Y 0.6 trillion. I am not offering an egg; I am offering a hen that will produce more eggs.

If provincial and municipal governments can also distribute the shares of the enterprises they own to residents, that distribution would produce a huge wealth effect and would help increase demand. That approach would not influence the government's control now because the government is still the largest shareholder. It would also not lead to the unfair distribution of wealth, which occurred during Russia's voucher privatization. Because the distributed shares would have a market price, owners could openly and fairly sell their shares, and shares could not be bought cheaply by only a few people.

Conversely, we could use the distribution of state-owned shares to reduce the income gap. The simplest method would be to give villagers two shares, urbanites one share, wealthy people one share (or no shares), and poor people two shares. Of course, the specifics need more detailed research, but at this time, we should give a portion of state wealth to the people. In the short term, it would induce the wealth effect and stimulate demand because people are willing to consume only if they have assets. In the long term, it could reduce the government's operational pressures and reduce the income gap.

Crises and the Rise of Great Nations

I would like to emphasize that enterprises also need to self-adjust. Insolvent businesses should go bankrupt, and those that ought to be sold should be sold. Thus, after the crisis, industrial integration could lead to large-scale, internationally competitive companies. I am certain that after this crisis, no matter what the industry, industrial structures and business structures will change drastically.

Businesses need to have their own core competence. Even if they get through this crisis, they will still have problems in the next crisis without a core competence. While conducting a survey, I discovered a very strange issue. For some large foreign companies, the original equipment manufacturer is not given directly to a Chinese business; it goes through an intermediary. One reason is that the information systems of Chinese companies are subpar. They have no way to monitor and control the items that they are given to manufacture. If China's enterprise information systems were to improve, more trust would exist, and we would receive more orders directly. That is a technological issue, but it also relates to our core competitiveness. Of course, ultimately, our desire is to have independent brands. During this crisis, businesses with independent brands faced fewer difficulties than did those that had performed original equipment manufacturer work without a brand. I believe that observation was a lesson.

As Chinese, we do not need to be so pessimistic. The potential of China's economy has yet to be released. After the crisis in 1929, the United States replaced Great Britain as the world's economic super-power. Perhaps after this depression, it will be China's turn. Before 1929, Great Britain was an economic superpower, and the British pound was the international reserve currency. However, Great Britain was a debtor nation, using money borrowed from the United States, because it wanted to sustain its empire.

Today, the United States is an economic superpower, and China is a great nation on the rise. China loans money to the United States. Perhaps the structural changes that occurred in the world after the 1929 crisis can recur after the 2009 crisis. After another 20, 30, or 50 years, China could possibly overtake the United States as the world's largest economy. Therefore, speaking on the significance of that possibility, this crisis may be a good opportunity for China. The rise of all great nations comes about by succeeding during an opportunity.

Of course, success requires our own hard work and our continued push for market reforms!

15. The Economy Is Not a Single Product of GDP

The severity of the current financial crisis that started in the United States and then spread over the entire globe was on a scale rarely seen since the Great Depression. As the Austrian economists have observed, each economic crisis has three basic characteristics.[1]

The Three Characteristics of a Crisis

First, essentially all entrepreneurs make the same mistakes at the same time. Entrepreneurs' main duty is to forecast the future and to make commercial decisions according to their forecasts. Forecasting means grasping the market's future prospects and judging which investments and products will make money. Profit is revenues minus costs, so entrepreneurs need not only to forecast the product market but also to forecast the factor market, including changes in the capital market.

To entrepreneurs, the larger the probability of forecasting correctly, the greater the opportunity is for survival. In contrast, the larger the probability of forecasting incorrectly, the smaller the opportunity is for survival. Normally, some entrepreneurs succeed in forecasting, and some fail. On average, the number of successful forecasters is larger than the number of unsuccessful forecasters. About 70–80 percent of businesses in all industries can make money. However, an economic crisis changes the situation. Basically, almost all businesses make forecasting mistakes, so all businesses lose money. Why do almost all entrepreneurs make the same mistakes at the same time? That issue is worth our consideration.

Second, capital goods industries are more volatile and experience bigger decreases in growth rate than do consumer goods industries. In general, during the economic cycle, products that are higher up in the production structure, such as raw materials, are more volatile. Midstream products are less volatile, and products that are lower in

Figure 15.1
GROWTH RATES OF CHINA'S INDUSTRIAL VALUE ADDED

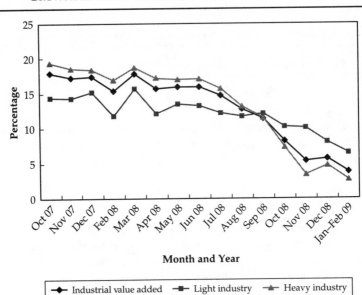

Month and Year

Industrial value added   Light industry   Heavy industry

SOURCE: National Statistics Bureau's website, http://www.stats.gov.cn/english/.

the production structure along with consumer goods are the least volatile.

Figure 15.1 shows that between October 2007 and August 2008, the growth of China's light industry was lower than the growth of heavy industry (calculated using value added). Starting in September 2008, the growth rate of heavy industry was lower than the growth rate of light industry. In general, during an economic boom, upstream industries—also called heavy industries—have higher growth rates. During an economic bust, light industry has a relatively higher growth rate (or a relatively lower decrease). As we view China's situation, we see that when industrial growth exceeds 12 percent, heavy industry grows faster than light industry. When industrial growth is below 12 percent, light industry will grow faster than heavy industry. During a financial crisis, even if both decrease, the rate of decrease will be different.

From the viewpoint of price, products higher upstream will have larger fluctuations (Figure 15.2). The production price of raw materi-

Figure 15.2
CHANGES IN VARIOUS MONTHLY PRICE INDEXES

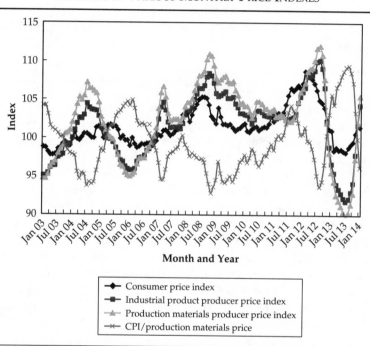

Month and Year

— ♦ — Consumer price index
— ■ — Industrial product producer price index
— ▲ — Production materials producer price index
— ✕ — CPI/production materials price

SOURCE: National Statistics Bureau's monthly report and website, http://www.stats.gov.cn/english/.

als will be more volatile than that of general industrial goods, and general industrial goods will be more volatile than will consumer goods. In the raw materials industry, prices in the excavation industry will be the most volatile. When an economic crisis occurs, the drop in the prices of production materials will be much larger than the drop in the prices of materials needed for subsistence. Prices in the excavation industry will drop the most. During January and February 2009, China's excavation industry prices already experienced a tremendous drop, falling tens of percentage points. That point is very significant for our understanding of economic cycles. It tells us that the crisis was more likely caused by overinvestment, not a lack of demand. At the same time, as the economic cycle spreads from one industry to another, there is an important time lapse in between.

317

Third, when a financial crisis occurs, the original funds suddenly disappear, and debt financing decreases. All businesses lack money, but no banks are willing to lend. Imagine a well with adequate water reserves suddenly going dry. How does such a situation come about?

Errors of Keynesian Economics

To the Austrian school economists, understanding a financial crisis requires a rational explanation of the three phenomena as listed in the preceding section. Actually, the current macroeconomic policies of all governments are built on a foundation of the Keynesian analytical framework, which has some problems.

First, we need to understand that the fluctuations mentioned before are not the fluctuations of one kind of product, but are the fluctuations of all markets simultaneously, even though the ranges are different. Only one factor could cause that kind of general fluctuation without causing a fluctuation in a single product or industry: a monetary fluctuation. Any economic fluctuation, or the simultaneous increase or decrease of product prices, is caused by money. Of course, for people in the business world, understanding the true meaning of money is not a simple matter. Even in academic circles, opinions differ about the definition of money.

Second, we need to grasp the importance of viewing the economy as a structure, as a value chain, composed of different industries and products, not just as a single product.

From here, we can see the problem with our macroeconomic policies. Currently, our macroeconomic policies are built on a foundation of Keynesian theory. A basic assumption of Keynesian theory is that the economy is in the form of a single product: the gross domestic product (GDP). In the analytical framework of Keynesian economics, there is the so-called circular flow of the economy. Households provide the factors of production and receive income in the form of wages, interests, profits, and bonuses (GDP). Businesses engage in production and sell their "products" (GDP) to factory owners for household consumption or investment. From the viewpoint of demand, GDP is broken down into consumption, investment, and net exports: the so-called troika.

According to that theory, economic recessions are caused by a shortage of general demand. The way to resolve problems is to increase demand. For example, in one year, the economy is composed of 60 units of consumption, 35 units of investment, and 5 units of net exports. But the next year, investment decreases by 15 units, and net exports decrease by 5 units. Keynesianism believes that the government could enlarge internal demand by increasing domestic consumption from 60 units to 80 units, and the economy would quickly recover. That theory is absolutely wrong.

In reality, GDP = consumption + investment + net exports is a formula, not a theory. The first economy and the second economy in the above example are completely different, even though their totals are the same. If residents increase consumption, will that resolve our problem with an overcapacity of steel production? No matter if we are discussing the world or China, we are currently facing structural issues. It is not that investment is insufficient so we can increase consumption or that consumption is insufficient so we need to find a way to increase exports.

The source of the issue is a lack of true understanding of the production structure. The goods and services that China exports are not necessarily goods and services that the Chinese can consume. China is the largest producer of wigs in the world, but how many Chinese can consume those wigs when the export market collapses?

Keynesianism provides a theoretical basis for trade protectionism. According to that theory, if a country's exports are greater than its imports, it has a trade surplus, and international trade makes a positive contribution to GDP. If its imports are greater than its exports, it has a trade deficit, and international trade makes a negative contribution to GDP. If exports equal imports, trade has zero effect on GDP. Therefore, the way to solve a financial crisis is to increase exports and reduce imports. It is no wonder that when Keynesian economists guide economic policy, trade protectionism will prevail.

CPI as a Bad Guide

As a counterpart of viewing the economy as a single product (GDP), Keynesian economists use the general price level, especially the consumer price index (CPI), as their main indicator for judging whether or not the economy is overheating. They also use it to set macroeconomic policy. The monetarist school of economics does the same.

Is the CPI, or a general price index, an effective channel for judging the macroeconomy? The financial crisis in the 1930s and the current crisis have a common point, and that is the stability of prices before the crisis. There were even suspicions of deflation (a decrease in the price level).

Speaking from the Austrian school's theory, we absolutely cannot focus our attention on the stability of the general price index. Instead, we need to consider relative price changes, especially changes in interest rates and the price of capital goods. Of all prices, only relative prices can transmit resource allocation signals; absolute prices cannot. To the Austrian school, when the economy has a big increase in technological advancement that leads to increases in productivity, it is only right that the general price level should have a corresponding decrease. If the monetary authority attempts to maintain the stability of prices, it will probably cause excessive amounts of currency to be injected into the economic system. Such an injection will lead to an excessive boom, and a crisis will soon follow.

Following William White, I stress again that the general price index (or the CPI) is a poor guide for macroeconomic policy.[2] Alan Greenspan's mistake was to use the general price level as a basis for judging the amount of money that should exist. He dropped interest rates by a large degree because he feared deflation. The result was a rapid increase in credit expansion, which led to a serious economic crisis. China's macroeconomic policy reasoning would be greatly transformed by not being fixated on the CPI but instead by focusing on credit and interest rates.

Worries about deflation are an important reason for governments to use expansionary monetary policy. If we look back on history, deflation and economic recessions do not have a strong relationship.[3] For example, from 1873 to 1896, the price level in many Western countries dropped by about 2 percent on average. It did not cause a recession, but instead the annual growth in the production level was 2–3 percent on average. In the 10 years between 1870 and 1879, the American price level dropped on average by 1.8 percent per year, but those 10 years were the golden age of growth in U.S. history. Currently, we are used to inflation, not deflation. When we see the price level drop, we get nervous and want to inject money into the system to help it climb back up. That approach is very dangerous.

Money Is Not Neutral

A related subject is our need to understand the nonneutrality of money. In theory, regardless of whether we are discussing monetarism or Keynesianism, they both believe that money is neutral over the long term. Milton Friedman proposed an idea that if the amount of money in the market doubles, prices will also double.[4] Austrian school economists disagree with that viewpoint. They believe money is not neutral, so currency injections will not cause all prices to rise together.[5] The reason is that the growth in money must enter the market through some privileged industry or product. Not all industries and products will receive the same proportional amount of money at the same time. Those that receive the money first benefit, and those that receive the money later lose. Therefore, a producer receiving the money first and a consumer receiving the money first are two completely different situations. From China's perspective, the industrial structures caused by state-owned enterprises receiving money first and private enterprises receiving money first are very different. The effect on the total economy is also very different.

Specifically, money embodies its nonneutral characteristics through changes in relative prices. If relative prices do not change, all prices rise and fall together, so resource allocation will not change. The changes in the general price level in many cases cannot reflect the actual change in resource allocation. A true wealth creator is influenced by relative prices to transform resources. At the same time, the market is an adjustment process. During that process, general price levels calculated by the year, quarter, and month are completely different.

The nonneutrality of money means an excessive amount of money will change the structure of production and cause a crisis.

How Monetary Expansion Causes a Crisis

To understand how excessive amounts of money cause a crisis, we need only to understand how the production structure is formed. Society's total goods can be divided into intermediate goods (capital goods) and final consumption goods. Modern society's production is a roundabout production process. Intermediate goods produce final consumption goods indirectly. Intermediate goods are the source of future growth in consumer goods. Given the status of technology and production, the proportion between those two categories of goods is decided by people's preference between current and future consumption.

After reaching a certain individual income, people will distribute their income between consumption and savings, in other words, between current consumption and future consumption. That distribution is very important because it determines what we commonly call the discount rate, or the natural rate of interest.

People who contemplate the future will leave more of their income to the future. That money composes the source of investment funds and decides the scope of production for intermediate goods. If people contemplated only the present, savings would not exist, and there would be no investment. The point is, the goal of investment is to increase future consumption, not to increase current GDP. Unfortunately, government policymakers often forget that basic bit of common sense. They invest to produce current GDP, which results in large amounts of meaningless investment. Such is the pernicious influence of Keynesian economics.

In a market economy, savers and investors are not usually the same people—especially because savings come mainly from households, but investment decisions are made by entrepreneurs. So what should we rely on to turn savings into investments while maintaining equilibrium between the two? We should rely on money (and debt).

It is precisely through a transfer of money that society is able to realize a transformation of savings into actual investment. The process of transferring savings into investments must pass through a very important signal: the interest rate of money. Here, we need to understand that the nominal interest rate and the natural interest rate differ substantially. When the government monopolizes the money supply, the interest rate on money is controlled by the government and can be changed by the government. The true interest rate, however, or the so-called natural rate of interest, is produced by the behavior of people. In reality, if the interest rate on money and the natural interest rate differ, the economy will be misguided and distorted.

The money rate of interest is an important factor when entrepreneurs set investment policies. It affects not only the decision to invest but also the investment scale. Generally speaking, the lower the interest rate is, the larger investment scales are. The money rate of interest level is directly related to the amount of money. In fact, the monetary authority can either use expansionary monetary policy to lower interest rates or use lowered interest rates to expand the scope of money.

When an entrepreneur invests in capital goods, the effects of that investment will not be evident for a few years. Therefore, greater room for speculation exists. Given that the money supply does not change, if consumers' preferences change so that they are willing to save money, the natural interest rates will decrease. Lowered interest rates will cause entrepreneurs to increase investment in upstream industries. More resources flow toward upstream industries, thus realizing a transformation of savings into investments. The further upstream an industry is, the more sensitive it is to interest rates.

According to the Austrian school's viewpoint, increased upstream investment will lengthen the production process and create more links in the chain. In essence, it will cause the division of labor to become more detailed, so future production will be more efficient. During the adjustment process, upstream products will increase in price, and downstream products will decrease in price. The economy will reach a new equilibrium step by step. Because growth in upstream investments promotes efficiency in the production of consumer goods, more consumer goods will be produced, and the transaction demand of money will increase. When the money supply does not change, the general price level will not increase; instead, it will decline. The living standards of the masses will be improved, and a crisis will be averted.

Now, let us discuss how the economy will react if households' real savings do not increase, but the government artificially decreases interest rates and expands the money supply. The amount of funds for investment will increase, and the cost of capital will decrease. The lower cost of capital will lure entrepreneurs into increasing production of intermediate goods, expanding investment scales, building new factories, upgrading facilities, and implementing raw materials development.

What do upstream industries rely on to attract the factors of production? They rely on price. When they do, raw materials prices and capital goods prices increase, as do land prices and wages. Those increases attract more factors of production upstream. For example, during the Internet bubble, graduates with master's degrees in business administration entered the information technology industry en masse. They did so because the industry's relative prices increased, so its attractiveness increased with it. The result was an overall increase in the wage level. The stock prices of those industries also increased, further luring more investment capital into those industries.

When stock prices increase and more capital is invested, people's nominal incomes increase, while real savings do not. Consumption demand will increase, and with it the price of consumer goods will also increase. Downstream industries will begin to compete with upstream industries for resources and factors of production. Because of the thriving demand in the consumer goods industries, wages will be pushed up, thus successfully attracting resources from upstream industries. Upstream industries will begin to be squeezed. Then, interest rates will also begin to rise.

Therefore, as we speak from the upstream, investments that were originally believed to be profitable will be found to be unproductive. When the original investment proves to be a mistake, there is no choice but to stop. Bank debt cannot be repaid, funds are in short supply, businesses immediately go bankrupt, and the number of unemployed people increases. Those outcomes will naturally lead to a decrease in incomes, which will ultimately affect consumer goods industries. A full-on crisis will have erupted, and all entrepreneurs will discover they have made mistakes!

After the crisis, if the government does not intervene, adjustment will automatically begin. Although prices have dropped in common, and nominal wages have adjusted downward, consumer prices will have a relative increase, thus transferring factors of production back to consumer goods industries. The economy will gradually recover its original state of equilibrium.

Why Artificial Prosperity Cannot Be Sustained

People may wonder why the government cannot continue increasing the money supply to sustain economic prosperity. In the short term, of course, that approach will work. In the long term, however, sustained growth of money will lead to a continuous increase in the wages and prices of the other factors of production. As soon as consumer prices begin to rise in common, the government's capital injections must stop.

Using monetary policy to solve financial crises often creates a bigger crisis. Using Hayek's metaphor, the government's injection of money to stimulate the economy is like grabbing a tiger by its tail. If one lets go of the tail, one will most likely be eaten. If one does not let go and runs with the tiger, one will most likely die of exhaustion. As soon as the government stops injecting money into the economy, a recession will occur. If it continues to inject money, the entire monetary system could possibly collapse.

Government capital injections basically caused the current crisis. The Internet bubble at the turn of the 21st century was in itself caused by excessive credit. After the Internet bubble collapsed, the correct policy would have been to allow the economy to naturally adjust through a small recession. It would have then recovered to its natural state.

However, the Federal Reserve led by Alan Greenspan and the George W. Bush administration did not want to allow the economy to enter a recession. They began to implement expansionary monetary policies, reducing the interest rate 11 times in succession. In 2003, the Federal Reserve's interest rate decreased to 1 percent, but the real interest rate was already negative. By the second half of 2004, problems started to arise, so the Federal Reserve began to increase interest rates. The crisis was unavoidable. To avoid a relatively minor recession, the Federal Reserve and the Bush administration instead brought on a much larger decline.

The consequences of government policies to handle today's financial crisis will also be very serious. The price to be paid for China's official policy of surpassing an 8 percent GDP growth in 2009 will become evident in a few years. We must prepare ourselves to meet the next crisis.

In all, economic decline is often the companion of artificial prosperity. A bust must follow a boom caused by monetary expansion. The source of this crisis was not "too little" but "too much": too much debt, too much money, too much investment, and too much consumption. Currently, there is no way to continue on smoothly. We must stop, but the problems brought about by stopping have already developed.

China's Role

During the formation of this financial crisis, what role did China play? The Federal Reserve expanded the money supply and lowered interest rates, thus creating a powerful investment and consumption demand. Someone with the ability to consume only $100 suddenly was able to consume $120. Who made up for that difference? China did.

The question is what was China doing filling the gap? There is a very large relationship between this gap filling and China's foreign exchange-rate system. Perceptively speaking, if China used a flexible exchange-rate system, the United States' expansionary policies would have caused a relative appreciation of the renminbi. The price of U.S. imported products would have increased. Alarm bells at the Federal Reserve would have sounded earlier, forcing it to contract the money supply and raise interest rates.

In reality, the renminbi exchange rate was fixed so Chinese companies (and foreign-invested companies producing in China) could export the products of hard-working Chinese laborers to the United States at a constant price. To satisfy Americans' huge appetite, China accepted huge amounts of foreign exchange and then loaned it back to the United States. That situation is the same as the United States' printing IOUs to buy Chinese products. In the end, the United States determines the value of those IOUs. The demand of Americans was excessive, but we were responsible for prices and interest rates not going up. We misled them.

Metaphorically speaking, the door was left open, and a thief stole something, but we ignored it. The next day, the door was still open, so the thief returned and stole some more, but we did not care. On the third day, the thief returned and stole everything of value. If the thief were ultimately caught, his punishment would be severe. If we had discovered the theft on the first day and added measures to curb further thefts, the thief would have received only a minor sentence, rather than being put away for years.

The crisis finally happened, but because the reasons for the crisis are not clearly understood, all countries' governments are tackling it with the same measures that caused the crisis at the beginning. Many countries have implemented low interest rates—even zero percent interest rates—and large-scale credit expansion. China is, of course, no exception. With regard to scale, China has embarked on the largest experiment in world monetary history.

The correct approach is to bring into play the market's ability to correct itself. That approach will have its hardships, but we can be certain that recovery will be quick. Our current solution is to cover up problems with money, instead of forcing businesses to implement structural adjustments. Pouring money on the problem will make structural issues more serious, not lighter.

Something worth pointing out is that the financial crisis had a large negative effect on China's exports, so the government is currently subsidizing them. Actually, the government should induce business transformation to develop the home market. The Chinese economy's excessive reliance on exports is not a positive matter. Continued trade surpluses have many disadvantages and few benefits. Renminbi undervaluation means Chinese incomes are being used to subsidize Americans, and it means exports are partly sold, partly given away.

I believe the renminbi's appreciation would be much more beneficial to China than to the United States. Renminbi appreciation would increase Chinese businesses' zeal for developing the domestic market. It would also create the wealth effect, thus reducing the income gap, and it would increase consumer demand. Some people believe that renminbi appreciation will produce losses on China's foreign exchange reserves. That view is self-deception and is similar to the worries of more than 10 years ago about state-owned enterprises' write-offs of bad accounts causing asset losses. The real indicator to measure wealth is our productivity and our standard of living, not how many IOUs issued by others we own.

An old adage says, "Wisdom must be bought." I worry that we have paid the price but are no wiser for it.

16. Financial Crises and the Development of Economics

We are currently experiencing the most serious worldwide economic crisis since the end of World War II. This crisis was ignited by the U.S. subprime crisis, which quickly spread to the entire financial system and the real economy, and then it engulfed the globe. No matter whether a country was developed or was an emerging market, no one was spared.

This crisis will probably have a very important effect on the development of economics. The Guanghua School of Management and the China Center for Economic Research convened an internal forum to discuss and exchange ideas about viewpoints with regard to financial crises and their influence on economics. We can be indifferent about the United States' 1987 Financial Crisis, Japan's economic bubble, the Asian Financial Crisis, and the Internet bubble, but we must be concerned about the current crisis. The goal of our discussions today is to make everyone aware of the changes that may happen to the world of economics.

Current economic research is becoming progressively more technical, but the effect of a large crisis on economics is not limited to technological aspects. After this crisis occurred, some people believed the free market failed again, and the "visible hand" of the government became more important. That view has presented a challenge to the direction of China's future reform. Some people even say that after 2009, Chinese socialism needs to save American capitalism. Although partly a joke, that notion reflects a very important issue. My viewpoint is simple: if there is a problem, it will come from the government, not the market.

The 1930s Crisis and the Austrian School

Both Friedrich Hayek and Ludwig von Mises forecasted the financial crisis of the 1930s, although they did not indicate the day on which it would occur. According to their theory, credit expansion happened in the 1920s, so the stock market and real estate bubble would experience a crisis. After the crisis, Hayek's 1931 book *Prices and Production* had an immense effect. The Austrian school of economics became a hot topic. Lionel Robbins, the head of the Department of Economics at the London School of Economics, wrote the introduction to *Prices and Production*. He praised Hayek's work and invited him to join the school's faculty.

However, soon after Keynesianism emerged, the direction of economics changed. Governments had already taken steps to increase internal demand, which Keynesians would have recommended, but Keynesian economics provided a theoretical basis for government intervention, so it was warmly welcomed. Because effective demand was scarce, governments had reason to intervene to rescue the economy. After World War II, Hayek refocused mainly on political philosophy research, not economics. The Austrian school was marginalized.

Starting in the 1970s, monetarism began to be taken seriously. In the 1980s, it surpassed Keynesianism to become mainstream economics. Milton Friedman's understanding of the 1929 crash was that the government did not provide enough money after the crisis. The crisis lasted so long because the Federal Reserve sought deflation when it should have loosened monetary policy. Interestingly, when we look back on history, we discover that Friedman was a Keynesian from the outset. He never challenged Keynes. When he was testing Keynes's demand function, he discovered that people's consumption changed with long-term changes in income, not short-term changes. Slowly, Keynesianism began to be considered irrational, so the Rational Expectations school of economic thought later emerged.

Austrian school research has endured. Murray Rothbard published *America's Great Depression* in 1962, one year earlier than Friedman and Schwartz's *A Monetary History of the United States, 1867–1960*. Rothbard believed the crisis in the 1930s was the result of the Federal Reserve's expansionary monetary policy and low interest rates that caused distortions in the investment structure and an asset bubble. Rothbard showed that Roosevelt's New Deal was actually a continuation of Hoover's policies. Hoover's policies included rescuing banks, implementing alliances between big businesses, prompting businesses to increase investment, limiting layoffs and wage decreases, interfering with prices, implementing budget deficits, building large-scale public infrastructure (such as the Hoover Dam), implementing trade protectionism (such as the Smoot-Hawley Tariff Act), and reducing immigration quotas. That series of measures caused the crisis to continue without recovery.

In his book *Vienna and Chicago: Friends or Foes?*, Mark Skousen separates faith in the market into four levels. The first level is no faith in the market economy, which is traditional Marxist economics. The second level is skepticism toward the market, which is Keynesian economics and economics that promotes government interventionism. The third level is an extraordinary faith in the market economy, but also the belief that sometimes government involvement is necessary. That level is the Chicago school of economics. Friedman believed that during an economic recession, governments should use extreme monetary policies to move the economy out of a slump. The fourth level is complete faith in the market. That is the Austrian school represented by Mises and Hayek, but today its representatives are mainly in the United States.

The Austrian school is fighting a three-front war, battling Keynesianism, the socialist planned economy, and monetarism simultaneously. Hayek received the Nobel Prize in Economics for his business cycle theory, yet his business cycle theory was criticized by monetarism. Although Friedman praised Hayek's *The Road to Serfdom*, he believed Hayek's business cycle theory was incorrect.

The Austrian School's Forecasting of This Crisis

Mises and Hayek forecasted the crisis in the 1930s. Other people also predicted the global financial crisis, with the most famous predictions coming from the Austrian school. Peter Schiff is an investor and financial commentator who wrote the book *Crash Proof: How to Profit from the Coming Economic Collapse*. During television interviews in 2006, he forecasted that the United States would have big problems, including subprime debt, the housing market, and even the entire economy. Now, except for the U.S. dollar not having collapsed, everything else has come to fruition.

William White is an Austrian school economist who was head of the Economics Department of the Basel-based Bank of International Settlements. Under his leadership, the research method of the Bank of International Settlements is primarily based on Austrian school theory. In 2006, White wrote a paper titled "Is Price Stability

Enough?" and forecast that the economy would likely have a problem. In the bank's June 2007 annual report, his viewpoint was more clearly demonstrated.

Krassimir Petrov, an economist at the Ludwig von Mises Institute, wrote an article in 2004 titled "China's Great Depression," forecasting that China would enter a depression in 2008–2009.

Ron Paul, a U.S. politician who ran for president, is also a staunch supporter of the Austrian school. At the end of 2008, he made a speech in Congress titled "The Austrians Were Right." Peter Schiff helped him write it.

Recently, Jesús Huerta de Soto Ballester, an Austrian school economist from Spain, wrote a book titled *Money, Bank Credit, and Economic Cycles*. It is believed to be the most integrated modern version of the Austrian school's theories about money and the business cycle.

The current crisis and the Great Depression in the 1930s have many similarities. On the one hand, the macroeconomy did not show any obvious symptoms before the crisis: prices were stable, economic growth was normal, and technological progress was good. On the other hand, problems arose with the stock market, the housing market, and investments. Therefore, this crisis could have been forecast using Austrian school theories.

The Great Depression had an immense impact on economics. At the time, two people could have prevailed: Hayek and Keynes. As noted earlier, ultimately, Hayek was marginalized, and Keynes became mainstream. The current crisis has two possible outcomes: (a) further strengthening of Keynesian dominance over economics and (b) completely discarding Keynesianism and resurrecting the Austrian school. I believe the latter outcome is possible. We must remember that according to Austrian theory, government bailouts can only postpone a crisis, and cannot truly solve the issue.

Different Understandings of Economic Crises

Keynesianism emphasizes scarcity of effective demand. The United States obviously does not have a scarcity-of-demand issue; instead, demand is excessive. Over the past 10 or so years, China's household savings rate also has not increased; it has decreased from 30 percent in 1996 to about 25 percent. Calculations from World Bank reports show that household savings as a proportion of gross domestic product (GDP) has decreased from 20 percent to 16 percent.[1] Theories based on Keynesianism will lead to trade protectionism. GDP is formed by consumption, investment, and net exports, so an increase in net exports will increase GDP. The simplest method to increase net exports is to impose tariffs and limit imports. Those ideals have already entered the statistical system because China's Statistics Bureau calculates the contribution rates of investment, consumption, and net exports to GDP.

According to the Austrian school's viewpoint, the deeper a crisis is, the more necessary liberalization becomes. Say's law of markets states that supply creates demand, as opposed to demand creating supply. Others will buy our products and services only if we buy the products and services of others. Therefore, free trade is the best policy, not what the Keynesians advocate.

It would be better to say that this crisis happened because China is too unfree than to say it happened because the United States is too free. If the renminbi could have appreciated five years ago, giving businesses a correct signal, business investment in setting up factories would have had a clearer direction. The renminbi continued to be undervalued, signaling that exports are always profitable, so businesses were export driven. If changes had been made earlier, the trade surplus and foreign exchange reserves would have been smaller, and currency issuance would have been lower, so China would not have experienced such a large problem.

Internationally, some people believe China's not spending money induced the United States to spend money, thus causing this crisis. That view is ridiculous. Overall, the United States does the moving, and China gets moved. However, if we analyze balance of payments, China has aided and abetted the United States. If the renminbi exchange rate had been suitable, a large amount of cheap goods would not have been sent to the United States. U.S. inflationary policies would have caused prices to rise earlier, and the Federal Reserve would have possibly adopted measures earlier. Because the renminbi was undervalued, U.S. currency's growth did not manifest as price increases. The Federal Reserve's monetary policies focused on price, so it saw price stability and believed there was no problem with the macro interest rate.

Asymmetry was a characteristic of Alan Greenspan's monetary policies. The Federal Reserve will use monetary policy to help the economy after the bubble bursts, such as after the 1987 stock market crash, the Asian Financial Crisis, and the Internet bubble. When there is a huge increase in stock prices, the Federal Reserve will not use deflationary monetary policy; instead, it will resort to more expansionary monetary policy.

White's *Is Price Stability Enough?* uses historical and theoretical bases to conclude that the price level cannot be used as the main indicator to judge macroeconomic conditions. According to Austrian school theory, changes in relative prices are most important, not the general price level. A relatively long time elapses between investment goods leading to consumer goods. When the prices of consumer goods begin to rise, a disaster is on its way, and it cannot be solved by taking measures against it.

The Austrian school believes a serious asymmetry exists between economic declines and rises. During an economic boom, upstream industries experience large increases, and downstream industries have relatively small increases. During an economic bust, upstream industries experience sharp declines, and downstream industries have relatively small decreases. In 2008, China's industrial production obviously had that experience, as the growth of heavy industry was much higher than light industry in the first half of the year, but it decreased by a much larger extent in the second half of the year. According to Keynes's theory on the scarcity of demand, that adjustment should appear as a faster decline in light industry. In reality, that is not the case, so using scarcity of demand is unjustified.

This crisis will have an immense effect on the economy. With regard to China, it will not only affect the economy but also the entire progression of reform. Now, some relatively extreme viewpoints are saying, "The United States collapsed, and the market economy failed, so why does China still need to liberalize?" or "The reason China has not had a problem is because the financial system has not been liberalized." Different understandings of the crisis will lead to completely different policies.

Resurrection of the Austrian School of Economics

Now that we are experiencing the most serious worldwide economic crisis since the end of World War II, I recommend that all economists, bureaucrats, and media personalities—even the common people—read Rothbard's *America's Great Depression*. It will help us reflect on the true causes of this crisis, and it will help us avoid the same mistakes in the future.

Although Austrian school economics is far from today's mainstream economics, ever since Hayek received the Nobel Prize in Economics in 1974—and especially after the collapse of the former Soviet Union and eastern European centrally planned economies—more attention has been paid to Austrian school theories on the free-market economy, entrepreneurship, and anti-interventionism. It has had an important effect on the formulation of government economic policy (including revisions to the Anti-Monopoly Law). Some popular textbooks have also started to introduce the viewpoints of the Austrian school. Together with the Chicago school, the Austrian school had a pivotal role in the resurrection of free-market ideas throughout the world in the second half of the 20th century.

In 2000, Federal Reserve Chairman Greenspan said, "The Austrian School [has] had a profound and . . . probably an irreversible effect on how most mainstream economists think in [the United States]." Even some Keynesian economists have started to pay attention to Austrian school ideas. (Actually, the Austrian school's influence on Keynesian macroeconomics has been ignored. Keynes himself even acknowledged Mises's viewpoint on the practical effects of nominal prices.)

Since the 1990s, *The Economist* and the Bank of International Settlements have used the Austrian business cycle theory to analyze asset bubble inflations. Especially after this crisis that engulfed the entire globe, the Austrian business cycle theory has once again attracted wide attention. On June 25, 2007, the *Wall Street Journal* published an article titled "Amid Financial Excess, a Revival of Austrian Economics." It introduced the Bank of International Settlements' annual report analyzing the world economic situation on the basis of the Austrian school's business cycle theory. (Canadian Austrian school economist William White led the analysis.) The report predicted that the asset bubble was a harbinger for a global economic crisis. In 2009, Thomas Woods, a senior fellow at the Ludwig von Mises Institute, published a treatise titled *Meltdown*, which explained this crisis and has already become a best seller.

The 1930s' crisis led to the success of Keynesian economics, a success that perhaps itself was a historical tragedy. Over the past few decades, the Chicago school, represented by Milton Friedman, has already defeated Keynesianism. Its victory represents tremendous progress in the history of human ideas. Since the outbreak of this crisis, Keynesian economic policies have again become popular. Perhaps after this crisis, Austrian economics will be truly resurrected—not Keynesian economics. The Austrian school's business cycle theory is the only business cycle theory to integrate general principles (especially the theories on the market process, entrepreneurship, and money) for a solid macroeconomic foundation and to forecast two depressions successfully. Possibly over the next 10 or 20 years, it will become the only mainstream business cycle theory. Of course, only time will tell.

PART FOUR

THE PROSPECT OF CHINA'S FUTURE

17. Taking the Pulse of Future Chinese Economic Growth and Systemic Reform

Each person's life or career has high points and low points. During low points, one can easily become overly pessimistic. During high points, one can easily become dizzy with success. The results of neither situation are very good. The same holds true for a country or society. Today's world economy should be considered at a low point. The effects of the global financial crisis have not been eliminated. The way to view China's future economy—and even the world's future economy—is a key issue that many people focus on. If one is to correctly understand that issue, it must be viewed from a longer historical perspective.

In View of Historical Conjectures: Countries with Large Populations Will Resurface as Countries with Large Economies

Humanity has 5,000 years of written historical records. According to the research of economist Angus Maddison, during a large span of human history, the ability to create wealth changed little.[1] For a relatively long period, per capita gross domestic product (GDP) did not grow, or it even decreased. It did not take off until the past two centuries. In addition, with regard to per capital GDP, the differences between countries in the past were not large. For example, in 1500 AD, the per capita GDP of the richest country was three times higher than that of the poorest country. Today, per capita GDP of a few developed countries is dozens of times, or even a hundred times, higher than that of underdeveloped countries.

In the relatively long history of humanity, the economic scale of each country (or region) was highly correlated with its population scale. In other words, population scale determined economic scale. The detachment of population scale and economic scale is a phenomenon that happened only in the past 200 years. In view of Maddison's data, we can calculate the correlation between population scale and economic scale. In 1500, it was 0.9873; in 1700, it was 0.964; in 1820, it was still high at 0.9423, but it later began to decline rapidly. In 1870, the correlation between population scale and economic scale was 0.6393; in 1913, it was 0.3404; in 1950, it was 0.1554; and in 1973, it was 0.148. In other words, by 1973, population scale and economic scale on a worldwide scope had almost no correlation. For example, Asia (excluding Japan) accounted for 54.6 percent of the world's population but produced only 16.4 percent of the world's GDP. Developed countries accounted for 18.4 percent of the world's population but produced 58.7 percent of the world's GDP. That circumstance began to reverse in the past 30 years. The correlation between population scale and economic scale had increased to 0.5185 by 2003, and it is projected to increase further to 0.733 by 2030 (see Figure 17.1).

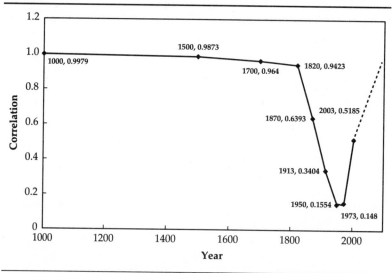

Figure 17.1
CORRELATION BETWEEN POPULATION AND GDP (1000–2030)

SOURCE: Angus Maddison, *Contours of the World Economy, 1–2030 AD* (Oxford: Oxford University Press, 2007), Statistical App. A.

Why did the difference between each country's per capita GDP increase over the past 250 years? Why did population scale and economic scale lose a reciprocal relationship? The simple reason is that different countries chose different systems. Some countries established market economies, and some did not. Even though the various details are debated, modern economic theory and social applications prove that the market economy is the most effective mechanism to develop an economy and people's livelihoods.

If the economic system did not have differences between the market economy and others—or to say that the entire world had implemented a market economy—then the differences in per capita GDP would slowly disappear. That is precisely what happened over the past 30 years. Market reforms in China and other countries have started to reverse the deviation in population scales and economic scales on a worldwide scope over the past 200 years.

Therefore, I have a bold prediction. According to current trends, over the next 50 to 100 years, the difference in the population scale and the economic scale between regions will perhaps return to its status before the 19th century. Because a country's economic scale will be related to its population scale, countries with large populations will have large economies. In today's world, in addition to China and India having the largest populations, Asia accounts for close to 60 percent of the world's population. Calling the 21st century the Asian century is simply the return to the relationship between population scales and economic scales. That is also the equalization between the Western and Eastern worlds that Adam Smith predicted in his 1776 work *The Wealth of Nations*.[2] Now, we can already see that trend.

Figure 17.2 shows Maddison's estimates for major countries as a proportion of world GDP. Essentially, according to calculations using adjustments for purchasing power, in 1 AD, during the Western Han dynasty, India's GDP accounted for about one-third of world GDP. By 1820, China's GDP accounted for about one-third of world GDP. By postwar 1950, the United States' GDP accounted for about one-fourth (27.3 percent) of world GDP. What will the future state of affairs be? Maddison predicts that by 2030, China's GDP will possibly account for 23 percent of world GDP, India will account for 10 percent, the United States will account for 17 percent, and Western Europe will account for about 13 percent.

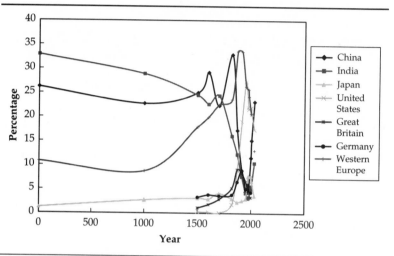

Figure 17.2
MAJOR ECONOMIC SYSTEMS AS A PROPORTION OF
WORLD GDP

SOURCE: Angus Maddison, *Contours of the World Economy, 1–2030 AD* (Oxford: Oxford University Press, 2007), Statistical App. A.

From those calculations, we can see China's huge change over the past 30 years. A country's weight and voice on the international stage are decided by its economic power. During the past few years, we have seen that the world cannot avoid China, regardless of whether we are discussing good or bad issues. Originally, no one invited China to "come out and play"; groups such as the G-7, G-8, and Organisation for Economic Co-operation and Development had no place for China. Now, everything is discussed with China. As a mainstream saying goes, "The 19th century was the European century, the 20th century was the American century, and the 21st century is the Asian or Chinese century."

Will the "Chinese century" really materialize? The answer depends on China's future economic growth. I believe that China's such growth will occur in three large transitions. First, we will transition from a reliance on export-driven growth to more balanced growth between the domestic and international markets. Second, we will transition from low-cost, cheap resources and cheap labor–supported growth to innovation and high value-added, industry-based growth. Third, we will transition from the model of enterprise organic growth to an integrated model of industrial growth. The progress of those transformations crucially relies on China's systemic reforms, including economic and political reform. Globalization is the background for those transitions.

Globalization's Effect on the World and on China's Economy

The globalization of the economy has been a long historical process. It is generally believed that the first high tide of globalization happened during the more than 40 years between 1870 and 1913. From the start of World War I to 1950 was the era of "deglobalization." For the measurement of exports as a proportion of GDP, the world average was 4.6 percent in 1870, but by 1913, it had increased to 7.9 percent. That process caused changes in the economic and political structure of the world.

In the United States, labor was scarce, so the wages of workers in manufacturing were relatively high. Globalization caused the wages of manufacturing workers to decrease as a percentage of the national income. That decrease caused an increase in trade union activity and immigration restrictions. Land in Western Europe was scarce, and the population was large, so rents were relatively high. Globalization caused the relative price of land to drop dramatically, which led to Europe's agricultural protection policies.[3]

After the eruption of the Great War, trade between belligerent countries basically stopped, even though the trade of neutral countries increased. After the Depression in 1929, trade protectionism became mainstream. With the added influence of World War II, by 1950, world exports as a proportion of GDP had decreased to 5.5 percent, only 0.9 percentage points above 1870 (as shown in Figure 17.3).

After 1950, there was a new wave of globalization. Especially after 1980, the globalization wave further accelerated. In 2007, world exports as a proportion of GDP were 25.6 percent. Also important is the fact that the present form of globalization has experienced a huge change. Before globalization, trade was in simple products, but now labor has been divided along the value chain. Originally, one person produced apples, another produced peaches, and then apples were exchanged for peaches. Now, one person grows the seedlings,

Figure 17.3
MERCHANDISE EXPORT VALUE AS A PROPORTION OF GDP
FOR THE WORLD AND MAJOR ECONOMIES

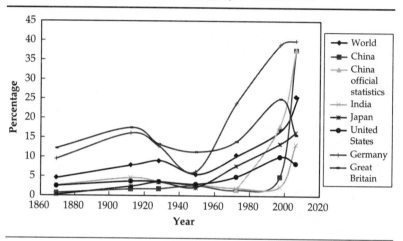

SOURCES: Data from 1998 and before come from Angus Maddison, *A Thousand-Year History of the World Economy* (Beijing: Peking University Press, 2003). Data for 2007 come from the *China Statistical Yearbook*, 2008.
NOTE: Because the data are not of the same caliber, 2007 data and pre-1998 data are not really comparable, but the general trend is the same.

someone else fertilizes them, and another person picks the fruit. The division of labor is becoming increasingly more specialized. The emphasis is no longer on trade between final products; it is on trade between different parts of the value chain. An enterprise can perhaps succeed by having the advantage in one part of the value chain. That is a characteristic of present-day globalization.

Globalization changed the political and economic structure of the world. If China was considered the biggest victim during the first period of globalization, China is now considered the biggest beneficiary during the current period of globalization. Although overall, every country has benefited from this period of globalization. Without present-day globalization, the Chinese economy could not have sustained 30 years of rapid growth. China would also not have the international status it has now. This period of globalization caused the separation of every link of production, so economic growth was attained by every country through nonintegrative production processes. China grabbed hold of that opportunity and became the number one manufacturing country. Therefore, the globalization of 100 years ago and of the next 100 years will affect China's destiny in completely different ways.

Will the 2008 Financial Crisis be followed by the same "deglobalization" that followed 1929? My personal judgment is that growth in exports as a proportion of GDP will stagnate—even decrease—but will not have a large-scale reversal. We have already learned from the past that trade protectionism does not work. In 1931, the United States enacted the Smoot-Hawley Tariff Act in an attempt to protect U.S. businesses. It caused a reversal in global trade and prolonged the crisis. The majority of trade protection policies allow a small group of people to seek private gain while waving the banner of national interests. That should be a lesson for this financial crisis. If each country reimplements trade protectionist policies, we will be stuck in a depression for a longer, not shorter, time.

China's Export-Driven Economy Is No Longer Sustainable

During most of the past 30 years, the growth rate of China's international trade has surpassed the growth rate of GDP. In essence, China's actual annual GDP growth rate has been about 10 percent, but the actual annual export growth rate has been about 15 percent. According to calculations using nominal values, 2008 exports were 553 times the amount of 1978 exports, but 2008 GDP was 83 times the amount of 1978 GDP. The former is 6.7 times the latter. The result is that trade as a proportion of GDP has risen dramatically. According to data from the National Statistics Bureau, exports as a percentage of GDP were 4.6 percent in 1978, 16.1 percent in 1990, 20.8 percent in 2000, and 37.5 percent in 2007 (Figure 17.4). In 2009, trade surplus was 8 percent of GDP, whereas the United States' trade deficit was 8 percent of GDP. At the end of 2008, China's foreign exchange reserve surpassed $2 trillion.

After 2001, China's export growth took off. It did so for many reasons, including China's entry into the World Trade Organization and increases in Chinese competitiveness. It cannot be denied that the export growth was related to the renminbi's exchange rate. Because the renminbi was undervalued, international trade was more

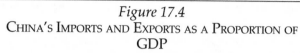

Figure 17.4
CHINA'S IMPORTS AND EXPORTS AS A PROPORTION OF
GDP

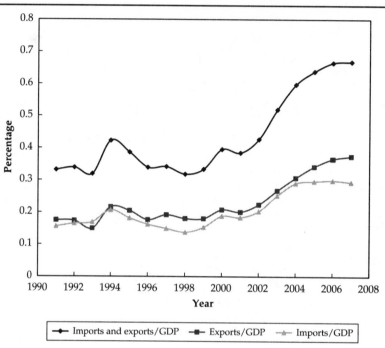

SOURCES: *China Statistical Yearbook* (related years) and National Statistics
Bureau website, http://www.stats.gov.cn/english/.

profitable than was domestic trade for businesses. After the start of
the 2008 Financial Crisis, the government continued subsidies for
exports. The benefits of those export subsidies were not considered;
the thinking seemed to be simply exports for the sake of exports. The
first half of 2009's export subsidies reached Y 800 billion, equal to
5 percent of GDP. Are those subsidies worth it? We need to seriously
research the issue.

After this crisis, China's exports were hampered. I personally believe that the crisis will not be short term; rather, it will be a long-
term adjustment process. My reason is that, generally speaking, the
larger the scale of the economy, the smaller trade is as a proportion

of GDP. (Speaking about extremes, if the entire world were united into only one country, that proportion of trade would be zero.) We can see from the data that among the world's 10 largest economies, only Germany's exports as a proportion of GDP (39.9 percent) are higher than China's (37.5 percent). Other countries—such as the United States at 8.4 percent, Japan at 16.3 percent, the United Kingdom at 15.7 percent, France at 21.6 percent, Italy at 23.4 percent, Spain at 7.4 percent, Canada at 29.2 percent, Brazil at 12.2 percent, and the world average at 25.6 percent—are all lower than China's figure (see Figure 17.5). What do those data mean? One possibility is that our GDP has been undervalued; another possibility is that our reliance on exports is too high.

Another point that deserves our attention is that, according to official Chinese statistics, 55 percent of the population is involved in agriculture. Therefore, exports as a proportion of GDP should not be as high. At the least, China cannot be compared with other industrialized countries because many of its agricultural products

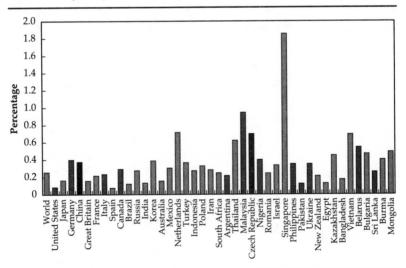

Figure 17.5
EXPORTS AS A PROPORTION OF GDP
(2007, RANKED ACCORDING TO ECONOMY SIZE)

SOURCE: *China Statistical Yearbook*, 2008.

are for personal consumption. Now, China's exports are a high percentage of GDP; at the same time, with so many farmers, there is a problem.

If this crisis is related to trade imbalance, then our export growth cannot be maintained. Regardless of whether other countries implement trade protectionist policies, it will be almost impossible for China to promote GDP growth through exports. What is the next step? There needs to be equilibrium between the two markets, which means developing the domestic market. Here, developing the domestic market does not refer to the "expansion of domestic consumption" that we often hear, to monetary expansion, or to government investment stimulus. Instead, it refers to expanding market liberty, releasing the entrepreneurial spirit, using resources more rationally, and fulfilling the actual needs of average people. That is a larger-scale, deeper degree of "Reform and Opening" for the Chinese economy. The question is how large is the potential of that domestic market?

China Itself Is a "World"

Let us first look at economic scales. Mainland China has 31 provincial-level economic regions. If we list each economic region as independent "countries" and then compare them with the economic scales of other countries, we will see very surprising results (Figure 17.6).

- The top four provinces by economic size are Guangdong, Shandong, Jiangsu, and Zhejiang. If Guangdong were its own independent economic entity, it would be the 18th largest in the world in 2008 (calculated using GDP exchange rates). It would follow Turkey (equaling 67 percent of Turkey's size) but precede Poland, Indonesia (the world's fourth-largest country by population), Belgium, Switzerland, Sweden, and Saudi Arabia.
- Shandong and Jiangsu are numbers two and three. They are larger than Norway, Austria, Iran, Greece, Denmark, and Argentina.
- Zhejiang, number four, is larger than Venezuela, Ireland, and South Africa.
- Henan, number five, is larger than Finland, Thailand, Portugal, and Colombia.

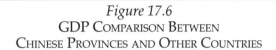

Figure 17.6
GDP COMPARISON BETWEEN
CHINESE PROVINCES AND OTHER COUNTRIES

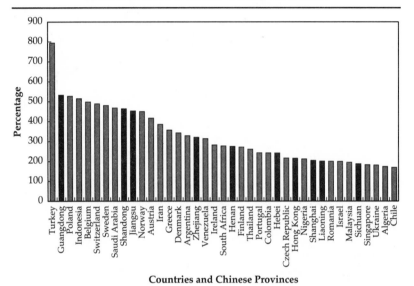

Countries and Chinese Provinces

SOURCES: Statistics for other countries came from the World Bank's online database. Statistics for regions of China came from the National Statistics Bureau.
NOTE: Calculations are based on the exchange rate at the end of 2008.

- Hebei, number six, is larger than the Czech Republic, Hong Kong, and Nigeria.
- Shanghai and Liaoning are numbers seven and eight. They are larger than Romania, Israel, and Malaysia.
- Sichuan, number nine, is larger than Singapore, Ukraine, Algeria, and Chile.
- Hubei, number 10, is larger than Pakistan and the Philippines.
- Hunan, number 11, is larger than the United Arab Emirates and Egypt.
- Fujian and Beijing are numbers 12 and 13. They are larger than Hungary.
- Anhui, number 14, is larger than Kazakhstan, New Zealand, and Peru.

- Heilongjiang and Inner Mongolia are numbers 15 and 16. They are larger than Kuwait.
- Guangxi, Shanxi, and Shaanxi are numbers 17, 18, and 19. They are larger than Libya.
- Jiangxi, number 20, is larger than the Slovak Republic.
- Tianjin and Jilin are numbers 21 and 22. They are larger than Vietnam and Morocco.
- Yunnan, number 23, is larger than Angola and Bangladesh.
- Chongqing, number 24, is larger than Croatia.
- Xinjiang, number 25, is larger than Belarus, Sudan, Luxembourg, Qatar, Serbia, and Bulgaria.
- Guizhou and Gansu are numbers 26 and 27. They are larger than Lithuania, the Dominican Republic, Sri Lanka, Uruguay, and Panama.
- Hainan, number 28, is larger than Cyprus, Tanzania, Jordan, Bolivia, and Iceland.
- Ningxia, number 29, is larger than Ghana, the Bahamas, and Uganda.
- Qinghai, number 30, is larger than Zambia, Honduras, Nepal, and Burma.
- Tibet is last but is still larger than Mongolia.

Let us look again at population. Population scale is a major deciding factor in market scale. For example, China Mobile became the world's largest telecommunications company because of China's large population scale. When Great Britain arose 200 years ago, the world's population had fewer than 1 billion people, and Great Britain accounted for less than 2 percent of the world's population. The reason Great Britain established colonies was partly because its own population was too small. When the United States arose 100 years ago, the world's population had fewer than 1.6 billion people, and the United States accounted for more than 5 percent of the world's population. Today, China's population has already surpassed 1.3 billion people, which is almost as large as was the total world population 100 years ago. It is higher than about one-fourth of the population of developed countries. For that reason, many countries focus on the Chinese market.

Looking at China's provinces separately shows that the population of some are larger than the total population of some major

Figure 17.7
A COMPARISON OF POPULATION BETWEEN SELECTED CHINESE REGIONS
AND SELECTED COUNTRIES (2007, MILLIONS)

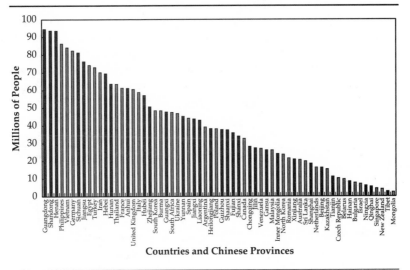

SOURCE: *China Statistical Yearbook*, 2008.

world powers (Figure 17.7). China's three most populated provinces
are Guangdong, Shandong, and Henan. The populations of each
are larger than the Philippines, Vietnam, and Germany (today's
fourth-largest economy). Sichuan and Jiangsu have larger populations than Egypt, Turkey, and Iran. Hebei and Hunan are larger than
Thailand and France (fifth-largest economy). Anhui is larger than
the United Kingdom (sixth-largest economy) and Italy (seventh-
largest economy). Hubei and Zhejiang are larger than South Korea
(13th-largest economy) and Burma. Guangxi is larger than South
Africa and Ukraine. Yunnan is larger than Spain (eighth-largest
economy). Liaoning is larger than Argentina. Heilongjiang is larger
than Poland. Guizhou, Shaanxi, Fujian, and Shanxi are larger than
Canada (ninth-largest economy). Chongqing and Jilin are larger than
Venezuela. Gansu is larger than Malaysia. Inner Mongolia is larger
than North Korea and Romania. Xinjiang is larger than Australia
(14th-largest economy) and Sri Lanka. Shanghai is larger than the

Netherlands (16th-largest economy). Tianjin is larger than the Czech Republic and Belarus. Hainan is larger than Bulgaria and Israel. Ningxia and Qinghai are larger than Singapore and New Zealand. Tibet is larger than Mongolia.

The purpose of comparing the economic scales and populations of the provinces is to show the inherent potential of the Chinese market. China's provinces vary immensely, so the potential exists for mutually beneficial trade and division of labor. If interprovincial trade can be accomplished well, then China itself can create a world-class market. More than 200 years ago, the father of economics, Adam Smith, marveled at the fact that "the extent of China's home market is not much inferior to the market of all the different countries of Europe put together."[4] Now is the time for us to truly develop this enormous market!

Development of the domestic market cannot be accomplished without developing the hinterland and western regions of the country. The economic growth led by coastal regions in the past went together with export-driven growth. Tomorrow, hinterland and western regions will become more important. It is encouraging that the regional structure of China's economic growth has already begun to transition to benefit central and western China. During the first and second decade after the start of Reform and Opening, the growth rate of the eastern region surpassed that of the central and western regions. However, over the past 10 years—or the third decade after Reform and Opening—especially during the past 5 or 6 years, the speed of growth in the central and western regions exceeded that in the eastern region.

During the first decade, the four fastest-growing provinces were Guangdong, Zhejiang, Fujian, and Shandong, all of which are in the east. During the second decade, the four fastest-growing provinces were Fujian, Guangdong, Zhejiang, and Shandong, which are coastal provinces. During the third decade, the four fastest-growing provinces were Inner Mongolia, Shaanxi, Tianjin, and Ningxia, three of which are in the central and western regions. During the past six years, from 2003 to 2008, Inner Mongolia was first, and Henan was second; the other fastest-growing provinces were Shaanxi, Shandong, and Shanxi.

Those facts show that a territorial transition is occurring in Chinese economic growth. They also show that interregional differences are decreasing, so the accounts saying China's regional disparity is getting progressively larger should not be believed without doubt. Development of the domestic market will certainly lead to equalization trends in the per capita incomes of the eastern, central, and western regions. There is hope that over the next 30 years, the gap between China's east and west will contract dramatically and slowly disappear.

What Will Domestic Market Development Rely On?

Generally speaking, a few major factors support the economic growth of a country: (a) property rights protections, (b) scientific and rational thought, (c) development of capital markets, and (d) transportation and communication.[5]

Over the past 30 years, China's transportation infrastructure has experienced a tremendous change. China built its first highway (100 kilometers) in 1988. By 1995, China had 2,100 kilometers of highways. By 2008, China already had 60,000 kilometers of highways and was expanding at a rate of 5,000 kilometers per year. Rough estimates claim that compared with 20 years ago, the travel time between two points has probably decreased one-half to two-thirds (of course, that does not include intercity travel). That reduction in travel time is very important because, for example, 20 years ago, conducting business between two areas was costly, but now it is possible.

After this economic crisis, China made huge investments in road construction (including highways and high-speed trains). Those improvements will have a tremendous effect on future economic development. Stated simply, decreases in transportation costs necessarily increase the development of the division of labor and exchanges. Without steam engines, railroads, and steamboats, the world economy could not have integrated. China's rapid development of transportation will create a good foundation for the integration of the Chinese economy.

Yet the main obstacle to developing the domestic market is not basic hardware infrastructure such as transportation or communications; it is transaction costs related to institutions. The main differences between international and domestic trade are the different transaction costs caused by separate sovereignty. Because international trade is conducted between sovereign countries, the formalities involved—

such as currency exchange, customs inspections, tariff protections, and nontariff protections—cause international trade to be costlier than domestic trade. Therefore, the main trend of world economic development has been to reduce the costs of international trade. Examples include the establishment of the European Union and the use of the euro. Thus, "international trade" between different European countries became "domestic trade." Now, there are discussions on how to integrate the East Asian economy or how to make trade between China, Japan, and South Korea as easy as domestic trade.

Regrettably, China's administrative divisions and government-led economic system create many circumstances in which the transaction cost of domestic trade is even higher than that of international trade. Consequently, the relative advantages of each region cannot be fully developed, which seriously affects the development of the domestic market and which is an important reason that China's economic growth rate overly relies on exports. Future adjustments and divisions of China's administrative areas should respect the inherent market attributes of a region and should reduce administrative functions. Otherwise, artificial administrative divisions will cut off rational market division of labor between areas. In addition, all forms of local protectionist policies must be abolished. When China waves the flag of free trade on the international stage, it should not forget that the domestic market is more in need of free trade.

Another obstacle to the development of the domestic market is commercial culture and business integrity. Ask a Chinese export manufacturer why 70–80 percent of its products are exported, instead of being sent to the domestic market. He will probably reply that the domestic market presents many difficulties such as these: (a) signing a contract, then (b) delivering the goods, but (c) having to wait a very long time to get paid. For exports, as long as a contract is signed, payment is received within the contractual limit.

Some enterprises are willing to sell exports at low prices, instead of selling to domestic clients at high prices, because there is too much uncertainty in the domestic market. We can see that if we do not strengthen the rule of law, effectively enforce contracts, and curtail rampant local protectionism, then Chinese entrepreneurs will have no confidence in expanding the domestic market.

Of course, we do not want to mistakenly believe that outward development is no longer important. Outward development was vital during the past 30 years of Chinese development, and it will still be vital in the future. Figure 17.8 shows exports as a proportion of each province's GDP. From the figure, we can see a very large difference. In 2007, Guangdong was 91 percent, Shanghai was 85.6 percent, Jiangsu was 61.3 percent, Tianjin was 57.4 percent, Zhejiang was 55.4 percent, and Fujian was 40 percent. The proportions for the next four provinces suddenly dropped to a little over 20 percent. Many provinces' international trade proportions were very low, such as Inner Mongolia, which was only 4.7 percent. Henan was China's fifth-largest economy, but its exports made up only 4.6 percent of its GDP. The statistics show that tremendous room still exists for international trade development in the central and western regions.

Figure 17.8
RANKING OF EXPORTS AS A PROPORTION OF
GDP FOR EACH PROVINCE (2007)

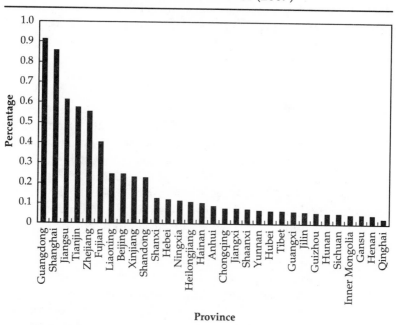

SOURCE: *China Statistical Yearbook*, 2008.

China's future economic development will also accompany urbanization. China's urban population now accounts for 45 percent of the total population, but at the start of Reform and Opening, it was only 18 percent. Perhaps over the next 30 years, it will increase to 75 percent. Such an increase should not be considered impossible; instead, it should be considered necessary. A country with the majority of its population engaged in agriculture cannot possibly become a truly developed country. What would such a change mean? Over the past 30 years, the number of cities in China with more than 1 million people increased by 200. Over the next 30 years, 400 million Chinese people will migrate from the countryside to the cities. If we consider a city as having 1 million people, then China needs to add 400 more cities.

Businesses that make market projections, including real estate developers, should look into that point. National development strategies, including the construction of the new countryside, should also consider that point. Because so many people want to move to the city, is it rational and profitable to spend so much money in the countryside? After the infrastructure is built, who will use it? Is there actually value in expending such a large amount of resources? Would it not be better to help the rural population move to the city? Those questions are all worth our consideration.

Industrial Innovation and Integration

In addition to developing the domestic market, the second transformation of economic development will be industry upgrades from low-cost advantage to high value added. Over the past 30 years, low prices were the reason that Chinese products could open up the international market. That reason is universally logical. Every country rose economically because it had an advantage in some industry and could dominate the market with low-priced products. The question is, with the development of the economy and with improvements in living standards, how long can China's low costs last?

A simple way to judge the degree of a country's development is to look at work and leisure time. People in developed countries work from Monday to Friday and rest on Saturday and Sunday. People in emerging markets work from Monday to Sunday. People in undeveloped countries rest from Monday to Sunday.

Hong Kong has not yet implemented the five-day workweek. Mainland China has already implemented it with frequent vacations and double or triple overtime. Our level of development is not low. We should say that more leisure time and higher pay are trends of economic development. Over the past three or four years, the wages of Beijing nannies have almost doubled. Coastal regions have experienced "migrant worker shortages." Because of the effect of the one-child policy, China will slowly experience a labor shortage, so wage increases are unavoidable. The issue is that when labor costs increase, how can China sustain its competitiveness? To do so calls for more innovation, thus producing higher value-added goods.

How innovative are Chinese enterprises? China's National Patent Office authorizes essentially three categories of patents: invention patents, utility model patents, and design patents. Of those, invention patents are a stern indicator of the core competitiveness of an enterprise. The other two categories are just window-dressing.

Figure 17.9 shows the percentage of invention patents as a proportion of all patents that were authorized for enterprises. We can see that in 2006, the proportion was 74 percent for foreign enterprises, but only 11 percent for Chinese enterprises. The entire time series indicates that the proportion for foreign enterprises is much higher than for Chinese enterprises. In reality, we all know that many Chinese patents are submitted only for comparisons and awards, and their technological content and commercial values are negligible. Therefore, the innovation of Chinese enterprises does not allow for optimism.

From the perspective of history, a country's rise certainly accompanies the appearance of revolutionary technology or industries. Examples include Great Britain's steam engine and textiles; Germany's chemical industries; and the United States' automobiles, electronic communication, and information technology. Those technologies changed industry, changed the economic structure, and thus changed the world.

A country that does not establish a new industry cannot possibly become a true economic superpower. However, the establishment of new industries does not rely on government investment. The future is uncertain, and comprehending market trends is not a strong point of government bureaucrats. For example, a domestic program for government investments spent a huge amount of money

Figure 17.9
INVENTION PATENTS AS A PERCENTAGE OF TOTAL PATENTS

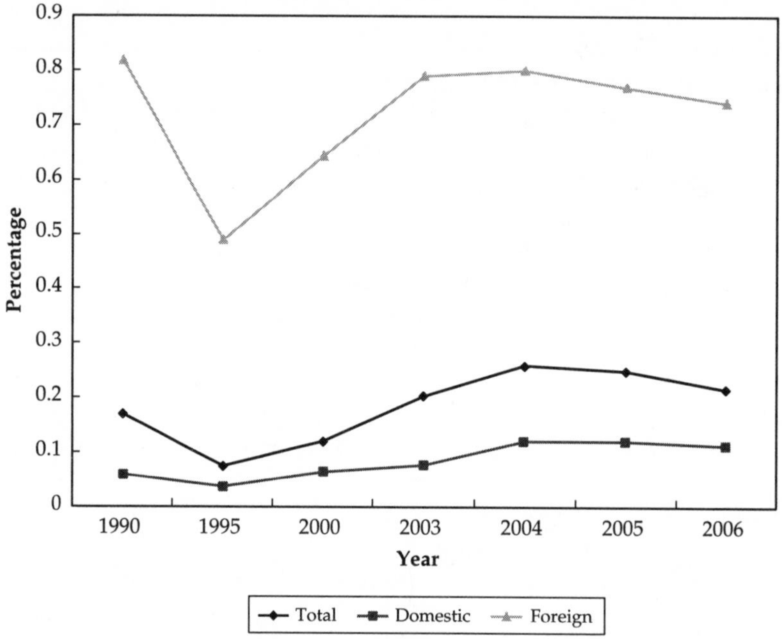

SOURCE: *China Statistical Yearbook* (relevant years).

on production lines for camcorders. Before the product was even finished, the market had already killed off camcorders. And let us not even address the opportunities for large amounts of corruption, waste, and deception hidden in government investment.

Industrial progression is a market process, and it relies on entrepreneurs. The advantage of the market is that it can always select entrepreneurs with the ability to adequately foresee trends. It turns them into the leaders of new industries. Chinese entrepreneurs must work hard to see the future's true colors if they are to understand the kinds of technologies that will have a deciding influence on future industries, as well as the kinds of industries that can lead economic development in the future. Unfortunately, Chinese entrepreneurs must still spend more energy on nonmarket, nontechnological aspects. Foreign entrepreneurs get together to discuss their industry and the future structure of their industry. Chinese entrepreneurs get together and spend the most time discussing political and policy issues. Therefore, government intervention in the market must be further reduced.

A speech made by leadership will not resolve the problem and increase a country's ability to innovate. The education system is especially important. We need to cultivate scientific and rational thought. Without such thinking, which appeared during the Enlightenment, the Western world would not have arisen. China's education has progressed, but the influence of ideology is still too great and has too much control over people's thoughts. Too much waste and too little efficiency exist in our education system, so education must undergo a huge reform in the future.

The final transition is from growth in the number of enterprises to industry consolidation. In essence, the past 30 years of Chinese economic growth has relied primarily on continuous increases in small and medium-sized enterprises. After this crisis, perhaps China will transition from growth in the number of enterprises to an increased enterprise scale. There will be a new wave of industry mergers and acquisitions (including domestic and international mergers and acquisitions), which will cause industry concentration to increase dramatically.

From the perspective of history, during the economic development of Western countries, large-scale multiregional and multinational enterprises emerged mostly after crises. In that sense, crises also have positive aspects. When a person dies, that is the end. When a business dies, a reorganization of assets occurs, which causes assets to be used more efficiently. China needs to adjust policies in that respect. Relying on loans to rescue enterprises is inappropriate. Bankrupt enterprises should be allowed to go bankrupt. Only then can truly outstanding enterprises develop and become the driving force of the economy.

Fully Implement Market Reforms to Guard against "State Progress and Private Decline"

The source of China's success of the past 30 years was Reform and Opening. Whether or not China can become the world's largest economic superpower will be decided by whether or not it fully implements market reforms. So-called market reforms refer to price liberalization, enterprise privatization, administrative decentralization, openness, and globalization. China's reforms did not come from meticulous planning or careful consideration; most of them were forced. When times are good, no one wants to reform; people want to reform only when times are bad. Therefore, we must not forget history or forget where we came from.

During the global financial crisis, a phenomenon appeared that has been called "state progress and private decline." Huge numbers of bank loans were given to state-owned enterprises so they could forcefully purchase private enterprises. We need to be vigilant about such actions. From a long-term perspective, the state-owned enterprises that had the easiest time receiving money will likely go bankrupt. According to experience, after a few years, the bad debts of those state-owned enterprises will increase, so banks will have to restructure debt.

Before 1990, state-owned enterprises went to the banks any time they needed money. They accumulated a huge number of bad debts, which ultimately could only be sold. We already restructured once. The reason China did not have a big crisis then is because a few years ago we spent trillions of yuan to resolve that issue. We should not believe that more money equals more strength because it only serves to expose more problems later. In addition, the government is promising increasingly more welfare. Future government revenue cannot possibly support those promises. The only way to resolve the funding issue is to sell off the shares of state-owned enterprises.

In my view, within the next 30 years, the state-owned sector of the economy should decrease to 10 percent of the total. Right now, it is about 36 percent; thus by 2040, it should be less than 10 percent. Whether or not we are willing, perhaps that is the only solution. I have said before that the basic tasks of state-owned enterprise reform have already been completed. We no longer need (a) to go to war over the issue or (b) to hold another National Party Congress to discuss the direction of state-owned enterprise reform. The largest state-owned enterprises are already publicly listed. The remaining issues are technical and operational with regard to how quickly state-owned shares can be reduced. Perhaps an organization such as China Central Television will also be privatized in the future. Because of competition from the Internet and local stations, its advantage will continuously decrease. Ultimately, perhaps no one will watch CCTV unless it is privatized.

Overall, I believe that even if short-term twists and turns occur, because of the fruits of the past 30 years of reform, the main trend of market reforms will not change. The state-owned enterprises that are doing well today rely basically on monopolies to earn money, but their efficiency is very low. State-owned enterprises hold two-thirds of society's economic resources, but they create only one-third of society's value. After they are privatized, we can imagine the kind of potential the Chinese economy will bring forward.

The Direction and Route of Political Reform

Of the emerging markets, the most valuable reference point from China's reforms is the fact that it chose to establish a market first and to establish democracy second. That was the brilliance of Deng Xiaoping. Countries that put democratic reforms before market reforms have few good results, including India. Market reforms certainly need to be made before democratic reforms because democracy is just a type of political system. Political systems will not solve problems on their own; therefore, they should not be the first choice.

What are the differences between market decisions and political decisions? Imagine a group of 300 people who want to eat. Market decisions allow everyone to choose individually, to buy whatever they want to eat. Thus, everyone's preferences are satisfied. In contrast, political decisions would require everyone to eat the same thing. Democratic politics would be like having everyone vote on whether to eat meat or fish. If more than 50 percent of people want to eat meat, everyone must eat meat. Democracy is a forceful method.

If a country has yet to establish property rights, and its government controls large amounts of resources but believes democracy will solve problems, then it is easy to give to the government the decisionmaking power that should have originally belonged to the market. That government decisionmaking power not only leads to efficiency losses but also breeds serious corruption. Therefore, we should first separate the functional scope of the market and the government, thereby giving as much decisionmaking authority to the market as possible.

The emergence of the middle class is very important to the healthy operation of a democratic political system. Without an enormous middle class, democracy could possibly turn into populism, or even mob politics. Democracy must be built on a rule-of-law foundation. That foundation requires every citizen to have a basic civil awareness and sense of responsibility. The so-called middle class is made up of those kinds of people: they have a certain number of private assets to protect, but they are not wealthy enough to do whatever they want. However, they are willing and have the ability to take responsibility for social stability.

If the absolute majority of people in society have nothing, but a minority of people are extremely wealthy, there will be trouble. Poor people may not respect society's rules because, as Karl Marx said, all they have to lose are shackles, but they can gain the whole world. Extremely wealthy people also do not have to respect society's rules because they can use the power of money to put down others. Such a society is awful. Therefore, the emergence of the middle class is very important. The middle class should emerge through free-market competition, so that becoming wealthy is a process of using individual endowments and working hard. People who become wealthy from market competition often have a stronger civil awareness and moral principles. Society views a person who becomes wealthy from individual ability and a person who becomes wealthy from fraud and violence very differently.

Of course, we cannot say that economic marketization can replace political democratization. In 1990, I participated in a conference in the United Kingdom. The topic was the mainstream tendency at the time for Western academic circles to praise Russia and belittle China. I made a prediction about the long-term progression of Chinese reform.

I believe that a tai chi diagram can be used as an analogy for China's reforms (see Figure 17.10). If an S-shaped curve is drawn down a vertical oval, splitting it in two, one side will be wide and become narrow, and the other will be narrow and become wide. The wide-to-narrow half is economic reform, and the narrow-to-wide half is political reform. That is the relationship between economic and political reform. The focal point for the first stage is economic reform, with a few small political movements. The focal point for the second stage is political reform, as economic reform slowly winds up. In the current stage of Chinese reform, the most important aspects of

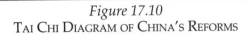

Figure 17.10
TAI CHI DIAGRAM OF CHINA'S REFORMS

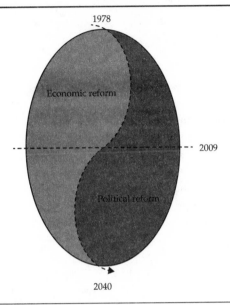

SOURCE: Author's compilation.

economic reform have largely been completed, with some remaining technical and operational issues to resolve and with political reform just beginning. After today's reforms, the contents of political reform will become progressively more important.

How a country with 1.3 billion people can build a democratic political system is still uncertain. I would like to emphasize the following few points:

First, China's political reforms should be gradual; we cannot use shock therapy. After the founding of the United States, the slaves were not freed for 89 years, women did not obtain the right to vote for 144 years, and black Americans did not have the right to vote for 189 years (not until 1965). In early elections in Great Britain, one had to have land and wealth to vote; not just anyone could vote. Because of the way China's society has developed, the country cannot possibly follow that path, but some lessons are worth considering.

363

Second, the rule of law must be established first, which requires an independent judiciary. Without a relatively independent judicial system, democratic politics are not possible. The authority of the law and the courts is the core of a rule-of-law society. Elections are an example. If we elect a provincial governor or a county leader, will the outcome be acknowledged? That is a very important question. If the results of the election are contested (even U.S. presidential election results are sometimes contested), an organization of authority is necessary to resolve the issue. If the authority of the courts cannot be established, disagreements will turn into violence. If the courts have authority, there can be disagreements, but everyone must acknowledge the courts' decisions.

Regrettably, many of the actions we are taking today weaken the authority of the law and the courts. That result is extremely dangerous. When the government selects a house to demolish, how can the owners protect their rights? If a conflict exists, the courts should resolve it. At the same time, our current methods are weakening the authority of the law; they are strengthening the coordination of government departments and government's authority. Many individual affairs are not handled according to legal procedures, so they become group affairs. That approach too is very dangerous. Many government departments are unaware of that consequence.

Now, many disturbances are resolved by finding an audience with the government, by coordinating with the government, or by paying money. Sooner or later, that approach becomes a large issue. If the courts use legal means to resolve private disputes, such as demolition compensation, not everyone has to accept it; but after the courts make a judgment according to principles, it must be enforced. If that is the case, social chaos will not ensue. I want to emphasize that the government is not completely aware of this issue. If the government uses administrative means to resolve those social contradictions, it will probably lead to social instability, or even chaos. Only with support of the judiciary can social issues be turned into cases and individual issues. Only at that time can society be stable. That point is very important.

The hardest issue faced by Chinese political reform is how to merge democracy and meritocracy. Democratic reform must not turn into either populism or a movement of hooligans. The United States is probably the best country to merge democracy and meritocracy. The structure of U.S. politics and law—including the Senate, the House of Representatives, and the Supreme Court—is designed to guard against hooligan movements and mob politics. China also needs to find a suitable electoral system, one that guarantees the merger of democracy and meritocracy. What we call "Party leadership" is actually a type of meritocracy. Given China's traditions and large population, its future challenges are immense. India was discussed earlier. Its political system reform came before its economic reform. But we should not belittle it, because no matter what happens, it has already gone through that turbulence. If India develops faster than China in the future, it will probably be because China's political system reforms were not handled well.

We need to investigate the next specific step. Unfortunately, the atmosphere for investigating those issues is not very good. Regardless of whether it was economic reform, price reform, or property rights reform, we have conducted open or private inquiries into all of them. However, for such a large transformation of the political system, we have not formed an open climate to discuss the issue.

There is talk of political mechanism reform, but it has gone no further than slogans, which is relatively troublesome. I believe we should inquire into the Taiwan and Hong Kong models to discuss such reform. Actually, our thought process in handling the Hong Kong issue is constructive for resolving many political system reforms on the mainland. For example, we could slowly proceed with functional constituency elections. That approach would be effective in guaranteeing elite politics and meritocracy during democratization. That judgment is not necessarily correct, but I think it should be discussed. The most suitable procedure for elections of any level of government leader or senior cadre should be discussed openly. We ourselves should seriously research that issue, and then we should see which way is best to maintain social stability and to have rule by elites under a democratic system. If such issues are not seriously considered, the process will appear rather passive.

After another 30 years, in about 2040, China's reforms should basically be complete. I draw lessons from historian Tekong Tong in that China will have had two truly large structural transformations. The first was from the feudal system to the imperial system. It took about 200 to 300 years, from the Duke Xiao of Qin until the Emperor Wu of Han. After the Emperor Wu of Han, the whole imperial political system was stable; only governance issues remained. The second transformation will have been from the imperial system to a democratic society, which will probably take 200 years. If we use 200 years as our benchmark, from the start of the Opium Wars in 1840 to 2040 is precisely 200 years.

The past 30 years and the next 30 years will possibly be the last act in China's 200-year history of transformation. Starting in 1840, events such as the Westernization movement, the *Wuxu* movement (a reform movement in 1898 led by Chinese scholars Kang Youwei and Liang Qichao), and the 1911 Xinhai Revolution, the Socialist Transformation, among others, were all trying to find outlets for China's transformation. In the end, Deng Xiaoping helped us find a route for economic emergence. In the next 30 years, we must find an effective route for political transformation.

To conclude, I would like to discuss our international strategy. China's influence grows by the day, especially after the financial crisis. In the future, China must participate in the international community to set the rules of the game, but Chinese people must not be arrogant. As Deng Xiaoping said, we must hide one's capacities and bide one's time. It is most important for China to develop itself and not vie with the United States for control of the world. Develop well, and others will come when they are in need. Nothing is wrong with that approach. China must certainly rely on economic development to increase its international status. From a historical perspective, any international status that has relied on military strength has been short-lived. Westerners emphasize China's responsibility, and that assessment is reasonable. We must be responsible in order to have international status.

In the next 30 years, perhaps China will become the world's largest economy. By that time, China's best enterprises will also certainly be world-class enterprises. China's leaders—regardless of whether they are government leaders, business leaders, or academic leaders—will all be world-class leaders. China's 100-year dream of superpower revival will come true at that time. Such a revival will be an honor for each Chinese citizen. Of course, the premise for doing so is that we build a democratic, rule-of-law market economy.

Notes

Introduction

The Introduction is a revised version of a speech the author gave on December 10, 2012, at the Shanghai Social Science Association's conference. An abridged version was published in 2011 in volume 2 of the *Tansuo yu Zhengming Magazine*.

1. See Gregory Clark, *A Farewell to Alms: A Brief Economic History of the World* (Princeton, NJ: Princeton University Press, 2007).

2. Also see Murray Rothbard, *Economic Thought before Adam Smith*, vol. 1 of *An Austrian Perspective on the History of Economic Thought* (Auburn, AL: Ludwig von Mises Institute, 2006), p. 26.

Chapter 1

The text of this chapter comes from a lecture titled "How to Comprehend the Market Economy" given to students at the Guanghua School of Management on October 10, 2007, along with revisions made after the question-and-answer session. It was first published on December 18, 2007, in the *Xuexi Shibao*.

1. William Oliver Coleman, *Economics and Its Enemies: Two Centuries of Anti-Economics* (New York: Palgrave Macmillan, 2002). Its Chinese translation was published by Shanghai People's Press, 2007.

2. See Eric D. Beinhocker, *The Origin of Wealth: Evolution, Complexity, and the Radical Remaking of Economics* (Boston: Harvard Business School Press, 2006), pp. 9–10.

3. Ibid., p. 9

4. Frank H. Knight, *Risk, Uncertainty and Profit* (Boston: Houghton Mifflin, 1921).

5. Joseph Schumpeter, *The Theory of Economic Development* (Cambridge, MA: Harvard University Press, 1934).

6. Hernando de Soto, *The Mystery of Capital: Why Capitalism Triumphs in the West and Fails Everywhere Else* (New York: Basic Books, 2000).

7. Niny Khor and John H. Penvacel, "Income Mobility of Individuals in China and the United States," IZA Discussion Paper no. 2003, Institute for the Study of Labor, Stanford University, 2005.

8. William Bernstein, *The Birth of Plenty: How the Prosperity of the Modern World Was Created* (New York: McGraw-Hill, 2004).

Chapter 2

The contents of this chapter are from a speech given by the author on April 14, 2007, at the 14th Annual Chinese Entrepreneur Growth and Development Survey Publication and Corporate Social Responsibility Forum. It was first published on August 19, 2007, in *Jingji Guanchabao*.

1. Frank H. Knight, *Risk, Uncertainty and Profit* (Boston: Houghton Mifflin, 1921).

2. Joseph Schumpeter, *The Theory of Economic Development* (Cambridge, MA: Harvard University Press, 1934).

3. Nicholas Carr, "IT Doesn't Matter," *Harvard Business Review*, May 2003, pp. 5–12.

Chapter 3

The paper on which this chapter is based was prepared for the International Economic Association Round Table on Market and Socialism, in the Light of the Experiences of China and Vietnam, Hong Kong University of Science and Technology, January 14–15, 2005. Substantial revisions have been undertaken since the presentation. The author thanks all participants and particularly Yijiang Wang for valuable comments.

1. For conceptual clarification of market socialism, see János Kornai, "Socialism and the Market: Conceptual Clarification," in *Market and Socialism*, ed. János Kornai and Yingyi Qian (New York: Palgrave Macmillan, 2008), pp. 11–24.

2. Most Chinese economists held this view either explicitly or implicitly up to the late 1990s, and it has been very much an official view that has guided the formation of reform policy during most of the reform period. Justin Lin may be the best-known representative of this school. See Justin Lin, Fang Cai, and Zhou Li, "Competition, Policy Burdens, and State-Owned Enterprise Reform," *American Economic Review* 88, no. 2 (1998): 422–27.

3. I have been cited as a representative of the ownership school. As early as 1986, I argued that it is impossible to separate firms from governments. See Weiying Zhang, "Entrepreneurship and Ownership" [Qiyejia yu suoyouzhi], Working Paper no. 30, China Institute for Economic System Reform, 1986; also see Weiying Zhang, *The Theory of the Firm and Chinese Enterprise Reform* [Qiye lilun yu Zhongguo qiye gaige] (Beijing: Peking University Press, 1999).

4. Joseph E. Stiglitz, *Whither Socialism?* (Cambridge, MA: MIT Press, 1994).

5. Louis Putterman, "China's Encounter with Market Socialism: Approaching Managed Capitalism by Indirect Means," in *Market and Socialism*, ed. János Kornai and Yingyi Qian (New York: Palgrave Macmillan, 2008), pp. 47–65.

6. Stiglitz, *Whither Socialism?*

7. Theodore Groves, T. Yongmiao Hong, John McMillan, and Barry Naughton, "Autonomy and Incentives in Chinese State Enterprises," *Quarterly Journal of Economics* 109 (1994): 202–26; Weiying Zhang, "Decision Rights, Residual Claims, and Performance: A Theory of How Chinese State Enterprise Reform Works," *China Economic Review* 8, no. 1 (1997): 67–82.

8. Weiying Zhang and Jie Ma, "Ownership Foundation of Vicious Competition" [Exing jinzheng de chanquan jichu], *Journal of Economic Research* [Jingji yanjiu] 7 (1999).

9. More generally, β may represent the right of control that the manager has over the firm, and α may represent the responsibilities that he must bear in the firm.

10. In this chapter, I also show that in a mixed economy, a private firm could survive if—and only if—its technological productivity is sufficiently higher than that of the state-owned firm.

11. Given that the manager had to bear the cost of the efforts, that reality led to the undersupply of such efforts.

12. Weiying Zhang, "Decision Rights, Residual Claims and Performance."

13. Bengt Holmström and Paul Milgrom, "Multi-Task Principal-Agent Analysis: Incentive Contracts, Asset Ownership, and Job Design," *Journal of Economic Behavior and Organization* 7 (1991): 24–51.

14. Steven Sklivas, "The Strategic Choice of Managerial Incentives," *Rand Journal of Economics* 18, no. 3 (1987): 452–58.

15. Weiying Zhang, "A Principal-Agent Theory of the Public Economy and Its Applications to China," *Economics of Planning* 31 (1998): 231–51.

16. Stiglitz, *Whither Socialism?*; Justin Lin, Fang Cai, and Zhou Li, "Competition, Policy Burdens, and State-Owned Enterprise Reform," *American Economic Review* 88, no. 2 (1998): 422–27.

17. Ironically, the Chinese experience is quite often taken as empirical support for the competition school's arguments.

18. János Kornai, "The Soft Budget Constraint," *Kyklos* 39, no. 1 (1986): 3–30.

19. Schumpeter, *The Theory of Economic Development*.

20. N. Gregory Mankiw and Michael D. Whinston, "Free Entry and Social Inefficiency," *Rand Journal of Economics* 17, no. 1 (1986): 48–58; Kotaro Suzumura and Kazuharu Kiyono, "Entry Barriers and Economic Welfare," *Review of Economic Studies* 54 (1987): 157–67.

21. John Vickers and George Yarrow, *Privatization: An Economic Analysis* (Cambridge, MA: MIT Press, 1988).

22. Xingmin Yin, "Industrial Concentration and Efficiency of Resources Allocation in Chinese Manufactories" [Zhongguo zhichaoye de chanye jizhongdu he ziyuan peizhi xiaolv), *Journal of Economic Research* [Jingji yanjiu] 1 (1996).

23. Weiying Zhang, "Nontransferability of Control Benefits and Property Rights Barriers to Merger and Acquisitions in State Sectors" [Kunzhiquan de buke buchangxing he guoyou qiye jianbing zhongde chanquan zhangai], *Journal of Economic Research* [Jingji yanjiu] 7 (1998).

24. Phillipe Aghion and Patrick Bolton, "An Incomplete Contracts Approach to Financial Contracting," *Review of Economic Studies* 59 (1992): 473–94; Oliver Hart, *Firms, Contracts, and Financial Structure* (New York: Oxford University Press, 1995), chap. 5–6.

25. In the standard model, in which only cash flow is concerned, it is assumed that the marginal firm merely breaks even. I believe that it is more realistic to take control benefits into account. However, if the owner-manager is liquidity constrained, the zero-profit condition might apply.

26. The case of listed private companies will be discussed later in the chapter.

27. This conclusion holds as long as the decisionmaker is not a 100 percent owner. It definitely holds when the manager claims a greater share in revenue than is borne in cost, as was assumed in the previous section.

28. Hongbin Li, Weiying Zhang, and Li-an Zhou, "Ownership, Efficiency, and Firm Survival in Economic Transition: Evidence from a Chinese Science Park," working paper, Guanghua School of Management, Peking University, 2005. Available from the authors.

29. George A. Akerlof, "The Market for 'Lemons': Quality Uncertainty and the Market Mechanism," *Quarterly Journal of Economics* 84 (1970): 488–500.

30. Jeremy Shearmur and Daniel Klein, "Good Conduct in the Great Society: Adam Smith and the Role of Reputation," in *Reputation Studies in the Voluntary Elicitation of Good Conduct*, ed. Daniel Klein (Ann Arbor: University of Michigan Press, 1997), pp. 29–45.

31. Yi Zhang, and Guang Ma, "Law, Economic, Corporate Governance, and Corporate Scandals in a Transition Economy: Insight from China," working paper, Guanghua School of Management, Peking University, 2005.

32. Weiying Zhang, *Property Rights, Governments, and Reputation* [Chanquan, zhengfu yu xinyu] (Beijing: Sanlian Publication, 2001).

33. David Kreps, "Corporate Culture and Economic Theory," in *Perspectives on Positive Political Economy*, ed. James Alt and Kenneth Shepsle (Cambridge: Cambridge University Press, 1990), pp. 90–143.

34. State Statistics Bureau of China, 1998, p. 99.

35. Shaomin Li, Shuhe Li, and Weiying Zhang, "The Road to Capitalism: Competition and Institutional Change in China," *Journal of Comparative Economics* 28 (2000): 269–92; Ross Garnaut, Ligang Song, and Yang Yao, "SOE Restructuring in China," in *China's Policy Reforms: Progress and Challenges* (Beijing: Tsinghua University and Stanford Center for International Development, 2004).

36. Xiao Zhao, "Competition, Public Policy and Institutional Change," CCER Working Paper no. C1999025, Peking University, 1999.

37. Unpublished report of the State Economic and Trade Commission, cited in Garnaut, Song, and Yao, "SOE Restructuring in China."

38. China Stock Exchange Executive Council, 2001:5.

39. Li, Li, and Zhang, "The Road to Capitalism."

40. Traditionally, ownership is defined by who can lay claim to the residual rights. Grossman and Hart define ownership as being rights of control over assets. Sanford J. Grossman and Oliver Hart, "The Costs and Benefits of Ownership: A Theory of Vertical and Lateral Integration," *Journal of Political Economy* 94 (1986): 691–719. Economists presently recognize that both residual claims and control rights are essential to ownership. Here, I omit control rights not because they are irrelevant but because of technical intractability. Nevertheless, it is my conjecture that my results apply to control rights as well. Furthermore, given that state-owned enterprise managers have obtained considerable autonomy of decision, I believe that the transfer of residual rights is just completion of privatization; that is, as the manager holds all the residue of the firm, he becomes the de facto owner of the firm.

41. Cao, Qian, and Weingast argue that federalism, Chinese style, has induced privatization. However, one question they do not address—at least not formally—is how cross-regional competition stimulates the rise of a private-ownership system. Yuanzheng Cao, Yingyi Qian, and Barry R. Weingast, "From Federalism, Chinese Style, to Privatization, Chinese Style," *Economics of Transition* 7, no. 1 (1999): 103–31.

42. Li, Li, and Zhang, "The Road to Capitalism."

43. World Bank, *Bureaucrats in Business: The Economics and Politics of Government Ownership* (Oxford and New York: Oxford University Press, 1995), pp. 31, 56.

Chapter 4

This text is a revised version of a presentation the author gave on October 13, 2007, at the "China's Competition Policies and the Anti-Monopoly Law" academic seminar.

1. Joseph Schumpeter, *The Theory of Economic Development* (Cambridge, MA: Harvard University Press, 1934).

2. David Kreps, "Corporate Culture and Economic Theory," in *Technological Innovation and Business Strategy*, ed. M. Tsuchiya (Tokyo: Nippon Keizai Shimbuunsha Press, 1986); also in *Perspective on Politive Political Economy*, ed. James Alt and Kenneth Shepsle (Cambridge, MA: Harvard University Press, 1990), pp. 90–143.

3. Joseph Schumpeter, *The Theory of Economic Development* (Cambridge, MA: Harvard University Press, 1934).

4. Dominick T. Armentano, *Anti-Trust and Monopoly: Anatomy of a Policy Failure*, 2nd ed. (San Francisco: Independent Institute, 1992).

5. Murray Rothbard, *Market and Power: Government and the Economy* (Menlo Park, CA: Institute for Human Studies, 1970).

Chapter 5

This article was completed on September 15, 2006, and published in *Wenhui bao* on September 18, 2006.

1. Also see Simeon Djankov, Rafael La Porta, Florencio Lopez-de-Silanes, and Andrei Shleifer, "The Regulation of Entry," *Quarterly Journal of Economics* 117, no. 1 (2002): 1–37.

Chapter 6

This text was adapted from the author's presentation at the opening ceremony of the 11th Annual Yabuli Chinese Entrepreneur Forum on February 15, 2011.

Chapter 7

This text is a revised version of a speech the author gave at Peking University and was titled "*Shichang jingji zui daode*." The original text was published in *Nanfang zhoumo*, no. 31, on July 14, 2011.

1. Adam Smith, *The Theory of Moral Sentiments*, ed. Knud Haakonssen (Cambridge: Cambridge University Press, 2002), p. 11.

2. Ibid.

3. See Ludwig von Mises, *The Anti-Capitalist Mentality* (Indianapolis: Liberty Fund, 1981), chap. 1.

4. H. Peyton Young, "The Economics of Convention," *Journal of Economic Perspective* 10, no. 2 (1996): 105–22.

Chapter 8

This article was completed on March 3, 2006. Most of the contents were published in the *Economic Observer* [Jingji Guanchabao] on March 11, 2006. The entire article was included in the book *Thirty Years of China's Reform: Thinking of Ten Distinguished Economists* [Zhongguo Gaige Sanshi Nian: Shi Wei Jjingji Xuejia de Sikao] (Shanghai: Shanghai People's Press, 2008).

1. John Rawls, *A Theory of Justice* (Cambridge, MA: Harvard University Press, 1971).

2. Ibid.

3. Martin Ravallion and Shaohua Chen, "China's (Uneven) Progress against Poverty," World Bank Policy Research Working Paper no. 3408, September 2004, http://ssrn.com/abstract=625285.

4. Zhiwu Chen, "Can State-Ownership and Government Regulation Promote Even Development?" *Economic Observer* [Jingji Guanchabao], January 2, 2006.

5. James Mirrlees, "An Exploration in the Theory of Optimum Income Taxation," *Review of Economic Studies* 38 (1971): 175–208.

6. James Heckman, "China's Investment in Human Capital," *Economic Development and Cultural Change* 51 (2003): 795–804; James Heckman, "China's Human Capital Investment," *China Economic Review* 16 (2005): 50–70.

7. Xavier Sala-i-Martin, "The World Distribution of Income: Falling Poverty and ... Convergence, Period," *Quarterly Journal of Economics* 121, no. 2 (2006): 351–97.

Chapter 9

This text was a cooperative effort with Gang Yi. The English draft was written in 1994, then presented at international academic conferences in Great Britain, the United States, Australia, and Hong Kong. It was printed as an internal manuscript for the Chinese Economic Society (China) and the Chinese Economic Research Center of Peking University, but it was formally published in *China's Economic Growth and Transition*, edited by Clement A. Tisdell and Joseph G. W. Chai (Commack, NY: Nova Science Publishers, 1997). The Chinese text was translated according to the formal English publication. Shaojia Liu, Dingding Wang, and Robert Sandy provided very valuable revision suggestions, which are appreciated. At the same time, the authors would like to thank the participants of the 1995 AEA meeting, as well as the participants of a series of seminars at Oxford University, the London School of Economics, and Hong Kong City University. A special thank-you is given to Mr. Zhijing Niu for translating the English version.

1. Hungary and Poland had implemented gradualism before the "Big Bang." Even the former Soviet Union had tried gradualism before its collapse.

2. For example, János Kornai says: "The reform process has a forty-year history in Yugoslavia, twenty in Hungary, and almost a whole decade in China. All three countries represent specific mixtures of amazing results and disastrous failures." János Kornai, *Vision and Reality, Market and State: Contradictions and Dilemmas Revisited* (Budapest: Corvina Books, 1990), p. 210.

3. See, among others, Alan Gelb, Gary Jefferson, and Inderjit Singh, "Can Communist Economies Transform Incrementally? The Experience of China," in *NBER Macroeconomics Annual 1993*, ed. Olivier Jean Blanchard and Stanley Fischer (Cambridge, MA: National Bureau of Economic Research, 1993), pp. 87–150; Gary Jefferson and Inderjit Singh, "China's State-Owned Industrial Enterprises: How Effective Have the Reforms Been?" Brandeis University and World Bank, 1993; John McMillan and Barry Naughton, "How to Reform Planned Economies: Lessons from China," *Oxford Review of Economic Policy* 8, no. 1 (1992): 130–43; Dwight Perkins, "China's 'Gradual' Approach to Market Reforms," paper presented at the Comparative Experiences of Economic Reform and Post-Socialist Transformation conference, El Escorial, Spain, July 6–8, 1992; Jeffrey Sachs and Wing Thye Woo, "Structural Factors in the Economic Reforms of China, Eastern Europe, and the Former Soviet Union," 1993 (copy in author's files); Gang Yi, *Money, Banking and Financial Markets in China* (Boulder, CO: Westview Press, 1994); and Gang Zou, "Modeling the Enterprises Behavior under the Two-Tier Plan/Market System in the PRC," University of Southern California, Davis, 1993.

4. See, for example, Kang Chen, "Crossing the River while Groping for Planned Stones: A Public-Choice Analysis of China's Economic Reform," 1992 (copy in author's files); Mathias Dewatripoint and Gérard Roland, "Economic Reform and Dynamic Political Constraints," *Review of Economic Studies* 59 (1992): 703–30; Mathias Dewatripoint and Gérard Roland, "The Virtues of Gradualism and Legitimacy in the Transition to

a Market Economy," *Economic Journal* 102 (1992): 291–300; Gang Fan, "Liang zhong gaige chengben he liang zhong gaige lujing," *Journal of Economic Research* [Jingji yanjiu] 1 (1993): 3–15; Shijin Liu, "Transition to Market Economy in China: The Course of Actions and the Public Choice," Institute of Industrial Economics, CASS, Beijing, 1993 (copy in author's files); Peter Murrell, "Public Choice and the Transformation of Socialism," *Journal of Comparative Economics*, 15, no. 2 (1991): 203–10; Peter Murrell and Mancure Olson, "The Devolution of Centrally Planned Economies," *Journal of Comparative Economics*, 15, no. 2 (1991): 239–65; Peter Murrell and Yijiang Wang, "When Privatization Should Be Delayed: The Effect of Communist Legacies on Organizational and Institutional Reforms," *Journal of Comparative Economics* 17, no. 2 (1993): 385–406; and Zhigang Wang, "Gradualism versus Big Bang: An Economic Perspective," paper presented at the ASSA-CES Joint Session of ASSA Meetings, Boston, January 3–5, 1994.

5. Shangjin Wei defines gradualism versus Big Bang as follows: Gradualism refers to a sequential implementation of minimum bangs, and a minimum bang is a simultaneous implementation of a minimum set of reforms that exhibit "strong interdependence"; Big Bang refers to a simultaneous implementation of all small bangs. Shangjin Wei, "Gradualism versus Speed and Sustainability of Reforms," 1992 (copy in author's files). Wei's definition has several defects, as pointed out by Zhigang Wang in "Gradualism versus Big Bang." First, Wei's is actually a gradualist's definition and is irrelevant for Big Bang economists because the definition per se excludes the underlying assumption of the Big Bang approach that all components of a reform program exhibit strong contemporaneous interdependence. Second, Wei's definition ignores the intertemporal interdependence among different components of reforms that is crucial for understanding reform processes. Third, Wei does not consider the evolutionary process of even a minimum bang. As Zhigang Wang argues, gradualism means not only a sequential but also an evolutionary process. According to Wang, Big Bang refers to a comprehensive reform program that is implemented with one stoke; gradualism refers to a comprehensive reform program that is implemented in a sequential, evolutionary fashion. Although Wang's definition captures two important elements of gradualism (i.e., sequential implementation and evolutionary process) and might be sufficient for setting up a theoretical model of gradualism versus Big Bang (as he did), it is far from explaining the major dimensions of China's gradual reform.

6. In the early period of reform (until 1984), the objective was to "perfect and improve the socialist planned economy by introducing some market elements." Some observers may argue that in the early stages, there was no objective at all. For example, Perkins wrote, "Most Chinese leaders did not have a clear reform objective in mind," in "China's 'Gradual' Approach to Market Reforms," p. 4. For a similar argument, see Gang Fan, "Dual-Track Transition: China's Incremental Approach to Market-Oriented Reform," 1993 (copy in author's files). The September 1984 Third Plenary Session of the 12th Communist Party of China Central Committee adopted "the socialist planned commodity economy" as the objective model of reform. Although it represented for many Chinese economists a revolutionary change in the reform objectives, interpretation of the "planned commodity economy" was controversial. Some emphasized its "planned nature," whereas others emphasized its "commodity nature." The "socialist market economy" was officially adopted as the objective model by the 14th Communist Party of China National Congress in 1992. Note that the official changes in the objective model do not necessarily represent the actual timetable of changes. Normally, they lagged.

7. In fact, SCRES was established in 1982, initially for drawing up the reform blue-print. The then State Economic Commission was assumed to be in charge of imple-menting annual economic reform programs. The predecessor of SCRES was the State Council's Reform Office, which was established on May 8, 1980, also for drawing up the reform blueprint. See Shangquan Gao, *Zhongguo de jingji tizhi gaige* (Beijing: People's Press, 1991), app.

8. It was drawn up by the then Economic System Reform Office under the State Council's Financial Commission and submitted to the State Council on December 3, 1979. The office was set up in June 1979. See ibid.

9. Jinglian Wu and Xiaochuan Zhou, *Zhongguo jingji gaige de zhengti sheji* (Beijing: Zhanwang Press, 1988); Xiaomin Shi and Jirui Liu, "Jingjixuejia bixu zunzhong lishi yu shishi," *Journal of Economic Research* [Jingji yanjiu] 3 (1989): 11–33.

10. Jinglian Wu and Jirui Liu, *Lun jingzhengxing shichang tizhi* (Beijing: Financial and Economic Press, 1991); David Newbery, "Sequencing the Transition," CEPR Discus-sion Paper no. 575, Center for Economic Policy Research, 1991.

11. Tian Jiyun, then vice premier, argued that the price reform should be conducted "from easy to hard and step-by-step." He wrote, "What is easy and what is hard must be judged according to its effects on people's direct interest." Tian Jiyun, "Jiji zuo hao jiage tixi gaige gongzuo," *People's Daily*, January 28, 1985.

12. Wu and Zhou, *Zhongguo jingji gaige de zhengti sheji*.

13. Although some mutations of the dual-track prices existed even in the pre-reform period, it was not until the early 1980s that the dual-track system became important—although it was not legalized in industrial sectors until 1985. The govern-ment's pre-1985 reform plans did not envisage this delay in application to industrial policy. Weiying Zhang was the first to propose the dual-track system as a transitional approach to a market price system. His ideas were "collectivized" by a conference of young economists held in September 1984 in Zhejiang Province (called the Mount Mogan Conference), which greatly influenced the government's 1985 policy. Weiying Zhang, "Jiage gaige zhong yi 'fang' weizhu de silu," *Zhongguo: Fazhan yu gaige, 1984–1985* (Beijing: Qiushi Press, 1984), pp. 500–8. For some analyses of the evolution of the dual-track system, see, among others, William A. Byrd, "Impact of the Two-Tier Plan / Market System in Chinese Industry,"*Journal of Comparative Economics* 11, no. 3 (1988): 295–308; McMillan and Naughton, "How to Reform Planned Economies"; and Wu and Zhou, *Zhongguo jingji gaige de zhengti sheji*.

14. Xinshen Diao, "Zhongguo shuanggui zhi jingji fenxi," *Zhongguo: Gaie yu fazhan*, no. 2 (1989): 12–20.

15. Cutting the planned allocations occurred much later than the introduction of the dual-track system; privatization of the state-owned enterprises is yet to come.

16. Gang Fan, "Liang zhong gaige chengben he liang zhong gaige lujing."

17. Zhengfu Shi, "Reform for Decentralization and Decentralization for Reform: A Political Economy of China's Reform," 1993 (copy in author's files).

18. At the beginning of rural reform, many town and village cadres opposed the reform because of the loss of their superiority. But they soon realized that they could do much better than ordinary peasants by using their accumulated personal connec-tions and knowledge of the outside world. They then became "reformers." Today, the richest people in the countryside are those former cadres. A similar phenomenon occurred during the urban reform.

19. It seems that they will continue to support the reform until they themselves become capitalists, either by taking bribes or by going into business (*xiahai*). The

Chinese experience shows that it is possible to compensate bureaucrats during the reform period. The intuition is simple: if the reform implies transfer of economic power from bureaucrats to entrepreneurs, let the bureaucrats become entrepreneurs; for those who are not qualified to become entrepreneurs, let them become "shareholders" (but don't worry about where they get their money). Because of improved efficiency of resource allocation, the entrepreneur in the market economy can enjoy higher returns than can the bureaucrat in the planned economy. Then, why should a bureaucrat oppose the reform? Weiying Zhang, "Decision Rights, Residual Claim and Performance: A Theory of How Chinese Economy Works," Nuffield College, Oxford, 1994 (copy in author's files).

20. Kang Chen, Gary H. Jefferson, and Inderjit Singh, "Lessons from China's Economic Reform," *Journal of Comparative Economics* 6, no. 2 (1992): 201–25.

21. Agriculture reform is a good example. The family farming system was first secretly adopted by some peasants in Anhui Province in 1978, but the central government implemented it nationally much later. Industrial reform was pioneered by Sichuan Province in 1978 under then Governor Zhao Ziyang. More recent examples of bottom-up initiatives that only later became accepted by the central authority include the stock exchanges in Shanghai and Shenzhen. Ibid.

22. The leadership promotion system also reflects the local government dominance of reform. From the very beginning of reform, reform performance became a very important mark for the promotion of local government leaders to the central level. Zhao Ziyang and Li Wang (the former governor of Anhui Province) are two examples. This incentive system further strengthened the local government dominance of reform.

23. Zhengfu Shi, "Reform for Decentralization."

24. A comprehensive reform program contains all aspects of reform, such as prices, enterprises, financing, taxation, housing, and so on.

25. Zhengfu Shi, "Reform for Decentralization"; Zhigang Wang, "Gradualism versus Big Bang."

26. The largest and the longest setback occurred after 1989. But it was followed by an unprecedented—and the most radical—push in 1992 and 1993.

27. Most outside observers would like to argue that setbacks are brought on by "conservatives." However, that argument might be too simple. If a push is always followed by a setback, there must be some reason beyond the political aspect. The observation is that "conservatives" blame "reformists" for problems following the push, whereas "reformists" blame "conservatives" for problems following the setback.

28. Quoted in Wu and Zhou, *Zhongguo jingji gaige de zhengti sheji*, p. 311. It might be safe to say that Zhao Ziyang was an advocate for the idea of a complete blueprint of economic system reform until 1986.

29. The most influential paper was Shuqing Guo, Jinrui Liu, and Shufan Qiu, "Zonghe jingji gaige yu zhengti sheji," *People's Daily*, September 9, 1985.

30. Peter Nolan, "Reforming Stalinist Systems: Chinese Experience," Faculty of Politics and Economics, University of Cambridge, 1992.

31. Kang Chen, "Crossing the River."

32. Critics say that "right prices" are a precondition for enlivening enterprises; therefore, price reform should be accomplished before enterprise reform. But China did take that route.

33. Xiaoqiang Wang, "Groping for Stones to Cross the River: Chinese Price Reform against 'Big Bang,'" Discussion Paper no. DPET 9305, Department of Applied Economics, Cambridge University, 1993.

34. Gang Fan, "Dual-Track Transition."

35. Of course, that fact does not mean that there were no radical proposals for reform. For example, as early as 1979, economist Zhuyao Yu proposed "the socialist market" as an objective model of reforms. Furen Dong argued for state-ownership reform. Furen Dong, "Guanyu shehuizhuyi suoyou zhi de xingshi," *Journal of Economic Research* [Jingji yanjiu] 1 (1979). Nevertheless, it is safe to say that in the early 1980s, the majority of leaders and economists had not lost their trust in the planned economy and public ownership. Their major consideration was how to make the public ownership–based planned economy more efficient. Even today, many economists still believe in the "advantages of public ownership."

36. Ren Shan, "China's Economic Reform and Chinese Economists," *Intellectuals*, Winter 1987.

37. Many influential young economists worked in the following four research institutes: the Economic System Reform Institute of China, the Rural Development Institute of China, the Institute of Economics of the Chinese Academy of Social Science, and the State Council's Development Center. World Bank economists also played active roles in the mid-1980s.

38. Weiying Zhang, "Decision Rights, Residual Claim, and Performance."

39. By applying Murrell and Olson's devolution theory to China, Kang Chen gives an excellent analysis, both theoretically and empirically, of how bureaucrats can use their power of collective actions to manipulate the reform process. Kang Chen, "Crossing the River"; Murrell and Olson, "Devolution of Centrally Planned Economies."

40. Wu and Zhou, *Zhongguo jingji gaige de zhengti sheji*; Shi and Liu, "Jingjixuejia bixu zunzhong lishi yu shishi."

41. World Bank, *China: Country Economic Memorandum, Between Plan and Market*, Report no. 8440-CHA, Washington, 1990.

42. Jiaxiang Wu, a philosophical economist, was the most famous advocate for new authoritarianism. It should be pointed out that although we argue that a strong reform-minded authority is necessary for implementing a reform blueprint, we do not believe that such an authority is necessarily good for the reform. The reason is that a strong reform-minded authority may implement a very bad blueprint. In this sense, lack of a strong reform-minded authority might be fortunate for China.

43. Karl Marx regarded the market mechanism as a "thrilling jump," the failure of which would destroy not just the product but also its producer.

44. As Gang Yi points out, it would be naive to argue that "the price reform is to change relative prices rather than to raise all prices; and it does not necessarily bring about inflation if the monetary policy is held tightly." Gang Yi, "The Price Reform and Inflation in China, 1979–1988,"*Comparative Economic Studies* 32, no. 4 (1990): 28–61.

45. Weiying Zhang, "Jiage gaige zhong yi 'fang' weizhu de silu."

46. Tian Jiyun, then vice premier, argued that the price reform should be conducted "from easy to hard and step by step." He wrote, "That what is easy and what is hard must be judged according to its effects on people's direct interests." Jiyun Tian, "Jiji zuo hao jiage tixi gaige gongzuo."

47. This example is worth an elaboration because it tells a story of how the one-track planned price system evolved first into a dual-track system and eventually into a one-track market price system. When the price of a box of matches was 2 cents, all match factories suffered losses. In the early 1980s, the government made several attempts to raise the price from 2 cents to 3 cents, but it failed to do so because it feared citizen opposition. Given that raising the official price proved impossible, the match

factories began to seek alternatives. Either they put fewer matches into a box and sold them at the same price, or they designed a new box and sold it at a much higher price (since it was a "new" product, it was legal to sell it at a new price). There were two match prices. The official price of the old box remained unchanged, but that box was hard to find in the market, and it eventually disappeared. As a result, all matches were sold at the market price.

48. Kevin M. Murphy, Andrei Shleifer, and Robert Vishny, 1992, "The Transition to a Market Economy: Pitfalls of Partial Reform," *Quarterly Journal of Economics* 107, no. 3 (1992): 889–906.

49. Initially, economists were divided into two groups. One group argued that the irrational structure was caused by an irrational system; reform was the only effective way to solve the structural problems; therefore, priority should be given to reform. The other group argued that although introducing market elements was in line with the reform, a precondition for markets to function was a "buyer's market." Reform may make matters worse when the serious structural problems are not solved first. Hence, in the first stage, the policy should "concentrate on rectification and delay reform" (*zhong tiaozheng huan gaige*). After a year's debate, consensus emerged among economists. That is, in the first stage of reform, priority should be given to rectification, and reform should serve the rectification; the overall reform should begin only after solving the major structural problems. See Guoguang Liu, *Lun jingji gaige yu jingji tiaozheng* (Jiangsu: Jiangsu People's Press, 1982); Jinlian Wu, "Guanyu gaige chuqi fazhan zhanlue yu hongguan kongzhi de wenti," *People's Daily*, February 12, 1985, p. 3.

50. William A. Byrd and Gene Tidrick, "Adjustment and Reform in the Chongqing Clock and Watch Industry," World Bank Staff Working Paper no. 652, 1984.

51. William A. Byrd, "Impact of the Two-Tier Plan/Market System in Chinese Industry," *Journal of Comparative Economics* 11, no. 3 (1987): 295–308.

52. *China Statistical Yearbook*, 1991, pp. 395, 377.

53. *People's Daily*, November 25, 1991.

54. Gang Fan, "Liang zhong gaige chengben he liang zhong gaige lujing."

55. Mingfeng Tang, *Gaige shi nian* (Beijing: Beijing Press, 1990).

56. See Wu and Liu, *Lun jingzhengxing shichang tizhi*. Professor Wu was a leading critic of the budgetary contracting system; for him, the system was anti-reform.

57. Zhengfu Shi, "Reform for Decentralization."

58. Ibid.

59. Weiying Zhang, "Decision Rights, Residual Claims, and Performance: A Theory on How the Chinese Economy Works," Nuffield College, Oxford, UK, 1994."

60. When official prices were not at equilibrium level but could not be violated, local governments created a "bundling system" to bypass them. The bundling system can be explained as follows. Suppose the official price of one ton of steel is Y 600, and its market price is Y 1,000; the official price and the market price of a bicycle are Y 100 and Y 200, respectively. Liaoning Province supplies steel and demands bicycles, whereas Shanghai Province supplies bicycles and demands steel. Then, when Shanghai buys 100 tons of steel, it must sell 400 bicycles to Liaoning. Both steel and bicycles are bought at the official prices. By doing so, the provinces comply with the official prices, but the transaction is dealt with at market prices. Note that this system differs from the barter system. How many bicycles are needed for one ton of steel depends on the ratio of the market price–official price gap of steel to that of bicycles, rather than the ratio of their market prices. For example, if the official price of a bicycle is raised to Y 150, Shanghai must sell 800 bicycles to buy 100 tons of steel.

61. This can be formally modeled as a Nash–Cournot game. See Zhang, *Decision Rights*.

62. A commonly cited example against the fiscal revenue contracting system is that when it was introduced, the less efficient provinces (such as Inner Mongolia) discontinued supplying raw materials to the more efficient provinces (such as Shanghai) and instead built their own manufacturing facilities to process raw materials. That argument seems anti-economical. If Shanghai is more efficient at processing than Inner Mongolia is, it could afford to pay higher prices. It would be foolish for Inner Mongolia to refuse a price offer that could bring residually more than that by self-processing. If Shanghai cannot offer a higher price because its residual is claimed by the central government, the central government must make a revenue contract with Shanghai rather than abolish the contract with Inner Mongolia. (Note: Shanghai was one of three municipalities to whom the revenue-contracting systems were not applied in 1980.)

63. China had 30 provinces, 2,181 counties, and 55,800 towns in the 1980s.

64. For empirical studies on the performance of state-owned enterprises, see, among others, Gary Jefferson and Wenyi Xu, "The Impact of Reform on Socialist Enterprises in Transition: Structure, Conduct, and Performance in Chinese Industry," *Journal of Comparative Economics* 15, no. 1 (1991): 22–44; Donald Hay, Derek Morris, Guy Liu, and Shujie Yao, *Economic Reform and State-Owned Enterprises in China: 1979–1987* (Oxford: Oxford University Press, 1993). For a theoretical analysis, see Weiying Zhang, "Decision Rights."

65. Shangjin Wei and Lian Peng, "Love and Hate: State and Non-State Firms in Transition Economy," 1993 (copy in author's files).

66. In addition, domestic private enterprises and rural enterprises are disadvantaged in financing, technology, and skilled labor when they start their businesses, partly because of the government's discriminatory policies. Their only advantage is freedom. A lag in the state-sector reform may strengthen their competitiveness in markets.

67. Yingyi Qian and Chenggang Xu, "Why China's Economic Reforms Differ: The M-Form Hierarchy and Entry/Expansion of the Non-State Sector," 1993 (copy in author's files); Chen, Jefferson, and Singh, "Lessons from China's Economic Reform."

68. Wu and Zhao wrote: "Undeniably, the development of a large number of township enterprises serves some purposes: increasing production, creating jobs for the rural population, and supplementing the output of state-run enterprises. But it is also evident that they are competing with the large enterprises for raw materials and energy. Therefore, one should not be surprised to see that occasionally the most well-equipped rolling mills or steel mills stand idle, while energy-consuming small township mills continue to produce, at much higher cost, simply because they have succeeded in obtaining raw materials and energy supplies." Wu and Zhou, *Zhongguo jingji gaige de zhengti sheji*, pp. 315–16.

69. Jinlian Wu, "Guanyu gaige chuqi fazhan zhanlue yu hongguan kongzhi de wenti," p. 3.

70. Zhigang Wang, "Gradualism versus Big Bang."

Chapter 10

This text is from a speech made at the Conference on China's Economic Transition, organized by Ronald Coase and held July 14–18, 2008, at the University of Chicago.

The manuscript was finalized on December 31, 2008. I am thankful for the valuable comments of Ronald Coase, Ning Wang, Lee Benham, Hong Sheng, and other participants. Many thanks are owed to Juzheng Yang for tidying up the statistics.

1. *China Statistical Yearbook*, 2007.

2. I developed this idea in 1984. At the time, I was a graduate student at Northwestern University of China, in Xi'an. I wrote two articles. One advocated the dual-track price system as a transition mechanism from the centrally planned price to the market price; the other exhorted the entrepreneur system. Both articles are included in Weiying Zhang, *Jiage, shichang yu oiyejia* (Beijing: Beijing Daxue Chubanshe, 2006).

3. Frank Knight, *Risk, Uncertainty, and Profit* (Boston: Houghton Mifflin, 1921).

4. Ronald Coase, "The Nature of the Firm," *Economica* 4 (1937): 268–405.

5. Joseph Schumpeter, *The Theory of Economic Development: An Inquiry into Profits, Capital, Credit, Interest, and the Business Cycle* (Cambridge, MA: Harvard University Press, 1934).

6. By "entrepreneurial talents," I refer to individuals who have a relatively elevated ability to foresee the future in an uncertain world and to innovate new products or services and modes of production. I believe entrepreneurial talents are to a large degree inherent, although education and experience can increase people's abilities.

7. William Baumol, "Entrepreneurship: Productive, Unproductive, and Destructive," *Journal of Political Economy* 97 (1990): 893–921.

8. Murphy, Shleifer, and Vishny also make a similar argument. Kevin Murphy, Andrei Shleifer, and Robert Vishny, "Allocation of Talents: Implications for Growth," *Quarterly Journal of Economics* 106, no. 2 (1991): 503–30.

9. Armen Albert Alchian, "Some Economics of Property Rights," in *Economic Forces at Work* (Indianapolis: Liberty Press, 1977), pp. 127–49.

10. In a market economy, the firm is one form of exchange. Coase, "Nature of the Firm." When property rights can be freely exchanged, firms will emerge. Ownership of the firm is a contractual arrangement among different participants. Armen Alchian and Harold Demsetz, "Production, Information Costs, and Economic Organization," *American Economic Review*, 62, no. 5 (1972): 777–95. Although theoretically ownership of a firm may be shared by all participants equally, the contractual arrangement is typically asymmetric: some become the owners (employers) with assignment of residual claim (profits and rents) and control rights, whereas others become employees, taking contractual income by agreeing to obey the employers' authority (within limits). This "profit system" can be understood as an accountability system. Weiying Zhang, 1995, *Qiye de qiyejia—Qiyue lilun* (Shanghai: Shanghai Renmin Chubanshe, 1995). In most industries and in most cases, such a system provides the best incentive for entrepreneurs to make efficient decisions.

11. Armen Albert Alchian, "Some Economics of Property Rights," *Il Politico* 30 (1965): 816–29.

12. Murphy, Shleifer, and Vishny, "Allocation of Talents."

13. All organizations structured according to rank offer progressive returns for ability. Sherwin Rosen, "Authority, Control, and the Distribution of Earnings," *Bell Journal of Economics* 13 (1982): 311–23. Using government as an example, returns not only include monetary compensation, but also—more important—include political power and social status. The difference between total returns of high-level and low-level positions is higher than the difference in ability.

14. This description is a bit exaggerated. During China's transition, local government managers of the economy competed with other local governments. Government

officials showed entrepreneurial talents and engaged in productive activities. China's story (and that of other countries) shows that interregional competition may make government officials more productive, not less productive. Steven Cheung, *The Economic System of China* (Hong Kong: Arcadia Press, 2008). Indeed, globalization already caused government officials all over the world to be more productive. The reason is that each government must improve institutional efficiency. Overall, businesspeople are better than government officials at creating value, which is explained in the remaining text. Therefore, reallocating entrepreneurs from the government to the private sector will, in general, increase efficiency.

15. William A. Niskanen, "Nonmarket Decision Making: The Peculiar Economics of Bureaucracy," *American Economic Review* 58, no. 2 (1968): 293–305.

16. Schumpeter, *Theory of Economic Development*.

17. Murphy, Shleifer, and Vishny, "Allocation of Talents."

18. An old Chinese proverb says, "An incompetent soldier harms himself; an incompetent general harms an army."

19. Robert Lucas, "On the Size Distribution of Business Firms," *Bell Journal of Economics* 9 (1978): 508–23.

20. See Robert Barro, "Economic Growth in a Cross-Section of Countries," *Quarterly Journal of Economics*, 106 (1991): 407–44; Stephen P. Magee, William A. Brock, and Leslie Young, *Black Hole Tariffs and the Endogenous Policy Theory* (Cambridge: Cambridge University Press, 1989); Kevin M. Murphy, Andrei Shleifer, and Robert Ward Vishny, "Allocation of Talents: Implications for Growth," issue 3530, National Bureau of Economic Research, Cambridge, MA, 1990.

21. Baumol, "Entrepreneurship"; Murphy, Shleifer, and Vishny, "Allocation of Talents."

22. Ibid.

23. Even though the commercial environment differed from one dynasty to the next, this description is tenable throughout history. Many people believe the Song dynasty was more commercialized, but the government was more attractive than was commercial activity.

24. My viewpoint was inspired by Professor Yushi Mao.

25. My concept of position-based rights is similar to Professor Steven Cheung's "rank order significance of rights." Cheung, *The Economic System of China*. However, when he sees this system as a type of contract, our views conflict.

26. Alchian, "Some Economics of Property Rights."

27. Even if the internal rights of an enterprise in the privately owned economy are based on position, because the ownership rights of the private company are based on the owners' contractual arrangements of the production factors and because those position-based rights in essence come from property-based rights, they can be defined as second-order position-based rights. In comparison, the position-based rights in the publicly owned economy are first-order position-based rights.

28. In Chinese, we refer to this as the "official standard," meaning everyone is judged according to his position in the government.

29. During the 10 years of China's Cultural Revolution, all property-based rights were destroyed. Following the Cultural Revolution, almost everything in the city was controlled by the government. The state became people's only source of food and clothing. Because agriculture was also controlled through the commune system, no one could leave the commune and survive.

30. State-owned enterprises were also quasi-government bodies because they were managed by bureaucrats.

31. Over the past few years, the media have reported on cases of some government officials murdering competitors.

32. Andrei Shleifer and Robert Vishny, "Corruption," *Quarterly Journal of Economics* 108, no. 3 (1993): 599–617.

33. To have a perspective on university students' opinions on careers, the study included "university student" as a career category. See the Social Research Office of the Chinese Economic System Reform Institute, *Gaige de Shehui Xinli: Bianqian yu Xuanze* (Sichuan: Sichuan People's Press, 1988), pp. 111–13.

34. Martin Weitzman and Chenggang Xu, "Chinese Township and Village Enterprises as Vaguely Defined Cooperatives," *Journal of Comparative Economics* 18 (1994): 121–45.

35. Weiying Zhang, "A Principal-Agent Theory of the Public Economy and Its Application to China," *Economics of Planning* 31 (1998): 231–51.

36. Zhejiang Province became famous for being the first to develop private enterprises. However, because private enterprises were illegal in the province during the 1980s, they often faced pressure. For example, at the end of 1981, the Zhejiang Provincial Committee investigated eight well-known private enterprises in Wenzhou City, which became known as the "Eight Kings." In April 1984, the central government decided to clamp down on "economic crimes." The Zhejiang government immediately brought legal proceedings against the eight. Seven of the entrepreneurs were sent to prison, and one fled. In 1984, when the political environment favored reform, the Wenzhou City government overturned their sentences, calling them heroes of economic development. Licheng Ma, *Datupo: Xinzhongguo siying jingji fengyun lu* (Beijing: Zhongguo Gongshang Lianhe Chubanshe, 2006).

37. Shaoming Li, Shuhe Li, and Weiying Zhang, "The Road to Capitalism: Competition and Institutional Change in China," *Journal of Comparative Economics* 28, no. 2, (2000): 269–92.

38. *South China Morning Post*, June 13 and 17, 1997.

39. Jianjun Zhang, *Marketization and Democracy in China* (London and New York: Routledge, 2008).

40. Mengfu Huang and Deping Hu, eds., *Zhongguo minying jingji fazhan baogao*, no. 3 (Beijing: Shehui Kexue Wenxian Chubanshe, 2006), p. 103.

41. Licheng Ma, *Datupo*, pp. 172–74.

42. An example is Guangjiu Nian of Wuhu City, Anhui Province. In the 1950s, he took over his parents' grocery store. In the 1960s, he was sent to prison for engaging in private commercial activity. After he was released from prison, he restarted his private business of selling fried watermelon seeds. Because his watermelon seeds were of such good quality, his market expanded quickly. By 1983, he employed more than 140 workers and had monthly sales revenues exceeding Y 500,000. According to the policy at the time, employing more than seven people was considered capitalist exploitation, not sole proprietorship. His case became provocative. Someone reported his case to Deng Xiaoping. On November 22, 1984, Deng Xiaoping stated, "Do not impede him; wait and see." The case was resolved.

43. Licheng Ma, *Datupo*, p. 201.

44. A well-known story is that of Weifeng Huang, Meiyi Wu, and Peiyun Lin, the three vice mayors in Wenzhou City who stepped down from political office to pursue private businesses. Ibid.

45. Government officials are often sent there to study when they will be promoted.

46. The well-known company SOHO, established in 1995 and listed on the Hong Kong Stock Exchange, is still owned by Feng's former partner, Shiyi Pan.

47. In 1990, the average urbanite's usable housing area was 13.7 square meters. By the year 2000, it had reached 20.3 square meters. The proportion of commercial housing increased from 10 percent in 1990 to 90 percent in 2000. *China Statistical Yearbook*, 2004.

48. In 1990, China had only 500 kilometers of highways. By 2000, the network of highways had increased to 16,300 kilometers, and by 2006, it had reached 452,000 kilometers. See *China Statistical Yearbook*, 2007.

49. See All-China Federation of Industry and Commerce, ed., *Zhongguo Siying Qiye Daxing Diaocha, 1993–2006*, (Beijing: China Industrial and Commercial United Press, 2007), p. 146.

50. See Huang and Hu, *Zhongguo minying jingji fazhan baogao*.

51. Perhaps those numbers have been underreported. See Huiyao Wang, *Huigui shidai* (Beijing: Zhongyang Bianyi Chubanshe, 2005).

52. Ibid.

53. Zhongguancun encompasses 30 universities and 130 research organizations. The local government introduced legislation in the 1980s to encourage the commercialization of research results. More than 1,000 scientists engaged in research and engineers started businesses, even though they were registered as collectives, or state-owned enterprises. For example, today's third-largest computer supplier in the world, Lenovo, was founded by Chuanzhi Liu and his engineering colleagues. They all worked in a computer research institute of the Chinese Academy of Social Sciences. Licheng Ma, *Datupo*. In a way, Liu epitomizes the three generations of Chinese entrepreneurs. In 1980, he engaged in private entrepreneurial activities, just like peasant-background entrepreneurs. Similar to the bureaucrat-background entrepreneurs, he even had a state-sector "iron rice bowl" (guaranteed job). And he was also an entrepreneur with an engineering background.

54. Examples include Baidu (Chinese search engine), Sina (the leading online media company), Sohu (the second-leading portal website), Easenet (the third-leading portal website), Tencent QQ (the leading Internet service portal), Shanda (the leading interactive entertainment media company), Asiainfo (the first to bring the Internet to China), UT-Starcom, Dandan (Chinese "Amazon"), Vimicro (central processing unit producer), and Neusoft (the leading software producer).

55. The Liu brothers from Sichuan are an example. In 1982, the four Liu brothers quit their jobs in the state sector to start a business. Two of them (Yongxing Liu and Yonghao Liu) are listed among China's richest people.

56. In 2004, Rupert Hoogewerf began publishing the "China Rich List," which ranks China's wealthiest each year and has become very influential. His list has always been controversial because China's wealthy fear publicity and being revealed, so the list has some inaccuracies. However, it aligns with the goal of this text. The list can be accessed at http://hurun.net.

57. Twenty-six of the people were eliminated from the calculations because the year they started their business or their backgrounds could not be found.

58. "Iron rice bowl" is a Chinese idiom meaning guaranteed employment with a steady income and benefits.

59. See All-China Federation of Industry and Commerce, 2007.

60. Since 2000, the *China Statistical Yearbook* has provided only production value data for all state-owned enterprises and "above-scale" nonstate-owned enterprises (those that exceed Y 5 million in annual sales revenue). It does not provide the total industrial output of all enterprises. Because most nonstate-owned enterprises are below the standard, data since 2000 have undervalued the importance of the

nonstate-owned sector. For example, in 1990, the total output of all industrial enterprises was Y 12.61 billion, but the industrial output of all state-owned enterprises and above-scale nonstate-owned enterprises was only Y 7.27 billion. The latter accounted for only 57.6 percent of the total. If all nonstate-owned enterprises are included, the state-owned sector as a proportion of industrial output is perhaps lower than 20 percent. In 2006, the state-owned sector accounted for 35.8 percent of added value of all state-owned and above-scale nonstate-owned enterprises. That is 4.6 percentage points higher than industrial output values. The reason is that state-owned enterprises have monopoly status in high value-added core heavy industries such as oil, gas, power, and telecommunications.

61. Baumol, "Entrepreneurship."

62. The Third Plenary Session of the 11th Communist Party of China Central Committee is widely viewed as the start of China's economic reform. However, the documents issued clearly prohibit the household-contract responsibility system. The system was not officially recognized until 1982, three years after it had first been tried in practice.

63. Here, "value" has been defined as social value, which includes any person's hoped-for value judgment.

64. Knight, *Risk, Uncertainty, and Profit*.

65. Schumpeter, *Theory of Economic Development*.

66. According to the *China Entrepreneur Survey System Annual Report*, Chinese managers on average spend 15.5 percent of their time interacting with government officials, with some managers spending as low as 11 percent and others spending as high as 24.4 percent. See Lan Li, ed., *Jingjixuejia vs. Qiyejia* (Beijing: Jizai Gongye Chubanshe, 2008), p. 275.

67. Baumol, "Entrepreneurship"; Murphy, Shleifer, and Vishny, "Allocation of Talents."

Chapter 11

This paper was written in 1998 and was first published in *Corporate Ownership & Control* 3, no. 4 (2006).

1. See Kuan Chen, Gary H. Jefferson, Thomas G. Rawski, Hongchang Wang, and Yuxin Zheng, "Productivity Change in Chinese Industry: 1953–1985," *Journal of Comparative Economics* 12 (1988): 570–91; Roger Gordon and Wei Li, "The Change in Productivity of Chinese State Enterprise, 1983–1987: Initial Results," unpublished manuscript, Department of Economics, University of Michigan, Ann Arbor, 1989; David Dollar, "Economic Reform and Allocative Efficiency in China's State-Owned Industries," *Economic Development and Cultural Change* 39 (1990): 89–105; Gary Jefferson, Thomas G. Rawski, and Yuxin Zheng, "Growth, Efficiency, and Convergence in China's State and Collective Industry," *Economic Development and Cultural Change* 40 (1992): 239–66; John McMillan and Barry Naughton, "How to Reform a Planned Economy: Lessons from China," *Oxford Review of Economic Policy* 8 (1992): 130–43; Theodore Groves, Hong Yongmiao, John McMillan, and Barry Naughton, "Autonomy and Incentives in Chinese State Enterprises," *Quarterly Journal of Economics* 109, no. 1 (1994): 202–6; Donald Hay, Derek Morris, Guy S. Liu, and Shujie Yao, *Economic Reform and State-Owned Enterprises in China: 1979–1987* (Oxford: Oxford University Press, 1994); and Theodore Groves, Hong Yongmiao, John McMillan, and Barry Naughton, "China's Evolving Managerial Labor Market," *Quarterly Journal of Economics* 103, no. 4 (1995): 873–92.

2. However, a study by Woo et al. based on survey data for 300 SOEs found that TFP growth was zero at best during 1984–1988. Wing Thye Woo, Hai Wen, Jin Yibiao,

and Fan Gang, "How Successful Has Chinese Enterprise Reform Been? Pitfalls in Opposite Biases and Focus," *Journal of Comparative Economics* 18 (1994): 410–37.

More recently, in a comparative analysis of Chinese industry using a survey data set including 967 state-owned enterprises, Huang and Meng also calculated negative TFP growth for SOEs in the 1985–1990 period. Yiping Huang and Xin Meng, "China's Industrial Growth and Efficiency: A Comparison between the State and the TVE Sectors," *Journal of the Asia Pacific Economy* 2, no. 1 (1997): 101–21.

3. More precisely, risks that a bureaucrat bears are very different from the risks that a capitalist bears.

4. Frank Knight, *Risk, Uncertainty, and Profit* (Boston: Houghton Mifflin, 1921).

5. Ronald Coase, "The Nature of the Firm," *Economica* 4 (1937): 268–405.

6. Knight, *Risk, Uncertainty, and Profit*.

7. Armen Alchian and Harold Demsetz, "Production, Information Costs, and Economic Organization," *American Economic Review* 62, no. 5 (1972): 777–95.

8. Weiying Zhang, "Entrepreneurial Ability, Personal Wealth, and Assignment of Principalship: An Entrepreneurial/Contractual Theory of the Firm," PhD dissertation, Oxford University, 1994.

9. According to Grossman and Hart, control rights result from contract incompleteness and, therefore, are residual rights. In this chapter, control rights are used more loosely. They consist of at least two components: (a) rights to make business decisions and (b) rights to select and monitor the marketing member. Sanford Grossman and Oliver Hart, "The Costs and Benefits of Ownership: A Theory of Vertical and Lateral Integration," *Journal of Political Economy* 94 (1986): 691–719.

10. Asymmetry of monitoring is quite intuitive. A glance at the producing members will reveal whether they are working, whereas a look at the marketing member may tell little about what he or she is thinking.

11. This argument can be sharpened by the following example. Suppose that there is a working team of two people, A and B. They work only at night when the moon is out. The production technology requires that A work in the moonlight while B works in the shadows. The output cannot be attributed to each worker's marginal effort. Then, obviously, it is preferable to let B claim the residual rather than A, because A cannot see what B does while B can easily see whether A works hard or shirks. In the context of the firm, the marketing member is a worker-in-the-dark, whereas the producing member is a worker-in-the-light. Yang and Ng argue that management's claiming the residual is indirect pricing of managerial services. Xiaokai Yang and Yewkwang Ng, "Theory of the Firm and Structure of Residual Rights," *Journal of Economic Behavior and Organization* 26, no. 1 (1995): 107–28.

12. Here, following Knight, we understand that the entrepreneur has dual functions: making decisions and bearing risks. Knight, *Risk, Uncertainty, and Profit*.

13. Capital abuse by management can take various forms, one of which is "overinvestment" for career concerns. See Bengt Holmström and Joan Ricart i Costa, "Managerial Incentives and Capital Management," *Quarterly Journal of Economics* 101, no. 4 (1986): 835–60. See also Andrei Shleifer and Robert Vishny, "A Survey of Corporate Governance," *Journal of Finance* 52 (1997): 737–87.

14. Focusing on a corporate governance mechanism in this chapter does not mean that product market competition is not important in disciplining management.

15. According to Knight: "With human nature as we know it would be impractical or very unusual for one man to guarantee to another a definite result of the latter's actions without being given power to direct his work. Conversely, the second party

would not place himself under the direction of the first without such a guarantee." *Risk, Uncertainty, and Profit*, p. 270.

16. Milton Harris and Artur Raviv, "Corporate Governance: Voting Rights and Majority Rules," *Journal of Financial Economics* 20 (1986): 203–35.

17. Mathias Dewatripont and Jean Tirole, "A Theory of Debt and Equity: Diversity of Securities and Manager-Shareholder Congruence," *Quarterly Journal of Economics* 109, no. 4 (1994): 1027–54.

18. For an excellent survey, see Oliver Hart and Bengt Holmström, "The Theory of Contracts," in *Advances in Economic Theory*, ed. Truman F. Bewley (Cambridge: Cambridge University Press, 1987), pp. 71–156.

19. Michael Jensen and William Meckling, "Theory of the Firm: Managerial Behavior, Agency Costs, and Capital Structure," *Journal of Financial Economics* 3 (1976): 305–60. The evidence of strong correlation between the managerial payment and the firm's performance suggests that the actual residual stake held by the manager is more than proportional to his nominal stake. For a survey and synthesis, see Sherwin Rosen, "Contracts and the Markets for Executives," in *Contract Economics*, ed. Lars Werin and Hans Wijkander (Oxford: Basil Blackwell, 1991), pp. 181–211.

20. Weiying Zhang, "Entrepreneurial Ability."

21. Philippe Aghion and Patrick Bolton, "An Incomplete Contracts Approach to Financial Contracting," *Review of Economic Studies* 59 (1992): 473–94; Dewatripont and Tirole, "Theory of Debt and Equity."

22. Dewatripont and Tirole, "Theory of Debt and Equity." The Dewatripont-Tirole model uses the well-known facts that the debt holders' welfare is a concave function of the firm's profit, and the equity holders' welfare is a convex function of the firm's profit. The party in control of the firm, then, uses a nonverifiable, that is, noncontractible, signal as the basis for deciding whether to allow the firm to continue to operate or to shut down. The manager prefers to continue rather than to shut down, because he enjoys the private benefit from continuing. When continuing to operate, the firm's profit distribution is "riskier" (in the sense of second-order stochastic dominance) than when shutting down. For that reason, the "risk-averse" debt holders will dismiss the manager more often than will the "risk-preferring" equity holders.

23. Shleifer and Vishny, "Survey of Corporate Governance."

24. Andrei Shleifer and Robert Vishny, "Large Shareholders and Corporate Control," *Journal of Political Economy* 94 (1986): 461–88.

25. However, unlike equity, debt in a peculiar way may be tougher when it is not concentrated. If a borrower defaults on debt held by a large number of creditors, renegotiating with those creditors may be extremely difficult, and the borrower might be forced to liquidate. Robert Gertner and David Scharfstein, "A Theory of Workouts and the Effects of Reorganization Law," *Journal of Finance* 46 (1991): 1189–222; Mathias Dewatripont and Eric Maskin, "Credit and Efficiency in Centralized and Decentralized Economies," *Review of Economic Studies* 62 (1995): 541–56; Patrick Bolton and David Scharfstein, "Optimal Debt Structure and Numbers of Creditors," *Journal of Political Economy* 104 (1996): 1–25. Costs of concentrated ownership are potential expropriation by large investors of other investors and stakeholders in the firm. For that reason, as argued by Shleifer and Vishny, a good corporate governance system should combine some types of large investors with legal protection of both their rights and those of small investors. Shleifer and Vishny, "Survey of Corporate Governance."

26. Erik Berglöf, "Capital Structure as a Mechanism of Control: A Comparison of Financial Systems," in *The Firm as a Nexus of Treaties*, ed. Masahiko Aoki, Bo Gustafsson, and Oliver E. Williamson (London: Sage, 1990), pp. 237–62.

27. Sanford Grossman and Oliver Hart, "Corporate Financial Structure and Managerial Incentive," in *The Economics of Information and Uncertainty*, ed. John J. McCall (Chicago: University of Chicago Press, 1982), pp. 123–55.

28. Thomas H. Jackson, *The Logic and Limits of Bankruptcy* (Boston: Little, Brown, 1986); Oliver Hart, *Firms, Contracts, and Financial Structure* (New York: Oxford University Press, 1995).

29. Hart, *Firms, Contracts, and Financial Structure*.

30. Michael C. Jensen, "Agency Costs of Free Cash, Corporate Finance and Takeovers," *American Economic Review* 76 (1986): 323–29; Hart, *Firms, Contracts, and Financial Structure*.

31. Milton Harris and Artur Raviv, "Capital Structure and the Informational Role of Debt," *Journal of Finance* 45 (1990): 321–49.

32. Theoretically, "all the people" are the principal (owner) of the firm, and the state is only a representative of all the people. But in this chapter, I will discuss the relationship between the original owner and the state. See Weiying Zhang, "Decision Rights, Residual Claim, and Performance: A Theory of How the Chinese Economy Works," Nuffield College, Oxford, 1993 (copy in author's files).

33. In a capitalist firm, the monitor is monitored by residual claim. Alchian and Demsetz, "Production, Information Costs." In a state enterprise, residual claim does not serve this purpose.

34. Gang Fan, "On Ongoing Reform of Property Rights of State Enterprises" [Guangyu danqian guoyou qiyi chanquang guangxi de gaige], *Journal of Reform* [Gaige zazhi], no. 1 (1995); Weiying Zhang, "China's SOE Reform: A View of the Modern Theory of the Firm," *Journal of Reform* [Gaige zazhi], no. 1 (1995a); Chenyao Zhang, "Insider's Control and Chinese Enterprises Reform" [Neiburen kongzhi yu Zhongguo qiyi gaige], *Journal of Reform* [Gaige zazhi], no. 3 (1995); Chunlin Zhang, "Reform of SOE's Corporate Governance: A Financial Perspective" [Cong rongzi de jiaodu kan guoyou qiyi de gongsi zili jiegou gaige], *Journal of Reform* [Gaige zazhi], no. 3 (1995); Chunlin Zhang, "State Enterprise Reform and State Financing" [Guoyou qiyi gaige yu guojia rongzi], *Journal of Economic Research* [Jingji yanjiu] 4 (1997).

35. Jinlian Wu, *Modern Corporate and Enterprise Reform* [Xiandai gongsi yu qiyi gaige] (Tianjin: Tianjin Renmin Press, 1994).

36. Weiying Zhang, "Decision Rights, Residual Claim, and Performance."

37. Bureaucrats enjoyed considerable freedom to expropriate public funds in various ways. One such way was to invest in their hometown. For example, suppose there is Y 100 million available for construction of a railway, which costs Y 90 million and generates Y 99 million in public benefit if it does not pass through the bureaucrat's hometown. If it passes through his hometown, the railway would still cost Y 100 million, but it would generate only Y 95 million in public benefit because the bureaucrat would receive Y 5 million in private benefit. If the bureaucrat can pocket his or her rent of Y 10 million, the best choice is to donate it to the hometown to build a school, which would generate Y 11 million in personal benefit. The remaining Y 90 million can be used only to construct the railway not passing the bureaucrat's hometown, and the net return rate of the total investment is 10 percent. However, because it is impossible for the bureaucrat to pocket the rent, the second-best choice is to invest all Y 100 million in constructing a railway passing through the hometown, which has a net rate of the

return of zero. The misallocation is possible because the public does not understand what the optimal route is or that it is too costly for them to stop the decision—Y 5 million net surplus might be the maximum they could get from monitoring. Otherwise, the investment generates Y 5 million for the bureaucrat, which is better than nothing. It pays for the bureaucrat to hire experts to prove that the detour is the best for the public's interest.

38. Jinlian Wu, "Hard Problems and Policy Options of Large- and Medium-Sized SOE Reform" [Dazhongxing guoyou qiyi gaige de nandian he duice], *Economic Daily*, February 26, 1995.

39. One survey shows that even by the end of 1987, 78 percent of all state-owned enterprises with independent accounting systems and 80 percent of large and medium-sized SOEs adopted the management contract system. Shijin Liu, "Reform of SOEs: Restructuring the Microfoundation of the New System" [Guoyou qiyi gaige: chonggou xintizhi de weiguan jichu], in *1978–1994 China Report of Reform and Development: China's Road* (Beijing: China Financial and Economic Press, 1995).

40. For details of contracts and case studies, see China Enterprise System Reform Research Group, *Contract System in Practice* (Beijing: Economic Management Press, 1988).

41. However, as pointed out by Groves et al., the average numbers conceal considerable variation across enterprises in marginal profit retention rates. Although some enterprises were retaining 100 percent of their marginal profits by 1989, others were still remitting all their profits to the state. Theodore Groves, et al., "Autonomy and Incentives in Chinese State Enterprises," *The Quarterly Journal of Economics,* 109 (1994): 183–209.

42. The 1988 SOE Law identifies 14 rights to define the sphere of autonomy of state-owned enterprises.

43. Weiying Zhang, "China's SOE Reform"; Weiying Zhang, "Rational Thinking of China's SOE Reform," *China Business Time,* January 13, 1995b; Weiying Zhang, "Decision Rights, Residual Claim, and Performance."

44. Groves et al., "Autonomy and Incentives in Chinese State Enterprises"; Geng Xiao, "Options Open to China's Financial Reform after Eastern Asian Crisis," *International Economic Review* no. 5–6 (1997).

45. Jinlian Wu, "Hard Problems and Policy Options."

46. According to the survey by China Entrepreneurs Survey System, the average monthly income of a manager was Y 1,024 in 1995, just 2.2 times the average monthly income of an urban worker. See *Almanac of China's Economy 1996* (Beijing: China Economic Publishing House, 1996), p. 955.

47. This idea is similar to one in which corruption and bribes can improve efficiency given that the government controls firms. Andrei Shleifer and Robert Vishny, "Politicians and Firms," *Quarterly Journal of Economics* 109, no. 4 (1994): 995–1025.

48. Setting up subsidiary companies is pervasive in China. In some cases, subsidiaries are even set up in foreign countries. A state-owned enterprise having 5–7 layers of subsidiaries is typical. The governments have little knowledge about how many subsidiaries their SOEs have. Sometimes, even the top manager of the SOE has no such knowledge. The author was once told that one SOE used 12 pages to print out its organizational chart.

49. Apart from this direct effect, the accounting manipulation has also generated an indirect incentive effect by hardening the budget constraints of all the state-owned enterprises. The soft budget constraint has been argued as a major reason for the SOEs' inefficiency. But the budget constraints can be soft only if the government can make

arbitrary transfers of profit between profit makers and loss makers (assuming that the loan supply is constant). If there are no profit makers delivering profit to the government, it is impossible for the government to subsidize the loss makers. Managers' ability to manipulate accounting has greatly restricted the government's ability to transfer profit; as a result, all enterprises face stronger pressure to improve their own efficiency. In this sense, a poor government might be a good thing. Weiying Zhang, "Decision Rights, Residual Claim, and Performance."

50. I collected many examples of underreporting. In one case, the manager of a state-owned enterprise in Shenzhen told me that the company made a profit of Y 1.04 billion in 1994, but it reported Y 600 million to the government. In another case, a state export-import company made more than Y 1 billion in profit, but it reported a loss of Y 14 million.

51. Barry Naughton, *Growing Out of the Plan: Chinese Economic Reform, 1978–1993* (Cambridge: Cambridge University Press, 1995); Thomas G. Rawski, "Chinese Industrial Reform: Accomplishments, Prospects, and Implications," *American Economic Review* 84, no. 2 (1995): 271–75.

52. Xiaolin Wu, ed., *Research Reports on Debt Restructuring of China's State Sector* [Zhongguo guoyou jinji zaiwi chongzu yanjiu baogao] (Beijing: China Financial Press, 1997).

53. Kaoru Hayashi and Yoshio Wada, "Comparing Enterprise Reform in China and Vietnam: Finance, Incentives, and Corporate Governance," unpublished manuscript, 1997 (copy in author's files).

54. The social security payment is also an important factor for the increase in administrative costs.

55. Huang, Yiping, Wing Thye Woo, K. P. Kalirajan, and Ron Duncan, "Enterprise Reform, Technological Progress, and Technical Efficiency in China's State Industry," 1998 (copy in author's files).

56. Harry Broadman, and Geng Xiao, "The Coincidence of Material Incentives and Moral Hazard in Chinese Enterprises," Development Discussion Paper no. 606, Harvard Institute for International Development, Cambridge, MA, 1997.

57. The Chinese retirement age is 60 for men and 55 for women. Chinese courts find that economic crimes committed by 59-year-old managers are disproportionately high. This trend is called the "59 phenomenon."

58. Although the contract duration is three to four years, the government is not bound by the contract in replacing the manager.

59. One source says that more than 80 percent of the managers are appointed by industrial bureaus. Groves et al., "China's Evolving Managerial Labor Market." In fact, 100 percent are appointed by industrial bureaus.

60. It should be pointed out that bureaucrats are multitask principals. Bengt Holmström and Paul Milgrom, "Multitask Principal-Agent Analysis," *Journal of Economic Behavior and Organization* 7 (1991): 24–51; Avinash Dixit, *The Making of Economic Policy* (Cambridge. MA: MIT Press, 1996). Even if they are "benevolent," they still need to balance between different tasks. It is hard to imagine that they consider only the manager's ability of enhancing profitability in their selections.

61. For example, a state-owned enterprise manager of Wuxi City in Jiangshu Province increased the firm's assets from Y 2 million to Y 700 million within a few years. Then, he was called into the government line department office and told that because he had no university degree, he was not qualified to run such a large firm. He was then replaced and given a new position in a much smaller firm.

62. *Beijing Youth Daily*, March 11, 1998.

63. *China Entrepreneur Magazine*, no. 9, 1997.

64. The Institute of Economics at the Chinese Academy of Social Science surveyed 769 state-owned enterprises over the years 1980–1989. The survey shows that only 11 percent of managers serving at the end of the period had been appointed before 1980, and 44 percent had been appointed since 1985. Among the current managers, fewer than a quarter (23 percent) replaced retiring managers. For the remaining group, 38 percent replaced managers who were promoted, 46 percent replaced managers who were moved laterally, and 16 percent replaced managers who were demoted. Those data were misinterpreted by Groves et al. as an indicator for development of managerial labor markets in China. Groves et al., "China's Evolving Managerial Labor Market." In fact, in China, SOE managers are frequently reappointed every three or four years. Turnover of managers has little to do with managerial labor markets.

65. More recently, the government launched a master of business administration program for managers of large and medium-sized state-owned enterprises.

66. In 1995, 79.6 percent of managers had college degrees, compared with 33.4 percent in 1985. See *Almanac of China's Economy 1996*, p. 955.

67. Many managers and government officials have purchased their university diplomas or have obtained them using their administrative privileges.

68. Chenyao Zhang, "Insider's Control."

69. To my knowledge, Wu and Jin were the first to propose the state shareholding system. Jiaxian Wu and Lizuo Jin, "Shareholding System: An Approach to Future Reform," *Economic Daily*, August 3, 1985. A similar idea was also proposed by the World Bank's China Mission. Professor Yining Li at Peking University has been known for his shareholding-dominated reform proposal. See Yining Li, "A Proposal of Ownership Reform for China" [Woguo suoyouzhi gaige de shixiang], *People's Daily*, September 26, 1986.

70. In Shenzhen, two of the three SAHCs were formed by upgrading the giant companies, and one was newly established. In Shanghai and Beijing, most of NAHCs were transformed from the original line departments.

71. Jinlian Wu, *Modern Corporate and Enterprise Reform*, p. 223.

72. *China's Management of Enterprise Assets: The State as Shareholder* (Washington, DC: World Bank, 1997). By the end of 1997, the number of listed companies reached 745, most of which were the incorporated SOEs, with a total market capitalization of US$222.4 billion. *Security Market Herald*, no. 1, 1998.

73. Harris and Raviv, "Corporate Governance." Here, "cheap voting rights" refer to the voting rights of holders who assume no responsibility for voting results. For example, if the Chinese people were to select an American president, the voting rights that they hold are the cheap voting rights. Whoever becomes the American president matters little to Chinese citizens.

74. In March 4, 1998, *China Security Daily* carried a report of a municipal government's circular on "target management of listed companies," which set up detailed rules of annual budget and resource allocation for 15 listed companies. The targets include the investment budget, new issuance of shares and bonds, and asset restructuring. The circular rules that if the set targets cannot be fulfilled, the government will dismiss management. The report shows that the 15 listed companies are tightly controlled by the municipal government.

75. Of course, if the state is a dominant creditor, it may expropriate small equity holders and other creditors. Or it may be too soft on management. For a detailed discussion

of transforming the state from a stockholder into a debt holder, see Weiying Zhang "China's SOE Reform"; Weiying Zhang, "Rational Thinking of China's SOE Reform."

76. For more analysis of changes in corporate finance, see Chunlin Zhang, "Debt Reduction, Bankruptcy, and Enterprise Restructuring in the Chinese State-Owned Sector," Department of Enterprises, State Economic and Trade Commission, 1998 (copy in author's files).

77. The debt–asset ratios in 1994 were 75.7 percent and 74.2 percent for medium-sized and small industrial state-owned enterprises, respectively. A survey by the State Assets Administration of 123,900 SOEs (including industrial, commercial, and financial firms) estimates that the average debt–asset ratio in 1994 was 75.07 percent, or 83.3 percent if bad assets were excluded. All figures are cited in Xiaolin Wu, *Research Reports on Debt Restructuring*.

78. Weiying Zhang, "Rational Thinking of China's SOE Reform." According to Guo and Han, households' share of national income increased from 64.4 percent in 1979 to 77.5 percent in 1988, whereas the total share of the government and enterprises declined from 35.6 percent to 22.5 percent. In the same period, the households' share of national savings rose from less than one-fourth to nearly two-thirds. The abnormal increase in households' income may partially reflect profit diversion. Shuqing Guo and Wenxiu Han, *Distribution and Use of GNP in China* [in Chinese] (Beijing: China People's University Press, 1991).

79. In 1994, the central government selected 18 municipalities for the capital structure optimization experiment. The experiment expanded to 58 in 1996 and to 111 in 1997. The experimental cities are granted special favored policies for reducing the debts of their SOEs. Those policies are also applicable to some selected SOEs, including 100 experimental SOEs of the modern enterprise system.

80. ICBC Bankruptcy Research Group, "A Survey Report on Bankruptcy Problems" [Guanyu qiyi pochan wenti de diaocha baogao], *Economic Research Journal* [Jinji yan-jiu], no. 4 (1997).

81. Ibid.

82. According to the May 27, 1997, *Asia-Pacific Economic Times*, only about 1.4 percent of bankruptcy cases in 1995–1996 were filed by banks.

83. Liu calls them "pseudo-debts." Li Liu, "An Analysis of Capital Structure of SOEs," *Economic Science*, no. 2, (1996).

84. Hao Lu, "Short-Term Efficiency and Viability of SOEs" [Danqi xiaoyi yu guoyou qiyi huoyusi], *Journal of Economic Research* [Jingji yanjiu] 11 (1996).

85. A similar problem is also found in other reforming socialist countries. See Janet Mitchell, "Creditor Passivity and Bankruptcy: Implications for Economic Reform," in *Capital Markets and Financial Intermediation*, ed. Colin Mayer and Xavier Vives (Cambridge: Cambridge University Press, 1993), pp. 197–224.

86. Chunlin Zhang, "Debt Reduction."

87. That is a typical multiprincipal problem in public enterprises. See Dixit, *Making of Economic Policy*.

88. *China Statistical Yearbook*, 1996, p. 403.

89. China Reform Foundation, "Xianshi de Xuanze: Guoyou Xiao Qiye Gaige Shi-jian de Chubu Zongjie" (Shanghai: Yuandong Press, 1997), p. 35. Note that these statistics account for only explicit, not implicit, privatization.

90. This issue can be explained as follows. Suppose you have a black horse and are unhappy with it. One day, you see a zebra and fall in love with it. You intend to exchange the horse for the zebra. However, doing so may make other members of your family un-

happy. One way to solve your problem is to buy some white paint and brush stripes on the horse's back. If your family questions why you got a zebra, you can point out that it is not a zebra, but your horse painted with stripes. Thus, you can eliminate their concern. After a time, you may sell the horse and buy a zebra without anyone even noticing.

91. Shaomin Li, Shuhe Li, and Weiying Zhang, "Competition and Institutional Changes: Privatization in China," Working Paper no. 1998E002, Institute of Business Research, Peking University, 1998.

92. Li, Li, and Zhang submit their theory to a vigorous empirical test using China's industrial census data, which cover all 2,000 counties and more than 400,000 firms in China from 1993 to 1995. The test strongly supports their postulation that cross-region competition is the driving force behind China's transition from public ownership to private ownership. Ibid.

93. Recently, Geng Xiao proposed that, as a first step, China should separate the bank's deposit business from its lending business by allowing foreign banks to make direct loans to Chinese enterprises with interbank financing from their Chinese counterparts who take deposits directly from households. That sounds like a good idea. But it still faces the potential problem of possible collusion between foreign private banks and Chinese state banks. Geng Xiao, "Options Open to China's Financial Reform after Eastern Asian Crisis."

Chapter 12

This article was finalized on October 6, 2008. It was first published in *Zhongguo Gaige Sanshi Nian (1978–2008)*. Mengkui Wang was the main editor, and the China Development Press also published it in 2009.

1. This chapter discusses only product market price reforms, not production factor market reforms. With regard to the factor market, labor market reforms have been basically completed, but reforms of the capital market and the land market are far from complete.

2. The dual-track system ideal has been used in a broader scope, such as the coexistence of the state-owned and nonstate-owned system, or the labor market dual-track system.

3. *China Statistical Yearbook*, 2007.

4. B. E. Yuexibofu, "Eluosi lianbang de jiage zhengce he jiage gaige," in *Zhongguo yu Eluosi: Liangzhong gaige daolu*, ed. Liu Meixun, Liewusi Yalishanda, and Yiwannuoweiqi Zhubian (Beijing: Qinghua Daxue Chubanshe, 2004).

5. Another reason is that under China's political structure, bureaucrats are often unwilling to take big political risks.

6. The first article to propose and systematically prove the "priority for liberalization" dual-track system price way of thinking was "Taking Price Reform as the Center of Systemic Economic Reform." Weiying Zhang, "Yi jiagge gaige wei zhongxin, daidong zhengge jingji tizhi gaige," *Zhuanjia jianyi(san)* 6 (1984); (see the appendix to this chapter). This ideal resonated with the audience at the first Youth Economic Reform Theory Seminar (the Mt. Mogan Conference) held in September 1984, and the organizers reported the results of the conference discussions. It was acknowledged by the State Council leadership. See Weiying Zhang, "Yi jiagge gaige wei zhongxin, daidong zhengge jingji tizhi gaige"; and Weiying Zhang, "Jingji tizhi gaige yu jiage," *Jingji yanjiu cankao ziliao* 1 (1985).

7. Cheng Zhiping, *30-Year Price Reform (1977–2006)* (Beijing: China Market Press, 2006), p. 18.

8. Zhang Zhuoyuan, "Jiage tizhi gaige," in *Zhongguo gaige yu fazhan baogao: 1978–1994, Zhongguo de daolu* (Beijing: Zhongguo Caizheng Jingji Chubanshe, 1995), p. 122.

9. Yang Jisheng, *Deng Xiaoping shidai: Zhongguo gaige kaifang jishi* (Beijing: Zhongyang Bianyi Chubanshem 1998), p. 91.

10. Ibid., p. 384.

11. *China Statistical Yearbook*, 1997.

12. The expansion of the rural farm output quotas for each household happened largely after the increase in agricultural sideline products.

13. To see how the government calculated the subsidies for urban residents after the price increase, see Cheng Zhiping, *30-Year Price Reform*, pp. 22–27.

14. Chen Xiwen, *Zhongguo nongcun gaige: Huigu yu zhanwang* (Tianjin: Tianjin Renmin Chubanshe, 1993).

15. See Investigation Team of State Commission for Restructuring the Economic System, "Development, Invigoration and Regulation: Implication of Price Reform in Wuhan," in *China: Development and Reform* by the National Economic Reform Research Institute (Beijing: Central Party School Press, 1987), vol. 1984–1985.

16. Foreign trade was another obstacle for planned prices. Because of differences in domestic and international prices, trading enterprises incurred huge loses. Those losses were all subsidized by the government. With an increase in trade, subsidies for trade losses were a burden the government could not handle. For the dialogues of the State Council leadership, see Cheng Zhiping, *30-Year Price Reform*, p. 44.

17. Ibid., pp. 44–48. In May 1985, the State Council Price Research Center was merged into the State Council Development Research Center.

18. In 1983, the government turned profits that it had received in the past into taxes paid to the government, which was referred to as "tax substitution." To alleviate the differences in profits between enterprises caused by irrational prices, the government mandated different tax levels for enterprises that produced different goods. A major reason for "tax substitution" was to alleviate the differences in profit levels among enterprises, which was assumed to create a relatively fair environment for competition among enterprises. See Wang Zhizheng, "Ligai Shui de xianzhuang yu qianjing," *Jingji lilun yu jingji guanli*, 6 (1985).

19. Cheng Zhiping, *30-Year Price Reform*, pp. 54–59.

20. William A. Byrd and Gene Tidrick, "Adjustments and Reform in the Chongqing Clock and Watch Industry," World Bank Staffing Working Paper, no. 652, 1984.

21. William A. Byrd, "Impact of the Two-Tier Plan/Market System in Chinese Industry," *Journal of Comparative Economics* 11, no. 3 (1988): 295–308.

22. Task Force on Price Reform, Chinese Academy of Social Sciences, "Retrospection of Price Reform in 7 Years," *Finance and Trade Economics*, 10–11 ed., 1986.

23. Diao Xinshen, "Jiage: Shuangguizhi de zuoyong he jinyibu gaige de fangxiang," *Fazhan yu tizhi gaige* 2 (1986).

24. *China Statistical Yearbook*, 1985, pp. 297, 376.

25. For example, in 1984, the state allocated 44.91 tons of steel to Guangdong, but only 39.8 tons actually arrived, which was 88.5 percent of the planned supply. See Wen Guifang, "Jiji de tuijin shengchan cailiao liutong he jiage gaige," *Chengben jiage ziliao* 4 (1985).

26. Because the market price was illegal, the seller did not dare mark up the price too much. After products left the production enterprise, they often went through several intermediaries before reaching the final enterprise, so the same type of product would have many market prices. See ibid.

27. In 1984, there were 259,203 illegal-price investigations. See Cheng Zhiping, *30-Year Price Reform*, p. 73.

28. The acceptance of the dual-track system reform ideal was related to the Third Plenary Session of the 12th National People's Congress of the Communist Party of China in October 1984 formally establishing "the "planned commodity economy." After the establishment of "the planned commodity economy," price liberalization was no longer a taboo.

29. According to Cheng Zhiping, in an attempt to resolve the long-lasting stagnant supply issue for crude oil, in 1981, the State Council implemented a contracting policy for the Oil Ministry, which was to assume responsibility for completing the task of producing 100 million tons, and the excess outputs of crude oil could be sold domestically at the then international market price, or it could be exported by foreign trade organizations. This was the earliest legal dual-track system for production materials. Cheng Zhiping, *30-Year Price Reform*, pp. 89–92.

30. According to the statistics of the Materials Department, the planned allocation rate of steel orders in 1985 was 96 percent; it decreased to 88 percent in 1989 and decreased to less than 80 percent in 1990. The fulfillment rate of steel order contracts was 98 percent in 1987, but it had decreased to 91 percent in 1989. The planned allocation order contract rate and contract fulfillment rate for other raw materials were lower. See ibid.

31. Yang Jisheng, *Deng Xiaoping shidai*.

32. Ibid.

33. Ma Kai, "Zhongguo jiage gaige 20 nian de lishi jincheng he jiben jingyan," *Jiage lilun yu shijian* 1 (1999).

34. Ibid.

35. Cheng Zhiping, *30-Year Price Reform*, pp. 158–63.

36. *China Statistical Yearbook*, 2007.

37. Lawrence Lau, Yingyi Qian, and Gerard Roland, "Reform without Losers: An Interpretation of China's Dual-Track Approach to Transition," *Journal of Political Economy* 108, no. 1 (2000): 120–43; Weiying Zhang and Gang Yi, "China's Gradual Reform: A Historical Perspective," in *China's Economic Growth and Transition*, ed. Clement A. Tisdell and Joseph C. H. Chai (New York: Nova Science, 1997). After implementing the dual-track system, in 1985, Shijiazhuang City tested a unified price for below-quota and above-quota steel and wood category products. In accordance with the planned price, the difference between the two prices was returned to the purchasing enterprise. See Shijiazhuang Municipal Commission for Economic Restructuring, "Enliven the Goods Market by Implementing the Same Price for Steel Products and Timber within and beyond the Plan," "Cost and Price" section, 1985.

38. Cheng Zhiping, *30-Year Price Reform*, pp. 103, 116.

Chapter 12 Appendix

This text was the earliest thesis to propose the dual-track system price reform. The earliest version, published here, was completed on April 21, 1984. It was printed in the State Council Technological Economic Research Center Energy Group's publication *Expert Opinions* (III) (June 1984). It was then selected as a conference paper for the First National Youth Economic Reform Theory Seminar at Mt. Mogan, Zhejiang Province, in September 1984 (called the Mt. Mogan Conference). After the Mt. Mogan Conference, the shortened version of this paper was published in the third edition of the *Economic Daily* on September 29, 1984, and was titled "Price System Reform Is the Central Link of Reform." The main contents were also published in *Inner Mongolia Economic Research*. 4 (1984). A revised version, titled "Economic System Reform and Price," was submitted as the author's thesis for a master's degree in economics from Northwestern University of China. It was published in *Economic Research Reference Material* 6 (January 1985); it was then selected for the Outstanding Economics Master's and Doctorate Theses, 1984–1985. It was also included in *China: Development and Reform (1984–1985)* (Beijing: Central Party School Press, 1987). The original English translation was titled "On the Line of Thoughts in Price Reform Guided Chiefly by the Notion of Letting Go," *Chinese Economic Studies 22*, no. 3 (1989): 50–66.

1. It should be pointed out that in this paper, the author adopted the then standard official terminology of the goal of the reform. Before September 1984, the official goal of the economic reform was to "perfect the planned economy," rather than to abolish it. Explicitly proposing the market economy would incur big political risks. However, if the reform follows the proposal of this paper, the planned economy would disappear.

Chapter 13

This text is a revised version of a presentation given by the author on January 12, 2008, to the Tenth Guanghua New Year's Forum. It was first published in the *Jingji Guancha Bao* on January 20, 2008. A revised version appeared in *Zhongguo Gaige Sanshi Nian: Shi Wei Jingjixuejia de Sikao*, edited by the author.

1. Weiying Zhang, "Research on Income Distribution Policies in the New Era," *Management World* 1 (1986).

2. Martin Ravallion and Shaohua Chen, "China's (Uneven) Progress against Poverty," World Bank Policy Research Working Paper no. 3408, September 2004, http://ssrn.com/abstract=625285.

3. Ibid.

4. Yining Li, *Li Yining Gage Lunji* (Beijing: Zhongguo Fazhan Chubanshe, 2008).

5. Niny Khor and John H. Pencavel, "Income Mobility of Individuals in China and the United States," IZA Discussion Paper no. 2003, Institute for the Study of Labor, Stanford University, March 2006.

6. All Gini coefficients of the provinces in the following discussion are for urban areas, provided by the well-known income distribution expert Li Shi of Beijing Normal University. All other data are calculated from the 2004 *China Statistical Yearbook*, unless otherwise stated.

7. Fan Gang, Wang Xiaolu, and Zhu Hengpeng, *NERI Index of Marketization of China's Provinces 2006 Report* (Beijing: Economic Science Press, 2007).

8. James Mirrlees, "An Exploration in the Theory of Optimum Income Taxation," *Review of Economic Studies* 38 (1971): 175–208.

9. Frank H. Knight, *Risk, Uncertainty, and Profit* (Boston: Houghton Mifflin, 1921).

Chapter 14

This text is a revised version of a speech given by the author on February 8, 2009, to the Chinese Entrepreneur Forum. It first appeared in the *Economic Observer* [Jingji Guanchabao] on February 16, 2009.

1. See Mark Skousen, *Vienna and Chicago: Friends or Foes?* (Washington, DC: Regnery Publishing, 2005). For the original contribution of Austrian business cycle theory, see F. A. Hayek, *Prices and Production and Other Works*, ed. Joseph T. Salerno (Auburn, AL: Ludwig von Mises Institute, 2008); Ludwig von Mises, *The Theory of Money and Credit*, 2nd ed. (New Haven, CT: Yale University Press, 1953).

2. Murray Rothbard, *America's Great Depression*, 5th ed. (Auburn, AL: Ludwig von Mises Institute, 2000).

3. Cited in Peter D. Schiff and John Downes, *Crash Proof: How to Profit from the Coming Economic Collapse* (Hoboken, NJ: John Wiley, 2007), p. xxi.

4. Beat Balzli and Michaela Schiessl, "The Man Nobody Wanted to Hear: Global Banking Economist Warned of Coming Crisis," *Spiegel Online*, July 8, 2009, http://www.spiegel.de/international/business/the-man-nobody-wanted-to-hear-global-banking-economist-warned-of-coming-crisis-a-635051.html.

5. Krassimir Petrov, "China's Great Depression," Ludwig von Mises Institute, September 2, 2004.

6. Thomas E. Woods, *Meltdown: A Free-Market Look at Why the Stock Market Collapsed, the Economy Tanked, and Government Bailouts Will Make Things Worse* (Washington, DC: Regnery Publishing, 2009).

7. Rothbard, *America's Great Depression*.

8. Benjamin Powell, "Explaining Japan's Recession," *Quarterly Journal of Austrian Economics* 5, no. 2 (2002): 35–50.

9. Louis Kuijs, "How Will China's Saving-Investment Balance Evolve?" World Bank Policy Research Working Paper no. 4, May 2006.

Chapter 15

This text is a revised version of a speech given by the author on February 20, 2009, to the Guanghua CEO Roundtable Forum of the Chinese Entrepreneur Forum.

1. Murray Rothbard, *America's Great Depression*, 5th ed. (Auburn, AL: Ludwig von Mises Institute, 2000).

2. William R. White, "Is Price Stability Enough?" BIS Working Paper no. 205, Bank for International Settlements, April 2006.

3. Ibid.

4. Milton Friedman, *The Optimal Quantity of Money and Other Essays* (London: Macmillan, 1969).

5. Ludwig von Mises, *On the Manipulation of Money and Credit*, ed. Percy L. Greaves Jr., trans. Bettina B. Greaves (New York: Free Market Press, 1978); F. A. Hayek, *Prices and Production and Other Works*, ed. Joseph T. Salerno (Auburn, AL: Ludwig von Mises Institute, 2008).

Chapter 16

This text is a revised version of a presentation given by the author to the Economic Crises and Economics Symposium jointly held by the Peking University Guanghua School of Management and the Chinese Economic Research Center, February 22, 2009. The last section was added for this publication.

1. Louis Kuijs, "How Will China's Saving-Investment Balance Evolve?" World Bank Policy Research Working Paper no. 4, May 2006.

Chapter 17

This text is a revised version of a 2009 lecture for the Guanghua School of Management Master's in Business Administration Program. The main content was published in an article titled "Taking the Pulse of Future Chinese Economic Growth" for *Nanfang Zhoumo* on December 4, 2009. The author would like to thank Cen Ke and Xiaoyong Fu for their editorial work on the early versions.

1. Angus Maddison, *Contours of The World Economy, 1–2030 AD* (Oxford: Oxford University Press, 2007).

2. Adam Smith's prediction is cited in Giovanni Arrighi, *Adam Smith in Beijing: Lineages of the Twenty-First Century* (London and New York: Verso, 2007), p. 2.

3. Kevin H. O'Rourke and Jeffrey G. Williamson, *Globalization and History: The Evolution of a Nineteenth-Century Atlantic Economy* (Cambridge, MA: MIT Press, 1999).

4. Cited in Arrighi, *Adam Smith in Beijing*, p. 4.

5. William Bernstein, *The Birth of Plenty: How the Prosperity of the Modern World Was Created* (New York: McGraw-Hill, 2004).

Index

corporate social responsibility and, 55
government regulation and, 132–33
measurement of, 82
rent-seeking and, 132
statutory, 132–33
morality
Confucius and, 102–3
education and, 108
free market and, 106–9
self-centeredness and, 101–3
Sima Qian and, 106–7
Smith and, 106
universal values and, 110–12
Morocco, 350
Mount Mogan Conference, 374n13
Mu, Qizhong, 182
multitask model, 66
murder, 381n31
Mystery of Capital, The (de Soto), 35

name, reputation and, 76
Nande Group, 182
Nanhai City, 179
nationalism, vested interests and, 100
natural rate of interest, 322
Neoclassical economics, xviii, xxi
Nepal, 350
Netherlands, 347f, 351f
New Deal, 308–9, 330–31
New Zealand, 347f, 349, 351f, 352
Nian, Guangjiu, 381n42
Nigeria, 347f, 349, 349f
Ningxia, 350, 351f, 352, 355f
North Korea, 351, 351f
Norway, 348, 349f

objective model, in reform, 138
opportunity
equality of, 126, 128
income distribution and, 128–29
opportunity cost, 47, 48, 50, 53
"overcapacity," 89
ownership
competition and, 66–67
concentrated, 385n25
control benefits and, 70, 370n40,
379n10
defined, 370n40
duplication and, 70

entry and, 70–71
private vs. state, 66
reputation and, 75–76
residual claim and, 78, 370n40
ownership distortion, 63
"ownership school," 60

Pakistan, 347f
Pan, Shiyi, 381n46
Panama, 350
papermaking, 2–3
Pareto efficiency. *See also* efficiency
competition and, 61–62
revolution and, 122–23
patents, 357, 358f
patriotism, 102
Paul, Ron, 332
peasant-background entrepreneurs,
176–80, 177f
peasants. *See also* rural enterprises
after Cultural Revolution, 143
in China's 200 wealthiest people, 188t
household-contract responsibility
system and, 266
land-rights and, 105, 123, 124, 171
as returnees, 189
Pencavel, John H., 286
Peru, 349
petroleum industry, 242, 393n29
Petrov, Krassimir, 305, 332
philanthropy, 37
Philippines, 347f, 351, 351f
physiocratic school, 6
Pin, Peiyun, 381n44
"planned commodity economy" reform
model, 59–60
planned economy. *See also* command
economy
efficiency in, 62, 267–68
income distribution in, 283
logic of robbery and, 104
market economy vs., 13
prices in, 235, 240–46, 269–71
rights in, 13–14
supply and demand in, 267–68
Poland, 347f, 348, 349f, 351, 351f
policy
academics and, 133–35
austerity, 149–50, 153–54

About the Author

Weiying Zhang was born in 1959 in Shaanxi Province. He received undergraduate and graduate training in economics from the Northwestern University of China. His radical ideas for price reform presented at the Mount Mogan Conference landed him a position at the Economic System Reform Institute. In 1990, he attended Oxford University and obtained his PhD in Economics in 1994.

Professor Zhang has taught economics at Peking University since 1997. He was Dean of the Guanghua School of Management between 2006 and 2010 and is currently the Sinar Mas Chair of Economics at Peking University's National School of Development. He has been the Chief Economist for the China Entrepreneurs Forum since 2001. Professor Zhang is widely regarded as the leading advocate of the free market in China as well as an authority on the theory of the firm and ownership reform. His insightful and provocative opinions about China's reforms have been widely reported both in Chinese and international media. The *Wall Street Journal* once called him "China's Anti-Keynesian Insurgent." In 2011, he received the China Economic Theory Innovation Award for his pioneering contribution to the dual-track price reform.

His publications include *An Entrepreneurial-Contractual Theory of the Firm* (1995); *Game Theory and Information Economics* (1996); *The Theory of the Firm and Chinese Enterprise Reform* (1999); *Information, Trust, and the Law* (2003); *Ownership, Incentives, and Corporate Governance* (2005); *Core Competence and Growth of the Firm* (2006); *Prices, the Market, and Entrepreneurship* (2006); *Thirty Years of Chinese Reform* (2008); *The Road to the Market* (2012); and *Games and Society* (2013).

Cato Institute

Founded in 1977, the Cato Institute is a public policy research foundation dedicated to broadening the parameters of policy debate to allow consideration of more options that are consistent with the principles of limited government, individual liberty, and peace. To that end, the Institute strives to achieve greater involvement of the intelligent, concerned lay public in questions of policy and the proper role of government.

The Institute is named for "Cato's Letters," libertarian pamphlets that were widely read in the American Colonies in the early 18th century and played a major role in laying the philosophical foundation for the American Revolution.

Despite the achievement of the nation's Founders, today virtually no aspect of life is free from government encroachment. A pervasive intolerance for individual rights is shown by government's arbitrary intrusions into private economic transactions and its disregard for civil liberties. And while freedom around the globe has notably increased in the past several decades, many countries have moved in the opposite direction, and most governments still do not respect or safeguard the wide range of civil and economic liberties.

To address those issues, the Cato Institute undertakes an extensive publications program on the complete spectrum of policy issues. Books, monographs, and shorter studies are commissioned to examine the federal budget, Social Security, regulation, military spending, international trade, and myriad other issues. Major policy conferences are held throughout the year, from which papers are published thrice yearly in the *Cato Journal*. The Institute also publishes the quarterly magazine *Regulation*.

In order to maintain its independence, the Cato Institute accepts no government funding. Contributions are received from foundations, corporations, and individuals, and other revenue is generated from the sale of publications. The Institute is a nonprofit, tax-exempt, educational foundation under Section 501(c)3 of the Internal Revenue Code.

CATO INSTITUTE
1000 Massachusetts Ave., N.W.
Washington, D.C. 20001
www.cato.org